FOREWORD

Memorials of marble or granite for our fallen – both military and civilian – commemorate our dead, but they cannot capture the human emotions and individuality of those left behind to grieve; nor the character of each person who died. This is what Jay Hyrons has so eloquently achieved in bringing everyone from the Falklands conflict once more to the front and centre of our lives.

This book crucially allows us to do four things:

- To remember those that we fought with and lost.
- To show respect for the families of the fallen – they are the ones who suffer and are 'left behind.'
- To remind ourselves – and politicians – that war should not be undertaken lightly. The object of war should always be a better peace.
- To reflect - I lived to see the dawn of a new day and have been lucky to do so every day since the 14th of June 82.

And as we ponder these, let us never forget the words of Herodotus: 'no one prefers war to peace. In peace, children bury their fathers; in war, fathers bury their children.'

Maj Gen (Retd) Chip Chapman CB

FALKLANDS WAR TIMELINE

2 April 1982	Argentine Forces Invade the Falkland Islands
5 April 1982	Task Force begins mobilisation.
23 April 1982	First British Casualty
4 May 1982	HMS *Sheffield* struck by Exocet Missile
19 May 1982	Sea King crash during cross-decking
21 May 1982	Loss of British Gazelle
21 May 1982	Attack on HMS *Ardent*
21 May 1982	Bombing of HMS *Argonaut*
23 May 1982	Bombing of HMS *Antelope*
25 May 1982	Attack on SS *Atlantic Conveyor*
25 May 1982	Bombing of HMS *Coventry*
27 May 1982	Bombing of Ajax Bay
28 May 1982	Battle for Darwin and Goose Green
6 June 1982	Loss of British Gazelle
8 June 1982	Bombing of RFA *Sir Galahad* and *Sir Tristram*
8 June 1982	Bombing of LCU F4
10 June 1982	British loss at Port Howard, West Falkland
11 June 1982	British casualties at Wall Mountain pre–Mount Harriet Assault
11–13 June 1982	Battle for Mount Longdon
12 June 1982	Exocet Missile strike on HMS *Glamorgan*
12 June 1982	Assault on Two Sisters
14 June 1982	Assault on Wireless Ridge
14 June 1982	Battle for Mount Tumbledown
14 June 1982	Argentine Surrender – Cease of hostilities
24 June 1982	British casualty during clean-up operations
1983	Falklands Families Pilgrimage for Bereaved Families
2022	40th Anniversary Commemorations, included the naming of places in the Islands for all 258 casualties

THE
FALKLANDS
FALLEN

To my late husband Lance Corporal Gary David Bingley MM, a natural leader, a brother, a father, a son, and a huge personality.

Also, each person who gave their life during the Falklands War along with the families and comrades they left behind...

Sed gratia dei ibi nos omnes.

THE
FALKLANDS
FALLEN

A DEDICATION TO THOSE
STILL ON PATROL

JAY MORGAN HYRONS

Pen & Sword
MILITARY

AN IMPRINT OF PEN & SWORD BOOKS LTD.
YORKSHIRE - PHILADELPHIA

First published in Great Britain in 2024 by
Pen & Sword Military
An imprint of
Pen & Sword Books Ltd
Yorkshire - Philadelphia

ISBN 978 1 03610 931 8

Typeset by SJmagic DESIGN SERVICES, India.

Printed and bound in the UK by CPI Group (UK) Ltd.

Pen & Sword Books Limited incorporates the imprints of Archaeology, Atlas,
Aviation, Battleground, Digital, Discovery, Family History, Fiction, History, Local,
Local History, Maritime, Military, Military Classics, Politics, Select, Transport,
True Crime, After the Battle, Air World, Claymore Press, Frontline Publishing,
Leo Cooper, Remember When, Seaforth Publishing, The Praetorian Press,
Wharncliffe Books, Wharncliffe Local History, Wharncliffe Transport,
Wharncliffe True Crime and White Owl.

For a complete list of Pen & Sword titles please contact

PEN & SWORD BOOKS LIMITED
George House, Units 12 & 13, Beevor Street, Off Pontefract Road, Barnsley, South
Yorkshire, S71 1HN, England
E-mail: enquiries@pen-and-sword.co.uk
Website: www.pen-and-sword.co.uk

or

PEN AND SWORD BOOKS
1950 Lawrence Rd, Havertown, PA 19083, USA
E-mail: uspen-and-sword@casematepublishers.com
Website: www.penandswordbooks.com

CONTENTS

INTRODUCTION

In life we live with rank and status where those things are important within the structure of society. In death, however, those things fall away as the veil between the 'here and there' dissipates.

The grief one person feels on the loss of another is individual, it depends on their attachment to them, rather than any status they may have held in life.

This book has been written in alphabetical order for that very reason. Compiled by a Next of Kin who experienced the 'knock on the door', it has been written with love and respect for both the fallen and their families.

Each person has a short piece, the aim of which is to paint a picture of them as a person rather than from just the military perspective. In a perfect world each story would be even in length, but information on some is easier to glean than others.

Every care has been executed during seven years of research to make this text as accurate as possible. Sometimes official records do not match, other times memory has faded over time. Writing this book has involved the piecing together of parts of the whole, just like an intricate jigsaw puzzle, over forty years after the event.

Either way, the fallen herein are immortalised as sons, brothers, partners, fathers and husbands. The only separation in the text is between the 255 service personnel and the three civilians.

With a Task Force of almost 30,000 the losses were minute, but to those individuals affected they were gargantuan in proportion, completely impossible to measure.

The ripples of War are extremely widespread in their effect...

THE SERVICE PERSONNEL

24547055 Private Richard John de Mansfield Absolon MM 3rd Battalion Parachute Regiment 13 July 1962 ~ 13 June 1982 Age 19

Richard John de Mansfield Absolon was born at the Bearsted Hospital, Stoke Newington, on 13 July 1962. Dickie, as he was known, was the only son of John and Tricia de Mansfield Absolon. His parents married at the Register Office in Haringey, they lived in Tottenham, North London. John was a Consultant Engineer at the time of their marriage.

Dickie's grandfather Leonard Ord Absolon served in the First World War in the Machine Gun Corps. Records indicate that Leonard was wounded, then discharged in 1919 after five years of service. Leonard was an Estate Steward to the Earl of Carnarvon in 1921, he married in 1922. By the time Dickie was born, Leonard was retired.

Military service was a theme throughout the family, Leonard's father Augustine De Mansfield Absolon served with the Royal Defence Corps in 1914.

It appears the De Mansfield name entered the Absolon family in 1837 when Mysie De Mansfield McGlenning married John Absolon, an artist, in St James Church, Piccadilly, London. Mysie was born in India, the couple went on to have a large family. Their youngest son Augustine was Dickie's great-grandfather.

Augustine married in April 1890 in *Norfolk*, his eldest son, Alfred George Absolon, was born in 1893. Records indicate that Alfred George served with the British Army and was awarded the Military Cross for his bravery during the Battle of Sharqat, Mesopotamia (now Iraq) in October 1918. Alfred survived the First World War and went on to have three sons, he ended his days in Southampton.

Leonard and Winifred Absolon had one son, John De Mansfield Absolon, born in June 1923. John served with the Royal Artillery in the Second World War, retiring a Major after over twenty years of service.

Dickies parents divorced, they both remarried. John left for New Zealand to take up farming, and the family settled in Marton. Dickie attended Palmerston North Boys High School from 1977 to 1979. The school presents the Richard Absolon Memorial Trophy each year to the young man who shows 'outstanding qualities of fitness, courage, determination, and dedication'.

After spending his teenage years living in New Zealand, Dickie came back to England to join The Parachute Regiment in 1980, having left school at the end of the sixth form. Dickie passed out with 461 Platoon on 6 June 1980, he was posted to 3rd Battalion The Parachute Regiment.

During the Falklands War Dickie, still with 3 Para, was a scout/sniper with Patrol Company.

Extract from the Citation, *London Gazette*

> *MONDAY, 11th OCTOBER 1982*
>
> *THE QUEEN has been graciously pleased to approve the Posthumous award of the Military Medal to the undermentioned in recognition of gallant and distinguished service during the operations in the South Atlantic:*
>
> *24547055 Private Richard John de Mansfield ABSOLON, The Parachute Regiment*
>
> *'During eleven days of operations in the Mount Longdon area of East Falkland Island Private Absolon was employed as a scout/sniper with the Patrol Company 3rd Battalion The Parachute Regiment which was tasked with the gaining of information on the enemy force deployed in defensive positions around the Mountain.*
>
> *On the night of 11th/12th June Absolon with his partner led B Company onto the Mount Longdon feature in the first part of an assault to capture the position by the Battalion. The route selected gave the Company the opportunity to take the enemy by surprise and a valuable foothold was gained before the enemy was aware of the attack. Once battle was joined, Absolon fought with determination, always probing ahead to locate the enemy, and sniping at every opportunity. He was responsible for killing one particular sniper who was preventing the Company Headquarters from moving forward to link up with its platoons. He continued to display dash and determination throughout the 12th in a manner which was an example to many about him particularly for one so young. Tragically he was killed by mortar fire the next morning.*
>
> *This young and promising soldier displayed coolness, determination, and bravery under fire in demanding circumstances that were outstanding.'*

His full citation speaks for itself, he was deservedly awarded the Military Medal posthumously, such outstanding bravery and dedication from such a young soldier.

Dickie's home at the time of his death was Weybridge, Surrey. He is hailed as the only New Zealander to die in the war, but he was in fact a Londoner by birth. Dickie is honoured with a memorial at St Mary's Anglican Church in New Plymouth, Taranaki, New Zealand. His father John, a retired Major, died in 2004, he is buried in Taranaki.

Dickie died exactly one month short of his 20th birthday. His body was repatriated, he was laid to rest in Aldershot Military Cemetery.

In 2022, as part of the Falkland Islands 40th Anniversary Place Names Project, Dickie was honoured with 'Absolon Bay', an inlet north of Main Point Creek, West Falkland.

His name lives on…

D076946L Petty Officer Air Engineering Mechanic (Electrical) Michael John Adcock HMS *Glamorgan* 11 March 1947 ~ 12 June 1982 Age 35

Michael John Adcock was born at 121 Highbury Road in Nottingham on 11 March 1947, one of fraternal twins, his sister was named Jean. Michael and Jean were the youngest children of Ronald George and Alice Adcock (née Davies). Michael had an older brother and two sisters.

Ronald was born in 1916 during the First World War, the eldest son of George William and Gertrude Adcock (née Moss). It appears that Ronald was one of twelve children including a set of fraternal twins, records indicate his father, George William Adcock, was one of thirteen children.

Grandfather George served in the First World War as a Pioneer in the Royal Engineers; he was medically discharged in June 1918. His brother Harry was a Sapper in the Royal Engineers Railway Troops Dept. Unusually, all the Adcock boys of that generation survived the First World War.

George's father John was it seems one of eleven children. The Adcock name is therefore prevalent in the Beeston area of Nottinghamshire.

At the time of Michael's birth Ronald was a Colliery Banksman in Beeston, the family were living in Fairfield Avenue.

Michael attended Beeston Primary School followed by Bramcote High School. Michael joined the Royal Navy when he was 16 years old. He enjoyed cricket, football, cross country running and boxing.

Michael was set for a life of travel, Christopher Greenhough says:

> I served with Michael on 737 squadron at RNAS Portland in 1978/1979, we trained together prior to joining our respective ships flights. A very social outgoing Senior Rate, with a fun spirit and sense of humour. I last saw Michael in Weymouth on a Glamorgan Flight run ashore that I was invited to prior to their flight embarking on Glamorgan for Spring Train in the Mediterranean, I then flew to the Gulf to join RFA Olna with Fleet Target Group.

Another former colleague knew Michael as 'Fred'. Prior to joining HMS *Glamorgan* Michael was with HMS *Norfolk*, he transferred when *Norfolk* was decommissioned in early 1981.

Michael married in Yeovil in 1970, he and his wife Ann had two sons; at the time of his death Michael lived in Portland, Dorset.

On 12 June 1982, Michael died when HMS *Glamorgan* was hit by an Exocet missile. Michael is remembered on the HMS *Glamorgan* memorial, made from Welsh Slate, in the Falkland Islands.

In 2022, as part of the Falkland Islands 40th Anniversary Place Names Project, Michael was honoured with 'Adcock Lagoon', a tidal lagoon at the south end of Lively Island, East Falkland.

His name lives on…

D176381K Air Engineering Mechanic (Radio) Adrian John Anslow 845 Squadron Fleet Air Arm SS *Atlantic Conveyor* 9 September 1961 ~ 25 May 1982 Age 20

Adrian John Anslow was born on 9 September 1961 in Rowley Regis, Staffordshire. Adrian's parents Alfred and Rosemary were married in 1958. Adrian had one younger sister Johann.

Adrian went to Coppice High School in Wednesfield, Wolverhampton. The Anslow family go back a few generations in the area, Adrian's great-great-grandmother was born in Wednesfield. One of his great-uncles was a Prisoner of War in Malaya in the Second World War.

Adrian joined the Royal Navy in 1979, he completed his training at HMS *Raleigh*. Adrian was a keen musician and athlete. He represented the Navy in swimming, shooting, running, fencing, and boxing. Adrian bought his mother a cherished silver dragonfly necklace, representing his squadron's emblem.

Adrian was able to pop home briefly on 1 April 1982, not knowing that he would never return again to his family. After flying to Ascension Island, he joined Fort Austin at first and like many of the guys travelling 'Down South' he enjoyed the wildlife, the whales and the turtles. He wrote home from HMS *Invincible*, he later transferred to the SS *Atlantic Conveyor*.

Atlantic Conveyor had sailed for Ascension on 25 April 1982 carrying Wessex and Chinook helicopters, having been requisitioned on 14 April and converted at Plymouth. On arrival, she embarked Sea Harriers and Harriers and departed again on 7 May for the Main Battle Group, whereupon the Harriers were transferred.

On 25 May, ninety miles north-east of Port Stanley en route to San Carlos Water, the ship was hit by an Exocet missile. The explosion and resulting fires caused her to be abandoned with the loss of twelve lives. She remained afloat but sank in heavy seas on 31 May while under tow.

Adrian rests with his comrades lost at sea, his life is commemorated on a number of memorials. Anslow Gardens in Ashmore Park is named after Adrian. At the time of his death Adrian was an Air Engineering Mechanic for 845 Squadron Fleet Air Arm.

Before he died Adrian told his family he was rescuing turtles on the beach at Ascension Island.

In 2022, as part of the Falkland Islands 40th Anniversary Place Names Project, Adrian was honoured with 'Anslow Harbour' a sheltered anchorage protected by North East Island and Lively Island, East Falkland.

His name lives on...

D170136A Marine Engineering Mechanic (Mechanical) 1 Frank Owen Armes HMS *Coventry* 13 January 1961 ~ 25 May 1982 Age 21

Frank's parents, Frank Sidney Armes and Rosemary Phelan, married in Norwich in 1956. Their first child Ann was born the following year in 1957, a sister Linda came along two years later. Lastly, the couple welcomed their only son Frank Owen Armes, born in Norwich on 13 January 1961, the family was then complete.

Frank attended Heartsease High school in Norwich. He was very sporty, partaking in long distance running, football, canoeing and abseiling. He also enjoyed shooting and was a good marksman.

Frank joined the Royal Navy on 17 January 1978, it had been his dream as a child to join the Navy, but he had one particular aspiration to join the 'Ark'. After Frank completed his training his first ship was indeed HMS *Ark Royal*.

HMS *Ark Royal* was the sister ship to HMS *Eagle*, an Audacious-Class aircraft carrier, she was the Royal Navy's last remaining conventional catapult and arrested-landing aircraft carrier. The ship's nickname was 'The Mighty Ark', she was commissioned on 22 February 1955, and decommissioned in 1979.

In 1977, under the flag of Admiral Sir Henry Leach KCB Commander-in-Chief Fleet, HMS *Ark Royal* led the Royal Navy's tribute to and celebrations of Queen Elizabeth II's Silver Jubilee at Spithead. HMS *Ark Royal* had also been featured in a major BBC documentary series, *Sailor*, made between February to July 1976. The series showed life aboard the ship and its theme tune *Sailing* by Rod Stewart became associated with the ship.

HMS *Ark Royal* visited Fort Lauderdale, Florida, from 30 May to 14 June 1978. Frank was with the ship on her farewell World Tour before she entered HMNB Devonport on 4 December 1978 prior to her decommissioning. During the time while the ship was in the Florida area Frank was able to visit Bermuda.

When the Falkland Islands were invaded Frank was in HMS *Coventry* off Gibraltar on exercise Springtrain. HMS *Coventry* set off 'Down South' as part of the huge Task Force. She had a Union Flag painted on the roof of her bridge and a black line painted through her funnel to her waterline to aid recognition. This because the Argentine Forces also had two Type 42 destroyers.

HMS Coventry had been one of three Type 42 destroyers providing anti-aircraft cover for the fleet, but by 12 May *HMS Glasgow* was damaged forcing her to return to the UK and *HMS Sheffield* was lost on 4 May. HMS *Coventry* was left to carry out the role alone until other ships could arrive from the UK.

On 25 May 1982, HMS *Coventry* was hit by three bombs just above the water line on the port side. Nineteen of her crew were killed and a further thirty injured.

Sadly, Frank Armes was one of those killed that day. Frank had served just over four years in the Royal Navy when he died.

His father Frank visited the Falkland Islands in 1983, Frank died in August 2003. Frank's mother Rosemary died on 21 October 2015; both his parents' ashes were scattered over the *Coventry*'s grave in 2016.

His sister Ann says:

> Frankie loved to travel but was a homebody at heart, very family minded and very loyal towards colleagues and friends. He had a terrific, dry sense of humour, always making us laugh with stories of his life in the Navy when he came home on leave. He always saw the funny side of life, except for when his beloved Norwich City lost a game!
>
> He was very proud to be in the Navy and enjoyed the camaraderie of the good friends he made there. He was a great brother, and his sisters still think of him every day and miss him terribly. We are so proud of him.

His friend and comrade Mark says:

> I can remember my last conversation with him, I said that we would have to lean over the side and put deep scratches in the paint work so we could spin bigger dits about our exploits, until that day May 25th we had been a lucky ship and I had every faith we would all return, there is not a day goes by without wishing that we all had. RIP Frank along with our other lost shipmates.

In 2022, as part of the Falkland Islands 40th Anniversary Place Names Project, Frank was honoured with 'Armes Point', the eastern most point of Long Island in Berkeley Sound, East Falkland.

His name lives on…

D171126C Able Seaman (Sonar) Derek Armstrong HMS *Ardent* 21 January 1960 ~ 21 May 1982 Age 22

Derek's parents, Thomas Armstrong and Edna Glendenning, married in 1956 in Northumberland. Derek was their third son born in Prudhoe, Northumberland. Derek attended Prudhoe High School.

Derek left school at 16 and went to work at Adams and Gibbens in Hexham before joining the Royal Navy when he was 18. He did his basic training at HMS *Raleigh*, then joined HMS *Vernon* to train as a Sonar Operator. In 1979 Derek joined HMS *Alacrity* and travelled the world, including a memorable visit to Shanghai. *Alacrity* became the first warship in thirty years to sail up the Yangtze River.

Derek then spent nine months with Second Submarine Squadron before joining HMS *Ardent* in 1981 as a trained deep-sea diver. HMS *Ardent* was a Royal Navy Type 21 Frigate which was launched in May 1975. Although *Ardent*'s war was brief, the ship played a key part in the Battle for Falkland Sound which resulted in the successful landing of British troops onto the Falklands. Every man played their part in this short and bloody War.

On 21 May 1982, HMS *Ardent* was attacked in at least three waves by Argentine Aircraft. The first attack took place when a lone A-4 Skyhawk dropped two bombs which straddled the frigate, both failed to explode.

The bulk of the air strikes began later and *Ardent* was ordered to proceed west of North West Island along with HMS *Yarmouth* to 'split air attacks from the south'. A group of three aircraft crossed Falkland Sound from the west and then turned to their left to attack from the north-east. Cannon fire and three bombs struck home as the Argentine aircraft pressed their attack from the port side. The only defensive weapons which reacted properly were the 20mm AA cannons.

During an intense couple of hours, the attack continued. While in full control of her engines and steering, but virtually defenceless, *Ardent* was told to head north, toward Port San Carlos. The attacks were relentless and by the time *Ardent* stopped in the shallow waters of Grantham Sound the fires in her stern were out of control. With the ship listing heavily, Commander Alan West decided to abandon the ship. HMS *Yarmouth* came alongside to take off survivors, the crew was then transferred to the *Canberra*. At that time, it was known that twenty-two men had lost their lives, sadly Derek was one of them. Able Seaman Derek Armstrong was on Fire Watch as they were attacked that fateful day.

Derek is remembered in Prudhoe Parish Church with a plaque dedicated to him and all his shipmates on HMS *Ardent*. Prudhoe High School also remembers him with the 'Derek Armstrong Memorial Award' presented each year to the best sportsperson, and a memorial plaque in the School Foyer.

In 2022, as part of the Falkland Islands 40th Anniversary Place Names Project, Derek was honoured with 'Armstrong Cove', a cove in the entrance to West Arm in Port Albemarle, West Falkland.

His name lives on…

24325221 Corporal Raymond Ernest Armstrong MID 22 SAS Regiment 17 August 1957 ~ 19 May 1982 Age 24

Raymond Ernest Armstrong was born on 17 August 1957 in Northern Ireland, he was known by his comrades as 'Paddy'. Paddy was the son of Robert Armstrong a shop manager.

When Paddy joined the British Army, he was initially Royal Green Jackets. In 1979 Paddy passed his SAS selection. When he went to take his Para Course at Brize Norton the first time, Paddy broke his leg and was on crutches for some time. In 1980, he took the Para Course again and was awarded his SAS wings. His Parent Unit remained the Royal Green Jackets.

Paddy married Carole, a State Registered Nurse, on 18 December 1981 at the Register Office, Hereford; the couple were living there when he left for the Falklands War.

In 1982 during Operation Corporate, Paddy was D squadron (19 Troop). Although he was technically still a Trooper, he was an acting Corporal at the time he died and is honoured as such in his Mention In Dispatches.

Exert from the Supplement to the *London Gazette* 8 October 1982:

> *'The QUEEN has been graciously pleased to approve the following names of those Mentioned in Dispatches in recognition of gallant and distinguished service during the operations in the South Atlantic: 24325221 Corporal Raymond Ernest ARMSTRONG, The Royal Green Jackets (Posthumous)'*

Paddy died in the Sea King crash on 19 May 1982 with many other servicemen who lost their lives that day. He is honoured in St Martin's Churchyard, Hereford, where the SAS Regimental Plot has a Memorial Plaque.

Paddy is remembered on all the usual main Falklands War memorials; however he is also remembered with a plaque at the Darling Street Methodist Church, Darling Street, Enniskillen, Co Fermanagh, Northern Ireland.

In 2022, as part of the Falkland Islands 40th Anniversary Place Names Project, Paddy was honoured with 'Armstrong Bay', a sandy bay west of Rabbit Point on Pebble Island, West Falkland.

His name lives on…

24221177 Sergeant John Leslie Arthy 22 SAS Regiment 27 October 1954 ~ 19 May 1982 Age 27

John Leslie Arthy was born in Essex on 27 October 1954. Barry Arthy and Joan Gyde married in Edmonton in 1953, the couple started a family the following year. John, it appears, was the eldest of three boys born to the couple over the next eight years.

John was a name passed down for generations on his mother's side of the family. Great Uncle Edward John George Gyde served with the 52nd Battalion, Rifle Brigade (Prince Consort's Own) during the First World War. Edward appears to have served until 1920. Edward was born in Forest Gate in 1900, one of nine children, sadly only four survived into adulthood.

John's maternal grandfather, John Charles Gyde, was born in 1907, one of twins, his brother died as a baby. The Gyde family lived for some time in Shoreditch. His mother Joan was born in 1933, the youngest of two girls.

John was known to his mates as 'Lofty'. Lofty served in Infantry Junior Leaders Battalion, Oswestry 1970s (Junior CSM)

Lofty's parent unit was the Welsh Guards, he joined the SAS in 1975. During the Falklands War he was serving with D Squadron (19 Troop). He died with his fellow servicemen in the tragic Sea King Crash on 19 May 1982.

Lofty is remembered at Hereford (St Martin's) Churchyard, Herefordshire SAS Regimental Plot on the Memorial Plaque. Lofty is also remembered with a plaque at the Allied Special Forces Memorial Grove at the National Memorial Arboretum, words include 'He was big in stature and even bigger in spirit'.

In 2022, as part of the Falkland Islands 40th Anniversary Place Names Project, Lofty was honoured with 'Arthy Rocks', prominent rocks south of Mt Usborne on mainland East Falkland.

His name lives on...

23969493 WO1 Malcolm Atkinson 22 SAS Regiment 6 July 1945 ~ 19 May 1982 Age 36

Two Malcolm Atkinsons were born 'up North' in the summer of 1945, both during the same week. Our Malcolm Atkinson was born on 6 July 1945 in Joseph Street, Grimethorpe Brierley, Hemsworth, to Housekeeper Alice Mary Atkinson (née Young). Malcolm was born during one war and died in another.

Known as 'Akker' to his mates, Malcolm joined the British Army starting his service with the Coldstream Guards in 1964 which eventually became his Parent Unit as he passed selection for the SAS.

In 1972, Akker was recommended for a Mention in Dispatches while employed as part of a group of SAS advisers in Oman. Though there was a citation it does not appear to have been actioned. The citation states that Akker showed bravery and calmness, his actions contributing to the success of the operation and the safety of his group.

By the time the Falklands were invaded Akker was serving with the SAS G Squadron (SSM) as a Warrant Officer Class 1.

Akker was sadly killed in the Sea King crash on 19 May 1982, he is remembered at Hereford (St Martin's) Churchyard, Herefordshire SAS Regimental Plot on the Memorial Plaque. At the time of his death Malcolm Atkinson lived in Shucknall, Hereford.

In 2022, as part of the Falkland Islands 40th Anniversary Place Names Project, Akker was honoured with 'Atkinson Rocks', prominent rocks south of Blue Mountain on mainland East Falkland.

His name lives on...

23834397 SSgt John Ivan Baker Royal Signals 3 July 1945 ~ 6 June 1982 Age 36

John Ivan Baker was born on 3 July 1945 at 27 Waterloo Crescent, Countesthorpe, a large village in Leicestershire. Joe was born at home to Gwendoline Marie Baker. Joe's mother was married to Spencer Joseph Baker in late 1939, later she remarried in 1952 in Kettering and lived to the splendid age of 91 years.

Joe joined the British Army in 1966, his service included time with 216 Parachute Squadron, Royal Signals. Joe also served as the Rear Link Detachment Sgt with 3 PARA Signals Platoon in Osnabruck (Quebec Barracks) from 1978 to 1980.

During the Falklands War Joe was under the command of Major Mike Forge the OC of 205 Signals Squadron. Joe was one of Mike's technicians.

Staff Sergeant Christopher Griffin and Lance Corporal Simon Cockton, of 656 Squadron Army Air Corps, had been ordered to fly equipment and personnel to a malfunctioning radio re-broadcast station on top of Pleasant Peak. The station had been established the previous day to provide a communications link between the 5th Infantry Brigade headquarters at Darwin, and the 2nd Battalion, Parachute Regiment at Fitzroy.

The crew departed from Goose Green in a Gazelle and collected the replacement equipment from the headquarters at Darwin. SSgt Griffin was the pilot of the Gazelle and Lance Corporal Simon Cockton his observer. They also took on board major Mike Forge and Staff Sergeant Joe Baker. Sadly, all four were killed in a friendly fire incident when they were mistaken for an Argentine aircraft.

Joe is remembered in many places on memorials in the Falklands and the UK. There is also a memorial at Mount Pleasant airport. The white rocks at the memorial spell the numbers '205' when they are seen from the air. They refer to 205 Signal Squadron. Joe died just a month short of his 37th birthday.

At the time of his death Joe resided in Rothwell, Northants. He is buried in San Carlos Cemetery, Falkland Islands. Joe married in 1970, sadly he left behind a young family.

In 2022, as part of the Falkland Islands 40th Anniversary Place Names Project, Joe was honoured with 'Baker Point', a westernmost point of Pleasant Island near Fitzroy farm settlement, East Falkland.

His name lives on…

C013406T Lieutenant Commander David Ian Balfour HMS *Sheffield* 9 July 1944 ~ 4 May 1982 Age 37

The Balfour name is thought to have originated from the 'Lands of Balfour' in the parish of Markinch, formerly belonging to a family which were long heritable sheriffs of Fife.

George William Balfour was born in Sorn, Ayrshire, on 2 June 1823, the son of the Rev. Lewis Balfour and Henrietta Scott. It is said that Dave was a relative of author/lawyer Robert Louis Stevenson, The Rev. Lewis Balfour was the Minister at Colinton.

George married Margaret Bethune Craig on 28 February 1854 in Cramond, Edinburgh, Scotland. The couple went on to have a large family. The family lived for many years in Edinburgh where all of the children were born. George was widowed in 1879, his wife had died at the age of just 49.

Dr George William Balfour, Dave's great-grandfather was a 'one time Physician in Ordinary to the King for Scotland and the late Queen Victoria', according to a memorial in Ratho Cemetery. Dr George William Balfour died in Colinton in August 1903, after working as a doctor well into his sixties, he also left behind a distinguished career. Though the family kept its Scottish roots, much travel was on the cards for the Balfour's.

At least four of George and Margaret's sons went into the Medical Profession, though sadly John MacIntosh, their second son, died in 1894 aged just 30 years. Sons Archibald and Henry followed in their father's footsteps to become doctors.

Youngest son Keith became a banker who, after much world travel, settled in Newton Abbot with his wife; he died in 1945. Henry married a South African from Durban after originally studying medicine in Edinburgh. Henry and his wife had two children before settling in Hampstead, he died in late 1963 aged 90.

Archibald married Margaret Ellen Spencer on 20 July 1905 in Winsham, Somerset, the couple went on to have three children. Archibald who saw service with 1st Battalion Northern Counties Highland Volunteer Regiment RAMC, was made Medical Officer and temporary Captain on 1 June 1918. Archibald died in 1950, he is buried with his wife at St Johns Church, Rothiemurchus, Inverness.

Thomas Stevenson Balfour (Dave's grandfather) was made 2nd Lieutenant of the Volunteer Battalion Prince Albert's (Somerset Light Infantry) on 26 August 1896. He married Ina Mary Tabuteau in Charlton Mackerel, Somerset, on 20 June 1900. Tom died on 6 September 1912, he is buried in the Municipal Cemetery, Chard, with his wife and only daughter. Tom and Ina's oldest son Harry became a schoolmaster, he died in 1992. The couple's youngest son, George Ian MacIntosh Balfour, was born in January 1912.

George Ian MacIntosh Balfour joined the Royal Navy as a cadet in May 1929. He was made a Sub Lieutenant on 2 September 1932, and Lieutenant in 1933. In August 1939 George married Pamela Forrester, in Alloa, Scotland, to a Navy Guard of Honour; the Second World War was about to break out. George was on the King's birthday honour list in June 1942, by then a Lieutenant Commander in HMS *Kelvin*. George was awarded the DSC on 10 September 1945 for 'brave or skilful conduct escorting or protecting a convoy (HMS *Scourge*)'.

During the Second World War, between 1942 to 1945 Lieutenant Commander Balfour served on Destroyers HMS *Decoy, Tuscan, Scourge* and *Solebay*. He was promoted to Commander on 31 December 1945 and five years later again to the rank of Captain. George saw a further promotion to Rear Admiral on 7 January 1960, he retired from the Royal Navy on 15 January 1963.

George and Pamela had three children; their eldest son Patrick was born two years after their wedding. Younger son David was born in 1944, the couple also had one daughter, Jane. Patrick and Dave were to follow their father into the Royal Navy.

David Ian Balfour was born in Haymarket, Edinburgh on 9 July 1944. Born during the Second World War within a Naval family, Dave was possibly already set for an outstanding Naval career. Educated at Radley College, a boarding school in Oxfordshire, it is no surprise Dave became a keen oarsman, doing well at the sport and in time becoming a member of Leander.

After Radley, Dave moved on to the Britannia Royal Naval College specialising as a Supply and Secretariat Officer. His postings afterwards included HMS *London, Brighton*, and *Chichester*. Later Dave found himself working inside the Ministry Of Defence as Assistant Secretary to the Vice Chief of Naval staff. By 1977 Dave had moved to the teaching staff of the Lieutenants Greenwich Course, an appointment which lasted three years.

Dave married Rosalind Raban-Williams in August 1975 at St Bartholomew the Great Priory Church, London. The couple had one daughter, born in May 1978. Rosalind's father had also served in the Royal Navy in the Second World War seeing a promotion to Lieutenant Commander in February 1948; her mother was the daughter of a civil servant.

Dave joined HMS *Sheffield* in 1980 as Supply Officer. HMS *Sheffield* (D80) was the second Royal Navy ship to bear the name *Sheffield*, after the city of Sheffield in Yorkshire. She was a Type 42 Guided Missile Destroyer laid down by Vickers Shipbuilding and Engineering at Barrow-in-Furness on 15 January 1970, launched on 10 June 1971 and commissioned on 16 February 1975. Her nickname was to be the 'Shiny Sheff'.

On 4 May 1982, HMS *Sheffield* was hit by an Argentine Super Étendard-launched Exocet missile south-east of the Falklands. That day twenty men died and twenty-six more were injured. One of the Exocets slammed into the *Sheffield*'s starboard side about 8ft (2.4 metres) above the waterline, ripping a hole 4ft high and 15ft long. It penetrated as far as the ship's galley. Dave sadly lost his life that fateful day.

Fleet Street newspapers informed their readers about this 'awesome, space-age weapon', and described it as 'a missile that couldn't miss'. In fact, it appears that later in the Falklands War, some were successfully deflected.

Though his grave is the South Atlantic, Dave is honoured with a memorial plaque in the family mausoleum at Colinton Cemetery, Edinburgh, which reads 'IN MEMORY OF LT CDR DAVID IAN BALFOUR RN KILLED IN ACTION IN HMS SHEFFIELD THE FALKLANDS 1982'. Dave is also remembered on The Scottish National War Memorial , the Castle, Edinburgh.

At the time of his death Dave resided in Hindhead with his family. His daughter married in 2003 and eventually settled in Devon. Dave's father, retired Rear-Admiral George Ian MacIntosh Balfour, died in October 1999 living well into his eighties, as did his mother Pamela who died in 2004. Dave's father-in-law died aged 93, his mother-in-law at the grand age of 101 … Sliding Doors. Both Dave's father George and his father-in-law lived through the Second World War serving in the Royal Navy, but fate was not so kind for Dave.

In 2022, as part of the Falkland Islands 40th Anniversary Place Names Project, Dave was honoured with 'Balfour Creek', a small inlet on the south shore of King George Bay West Falkland.

His name lives on…

CO19615Y Lieutenant Commander Richard William Banfield HMS *Ardent* 14 January 1952 ~ 21 May 1982 Age 30

The Banfield name can be traced back to the eighteenth century in Devon, where generations back the family were Yeoman Farmers. The name William and Henry, or Harry, had also been in the Banfield family for generations.

Richard's paternal grandfather, William Henry Banfield, was born in Honiton in September 1885, the seemingly eldest son of Harry Banfield and Jessie Maude Webb, who married earlier that year. Jessie was born in Honiton though her mother, also Jessie, was from Scotland and her father William hailed from Staffordshire. Jessie Maude was the fourth child of eight children, born before her mother died in 1872 after delivering fraternal twins. Jessie's father worked for the Inland Revenue; he remarried in London in 1875 and had two more children, later retiring to live in Worcestershire.

Harry Banfield was born in Honiton in early 1862. It appears that Harry was the fourth child of William Henry Banfield and Mary North who married in Gittisham, Devon, on 18 October 1854, though not all survived into adulthood Harry was one of possibly seven children. Harry had a cousin who was a year younger, also named Harry.

William Henry, Richard's great-great-grandfather, was born in 1830 in Awliscombe, Devon, the son of John Banfield, a farmer, for a while he worked on his father's farm. After William and Mary married, they went into the hotel trade, the couple ran the Dolphin Hotel in Honiton for many years. They remained there after retirement, still living in the High Street. William died in September 1895, Mary continued to live with her family in the High Street, she died in 1913 aged 84.

Harry followed in his father's footsteps running the Dolphin Hotel after his father retired, he was also a wine merchant by the 1890s. Harry and Jessie had one other son, Percy, born in 1888. William Henry, their oldest son, married Amy Rosalind Trant in Croydon in late 1906. Amy was born in Catford in 1883, the daughter of Henry Trant and Eveline Lamont. Eveline was born in Devon, and married Henry Trant in Portsea Island in 1880. Henry Trant was a Stock Exchange Clerk.

William and Amy set up home in Reigate where William continued to manage a wine merchant business. Their first child, a daughter, was born in 1908, with Eric Harry following close behind in 1910; though he was born in Reigate, Eric was baptised in Devon in September that year. Altogether, William and Amy had six children between 1908 and 1918, three of them born during the First World War.

Whenever William Henry left Devon, it seemed the West Country was never far away from this branch of the Banfield family. By 1921, William and Amy were running the Montague Arms in Slough with most of their children living with them, Amy's parents also lived at the establishment. Eric, however, was living in Bournemouth with his grandparents.

It is through Eric Harry Banfield that we first see the Navy creep into the Banfield line. During the Second World War Eric served as an officer with the Royal Naval Volunteer Reserve. Eric married Mary Patricia Anne Freeth in Worthing in 1947. Though Mary was born in Blackpool, her father Matthew, an architect's assistant, had a military background. Matthew was the grandson of Ronald and Christina Macpherson. The Macphersons were originally from Scotland but spent many years in the East Indies.

Helen Lushington Macpherson was born in September 1851 on Prince of Wales Island, also known as Penang Island. The island was renamed Prince of Wales Island in August 1786 by Captain Francis Light of the East India Company. At the time of Helen's baptism, it came under the British Presidency of Bengal.

When Helen was just 18 years old, she married William Freeth in September 1869 in India. William Freeth was ten years older than Helen; born in India on 31 March 1841, the son of Major William Freeth who later retired a Lieutenant Colonel and died in December 1886. William and Helen lived on the Isle of Man for some time in the late 1800s, by which time William was a retired Colonel and employed as Chief Constable to the Isle of Man.

Matthew Logan Freeth was born in August 1883, he followed in his father and grandfather's footsteps, joining the British Army as a young man. Aged just 17, Matthew was an Officer Cadet at the Royal Military College, Sandhurst in 1901. Matthew joined the South Staffordshire Regiment (38th and 80th Foot), by 1903 he was a Lieutenant and by September 1914 made Temporary Adjutant of 9th (Service) Battalion Staffordshire Regiment. By 1916 Matthew was a Major when he was unfortunately wounded in January 1916 in France and Flanders, and thus entitled to wear a 'Wound Stripe'.

Matthew Logan Freeth married Mary Veronica Corrigan in Lancashire in 1919 after the First World War had ravaged the world; their daughter, Mary Patricia Anne Freeth, was born in September 1919. Mary Corrigan was born in Liverpool in May 1899. The couple also had a younger son, William Logan, who was a partner in a café in Notting Hill in the 1950s. William Logan Freeth also seemed to be an adventurer, setting sail for New York in 1938, on the Queen Mary.

William and Helen settled in Sussex after William retired as Chief Constable, and William Logan was born there in January 1922. He appeared to serve for a short time in the Royal Air Force in the Second World War but spent a fair amount of time on board ship, at one time working for Cunard. William Logan settled in London where he married in Fulham in 1947.

After leaving the British Army, Matthew Logan Freeth became an architect's assistant, living with his young family in Blackpool in 1921. He worked for Jacob Parkinson & Sons Ltd at Talbot Saw Mills, which later became Sir Lindsay Parkinson and Co. By 1939 the couple had moved to Croydon where Matthew continued to work as an architect's assistant. Matthew's father William died in February 1919; his mother Helen continued to live in Preston Park, Sussex until her death in January 1930.

At some point the Freeth family moved to Portsmouth after Matthew's death in 1946, Eric Harry Banfield and Mary Freeth married the following year. Richard William Banfield was born in Portsmouth on 14 January 1952, although he appears to be their only child records indicate that he had two half-siblings by his father's first marriage.

Eric Harry Banfield became a Temporary Lieutenant on 22 March 1940, he was appointed for Aeronautical Technical duties in the Fleet Air Arm. On New Year's Eve 1951, Eric was promoted to the rank of Commander, still serving with the Royal Navy. Eric moved around during his life; he was living in Bournemouth in 1930 and it seems he married his first wife in 1931. After their first child was born, they moved to Sussex.

Richard was educated at Allhallows School, Rousdon commencing his education there at 13 years old. According to Margaret Lewis, Curator of the Allhallows

Museum in Honiton, Richard is remembered as a boy with a strong character and a likeable personality. Distinctions for his work included French, Biology, Latin and Divinity, he also excelled in Geography, Mathematics and Physics. Richard later became a Prefect in Venning House.

He was a member of the Combined Cadet Force and appointed the senior member of the Naval Section, therefore in charge of the school's sailing boats. Richard was awarded a scholarship to the Royal Naval College, Dartmouth, and joined the Royal Navy in 1970. He served on HMS *Blake*, HMS *Fearless*, HMS *Sovereign* and latterly HMS *Ardent*.

Richard was killed on 21 May 1982 aboard HMS *Ardent* when the ship was bombed in Falkland Sound. At the time of his death, he lived in Menheniot, Liskeard, Cornwall. He is remembered on all the Falklands Memorials, also on the War Memorial in Menheniot, Cornwall. Eric died in February 1985, just three years after his son; at the time he was living in East Lee on the Solent. Richard's mother Mary died in Sussex on 23 July 2001.

This Banfield line began in the West Country, Richard found himself back there after the family had many worldwide adventures.

In 2022, as part of the Falkland Islands 40th Anniversary Place Names Project, Richard was honoured with 'Banfield Island', a small tussac island at the entrance to Brown Harbour in Port Philomel, West Falkland.

His name lives on…

D171207C Able Seaman (Sonar) Andrew Robert Barr HMS *Ardent* 14 November 1961 ~ 21 May 1982 Age 20

Andrew ('Andy') Robert Barr was born in Bridgwater, Somerset on 14 November 1961. His parents, James Dunnachie Barr and Loraine Elizabeth Ball, married in Bridgwater in early 1957.

James Dunnachie Barr was born in Bothwell, Scotland, in 1930. The name Robert appears to go back for a few generations and is of Germanic origin, meaning 'bright fame'; the name of Barr has more than one origin but in Scotland it is from the Gaelic meaning 'height' or 'hill'. Going back generations it seems that Andy's great-great-grandfather was a coal miner who lived in Baird's Square in Bothwell, a mining village.

On his mother's side, the Ball family had a long history in the Bridgwater area of Somerset. Loraine was born in Bridgwater in May 1931; her father was a carpenter/joiner, his father before him a bricklayer as was his father before him. The Ball family lived in Lyndale Avenue, Bridgwater for many years.

Andy joined the Royal Navy at 16 years old; he had served for approximately four years when he set sail with the Task Force headed for the Falkland Islands. Andy was killed on 21 May 1982 when HMS *Ardent* was bombed and sunk in Falkland Sound, he was just 20 years old. Like many, the Barr family received that dreaded 'knock on the door' to deliver the spine-chilling news. Andy's grave, as with so many, is the sea.

Andy left behind a girlfriend, his parents and brother Robin. At the time of his death, he lived in Kendale Road, Bridgwater, Somerset. Andy's mother Loraine died in 1999, his father in April 2020.

Andy is remembered on various memorials including a bench at St Georges Church, Church Road, Wembdon, Somerset. The inscription on a brass plaque reads 'IN MEMORY OF A.B. ANDREW BARR KILLED IN ACTION HMS ARDENT FALKLANDS CONFLICT 21ST MAY 1982'.

In 2022, as part of the Falkland Islands 40th Anniversary Place Names Project, Andy was honoured with 'Barr Creek', the innermost reaches of Victoria Harbour on Walker Creek land, East Falkland.

His name lives on…

502379 Lieutenant James Anthony Barry Royal Signals/2nd Battalion Parachute Regiment 3 June 1957 ~ 28 May 1982 Age 24

Most of the Barry families who settled in London were originally from Ireland, so possibly going back a little further, Jim's roots may well have been there too.

It appears that Jim's grandfather, William Peter Barry, was born in February 1886 in London; his parents, William and Hannah, had married the year before. Communications had for a long time played a part in the Barry family. By 1901 William senior was a 'letter carrier' and William junior a telegraph messenger, the family lived in Islington, London.

William Peter Barry married Dorothy Tisdall in 1917, towards the end of the First World War. Dorothy's father Frank served in a Rifle Brigade during the First World War. William and Dorothy's younger son, Desmond Anthony Barry, was born on 21 April 1925. Des was still at school when the Second World War broke out, but he later joined the Royal Signals and by 1956 was a Captain. Des married Audrey Foster in 1953 in Kent, and as a service family there was some mandatory relocation.

James Anthony Barry was born in Surrey on 3 June 1957. He was known among his comrades as Jim.

First commissioned into the Royal Signals in 1976, Jim served in Germany with the British Army of the Rhine. Later he served with 249 Signal Squadron AMF (L), during his time with them he received the Whistler Trophy for the best junior officer in his year. A high achiever, Jim came first when he completed his Norwegian army winter warfare course. He qualified as a military parachutist and in 1981 was seconded to the 2nd Battalion of The Parachute Regiment as a platoon commander.

In April 1982, just over three weeks after the Falkland Islands were invaded, Jim made his way 'Down South' as the officer in command of 12 platoon, D Coy, 2 Para. His potentially bright future was cut tragically short in the famous 'White Flag' incident at Goose Green on 28 May 1982.

Jim was killed in a confused situation where the Argentines thought he was going to surrender. Jim in turn thought the Argentinians were about to surrender.

The circumstances were made more complex by friendly fire coming from Darwin Hill.

Jim was 24 when he died – just a week short of his 25th birthday. He is buried in Aldershot Military Cemetery.

In 2008 a bronze-cast plaque bearing the names of Captain James Philippson killed in Afghanistan and Lieutenant James Barry, both from Bricket Wood, was unveiled at the Park Street War Memorial during a special service organised by St Stephen Parish Council. Parish Councillor Mick Freeman made the proposal to honour the men. Father Richard Tillbrook conducted the ceremony, both soldiers had served with The Parachute Regiment.

Jim may have lived in Bricket Wood near St Albans when he died, but it appears he may well have attended Welbeck College in Leicestershire where a memorial was made for him. The wooden board in a moulded frame badge of Welbeck College was inscribed 'IN MEMORY OF JAMES ANTHONY BARRY 42 ENTRY LT ROYAL SIGNALS BORN 3RD JUNE 1957 KILLED IN ACTION FALKLAND ISLANDS 28TH MAY 1982'.

Jim's grandmother Dorothy died in 1987 aged 90. His father Des died on 30 December 2010 by which time the family were settled in Swindon, Wilts.

In 2022, as part of the Falkland Islands 40th Anniversary Place Names Project, Jim was honoured with 'Barry Bay', a small bay at the entrance to Fish Creek at Beaver Island, West Falkland.

His name lives on…

C015622P Lieutenant Commander Gordon Walter James Batt DSC 800 Squadron Fleet Air Arm HMS *Hermes* 10 February 1945 ~ 24 May 1982 Age 37

Gordon ('Gordy') Walter James Batt was born on 10 February 1945 in Bircotes, Worksop, Nottinghamshire. His parents, Rose Calvert and Alfred James Batt, had married there in 1943, he was to be their only son. It appears Gordy was the only son of an only son. At the time of Gordy's birth his father, known as James, was serving in the RAF and the Second World War was yet to see an end.

Gordy's father was born in November 1915 in Andover, Hampshire, to George and Maria Batt. Rose Calvert was born in October 1921 in Yorkshire to George and Edna Calvert. George Calvert married Edna, a young widow with a daughter, in early 1921. The family settled in Bircotes, Nottinghamshire, where George worked as a coal miner. Rose worked as a 'domestic' in 1939 at the Hemsworth Colliery Institute in Bircotes. After Gordy's birth the couple settled in Andover, Hampshire.

Gordy's grandmother Edna died in 1968, during his early days in the Royal Navy, after which time Rose's father George saw out his days in Andover; he died in 1975.

Gordy was educated at Andover Grammar School, and as a member of the local Air Training Corps he took an early interest in aviation. Gordy joined the

Royal Navy at HMS *Fisgard* in Cornwall as an Artificer Apprentice, but he was then selected in 1964 for Officer Training. At the Britannia Royal Naval College, Dartmouth, as an 'Upper Yardman' Cadet, he became interested in diving and sailing.

As a Midshipman, Gordy saw service in the Far and Middle East. He returned to Dartmouth in 1967 to continue his studies. Once commissioned as a Sub Lieutenant, he became the First Lieutenant of HMS *Brave Swordsman*. Gordy married Diana in 1970, and in the same year started pilot training. Gordy and Diana's eldest son was born in 1971, and in July of that year Gordy was awarded his Fleet Air Arm 'wings', as well as the Ground School Training Prize.

After completing Advanced Flying Training and Operational Training on Sea King helicopters, Gordy joined 824 Squadron, where he served in HMS *Ark Royal* until Easter 1973. At that time, it became clear that despite the rundown of its 'big carrier' expertise, the Royal Navy would need to maintain a nucleus of fixed-wing pilots to crew the forthcoming Sea Harrier; Gordy Batt was among the first of a small number of helicopter pilots selected to train on fast jets.

For Gordy it was to be a five-year secondment to the Royal Air Force, initially for training on Jet Provost, then the Gnat and Hunter, before qualifying on the F-4M Phantom. Gordy was then operational with 43 Squadron – the Fighting Cocks – at RAF Leuchars, where he lived with his family from late 1974 to August 1977.

Gordy then returned to the Royal Navy as a student at the Naval Staff College, Greenwich, until February 1978. A resumption of flying duties led to a two-year exchange appointment with the United States Navy, in the highly esteemed VX4 Squadron at the Pacific Missile Test Centre, Point Mugu, California. He is still remembered there for his great skill in saving an F14 Tomcat after a dramatic low-level engine failure. For this he was awarded the US Secretary of State's Commendation for Meritorious Services in the Air.

On return from the United States in 1980 he began his Sea Harrier conversion with 899 Squadron Naval Air Command and moved to the Royal Naval Air Station at Yeovilton, in Somerset. He was due to become Senior Pilot of 800 Squadron in late 1982.

The Falklands War had other ideas and Gordy deployed 'Down South' in HMS *Hermes*, with the integrated 800/809/899 Sea Harrier component of that carrier's Air Group. He flew several important missions as strike leader. For these services and his outstanding leadership, Gordy was nominated for the award of a Distinguished Service Cross.

On 23 May 1982, about an hour before midnight, he launched from *Hermes* with three other Sea Harriers, to attack Stanley Airfield once more. His aircraft was last off the deck but was then seen to explode ahead of the carrier. The cause of this accident, which occurred about ninety miles north-east of Port Stanley, was never established. He was awarded the DSC posthumously.

That year was to prove a devastating one for Gordy's mother Rose; her husband James died in January, and just four months later Gordy was killed in action.

Gordy Batt was a hugely respected, highly experienced, and much-admired figure in the demanding world of Naval aviation. Gordy left behind his wife Diana and their three children: Christopher, Andrew and Joanna. At the time of Gordy's death, he lived in Martock, Somerset. Gordy is remembered with a plaque on the Martock War Memorial which simply reads 'FALKLANDS WAR 1982 GORDON W J BATT'.

In 2022, as part of the Falkland Islands 40th Anniversary Place Names Project, Gordy was honoured with 'Batt Islet', the southernmost islet in the Rabbit Island Rocks group in King George Bay, West Falkland.

His name lives on...

24122095 Acting Corporal William John Begley 22 SAS Regiment 15 April 1950 ~ 19 May 1982 Age 32

William John 'Paddy' Begley was born on 15 April 1950 in Stranorlar, a town in the Finn Valley of County Donegal, Ireland. The name Begley is of Irish origin, an Anglicisation of O Beaglaoich, meaning 'descendant of Beaglaoch'. Beag means small and laoch means hero, the name translates as 'small hero'. There are many Begleys to be found in County Donegal.

Bill was the youngest of seven children born to Robert and Susan Begley, who married in Stranorlar, Donegal, on 22 April 1936. It seems that the family previously lived in nearby Letterkenny going back a few generations. Tragedy was not unfamiliar to the Begley family, one of their children had died of bronchitis aged just 4 months.

Robert Begley was a carpenter as was his father before him, before that great-grandfather Robert was a farmer. Robert had been a widower when he married Bill's mother, his first wife died from complications following childbirth. Sadly, Bill's father died from pneumonia in 1965; he did not live to see his son marry.

Bill joined the Royal Corps of Transport; he was first attached to the SAS in 1978 becoming fully badged in August 1979. Bill was acting corporal when he died on 19 May 1982 in the tragic Sea King helicopter crash.

Bill married Stella on 29 July 1977 at the Register Office in North East Hampshire, at the time the couple resided in Fleet. Stella's family were originally from Wokingham, where she was the daughter of an electrical engineer.

Bill and his wife later settled in Hereford, living in Tupsley; they had two children, a daughter born in 1979 and a son named after his father, born in 1982 after Bill's death.

Bill is honoured in Hereford (St Martin's) Churchyard, Herefordshire SAS Regimental Plot on the Memorial Plaque. There is a pot next to the memorial plaque which reads 'BILL YOUR LOVE LIVES WITHIN MY HEART UNTIL OUR SPIRITS TOUCH STELLA'.

At the National Memorial Arboretum in the Special Forces Grove Bill's name proudly shines with his other SAS comrades.

In 2022, as part of the Falkland Islands 40th Anniversary Place Names Project, Bill was honoured with 'Begley Island', a tussac-covered islet at the northeast entrance to Brenton Loch, East Falkland.

His name lives on...

24347663 Lance Corporal Gary David Bingley MM 2nd Battalion Parachute Regiment 28 February 1958 ~ 28 May 1982 Age 24

Gary was born on 28 February 1958 at 11 Alexandra Park Road, Muswell Hill, London. Gary was the eldest son of David ('Dave') Alfred Bingley and Marina Bessie Eates who married in 1957.

Dave was the youngest son of Harold Edwin and Edith Bingley (née Tunster). The couple married at Hendon Register Office in July 1933; they had three sons together. Dave was born in September 1936 in Stanmore; at the time of his birth his father was a bank clerk. In 1939 the Bingley family were living at Wall Hall Lodge in Radlett, Hertfordshire. Edith lived with the boys and her mother-in-law, Ada.

Marina was the youngest of thirteen children, so Gary had many cousins. His favourite 'Aunty Pat' was in fact his cousin. At the time of Gary's birth his father Dave was a bus conductor; he later went on to become a bus driver. Gary's mum also wore a uniform, she was a 'Clippie' as they were known in those days.

Gary's paternal grandfather Harold was the son of Edwin Bingley, originally from Lincolnshire. Edwin enlisted into the British Army in July 1898, he stood just over 5ft 11in tall and had dark hair and blue eyes, similarities with Gary. Edwin served with the Royal Artillery, spending 162 days of his service in Australia between 1900–01, arriving back in the United Kingdom for his 21st birthday.

Edwin Bingley married Ada Hale on 12 October 1904 in St Mary's Church Sundridge, Kent. At the time of their marriage Edwin was a serving soldier based in Farnham, Surrey. The couple had three children; Harold was their first son, born on 7 December 1906 at Wheatsheaf Cottages in Fernilee, Derbyshire. His birth was registered by Ada's sister Amy, Harold was born at home. Edwin was a domestic butler for much of his working life.

Gary was stationed in Aldershot when the Falkland Islands were invaded. Both he and his great-grandfather Edwin had served in the British Army; both had been stationed in similar locations. Gary had also served for a brief time in the Officers' Mess while stationed in Berlin, but in contrast to his great-grandfather he hated mess life and could not wait to get back to soldiering, to him a 'dickie bow' was only for dinner dances.

By 1911 Edwin was living and working as a butler in Little Cadogan Place in Chelsea, records indicate that he had been discharged in July 1910. By 1911 Edwin and Ada had two children, their third child, a daughter, was born in April that year. In June 1916 there is a record of Edwin re-attesting into the Royal Flying Corps. Edwin survived the First World War and by 1921 the family were living in St Mary's Cottages, Hayes near Bromley, now Grade II listed buildings.

As the Second World War began, Edwin it seems was working as a House Steward at the United States Embassy in Grosvenor Square, Knightsbridge. Harold, it appears, attested into the Royal Artillery in 1936, following in his father's footsteps.

Though Edwin's father was a gardener, future Bingleys were to continue with service to their country in different ways. Gary's father served with the Territorial

Army for many years. Though Gary and one of his brothers were born in London, the Bingley family later settled in Coventry.

Gary attended school in Walsgrave followed by Caludon Castle, the family lived in Arch Road, Wyken, Coventry. After leaving school, Gary joined The Parachute Regiment earning his maroon beret through Junior Leaders. Two of his school friends joined up around the same time.

A Junior Leader in Inkerman Company 1 JLB Shorncliffe, Gary was in 416 Recruit Platoon, he passed out in October 1975. Gary was posted to the 2nd Battalion, Parachute Regiment. School friends Gordon, and Dinger served with 3 Para.

In 1976/7 Gary did his first Northern Ireland tour in Belfast. During his 'R & R' he celebrated his 19th birthday which coincidentally was the day he met his wife. After a whirlwind romance, during which time he was posted to Berlin for two years, Gary and Jay married at Taunton Register Office, on 9 July 1977. The same weekend the couple married, Gary's family moved to Beverley in Yorkshire. Dave had secured a job as a civilian driving instructor at the Defence School for Transport, Normandy Barracks, in Leconfield.

Gary was passionate about football, a lifelong supporter of Tottenham Hotspur. During his time in Berlin, he usually played right wing for both the battalion and Combined Services football teams. He loved his life, being able to combine parachuting with his love of football.

Though known as 'Gaz' or 'Bing' to his friends, he was known as Gary to his wife and family. After Berlin, Gary was posted to Ballykinler for eighteen months. He was by then in A Company, who took a huge hit on 27 August 1979 with the Narrow Water bombing at Warrenpoint, The Parachute Regiment lost sixteen men in a heinous attack.

In 1981 the battalion were posted to Aldershot where Gary and his family lived in married quarters in North Camp. They spent a year there before the invasion of the Falkland Islands, during which time Gary spent six weeks on exercise in Kenya.

Gary was an unusual combination of a sagacious and capricious character who had the most amazing sense of humour, able to carry off impersonations of John Travolta or John Inman with equal aptitude.

A lover of Jacque Cousteau, the trip 'Down South' was full of adventure for Gary as he relayed home stories of dolphins and flying fish. Some of his last words to his wife were 'I've waited six years for this', and 'Goodbye Girlie', and in that moment Jay knew she would never see her husband again.

Gary died during the Battle for Goose Green. He was edging forward when he came across an Argentinian Machine Gun nest. As Section Leader of 11 platoon D company, he was right up front just the way he liked it. Gary received a catastrophic head injury; his gunner Baz Grayling was also injured. Three men in his platoon received the Military Medal for bravery, their actions enabling D company to move forward.

It is only when you see that terrain that it you can comprehend how impossible the Battle for Goose Green and Darwin was. It is said that 2 Para's victory turned the war around.

Jay had promised Gary that she would carry out his wishes for a cremation should he die before her. Neither of them thought of the logistics of a war 8,000 miles away. For the first time in history families were eventually given the choice of repatriation. The press made the announcement on 9 July 1982, ironically the day the couple would have celebrated their fifth wedding anniversary.

In November 1982 Gary was given a full military funeral followed by a cremation. Jay and Padre David Cooper held a private service to inter his ashes a few days after the funeral. His ashes are at rest with his brothers in arms in the Falklands Plot in Aldershot Military cemetery.

Gary and Jay had one daughter, born while stationed in Berlin.

In 2022, as part of the Falkland Islands 40th Anniversary Place Names Project, Gary was honoured with 'Bingley Bay', a bay on the west coast of Cape Dolphin on mainland East Falkland.

His name lives on…

D184194V Able Seaman Iain Macdonald Boldy HMS *Argonaut* 30 September 1961 ~ 21 May 1982 Age 20

Arthur Benjamin Boldy married Martha McBryde Morris in Alloa, Clackmannanshire, Scotland, in 1945, their first son, Keith, was born in Alloa the following year. Sons Ron and Iain followed over the next few years. During their marriage the couple relocated twice, the first time was from Scotland to Derby.

Martha McBryde Morris was born in Bathgate, Scotland in 1924, the oldest child of Thomas Morris and Elizabeth Graham McBryde. The couple had another daughter in 1929 after which they moved to Alloa, where youngest child Thomas John was born in 1934.

Iain Macdonald Boldy was born in Derby on 30 September 1961, the youngest of three boys. Iain was baptised at St Joseph's Catholic Church, later he attended St Joseph's Primary School in Gordon Road, Derby. The family moved to a little village called Darley Abbey where Iain became active in the Darley Abbey Methodist Scouts group and the youth club. After passing his eleven-plus, Iain attended Bemrose Grammar school from 1972.

After leaving school Iain aspired to join the Royal Navy but first on the agenda was a visit with brother Ron, by then living in Australia. Iain worked in a Printing Works, also attending day college on a book binding course, which he passed with flying colours. He made the trip to Australia and spent a very happy month there.

On returning home to the UK, papers were waiting for Iain to report to HMS *Raleigh* for training, he completed his Seamanship at HMS *Drake*. From there Iain was drafted to HMS *Argonaut*. He served six months in the Gulf, Africa, and the Vatican where he met the Pope.

In February of 1982 Iain married his fiancée Margaret, a nurse at the Derbyshire Royal Infirmary. Just weeks later HMS *Argonaut* was sent to the Falkland Islands, sailing on 19 April 1982 as part of the Task Force. HMS *Argonaut* (F5) was a

Leander-class frigate used by the Royal Navy from 1967 to 1993. Though she sustained damage during the Falklands War, *Argonaut* lost just two men and unlike other ships she remained afloat.

On 21 May, HMS *Argonaut* along with other frigates and destroyers was providing close escort for other amphibious vessels. The Task Force were expecting an opposed landing at San Carlos, it was a busy day for all.

HMS *Argonaut* was standing off 'Fanning Head' within Falkland Sound, guarding the northern approaches. The ship came under attack by Argentine aircraft, the first successful attack came at 10.15; a lone Argentinian aircraft, an Aermacchi MB-339 flown by Lieutenant. Guillermo Owen Crippa, attacked *Argonaut* with cannon-fire and rockets, causing damage to her Type 965 radar.

The second air attack came at 13.37 hrs by way of five Argentinian A4-Skyhawks from the Argentinian Air Force 5th Brigade. They hit *Argonaut* with two bombs, neither of which exploded although one killed two sailors when it entered the ship's Sea Cat missile magazine, detonating two missiles. The other did severe damage to the boiler room, knocking out the ship's power. Left dead in the water, *Argonaut* was vulnerable; she was towed away from immediate danger by HMS *Plymouth*. Both bombs were still live, taking days to defuse.

Iain Boldy was killed along with Matthew Stuart that day; other ships were not so lucky during this brutal war, but to every family the loss is beyond words.

Iain had not been married long enough to have any children but left behind a bereft widow, his parents, and brothers. The priests from the Catholic and Methodist Churches officiated at Iain's memorial service. Iain is now added to the Roll of Honour at his old school where his page sits in a Remembrance Book situated in the school library.

Totally devastated by the loss of Iain, his parents were unable to stay in the house which had been Iain's home. Martha and Arthur emigrated to Australia in 1988, making the long journey from Darley Abbey, Derby. They settled on Macleay Island, Queensland, off the coast of Brisbane. With second son Ron settled in Oz ten years earlier, it seemed like a plan to leave their pain behind. Life and emotions are not that simple; however, it remained their dying wish that their ashes be scattered in the place where their son Iain died, to reunite them with their lost son.

Sadly, Arthur died age 76 in 1997 from cancer, Martha kept his ashes in her bedroom for nineteen years until she herself passed from a stroke in 2016 Aged 91.

Martha was indeed a strong woman; at the age of 86 she made the 12,000-mile journey to the UK to stay with her eldest son Keith and to collect the Elizabeth Cross, all after she had undergone a triple heart bypass operation. Her ashes, with those of her husband, were to travel a bit further though some years later, 20,000 miles to be exact. The Boldys' ashes journeyed from Brisbane to the UK and then from Brize Norton down to the Falkland Islands with one of Iain's shipmates Paddy, who was visiting the Islands with the 'Not Forgotten Association' in November 2017.

Bad weather meant that Paddy himself was unable to complete the task, he left the ashes in the safe hands of the 1st Battalion Irish Guards who were stationed on the Falkland Islands at the time. The Guards passed the ashes on to the Royal Air Force who agreed to lower them on the exact coordinates where Iain had died in the Bay.

Iain's widow Margaret remarried in 1987; she has continued to help others with her Volunteer work at the National Memorial Arboretum at Alrewas.

Ron, who had also served with the Royal Navy, remained in Australia; Keith used his talent in life to become an amazing artist. In 2021 he donated the proceeds of a pencil drawing of 'Captain Tom' to a fundraiser Jay undertook for Veterans in Action.

In 2022, as part of the Falkland Islands 40th Anniversary Place Names Project, Iain was honoured with 'Boldy Island', a small tussac island south of Inner Northwest Island in the North West Island group just north of Falkland Sound.

His name lives on…

D1348157 Petty Officer Marine Engineering Mechanic (Mechanical) David Richard Briggs DSM HMS *Sheffield* 18 May 1956 ~ 4 May 1982 Age 25

David Richard Briggs was born in Balham, South London on 18 May 1956. David's parents Richard Horace Briggs and Jean Mary Gilby married in 1953. Jean was the daughter of Thomas and Annie Gilby, her father was a wharf labourer.

Richard was the son of Sydney and Ida Briggs, Sydney was a sheet metal worker, both families lived in the same block of flats in Balham.

Sydney Frank Christian Briggs was the eighth child of Joseph and Mary Jane Briggs who married in Bethnal Green in 1868. Most of their children were born in Woolwich; Sydney was a driver on the railway. The Briggs family has a lot of history in the London, Kent and Sussex areas. Great-uncle Henry, a commercial clerk, married in Woolwich but moved to Erith. Henry married Esther and had three children. Great-aunt Alice married in Woolwich in 1893, she also moved to Erith. Great-uncle Frederick married Louisa in 1895 in Woolwich, they had a family and ended up living in Crayford. Great-aunt Amy married in Woolwich in 1898, where three of her children were born before the family moved to Welling. Great-uncle Joseph married in 1904 and lived with his family in Erith. Great aunt-Helen married in 1912, but sadly her husband died in 1918; Helen was a nurse in Kent in the late 1930s. Great-aunt Edith married in Dartford in 1911, and lastly, great-uncle Stanley married in 1916, he was an inspector with London Transport and lived in Bexley in 1939.

Sydney and Ida married in Eastbourne, Sussex, in 1916; they had three children, of whom Richard was the youngest. When Sydney died on 28 February 1955, the year before his grandson David was born, he was still living in London. David's family moved to Crawley in Sussex not long after his birth.

David's father Richard served in the Royal Air Force from 1942 to 1947.

David was a keen touring cyclist, at the age of 13 he cycled over 1,000 miles in a fourteen-day round-trip from Sussex to the Peak District and Yorkshire Dales. His last cycle was hand-built, it was lost with his ship.

David joined the Royal Navy straight from school and soon reached Leading Rate. His first brush with danger was while serving in HMS *Egeria*, when he single-handedly extinguished a dangerous engine-room fire at sea, for which he received a Flag Officer's Commendation.

On 23 July 1977, 'Basher', as he was known to his mates, married Christine at St Andrew's Church, Burgess Hill. They subsequently set up home in Lee on the Solent to be near to his ship. Basher was promoted to Petty Officer and returned to HMS *Sultan* in Gosport for a spell as an Instructor before his final draft to HMS *Sheffield*.

HMS *Sheffield* sailed from Portsmouth on 19 November 1981 for a patrol in the Arabian Gulf followed by a major Mediterranean exercise. On 2 April 1982, four days before her planned return to Portsmouth, the ship was diverted to the South Atlantic.

Sheffield was on forward radar picket duty about seventy miles south and east of Stanley, on 4 May 1982 when she was struck amidships by an Exocet missile fired from Argentine Naval Super Étendard aircraft. The order to abandon ship soon followed as fires raged. Basher's firefighting second time around was to lead to his death.

Basher was awarded the Distinguished Service Medal posthumously, his citation:

> '*The QUEEN has been graciously pleased to approve the Posthumous award of the Distinguished Service Medal to the undermentioned in recognition of gallant and distinguished service during operations in the South Atlantic:*
>
> Petty Officer Marine Engineering Mechanic (M) David Richard BRIGGS D1348157
>
> *On 4th May 1982, HMS SHEFFIELD was struck by an Exocet missile fired by an Argentine aircraft. Petty Officer Marine Engineering Mechanic Briggs was in the vicinity of the After-Section Base and set in motion the initial fire-fighting effort.*
>
> *He then moved forward to his action station at the Forward Section Base but at this stage personnel were being evacuated from this area on to the forecastle. However, he led his team back to recover important equipment which was necessary to continue the fire-fighting operation. Unable to wear breathing equipment due to restricted access through a hatch, Petty Officer Marine Engineering Mechanic Briggs and his team re-entered the smoke filled forward section. In conditions of increasing smoke and almost no visibility Petty Officer Marine Engineering Mechanic Briggs made several journeys to the Forward Section Base to pass out much valuable equipment. Sadly, on the last attempt he was overcome by smoke and rendered unconscious, subsequent attempts to revive him proving unsuccessful.*
>
> *Petty Officer Marine Engineering Mechanic Briggs demonstrated leadership, bravery, and devotion to duty in trying to save his ship.*'

Basher's was the only body recovered from the 'Shiny Sheff'. He was buried at sea on 6 May 1982 in a ceremony witnessed by the aircraft carrier's ship's company in the presence of his Captain, 'Sam' Salt, and Commander Bob Rowley. The service was conducted by the Reverend Roger Devonshire, Flag Chaplain.

In 2022, as part of the Falkland Islands 40th Anniversary Place Names Project, Basher was honoured with 'Briggs Beach', a long sand beach on mainland East Falkland south of Dutchman's Island.

His name lives on…

D089826M Petty Officer Marine Engineering Mechanic (Mechanical) Peter Ian Herbert Brouard HMS *Ardent* 2 July 1950 ~ 21 May 1982 Age 31

Peter Ian Herbert Brouard was born on 2 July 1950, he was originally from Guernsey where the family name is well known.

Peter married Anne in Gosport in 1972, the couple had one son born in 1982 after his father's death. At the time Peter died, the family lived in Crewkerne in Somerset.

There is a memorial tree in the Le Foulon Cemetery in Guernsey dedicated to Peter. It says:

'This plaque and tree are dedicated to the proud and honoured memory of Guernsey man Petty Officer AEM Peter Ian Herbert Brouard RN Aged 31 years who was killed in action on board HMS Ardent in Falkland Sound, Falkland Islands on 21st May 1982 during the conflict in the South Atlantic. He was serving with 815 Naval Air Squadron as a member of the ships flight and died as his ship provided protection to the landing forces which liberated the Falkland Islands'.

On the 30th Anniversary of the war, Bailiff Richard Collas from Guernsey laid a wreath on behalf of Peter on the water near where HMS *Ardent* sank. He was visiting the Falkland Islands and while there visited sheltered accommodation built using funds donated by Guernsey.

Peter was finally added to the War Memorial on 22 May 2022, when a plaque for the Falklands War was unveiled by the Lieutenant-General of Guernsey, Lt General Richard Cripwell and Richard MacMahon, the Bailiff of Guernsey. Peter's widow Anne and a relative were in attendance.

In 2022, as part of the Falkland Islands 40th Anniversary Place Names Project, Peter was honoured with 'Brouard Creek', a creek running southwest at the head of Kelp Harbour on the Falkland Sound side of East Falkland.

His name lives on…

P029435P Corporal James Gardner Browning HQ 3 Commando Brigade Royal Marines 20 May 1951 ~ 11 July 1982 Age 31

James Gardner Browning was born on 20 May 1951 in Whitburn, West Lothian, an area with long association for the Browning family. The name James Browning goes back many generations in Scotland.

In 1867, James Browning and Janet Russell married – James was born in Larkhall, Lanarkshire, in 1845. The couple had a large family, it appears their first son James died in 1882, aged just 14. A son born a year later was named James Gardner Browning, he was second to youngest of nine children. In 1901 James Gardner was a cab driver, but within four years he had set up a business as a Funeral Director. Browning's Funeral Directors still operates today.

James Gardner Browning married Agnes Burton in Whitburn in 1902; they too had a large family. David Russell Burton Browning was one of their younger children, born in 1921.

David enlisted into the Royal Air Force in Padgate during the Second World War; he was a Leading Aircraftsman when he was awarded the British Empire Medal for risking attacks by sharks when he dove twice from a jetty at night to save two men whose boat had capsized off the West African Coast.

David married Robina Hunter Watt in Haymarket in 1948; Robina was born in Falkirk in 1928. David and Robina went on to have ten children, James Gardner Browning born in 1951 was the couple's third son.

James Gardner Browning was known to family and friends as either 'Jimmy' or 'Gardner'. Jimmy attended Armadale Primary School, followed by Bathgate Academy. From a young age Jimmy worked on farms, he was particularly close to his brother David.

After joining the Royal Marines circa 1970, Jimmy found himself posted to Poole in Dorset; it was during this posting that he met and fell in love with Barbara. Barbara was older than Jimmy with a family of three girls, he readily took on the role of stepfather to Mandy, Sally, and Tara. Jimmy and Barbara married in Bournemouth in 1978. Jimmy's mother remarried in 1978, and so Jimmy acquired a stepfather just as he became one himself.

Jimmy had quite an effect on Sally, encouraging her to join the Royal Air Force – he gave quite a good argument for the RAF. Though Sally had no knowledge that Jimmy's father had served in the RAF, she joined the service in 1983, the year after Jimmy's death.

For the family in Scotland, their last family get together was for the wedding of Jimmy's brother David and his bride Mima on 1 May 1982. As the Falklands War heated up the QE2 was also requisitioned, setting sail on 12 May 1982 with Jimmy on board. That wedding day was to remain among treasured memories in the years to come.

By Lonnie Donoghue:

> Jim enlisted into the Royal Marines in 1970. He elected to transfer to the engineering role as a vehicle mechanic training at Bordon, Hampshire, returning to Poole to serve in 3 Commando Brigade Workshop. During his time in Commando brigade, he served a long-term detachment with 45 Commando.
>
> In May '82 James was seconded to 10 Field Workshop REME joining the Unit on the QE2 for the journey south. During this time, we formed a weapon training team, and between us we trained

the whole workshop on every weapon available to them in every winterised guise.

James was a very fit, witty and humble Scotsman who didn't waste a moment raising banter with the Para trained element of the Workshops. His arctic warfare training stood him in good stead in the early days at San Carlos and he readily directed and advised in the early digging-in processes before the Workshop finally stabilised its location at Blue Beach.

On the evening of 11 July James was tasked with transferring troops by Gemini craft from the MV *Baltic* to HMS *Arrow* for a liaison function. On moving out of the Falkland Sound the sea was like a mill pond, unfortunately during his return journey the weather closed in and during the ensuing very heavy storm James was washed overboard.

Unfortunately, his body was never recovered. James was listed MIA until 1983 when he was formally listed as KIA although it was after cessation of hostilities.

Jimmy's grandfather, who began the family funeral business, died in 1972, it remains a family concern. Robina passed in 1993, Jimmy's father David in 2011 aged 89. Barbara died in Cornwall in January 2021; she had not remarried and treasured many memories of Jimmy until her passing.

Jimmy is honoured on the Armadale War Memorial. The Browning family have mainly stayed in the same area of Scotland.

In 2022, as part of the Falkland Islands 40th Anniversary Place Names Project, Jimmy was honoured with 'Browning Bay', a small bay north of Ajax Bay in San Carlos waters, East Falkland.

His name lives on…

24599688 Private Gerald Bull 3rd Battalion Parachute Regiment 11 November 1963 ~ 12 June 1982 Age 18

Gerald ('Ged') Bull was born in Brixworth, Northamptonshire, on 11 November 1963 to Amos Albert Bull and Rosalie Kitty Brown, who had married in 1951. Amos was born in January 1922 in Buckinghamshire; the family were farm workers from Hanslope. Grandfather Joseph and his wife Sarah Ann had eleven children.

Amos, it appears was named after his maternal grandfather Amos Newbury Lovell, who married Mary Ann Lovell on 27 September 1890 in Emberton, Buckinghamshire. Ellen Elizabeth Lovell was Amos and Mary Ann's oldest child. Amos, born in January 1872, was the son of George and Mary Lovell from Emberton. In 1901 the family were living in Towcester, Northamptonshire, where Amos was employed as a shepherd. Most of their children were born in Emberton, including son Amos Newbury junior who was born in January 1895. Amos joined the Oxfordshire & Buckinghamshire Light Infantry in 1914 at the start of the First World War. Sadly, he died on 27 April 1916 in France & Flanders, Amos junior is remembered on the Hanslope War Memorial.

Ellen Elizabeth Lovell married Robinson Haw at the beginning of 1913. Robinson joined the British Army in 1895, by the following year he had transferred to the Grenadier Guards. When the First World War commenced, Robinson was called up as a reservist. Having survived the Battle of Omdurman during the Egyptian Campaign in 1898, Robinson had settled with Ellen after seeing service in South Africa, Canada and Australia, returning to Morley around 1911. Ellen and Robinson had two daughters, Ellen and Myra. After losing her brother in 1916, just over a year later Robinson was also killed in 1917.

Ellen became a Bull, marrying into the family in late 1917. Her husband was one of eleven children.

Ged's great-uncle Octavius Thomas Bull DCM died in October 1918 at Horton War Hospital, Epsom. Great-uncle Charles Daniel Bull, 5th Battalion Oxford & Buckinghamshire Light Infantry, was killed in action on 25 September 1915 in France & Flanders, he is remembered at Ypres, Menin Gate. Great-uncle Fred joined the Northamptonshire Regt in 1906, in 1911 he was stationed in Malta. Albert Joseph Bull survived serving in the Northampton Regt in the First World War, though he was discharged in 1916 after being wounded.

Ged's father Amos also served in the British Army, listed as a 'soldier' on the 1939 register, his mother Ellen was a land worker at the Nurseries in Olney, Buckinghamshire; she died the year before Amos and Rosalie married. Records indicate that Ellen may have had as many as thirty grandchildren from her six children, though many – including Ged – were born after her death.

Gerald Bull was the fourth child of Amos and Rosalie who also had a set of fraternal twins two years after Ged was born. Ged was born in Brixworth, though he has a fabulous family history, he was the first to wear the maroon beret, passing P Coy and serving with the 3rd Battalion, Parachute Regiment. Ged also loved football; his preferred position was goalie.

Sadly, Ged was badly injured in the battle for Mount Longdon; he died of his wounds aged just 18.

Ged's body was repatriated, he is buried at All Saints Cemetery, Brixworth, Northamptonshire. He is buried in a Commonwealth War Grave, though he is not too far from his father Amos who died in 1985, brother Steve who died in 1988, and his mother Rosalie who died in 2011.

Ged is remembered on many Falklands memorials; he is also listed on the Brixworth War Memorial in Brixworth.

In 2022, as part of the Falkland Islands 40th Anniversary Place Names Project, Ged was honoured with 'Bull Islet', a small tussac island off mainland West Falkland near Port Edgar in Falkland Sound.

His name lives on...

24364397 Lance Corporal Barry Charles Bullers Army Catering Corps RFA *Sir Galahad* 22 March 1956 ~ 8 June 1982 Age 26

Barry Charles Bullers was born at 183 Chester Road, Shire Oak, Brownhills, Walsall Wood, Staffordshire. His parents Joseph Charles and Florence Bullers (née Pratt) married in 1933.

Joseph Charles Bullers was a coal miner when the couple married. Florence was the daughter of Harry Pratt, also a coal miner, who worked at Aldridge Colliery. Harry was also the son of a coal miner, born and raised in Walsall Wood. Harry worked at an iron foundry prior to coal mining, he ended up in the 1930s working above ground. Many of the men in the Second World War remained on home soil as mining and many other professions were vital in keeping the home fires burning; some joined up as reservists.

Florence's family lived in Chester Road; it was a street she remained living on after her marriage to Barry's father.

Joseph Charles Bullers was born at 13 Gladstone St, Walsall, the only son of Joseph and Florence Bullers (née Sturmy). Joseph Bullers was part of a family who had served their country during the First World War. Barry's grandfather Joe was born in Walsall, Joe's father, also Joseph, had married for a second time after being widowed in 1870. Having moved from Hampshire to Walsall, Joe was one of four sons born to Joseph and his new wife. Three of their sons served during the First World War as did half-brother Francis Frederick.

Private Francis Frederick Bullers served with the 3rd Battalion, South Staffordshire Regiment, until 23 March 1916 when he was deemed no longer physically fit for service. His Silver Star was issued on 15 September 1920. Charles Bullers attested into the 3rd Derby Regiment in October 1898, he transferred into the 1st South Staffordshire Regiment in 1915. Ernest George Bullers served as a Private with the Royal Welsh Fusiliers and the Army Service Corps during the First World War. All survived the war, married, and went on to have families of their own. Charles' son, also named Charles, served with the Royal Tank Corps enlisting in January 1931.

Joe Bullers was born in Walsall in early 1879, he attested into the South Staffordshire Regiment in January 1897. Joe married Florence Sturmy in Walsall in 1903. The couple had just one son, Joseph Charles Bullers, known as Charlie. Joe died in 1908 leaving Florence to bring up their son alone. Sadly, Florence died in 1912. Charlie, orphaned by the age of 7, went to live with relatives. Charlie was working for Conduit Colliery Co Ltd by the time he was 15.

Charlie and his wife Florence had four children between 1935 and 1956. Barry Charles Bullers was their youngest, eight years younger than his brother; he also had two older sisters. Barry had nieces and nephews almost the same age as him. Barry grew up in the Brownhills area of Walsall, later joining the British Army serving with the Army Catering Corps.

During the Falklands War, Barry was attached to the 1st Battalion Welsh Guards, he tragically died when the *Galahad* came under attack. Three A-4 Skyhawks targeted *Galahad*, which was hit by three bombs released from the Skyhawk flown by First Lieutenant Carlos Cachón. The second Skyhawk was unable to drop its bombs, and the third overshot the British ship. The damage was done however, it was to be the biggest loss of life for British Troops during Operation Corporate.

When Barry died, he was single and still living at home when on leave.

Barry is remembered with a plaque at Brownhills Memorial Hall, in the area where he grew up. Another plaque is situated in St Peters Church, Stonnall, in Staffordshire, a rectangular marble tablet is inscribed 'IN LOVING MEMORY OF LCPL BARRY CHARLES BULLERS ACC ATT WELSH GUARDS WHO GAVE HIS LIFE IN THE FALKLAND ISLANDS WAR 8 JUNE 1982 AGE 26'.

In 2022, as part of the Falkland Islands 40th Anniversary Place Names Project, Barry was honoured with 'Bullers Island', a small tussac island at the entrance to Brown Harbour in Port Philomel, West Falkland.

His name lives on…

24145047 Acting Sergeant Paul Alan Bunker 22 SAS Regiment 26 January 1954 ~ 19 May 1982 Age 28

Paul Alan Bunker was born Paul Alan Frank on 26 January 1954 in Plymouth, Devon. His parents, Leslie Andrew Frank and June Bunker, married in 1953, also in Plymouth. Tragically Paul was to be their only child as Paul's mother died in 1956, she was just 21 years old.

Paul's father Leslie was born in Devonport on 30 November 1930, the eldest child of Leslie Frank and Kathleen Byrne. Leslie died in the West Middlesex hospital on 13 October 1985, just a month short of his 55th birthday.

Paul Alan Bunker was a Junior Leader with the Royal Army Ordnance Corps between 1969-1971. Paul joined 22 SAS Regiment in August 1976 and was posted to 16 (Air Troop) initially.

Paul married in 1979; in May that year he joined with 19 (Mountain) Troop. Prior to the Falklands War he saw service in Northern Ireland, West Virginia, Florida and Bavaria.

During the Falklands War Paul served with D Squadron (19 Troop), he survived a crash on the Fortuna Glacier, South Georgia. He and his comrades had gone on to lead advance elements which led our forces to capture the main enemy positions in Grytviken. The surrender of the enemy in South Georgia followed.

Just ten days later he took part in a successful raid on Pebble Island which led to destruction of enemy aircraft.

On 19 May 1982, 22 SAS Regiment took a huge hit in the Sea King disaster, Paul was one of the casualties that day.

In 2022, as part of the Falkland Islands 40th Anniversary Place Names Project, Paul was honoured with 'Bunker Islet', a tussac islet off the south end of Sand Bay Island in the Arch Islands, West Falkland.

His name lives on…

24422490 Lance Corporal Antony Burke 1st Battalion Welsh Guards 6 January 1959 ~ 8 June 1982 Age 23

Antony was born in Wrexham, Denbighshire, on 6 January 1959, the eldest child and only son of Ronald and Marilyn Burke (née Hughes). Tony had a younger sister Gail. As a young man Tony joined the 1st Battalion Welsh Guards.

Tony married Diane Parry in 1980 in Rhuddlan, Denbighshire.

Tony was a Lance Corporal in the 1st Battalion of the Welsh Guards during the Falklands War. He was killed the day the *Sir Galahad* was bombed at Fitzroy on 8 June 1982, he was 23 years old.

Tony is remembered in St Margaret's Churchyard, Bodelwyddan, Denbighshire, with a gravestone. The inscription reads *'FOR MY SAKE AND IN MY NAME LIVE ON AND NEVER BE AFRAID TO DIE FOR I AM WAITING FOR YOU IN THE SKY'*

For many young men who perished in the Falklands War, their bodies lost to the ocean, a memorial stone is a place for family and friends to visit, a place to honour them, a place of reflection.

In 2004 a new funeral pall for the Welsh Guards was formally blessed at a special service at St Margaret's Church at Bodelwyddan (also known as the Marble Church), the service was led by Rev Berw Hughes. The pall is used in the funerals of former Welsh Guardsmen. Former guardsmen laid a wreath for Tony after the service.

In 2022, as part of the Falkland Islands 40th Anniversary Place Names Project, Tony was honoured with 'Burke Lagoon' at the innermost basin of Volunteer Lagoon, East Falkland.

His name lives on…

24369281 Corporal Robert Allan Burns 264 SAS Signal Squadron, 22 SAS Regiment 31 July 1959 ~ 19 May 1982 Age 22

Robert Allan ('Rab') Burns was born on 31 July 1959. Rab was the only son among four children, he was known to his family as Allan, but to his comrades he was Rab. The Burns family hailed from Dundee, Scotland.

Rab attended St Johns RC High school, Harefield Road, Dundee after which he joined the British Army aged just 16. Rab's parent unit was the Royal Corps of Signals, but he aspired to do great things, passing SAS selection in March 1979. A lover of the outdoors in general, Rab had shown his determination and grit previously when tabbing home nearly 100 miles after attending a camping trip to Rannoch Moor.

Rab is remembered as 'understated'; a lover of music known to play the bagpipes on occasion. Like many SAS service personnel, he kept low key around those activities, like many, he was destined for great things had his life not been so cruelly cut short.

When the Falklands were invaded on 2 April 1982, Corporal Burns was serving with 264 SAS Signal Squadron (attached G Squadron). He sadly lost his life during the Sea King crash on 19 May 1982.

In April 1983 Tam Dalyell, then MP for Linlithgow & West Lothian, addressed parliament with a follow up to his speech of December 1982, still seeking answers around the sinking of the *Belgrano*. He stated that an article by journalist Margaret Vaughan had riveted his attention with a passage headed 'Tears on the SS *Pilgrimage*' about corporal Robert Allan Burns.

In the article the journalist stated that Rab had confided in his father that he was expecting to be involved in an overseas conflict. It seems that a telegram to his father after his final leave in February 1982, indicated in a coded message that his destination was the Falkland Islands. It raised questions in the 'House' as to who knew the 'what and when'.

There are always questions after the event. Whether Rab or his comrades knew or not weeks before the rest of the public knew, it takes nothing away from the bravery of our forces, nor does it diminish the loss for families. Public record just means we can read those conversations for ourselves.

One of Rab's sisters is an established Jazz musician, sharing a love of music with her brother. He had been known to underplay his SAS role, suggesting that he was just a pen-pusher. He was certainly a lot more than that.

Just nine men survived the horrendous crash that day. Rab's grave is the South Atlantic Ocean.

In 2022, as part of the Falkland Island 40th Anniversary Place Names Project, Rab was honoured with 'Burns Lagoon', a tidal lagoon between Muddy Creek and Kings Creek at the northwest end of Port Salvador, East Falkland.

His name lives on…

24576615 Private Jason Stuart Burt 3rd Battalion Parachute Regiment 28 July 1964 ~ 12 June 1982 Age 17

Jason Stuart Burt was born in Hackney on 28 July 1964, the oldest son of Syd and Terry Burt, who for many years ran a market stall. Syd was of Jewish heritage, and Terry, Irish. The couple between them were made of strong stuff but nothing could have prepared them for the future and the heartbreak it would bring. Syd had been for some time in business with a partner in Mare Street, they were hardworking 'salt of the earth' people. Their second son, Jarvis, was born three years after Jason.

The couple settled in Walthamstow where Jason attended Chapel End Junior school. He is remembered fondly by classmates there as funny, entertaining, very good looking and a practical joker. Many girls would be drawn to Jason's good looks, but just as many to his charismatic personality. Prior to joining the army, Jason attended Sir George Monoux College in Walthamstow.

On leaving school at 16, Jason seemed determined to don a uniform. He joined The Parachute Regiment in September 1980, arriving at Browning Barracks,

Aldershot, to commence his training. Anyone who has attempted P Coy will understand it is a gruelling experience, many fail. Though Jason was a small lad compared to others it is not size but sheer grit that gets boys through such demanding training on their way to becoming men.

Though Jason's father initially declined to sign the application papers, Jason was not giving up; eventually Syd relented.

After successfully completing his training, Jason was sent to B Coy 3 Para, passing out just a few weeks before the invasion of the Falkland Islands. When the invasion came, Jason had a choice to make. At just 17 he was not allowed to vote, to give blood, have a drink in a pub or serve in Northern Ireland, but he did have the choice to serve on active service elsewhere and he chose to go. There were several young men who were the same age who left to travel 'Down South' on the SS *Canberra* which set sail with 3 Para on board on 9 April 1982. Jason was sadly to become the second youngest to be killed in the war.

Jason died during the Battle for Mount Longdon on 12 June 1982 alongside another 17-year-old, and a third friend who died the day after his 18th birthday. Just prior to his death he had administered first aid to his section commander Corporal Brian Milne, who had stepped on an anti-personnel mine. Jason administered morphine to the wounded soldier as machine-gun tracer rounds rained down and flares lit up the sky. This brave young man gave away his own morphine in an act of kindness that was way beyond his years.

After making it back to his lines unwounded, Jason followed Sergeant Des Fuller's command for a combined 4 and 5 Platoon group to charge, he stumbled, climbed back to his feet, and was killed by a 50-calibre machine gun round.

Jason was repatriated and buried in Aldershot Military Cemetery, his grave can be seen from right at the top of the hill, covered in flowers in the colours of his favourite football team, Chelsea. The grave bears the Star of David, denoting his Jewish roots.

On 22 June 2022, AJEX the Jewish Military Association held a service at the National Memorial Arboretum ahead of Armed Forces Day. In a poignant service, Jason in particular was remembered for his bravery in 1982 on the 40th Anniversary of the Falklands War.

It has been 125 years since the first service for Jewish Servicemen, by 1892 the growing numbers serving warranted Jewish Military Chaplaincy. Five years later in 1897, Rev. Cohen obtained the sanction of the British Admiralty and the War Office to hold an annual service for Jewish men in the Forces.

Syd and Terry continued to live in the same house in Walthamstow, keeping Jason's bedroom as a shrine. Such is grief for some, holding onto what was, we need not fear forgetting our loved ones though for the memories will always remain. Syd died in January 2012.

In 2022, as part of the Falkland Islands 40th Anniversary Place Names Project, Jason was honoured with 'Burt Creek', a creek close to the west entrance to Horseshoe Bay in Port Salvador, East Falkland.

His name lives on…

D075562M Acting Chief Weapons Engineering Artificer John David Law Caddy HMS *Coventry* 19 June 1947 ~ 25 May 1982 Age 34

John David Law Caddy was born in the district of West Hartlepool, Cleveland, on 19 June 1947. His parents, Robert Simpson Caddy and Doreen Law, married in 1941.

John was named after his paternal grandfather John Robert Caddy, who married Isabella Simpson in the district of Chester Le Street, Durham, in 1912. Their eldest son Robert Simpson Caddy was born on Christmas Day in 1913 in Newfield, Durham. Brothers John and Thomas followed over the next four years. In 1921 John, originally from South Bank, Yorkshire, had settled with his family in Pelton, Durham, where he worked for Pelton Fell Coal Company.

By 1939 the Caddy family lived in Central Avenue, Billingham. Robert was a heavy chemicals records clerk, his father John a heavy chemicals process manager. Robert died in 2000 in Nottingham.

John David Law Caddy married his wife Mary in 1972 in Teesside. They had one child.

From his friend Tony Babb:

> I served with John in HMS *Collingwood* while under training, he came to my 21st Birthday Party and had to watch my team Wolves, thrash his beloved Newcastle 5-0. He was then sent to submarines as a reluctant submariner, and we lost touch until I met him again on HMS *Coventry* just before the Falklands. I was doing some maintenance on the Sea Dart System. We had a good few beers in the mess at that time and a fantastic 'catch up'. A great guy who will have to wait a few years until we meet again elsewhere, and I can repay his kindness. The wets will be on me then.

John was Acting Chief Weapons Engineering Artificer serving on HMS *Coventry*, he is remembered as a tough but fair man who looked after his team.

On 25 May 1982, HMS *Coventry* and HMS *Broadsword* were ordered to take up positions to the north-west of Falkland Sound. The plan was for HMS *Coventry* to act as decoy to draw the Argentinian aircraft away from other vessels at San Carlos Bay. Though initially effective, the position of the ship meant that her Sea Dart missiles would be less effective. One Skyhawk was shot down before the two ships came under attack by four further A4 Skyhawks.

The Skyhawks flew so low that HMS *Coventry*'s targeting radar could not distinguish between the aircraft and land, it failed to lock on. Though *Broadsword* was hit, the bomb that hit her flight deck failed to explode, just a Lynx Helicopter was destroyed. During the attack of the second pair of Skyhawks HMS *Coventry* was hit by three bombs just below the waterline on the Port side.

Though the third bomb did not explode, the first two had done more than enough damage and within twenty minutes the ship was evacuated, soon after she had completely capsized, she quickly sank. Nineteen men died that day and a further thirty were injured.

John was killed in the computer room.

In 2022, as part of the Falkland Islands 40th Anniversary Place Names Project John was honoured with 'Caddy Rock', a prominent unvegetated rock in the passage between Rabbit Island and mainland West Falkland. (Rabbit Island is in King George Bay).

His name lives on…

P041627B Marine Paul David Callan 45 Commando Royal Marines 9 March 1961 ~ 10 June 1982 Age 21

In 1960, David Roy Callan and Pamela Elizabeth Sneddon married, a year later they welcomed their first born, a son. Paul David Callan arrived on 9 March 1961, born in Liverpool. The family grew rapidly as Paul's siblings followed, Andrew, Michael and Jacky were also born in Liverpool during the next four years. By the time Paul was 5 years old the family had moved to Wigan, where his youngest sibling Michelle was born.

The family made another move in 1971 to Ellesmere Port. Paul attended Parklands Junior School followed by Mill Lane Secondary School in Ellesmere Port. On leaving school he briefly worked for a local firm of industrial painters while waiting to join the Navy. Paul served six months in the Royal Navy passing out at HMS *Raleigh*, however he had other ambitions, his ultimate goal was to attain a Green Beret.

Within eighteen months Paul had earned his Green Beret; he became a Marine, passing his Royal Marines Commando Training, he was then posted to 45 Commando. Paul saw service in Northern Ireland, as a Chef he was involved in the team that made Princess Diana's wedding cake. Life was falling into place and when he met his partner Jackie Dowling, he soon had his own wedding to plan.

Jackie and Paul welcomed their son Jamie into the world at the end of 1981, they had their wedding date set for 14 August 1982 until fate intervened in the cruellest of ways. In April of 1982, Paul was home on leave. He was called back to base with 45 Commando in Arbroath as the Falkland Islands were invaded and all leave was immediately cancelled. Paul, like many, did not know where the Islands were, but he was soon to find out.

45 Commando under the command of Lieutenant Colonel Andrew Francis Whitehead, were hastily deployed to the Falklands between Royal Navy and Royal Fleet Auxiliary ships. Paul travelled the 8,000 miles on the RFA *Stromness*, arriving on 21 May 1982. As a Chef, Paul found himself based with the unit support group at Ajax Bay, at one end of a building that was later to become famous as the 'Red and Green Life Machine', the field hospital.

Tragedy was about to strike for young Paul though as two Argentinian Skyhawks attacked the once disused refrigeration plant at dusk on 27 May 1982. The young Marine sustained severe injuries to his upper torso. His spirit was strong, he was transported to the hospital ship HMHS *Uganda*, where he received both amazing medical treatment and devotional nursing care. Sadly, despite more than one surgery and many pints of blood, this young marine lost his life from the catastrophic wounds incurred. Paul died on 10 June 1982. The Reverend David Barlow of the Royal Navy gave Paul his last rites before his death, though he was careful not to let Paul know of his fate.

Surgeon Rick Jolly was a regular visitor to *Uganda*, the nurses asked that Paul be taken back with him to Ajax Bay rather than be buried at sea. The request was agreed upon immediately, Paul was temporarily interred there in a simple ceremony the day he died. Upon his repatriation in November 1982, Paul was finally laid to rest with his other comrades in the 45 Commando cemetery in Arbroath, Scotland.

There is a strong military presence in the Callan family. Paul's brothers Andrew and Michael were in the Cheshire Regiment, they sounded the last post at his memorial service. One of his grandfathers was a Dunkirk veteran and his other grandfather served for some time in the Staffordshire Regiment. A history to be proud of for sure.

Paul's mother had remained settled in Ellesmere Port; in October 2010 the young marine's name was added to the Memorial Stone in Great Sutton. There was an accompanying service that day with Royal Marine Reservists and Standard Bearers in attendance along with a presence from the Sea Cadets.

In 2022, as part of the Falkland Islands 40th Anniversary Place Names Project, Paul was honoured with 'Callan Point', a point at the end of little Rincon on mainland East Falkland near Blue Beach Farm Settlement in San Carlos Waters. The site is known as 'Kelly's Garden'.

His name lives on…

D145600D Marine Engineering Artificer (Mechanical) 1 Paul Brian Callus HMS *Coventry* 10 January 1958 ~ 25 May 1982 Age 24

The family military history of the Callus family runs deep indeed, through at least three Wars.

Victor John Callus (Paul's grandfather) was the third son of Henry Joseph Callus and Christine Josephine Pouhalski, who married in Cardiff in 1885. Some records suggest Turkish roots, although Naval records indicate that Henry was born in Malta; Callus is certainly a well-known name in Malta. Henry was a marine engineer who was widowed in 1901 when Christine died, aged just 47. The couple had four sons: Harry Mary Edward, Andrew Theodore, Victor John and Charles Albert.

Records indicate that Harry Mary Edward joined the Royal Navy in July 1900 as a Boy Cadet and served as such until July 1902. By 1914 he was a Colour Sergeant with the Royal Welsh Fusiliers. His citation for a DCM dated 28 October 1918 reads:

> *'For conspicuous gallantry and devotion to duty. For upwards of three years, he has consistently performed distinguished service, invariably displaying great coolness and courage under fire, and at times setting an example of devotion to duty worthy of the highest praise.'*

By 1921 Harry was a Sergeant Major 4th Battalion, Royal Welsh Fusiliers. It appears he continued employment with the British Army through the Second World War with a 3rd Service number. Harry married in 1924; the couple had two sons. He died in 1961.

Andrew Theodore Callus was born in September 1886, he married in Wigan in 1913 just before the First World War and appears to have served with the Royal Engineers. Andrew and his wife had seven children. After the war Andrew worked as a commercial traveller, settling in Rotherham. Andrew died in 1961, he is buried in Masbrough Cemetery, Rotherham, his widow was also buried there in 1979.

Charles Albert Callus served with the Royal Engineers in the First World War, he also survived and married in 1924; he had five children. Charles became a train driver for Great Western Railways, he saw out his days in Cardiff and died in 1977.

Victor John Callus was born on 6 December 1887 in Roath, Cardiff. Victor enlisted into the British Army in August 1906 and served with the Royal Welsh Fusiliers until 1913. When the Royal Flying Corps was banded, men were drafted in from many different regiments, Victor was one such man. Victor married Mary Taylor in London in 1920.

Victor survived the First World War and by 1921 was posted to the Instrument Design Establishment, RAF Biggin Hill. Victor retired from the RAF in 1931 but carried on working as a civilian technical instructor, settling in Stoke Mandeville with his family.

Victor and Mary had six children between 1921 and 1941: Paul's father, known as Brian, was their fourth child born in 1924. Victor died in Stoke Mandeville in October 1963. Vivien, their youngest daughter, married Gerard McMellon in Aylesbury, Buckinghamshire in 1961. Gerard was the son of John Dunstan McMellon, a Pioneer in the Royal Engineers in the First World War.

Brian Callus joined the Royal Navy in 1940 as an Electrical Artificer, by 1957 he was a Chief Electrical Artificer. Brian had a long career in the Royal Navy, retiring thirty-four years later as a Lieutenant Commander. Brian and June had three sons: Peter John, Stephen Victor and youngest son Paul Brian Callus, born in Gillingham on 10 January 1958. Brian crossed the bar on 6 October 2020, living well into his nineties. He lived out his days in Blandford Forum, Dorset.

Paul attended St Johns College in Southsea; he joined the Royal Navy at HMS *Fisgard* in 1974 as an Artificer Apprentice. While serving with HMS *Bristol* he met and fell in love with an American, Cynthia ('Cindy') Humphrey, they married in Salem, Virginia, in December 1980. Paul was then appointed to HMS *Coventry*. Sadly, unlike generations before him, he was not to survive his involvement with war.

HMS *Coventry* was bombed on 25 May 1982; she sank within the hour. Paul was one of those who died that day. Paul resided with his wife in Emsworth, Hampshire, at the time of his death; he is remembered on the War Memorial there. There were no children from his marriage, Cindy returned to live in America.

Cindy was a deeply spiritual woman; she devoted her life to the Church and helping others. Though she did not remarry or have children of her own, Cindy spent nine years teaching English to Chinese students one – of which she regarded as a surrogate daughter. Chelsey Zheng was by Cindy's side when she died on 21 December 2023, after a long illness.

In the summer of 1982, a memorial service was held at Emsworth RC church for Paul which was attended by some of his former classmates. A former choir boy and rugby player, he is also remembered as a loving husband. Paul had at least thirteen cousins from his father's siblings.

In 2022, as part of the Falkland Islands 40th Anniversary Place Names Project, Paul was honoured with 'Callus Island', a small tussac island in Lake Hammond, West Falkland.

His name lives on…

24332979 Lance Serjeant James Russell Carlyle 1ˢᵗ Battalion Welsh Guards 8 June 1956 ~ 8 June 1982 Age 26

James Bruce Carlyle married Gwyneth Jones in Ruthin, Denbighshire, Wales, in 1955. Eldest son James Russell Carlyle was born a year later on 8 June 1956 in Wrexham. James senior was known as Bruce, he and Gwyneth went on to have two more children David and Gillian.

The name James has been passed down for many generations in the Carlyle family.

Jim's great-grandfather James Beck Carlyle was born in Dublin in 1870, the son of James Carlyle, a bookkeeper, and his wife Margaret (née McArthur). James Beck married Emily Salmon (originally from Norfolk), the couple's eldest son was born on Christmas Eve 1897 in Ballyclare, Co Antrim, he was named James McArthur ('Mac') Carlyle. By 1921 the couple had settled in Cheshire and both their sons were working; just before the Second World War, Mac worked for the Board of Trade.

Mac married Elsie in 1925, the couple had two children, James Bruce Carlyle, and a daughter who was slightly older. During the Second World War Mac served his country, he is listed as a Lieutenant Commander for the Royal Naval Reserve, in 1939 he served as Paymaster on SS *Arandora Star*. The ship had been requisitioned by the British Government, converted into a troop carrier and painted grey with added gun placements.

SS *Arandora Star* was a target as she set sail on 30 June 1940 carrying hundreds of Italian internees and some German POWs. Canada had reluctantly agreed to take the internees from Warth Mills. A ship meant to carry 500 men was crammed with around 1,678 men. On 2 July 1940, SS *Arandora* was torpedoed by a German U-Boat off the coast of Ireland, many were killed instantly. Eventually, survivors were rescued by the Canadian Destroyer HMCS *Laurent* and taken to Greenock in Scotland.

Mac was not one of the 800 who died that fateful day; it was not the only time he survived a torpedo attack. Mac's brother had been an apprentice to a timber merchants, he went on to work as a commercial traveller in the trade. By 1939 James Beck Carlyle, now widowed, had moved to Denbighshire, where his great-nephew was homed during the war. James Beck died in 1945 as the war was coming to an end. Mac sadly died in March 1958, just two years after his grandson James Russell was born.

Known as Russ to his schoolmates and friends, he started school at Pentrecelyn, six miles from Ruthin. After the family moved to Ruthin, Russ attended Brynhyfryd School, Mold Road, Ruthin, from 1967 until 1972. Russ loved sports and also joined the school band. He also enjoyed fishing and golf. Russ left school at 16, he joined the Welsh Guards in 1973.

Jim, as he was known to his mates in the 1st Battalion Welsh Guards, saw service in Cyprus as part of the United Nations. Jim served a two-year tour in Berlin stationed at Wavell Barracks. Jim also saw service in Northern Ireland and an attachment to the Household Division.

In 1982, Jim travelled to South Georgia on the QE2, later he transferred to the *Canberra* arriving in the Falklands on 2 June 1982. The Unit transferred to the logistic ship RFA *Sir Galahad* for the journey around to Fitzroy on 7 June. The following day, the ship was attacked by Argentine Air Force A-4 Skyhawks, two bombs exploding in the tank deck.

Sadly, Jim was one of the Welsh Guards who did not make it. His mum and dad received the Elizabeth Cross in a May ceremony in Cardiff in 2011. The medal was presented by the Lord Lieutenants of South Glamorgan, Mid Glamorgan, West Glamorgan and Gwent. His parents James and Gwyneth were both there to receive the award, his dad said they were very proud to be there. The family understand the pain of losing someone special, the unseen cost of war.

Jim's parents by then had been to the Falklands three times, remaining immensely proud of the son they lost.

Brynhyfryd school has a plaque, a marble tablet which is inscribed 'In memory of Lance Sgt James Russell Carlyle a pupil here from 1967–1972, Killed in Action on his 26th Birthday 8 June 1982.'

In 2022, as part of the Falkland Islands 40th Anniversary Place Names Project, Jim was honoured with 'Carlyle Rock', an unvegetated rock south of Albemarle Rock in Falkland Sound.

His name lives on…

D136093W Petty Officer Aircrewman Kevin Stuart ('Ben') Casey 846 Squadron Fleet Air Arm HMS *Hermes* 23 January 1956 ~ 23 April 1982 Age 26

Someone always has to be first, whether its winning a race or dying in war. Here is the story of our first British Casualty from the 'Class of 82'.

Dennis Charles Casey and Margaret Bayliss married in 1953 in Rugby, Warwickshire. The couple had two children, both given the same initials of KS.

It appears that generations before, Kevin's maternal great-great-grandfather, Lewis Peverelle, had also worn a uniform, he was a Police Constable. His parents, Franciscus Peverelle, a groom, and Susanna Doust, married in August 1849 at St Peter's in Birmingham. Sadly, by 1881 Susanna was a widow. This was the Italian side of Ben's family.

Lewis Peverelle, the couple's oldest son, married Mary in 1871. Their second son Joseph Hollis Peverelle was born in 1880. He married Jane Allison Sutton in 1906, their second child Elizabeth Mary, Ben's grandmother, was born in 1908.

Elizabeth Mary Peverelle married Thomas Ward Bayliss on 2 August 1930 at Monks-Kirby, a village near Rugby. Ben's mother Margaret was born in Rugby on 3 September 1932, she was the eldest of six children.

The paternal side of Ben's family had Irish roots. Dennis Charles Casey was born in 1926 in Warwickshire. He was the second son of Thomas Casey and Ethel Annie Bingham. Ethel came from a large family, born in Nuneaton in the late 1800s to William and Emma Bingham.

Ben's paternal great-grandfather Thomas Casey married Charlotte Smith in 1894 in Lichfield. Thomas was the oldest son of James (John) Casey and Mary who were born in Ireland. The Casey family were miners for a few generations. (Interestingly, Ben's father Dennis was a Bevan Boy before he joined the Royal Navy.) Thomas and Charlotte had three children: Thomas (Ben's grandfather), Lilian and Wilfred. Thomas was born on 16 December 1895, he was baptised on 12 January 1896 at St Mary & St Modwen, Burton-on-Trent, Staffs. Sadly, Thomas senior died, leaving Charlotte a young widow with three children.

Kevin Stuart (Ben) Casey was born 23 January 1956, his sister Kim followed two years later. Although Kim married in 1980 her children, Sophie and Charlotte, weren't born until 1987 and 1989, so sadly Ben did not get to meet his nieces.

Ben was brought up in Long Lawford near Rugby. He went first to Long Lawford Primary School followed by Newbold High School. As a schoolboy he liked football and cross country running.

Ben joined the Royal Navy on 31 October 1972 as an Aircraft Mechanic and was posted to RNAS *Culdrose*, it was here that he was to meet a Wren, Ellen Wallbank, known as 'Elly', who became his wife in 1975. Ben had gone on to join 820 squadron on HMS *Ark Royal*, he had proposed before he set sail, and the couple married in Rugby on his return.

In February 1976 Ben joined HMS *Daedalus*, where he started training to become a Helicopter Crewman. Further training took place at RNAS *Culdrose* and

HMS *Osprey*. Ellen managed to join him at HMS *Osprey*, by which time she had been promoted to Petty Officer.

Ben was presented with his wings in September 1977, his first draft was to HMS *Nubian*, where he was a missile aimer on a Wasp flight. In November of the same year, he had just one weekend between leaving HMS *Nubian* and joining HMS *Alacrity*. The destination was the Falkland Islands as part of Operation Journeyman.

Ben remained with *Alacrity* until January 1979 when he joined 772 Squadron to fly on search and rescue operations. In March 1980 he completed his Petty Officer Aircrewman Course and stayed with 772 Squadron until July of that year. In September 1980 he joined 707 Squadron for his Commando course. Once the course was completed, he joined 846 Squadron flying Sea King MK 4s from HMS *Hermes*.

On the night of 23 April 1982, Petty Officer Aircrewman Kevin Stuart Casey became the first casualty of the 'Class of 82' when his Sea King crashed into the sea in the dark, in bad weather. The pilot survived, being picked up by another helicopter from HMS *Hermes*. Ben was pronounced 'missing presumed drowned' after an extensive search.

Ben's dad Dennis died the following year, on 16 July 1983, after which his widow went to live with her daughter. Dennis had been broken hearted after Ben's death. Ben and Elly had no children when he gave his life for his country.

In 2022, as part of the Falkland Islands 40th Anniversary Place Names Project, Ben was honoured with 'Casey Cove', a small cove on the east coast of Pebble Island, West Falkland.

His name lives on…

Assistant Laundryman Chi Shing Chan SS *Atlantic Conveyor* 16 May 1940 ~ 25 May 1982 Age 42

Chi Shing Chan was born on 16 May 1940, he was from Hong Kong. Chan, Chi-Shing had seemingly served with the Royal Fleet Auxiliary since 1964.

The Chinese served in various capacities supporting the Royal Navy, as civilians they were given the choice to disembark at Ascension Island or to continue at their posts; many stayed.

Reports vary about the numbers of Chinese serving as part of the Task Force. Some say sixty, others over 300. Many survived to return home to Hong Kong, eight men did not make it for a variety of reasons.

Chan died when the SS *Atlantic Conveyor* was attacked on 25 May 1982, his body lost to the sea.

In 1986 a plaque was unveiled by Rear Admiral Robin Hogg at the Mariner's Club, Tsim Sha Tsui in Hong Kong. All eight men were honoured, the families did not want the event publicised, preferring a private ceremony.

In 2022, as part of the Falkland Islands 40th Anniversary Place Names Project, Chan was honoured with 'Chan Point', the northwest point of Flat Jason Island, in the Jason Islands Group.

His name lives on…

24398996 Lance Corporal Simon Jeremy Cockton 656 Squadron Army Air Corps 8 April 1960 ~ 6 June 1982 Age 21

Simon Jeremy Cockton was born in Ealing on 8 April 1960, the eldest son of John and Winfred Joyce Cockton (née Bailey).

The Cockton family had its roots in Cumberland prior to John making his home in London. Going back to the middle 1800s, Joseph Cockton was a master shoemaker, the names of both Joseph and John were to feature often in the Cockton family.

Joseph Cockton, born in 1829, was the son of John and Mary Cockton (née Strong). Joseph married Eleanor Mitchinson in September 1858; the couple lived in Tallentire Village just north of Cockermouth, where they continued the family shoemaker business of Joseph's father, John. Their son, John Mitchinson Cockton, was born in 1863 and followed into the family business of shoemaking. Joseph was widowed twice before he died in 1904.

In 1892 John Mitchinson Cockton married Annie Bank, the couple's eldest son Joseph Bank Cockton was born the same year. By 1911 the family were living in Kirkgate, Cockermouth, where some of their children were born. Joseph Bank Cockton served in the Machine Gun Corps in 1916, later in the Tank Corps, School of Gunnery, where he is recorded as still serving in 1919.

John and Annie had four sons altogether: Joseph, John, James, and Harold. Second son John Mitchinson Cockton was born in Kirkgate in 1894; during the First World War John served in the King's Regiment, Liverpool. John married Ida (née Gibson), and they had one daughter born in late 1919. John Mitchinson Cockton died on 6 August 1921; he is buried in Cockermouth Cemetery in a CWGC grave, which suggests that he sadly died of a cause attributable to his service.

John and Annie's third son, James Fletcher Cockton, served with the Machine Gun Corps, Motor Machine Gun Service, Royal Artillery in the First World War, he survived the war and returned to Kirkgate where he worked in the family business. Youngest son Harold was born in October 1900, too young to serve initially in the First World War, he also went into the family business, he married in 1930 and had four sons.

Joseph Bank Cockton (Simon's grandfather) became a joiner after the war, he married Agnes Hannah Hodgson, and their eldest son John Cockton was born in February 1916. John initially grew up in Kirkgate, but by 1939 he was a turner and living in High Wycombe.

Simon's mother, Winifred Joyce Bailey, was born in January 1924, the eldest child of John Barnard and Vera Bailey (née Gomme). John Barnard

Bailey was born in Newport Pagnell in December 1900, he attested into the Royal Air Force on 19 August 1918 as a carpenter, aged just 17. John's father, another John Barnard, was a joiner. By 1921 the family were living in Princes Risborough, Buckinghamshire. At the beginning of the Second World War up until his death, John Barnard was a chair maker, he died in 1961, the year after Simon was born.

Simon's grandmother Vera was born and raised in Princes Risborough, where her family lived for many years. It was second time around for both John and Winfred Joyce Cockton, who carved out a life for themselves in Ealing, West London. Simon's mother worked as a clerical officer for the Ministry of Overseas Development. Simon was their only son; it appears they had one daughter .

Simon joined Junior Leaders Regiment Royal Armoured Corps at Bovington Camp in Dorset in January 1977. He joined 656 Squadron AAC in 1978 where he was a member of the signals detachment going on to be promoted to Lance Corporal in 1980. Simon attended his Air Crewman course in 1982.

When the Falklands were invaded Simon was just about to celebrate his 22nd Birthday. Simon married his sweetheart the day before he set sail, leaving his wedding reception to re-join his unit and deploy aboard the QE2.

On the night of 5 June, HMS *Cardiff* was stationed to the east of the islands to provide gunfire support to the land forces and intercept enemy aircraft. At around 02:00 hrs on 6 June, a radar contact was detected; a British Army Air Corps Gazelle helicopter was making a routine delivery of personnel and equipment to a radio re-broadcast station on East Falkland. From the contact's speed and course, *Cardiff*'s operations room crew assumed it to be hostile. One Sea Dart missile was fired, destroying the target. The Gazelle's wreckage and crew were discovered the next morning, and the loss was attributed to enemy fire. Although *Cardiff* was suspected, later scientific tests on the wreckage proved inconclusive.

Simon's mother was not prepared to accept the findings of the first inquest. It took until 1988 when finally, a second inquest stated that her son's death was indeed a 'blue on blue'.

Simon's father John died in 1985 before the news became public. Winifred was honoured with an award in 1990 by the Campaign for Freedom of Information for persistence in obtaining information in the face of obstructive bureaucracy. The award was presented by Ludovic Kennedy. Winifred died in 2005.

Simon liked to write poetry and though he did not live long enough to have any children he did know the joy of marriage during his short life. Simon's body was recovered to Ajax Bay and temporarily interred there, later repatriated he was laid to final rest in Frimley at the church where he married.

In 2022, as part of the Falkland Islands 40th Anniversary Place Names Project, Simon was honoured with 'Cockton Creek', a creek between Island Point and Devil's Point in the Bay of Harbours, East Falkland.

His name lives on…

24579323 Private Albert Mark Connett Army Catering Corps RFA
Sir Galahad 26 July 1962 ~ 8 June 1982 Age 19

Albert Mark Connett was born on 26 July 1962 in Manchester, the eldest child of Albert and Elizabeth Patricia Connett (née Wall), named after his father and grandfather before him. Albert and Elizabeth married at St Michaels Church, Hulme, on 20 May 1961. Although their first son was called Albert Mark, he was known as Mark. The couple went on to have two more sons, David and Andrew, later a daughter Janice completed their family.

Though Mark's mother was born in Barton, her family had moved to the Manchester area from County Durham courtesy of her grandfather, George Wall. The Wall family had been coal miners in Durham and South Shields; for many years before that, they were butchers.

George Wall, Mark's maternal great-grandfather was born at Boldon Colliery on 20 February 1885, one of possibly thirteen children. George went on to work at Boldon Colliery as a teenager, but life was about to change. George began playing football, a sport in which he excelled. As a fast and skilled outside left, he joined his local team, Boldon Royal Rovers, as a junior. His next team was Whitburn, based in Jarrow, a team player by 1901. Two months later, second division Barnsley had taken him to South Yorkshire. In 1903, George married Isabella Headley, a miner's daughter, in South Shields.

After three seasons at Oakwell, George transferred to Manchester United for a fee of £175, making his debut on 7 April 1906. This transfer saw his family move to Manchester, initially Stretford and later Old Trafford.

In 1915, the game was suspended for the duration of the First World War, by then George had played 316 league games scoring ninety-eight goals. As the First World War raged, George joined the British Army in the summer of that year, serving with the Black Watch, Royal Highlanders, posted to the 11th (Reserve) Battalion in Tain, Scotland, for basic training. Four weeks later, his battalion moved to Catterick. George was known to have returned to Manchester on recruiting business.

In 1916 George's battalion became the 3rd, 10th & 11th Service Battalion, Argyll & Sutherland Highlanders, he remained in service until 1918. After the First World War George resumed his football career, going on to play for Oldham Athletic for a fee of £200. By 1921, the family were settled in Old Trafford, George was playing for Hamilton Academic, Scotland. George's professional football career came to an end in the 1922/3 season, he had played more than 500 league and cup games.

George and Isabella's first three children were born in Boldon Colliery, but son Leslie Wall was born in September 1912 after the family had settled in Manchester. After George retired from professional football he remained in Manchester and continued to play football; he worked at the docks at Salford Quays. Leslie, Mark's maternal grandfather followed his father into dock work as a timekeeper.

Leslie married Edith (née Mountain) in 1937, the couple had two daughters, Elizabeth and Linda.

Elizabeth became a shorthand typist and married Albert Connett, a clerk. His father, also Albert, was the son of a greengrocer; he married in 1929. Sadly, grandfather Albert died in 1938, the same year his son Albert was born, he was just 31 years old.

Mark was schooled at Wilbraham High School in Chorlton. As a young lad he loved a game of darts. Mark is remembered as friendly, happy, kind, and caring. Mark joined the Army Catering Corps; at the time the Falkland Islands were invaded he was attached to the Welsh Guards.

The RFA *Sir Galahad* sailed from Devonport on 6 April 1982, originally with 350 Royal Marines on board. She had landed in San Carlos water on 21 May 1982. Three days later she was attacked by Skyhawks from the Argentine Air Force. The ship was hit by a 1,000 lb bomb which did not detonate. Royal Marine volunteers returned to help the Royal Navy EOD team in defusing and removing the bomb.

On 8 June 1982 when the *Galahad* came under attack again at Fitzroy, forty-eight soldiers and crewmen were killed, with many more injured. Mark was one of the fallen on a truly tragic day. On 21 June, the hulk was towed out to sea and sunk, it remains an official War Grave.

In 2022, as part of the Falkland Islands 40th Anniversary Place Names Project, Mark was honoured with 'Connett Peak', the summit of Elephant Jason Island, in the Jason Island group, it has a 682-foot elevation.

His name lives on…

D168369Y Catering Accountant Darryl Marvin Cope HMS *Sheffield* 27 May 1961 ~ 4 May 1982 Age 20

Darryl Marvin Cope was born in Kidderminster on 27 May 1961. Darryl was the middle child of three children. Don and Marge Cope (née Elliott) married at Wesley Methodist Church in Stourport-on-Severn. Darryl had a brother, Steven, who was one year older; he also had a younger sister, Rebecca.

The Cope family had migrated to Kidderminster, prior to that they had roots in Derbyshire for some years. Don's father, George Edward Cope, was a Sapper in the Royal Engineers in the First World War with 266th Railway Company. George worked for the Great Western Railway Company after the war.

George was the son of Charles Cope, a Manager of a Public House. Charles married Rachel Panther in 1872, the family were living in Bewdley, Kidderminster by 1901. George's oldest son Samuel attested into the Royal Artillery in 1926. George and Alice Cope (née Crew) had a large family, Don was their youngest, born in 1932.

Marge was born in 1937 in Gloucestershire, her father, Gilbert Ralph Elliott, was born into a large family in Minchinhampton, Gloucestershire in 1909; his birthday coincidentally is 2 April…

Darryl grew up in Stourport-on-Severn, first attending the junior school there, later the Grammar School in Hartlebury. Darryl was known as Daz to his friends, he joined the Royal Navy at 16, first training at HMS *Raleigh*. Daz then progressed to Catering and Accountancy courses at HMS *Pembroke* (Chatham) and HMS *Daedalus* near Portsmouth.

Daz joined his first ship the Type 42 destroyer HMS *Sheffield* in July 1979. The 'Shiny Sheff' as it became known had some problems. As the first of her class of Royal Navy destroyers, *Sheffield* spent her first years trialling the new systems and the Sea Dart Missile system. She had cost over £23 million to build and was launched on 10 July 1971 by Queen Elizabeth II.

During a refit of the 'Shiny Sheff' Daz was seconded for a tour of the Mediterranean onboard the assault ship HMS *Intrepid*. Daz was back on-board *Sheffield* when she sailed on 19 November 1981 to undertake patrols in the Indian Ocean and Persian Gulf. His Naval journey saw operations in March 1982 when the ship transited north through the Suez Canal to participate in Exercise Spring Train. Four days before the ship was due to return to Portsmouth, there was a change in plan, the 'Shiny Sheff' was ordered to divert and join the Task Force headed 'Down South' to participate in retaking the Falkland Islands.

While on forward radar picket duty about seventy miles south and east of Stanley, on Sunday 4 May 1982, the Type 42 destroyer was struck amidships by an Exocet missile fired from Argentine Naval Super Étendard aircraft.

Daz is honoured by the Darryl Cope Memorial Trophy handed out annually to an outstanding Catering Trainee. There is a bench dedicated to Daz also in the Memorial Gardens in Mitton Street, Stourport On Severn. The brass plaque reads 'THIS SEAT IS A MEMORIAL TO DARRYL COPE KILLED WHILE SERVING ON H.M.S. SHEFFIELD IN THE FALKLANDS CAMPAIGN 4TH MAY 1982'.

Over in the Falkland Islands there is a wooden pebble which was placed at the memorial to HMS *Sheffield* on Sea Lion Island in 2011. Darryl's mum, Marge, asked if a memorial could be taken to the Falkland Islands on her behalf after reading in a local paper that Mr Alan Rowe was due to run the Stanley Marathon. A friend of Alan's, Colonel Richard Sidwell RM, immediately offered to help, overnight he turned a beautiful piece of East Devon Oak as a gift to Marge and her family, a lasting memory to Darryl. These acts of kindness are very moving for families.

Daz's father, Don, died in late 1992.

In 2022, as part of the Falkland Islands 40th Anniversary Place Names Project, Daz was honoured with 'Cope Point', a point on mainland East Falkland opposite Tussac Island in Port Fitzroy.

His name lives on…

24438937 Lance Corporal Anthony Cork 2nd Battalion Parachute Regiment 5 October 1960 ~ 28 May 1982 Age 21

Anthony Cork was born in Colchester, Essex on 5 October 1960, the second child of Michael and Zilpha Cork (née Dickinson). Michael Cork, originally from

Canterbury, Kent, was a PT instructor with the Royal Artillery. Zilpha, a Yorkshire lass, was working as a WRAC cook when their paths first crossed.

Michael was born on Boxing Day in 1936, the third child of Leslie James and Mabel Alice Cork (née Foord). Leslie was a greengrocer, and the couple had six children altogether. Mabel was the youngest child of Joseph and Mary Ann Foord (née Morris), their only son, Joseph Thomas Henry Foord, was a Sapper in the Royal Engineers in the First World War, sadly he died in 1923.

Anthony's grandfather Leslie was the youngest child of Alfred and Emily Cork (née Leeds). Alfred was a builder, two of his sons went into the building trade, one became a baker. The Cork family had a long history in Kent.

Zilpha Dickinson was born in Huddersfield on 4 January 1938. Life was not kind to Zilpha, she had lost both her parents to cancer by the time she was a teenager, after which she lived for a while in a children's home. As a young woman she worked in the cotton mills until she was 18 years old, she then made the decision to join the British Army.

Michael and Zilpha married in Woolwich in 1957, their eldest son Brian was born a year later. After Anthony was born in Colchester the couple had another son, David, in 1964; Kim completed their family, she was born in Hanover in 1967.

Before joining the army, Anthony had a girlfriend who lived across the road, the couple had a daughter in March 1977.

Anthony Cork ('Corky') joined JPC 27 Platoon in 1977, he is fondly remembered by a friend who called him 'A little dynamo'. His friend says about Corky:

> He was outgoing but also quite private and chose his friends carefully. He was very friendly, loyal, and well respected. Very fit and very motivated and enthusiastic, driven in a focused way. He was immensely likeable which came from confidence not arrogance. Had he not died he would have gone far.

When they passed out, they went to separate battalions, him to 3 Para and Corky to 2 Para. He heard of Corky's death while on the *Uganda* after being injured on Mount Longdon, reading of Corky's demise at Goose Green in a newspaper. He remembers reflectively, they stopped dishing out newspapers to the injured after that.

Corky was in 10 Platoon D Coy at the time of the Falklands War and went 'Down South' with 2 Para on the MV *Norland*. He was married to Irene (née Beattie), they had a young son, Christopher Anthony, when Corky left. He was about to be a father again; Irene was just two months pregnant when Corky died. Daughter Antonia was yet another Falklands baby who would never know her father.

Anthony was killed on 28 May 1982 during the Battle of Goose Green. He was killed by machine-gun fire during the night advance towards Darwin Hill. His family like many were very vocal about his burial at Ajax Bay on Sunday 30 May 1982. His father thought it was disgusting and his brother Brian felt that if they were sent out there it was only decent, they be brought back.

Many families felt that way, the reality hitting so hard as footage of the mass burial was constantly shown by the media, which continues to date. Anthony's body was repatriated; he is buried at Lisburn New Cemetery, Blaris, Co Antrim, where Irene had returned to her family roots.

Tony is remembered with his own plaque in St Nicholas Church, Ashford Road, Thanington, Canterbury in Kent.

In 2022, as part of the Falkland Islands 40th Anniversary Place Names Project, Tony was honoured with 'Cork Lagoon', a large tidal lagoon west of Salinas Beach at the head of Brenton Loch, East Falkland.

His name lives on...

24469595 Private Jonathan Douglas Crow 3rd Battalion Parachute Regiment 17 December 1960 ~ 12 June 1982 Age 21

Jonathan Douglas Crow was born in Falkirk on 17 December 1960 to Geoffrey and Barbara Crow (née Nott). The couple had one other son, Paul, born three years later.

Great-grandfather William Crow was born in Hatfield, Hertfordshire, in 1858; he married Ellen Moule in 1892, the couple went on to have six children. William had a jewellers' shop in Stratford, East London. Aubrey Everard, Jon's grandfather, was the couple's fifth child.

By 1939 two of the children were teachers, living in Leek, Staffordshire. Eldest brother William was a Liberal Catholic Priest and lecturer, sister Ida was a secondary school teacher, she remained single. Aubrey was teaching and living in Weymouth as the Second World War was about to erupt. Aubrey married Ivy Marion Warltier in 1926, the couple had two children, the youngest, Geoffrey, born in 1927. Ivy was the daughter of a turner manufacturer of guns; she became a teacher.

Jon's father Geoffrey married Barbara in Leek, Staffordshire in 1951. Jon went to primary school in Petersham, followed by Sheen Grammar School. During his early schooldays Jon was a sea scout. A natural athlete, he was a member of the Kingston Wheelers cyclocross team, and by 1974 he had won a national championship. After a year at Kingston Polytechnic Jon left his schooldays behind and enlisted in the British Army on his 17th birthday; he wanted to be a Paratrooper.

Jon passed out of 444 Platoon Depot; the Para platoon was under the command of David Benest in July 1978. His passing out aptly coincided with Airborne Forces weekend, and it was also the first time the then Prince Charles officiated, taking the salute and carrying out the inspection. Unfortunately, Jon was unable to parade owing to a uniform failure, he kindly let his friend use his boots that day.

The majority of 444 platoon went to either 3 Para or 1 Para, Jon went to 3 Para along with the friend who borrowed his boots. Jon also enjoyed fishing, gliding and downhill skiing. He quickly passed the aptitude tests for Helicopter Pilot Training and there was a potential officer in the making.

When the Falkland Islands were invaded in April 1982, Jon travelled the long journey 'Down South' on the *Canberra*, setting sail on 9 April 1982. 3 Para landed at Port San Carlos on 21 May ready to begin their long tab across the island; their objective: Port Stanley. Jon was in the Anti-Tank Platoon, Support Company, at the time.

The Battle for Mount Longdon began on 11 June 1982. Given the terrain, it was a seemingly impossible task; the Argentinians were well dug in. Paratroopers, however, do not hear 'impossible', it is not in their vocabulary; three days of fighting lay ahead before they triumphed. Jon was killed early on in the battle on 12 June. After a temporary burial his body was repatriated, he was laid to rest in Aldershot Military Cemetery.

There is a plaque dedicated to Jon in the Royal Star and Garter Care home in Richmond. Funds raised in his name were used to refurbish the library. The family had a long association with the area.

In 2010 Jon's father was presented with the Elizabeth Cross by Richard Jewson, the Lord Lieutenant of the County. The service took place at the Great Hospital, Norwich, the family having relocated to Sheringham by then.

In 2022, as part of the Falkland Islands 40th Anniversary Place Names Project, Jon was honoured with 'Crow Beach', a sandy beach immediately south of McBride Head, mainland East Falkland.

His name lives on…

23948859 Acting Staff Sergeant Philip Preston Currass QGM MID 22 SAS Regt 23 November 1947 ~ 19 May 1982 Age 34

Philip Preston Currass was born on 23 November 1947 in Worksop, Nottinghamshire, the only son of Arthur Edwin and Gladys Beryl Currass (née Cashmore). Phil had two sisters.

For generations the Currass family had been coal miners mainly working and living in the Worksop area. Gladys, from Warwickshire, was a book binder prior to her marriage, Arthur worked in an Ironmonger's.

Arthur, born in 1921, was the youngest son of William Ernest and Sarah Hannah Currass (née Shooter). Arthur had one older brother, Ernest Nicholls Currass, born in 1914. Ernest was named after his grandmother, Mary Ann Nicholls, who married into the Currass family in 1883.

Phil originally started his Army career in the Royal Army Medical Corps. He joined D Squadron 22 SAS in 1972 and completed operational tours in Dhofar (Oman) and Northern Ireland. In 1979 he was awarded the Queen's Gallantry Medal.

Phil married Jenny in Aldershot in 1966, the couple started a family the following year.

During the Falklands War Phil helped liberate South Georgia during the raid on Pebble Island to destroy enemy aircraft. He was MID as follows…

Supplement to the London Gazette 8th October 1982

The QUEEN has been graciously pleased to approve the following names of those Mentioned in Despatches in recognition of gallant and distinguished service during the operations in the South Atlantic: 23948859 Staff Sergeant Phillip Preston CURRASS Q.G.M., Royal Army Medical Corps (Posthumous)

Mountain Troop was inserted onto the Fortuna Glacier, tasked with establishing the enemies strength & dispositions in the Leith area of South Georgia. It became necessary to evacuate the troops prior to any environmental casualties, during the evacuation Phil sustained injuries to his face and a concussion in a helicopter crash. Phil nevertheless continued to organise the rescue; he went on the spearhead the advance of British Troops in the retake of Gritvykin along with the organisation of Prisoner of War handling. His troop were then tasked with destroying enemy aircraft during a pre-invasion raid of Pebble Island. Phil ensured the evacuation of two men who sustained minor injuries during this action.

Phil was tragically killed in the Sea King crash on 19 May 1982. Like many men he fought alongside during the Falklands War Phil was a husband, father, son, brother and soldier; his loss was felt by his whole family.

In 2013, thirty-one years after his death, a memorial was unveiled at the National Memorial Arboretum. The modern stainless-steel sundial is set on a piece of Radnorshire stone. It takes pride of place in the Allied Special Forces Grove at the Arboretum in Alrewas, Staffordshire.

Phil's parents eventually settled in Market Drayton, Shropshire.

In 2022, as part of the Falkland Islands 40th Anniversary Place Names Project, Phil was honoured with 'Currass Creek', the south-west arm of Quaker Harbour, on the west coast of Weddell Island, West Falkland.

His name lives on...

C027154R Lieutenant William Alan Curtis MID 801 Fleet Air Arm HMS *Invincible* 11 July 1946 ~ 6 May 1982 Age 35

William Alan Curtis was born on 11 July 1946 in Lancashire, the eldest son of William Ernest and Joyce Curtis (née Dixon). The couple married in Lancashire in 1941. William Ernest Curtis was known as Bill, he was the only son of Ernest and Sarah Curtis (née Fish). Bill was a schoolmaster living in Poulton-Le-Fylde, Lancashire, in 1939.

In 1949, Bill and Joyce moved to the village of Cookley, where he became the Head of Cookley Seabright First School. He remained there for the next thirty years, retiring in 1976. Bill and Joyce had a younger son Tony in 1952. Bill was very well known locally where he taught generations of villagers. Bill was a keen sportsman, known as a prolific batsman and wicket-taker for Cookley in the Kidderminster Cricket League.

Joyce, from Penwortham, Lancashire, was an assistant teacher before marrying Bill; she was the daughter of a plumber who worked at Preston Airport. Joyce's grandfather was a postman, his wife was originally from Ireland.

William Alan Curtis was known as Alan or Al. He joined the RAF in the 1960s, his original service number was 4232269; he started his pilot journey flying V-Bombers. Al served for some time with the Royal New Zealand Air Force as a qualified Flying Instructor, flying Skyhawks.

Al was serving with 801 Squadron Fleet Air Arm in 1982, he was known as a gentleman, a great team member and an excellent tactician. Al was a real life 'Top Gun', a role that would always carry danger.

Based with 801 Squadron on HMS *Invincible* flying Sea Harriers equipped with Blue Fox radars, Al had already proved himself during the war with a *Canberra* aircraft interception. On 1 May 1982, Al took down a *Canberra* B62 of FAA Grupo 2, north of the Falkland Islands using a sidewinder, the Argentine pilots ejected but were not recovered.

According to Nigel 'Sharkey' McCartan-Ward, Commander of 801 Squadron, Al coped immensely well with the pressure of the moment despite his fuel being very low. Al received a posthumous Mention In Dispatches.

The day Al died he was attempting an interception of a very fast-moving low-level target; the weather conditions were awful with much low cloud.

Al died on 6 May 1982 in an extraordinary mid-air collision; two great pilots died that day. Al and Lieutenant Commander Eyton-Jones were flying a night patrol in two Sea Harriers. They were sent to investigate a suspicious radar contact near the hulk of HMS *Sheffield*, neither pilot returned.

Al is remembered with a plaque in St Peter's Church, Lea Lane, Cookley, Worcestershire. Joyce died in 2001, Bill in 2002, they are both buried in the cemetery in St Peter's, their son remembered close by.

At the time of his death Al's home was in West Chinnock near Crewkerne, Somerset. Al has a plaque in West Chinnock Parish Church in Somerset, it reads 'IN MEMORY OF LIEUTENANT WILLIAM ALAN CURTIS, RN KILLED IN ACTION IN THE FALKLAND ISLANDS ON 6TH MAY 1982 GIVEN BY THE VILLAGERS OF WEST CHIINNOCK.'

In 2022, as part of the Falkland Islands 40th Anniversary Place Names Project, Al was honoured with 'Curtis Island', a tussac island off John Point on the north side of Choiseul Sound, East Falkland.

His name lives on…

24513849 Guardsman Ian Antony Dale 1st Battalion Welsh Guards 13 March 1963 ~ 8 June 1982 Age 19

Ian Anthony Dale was born in Pontypridd on 13 March 1963, the son of Mervyn and Shirley Dale (née Webb).

Many families have no military history; however, the Dale family had served for more than one generation. Grandfather Peter James Dale was born in Barton Regis in January 1891, the son of Peter and Mary Jane Dale (née Sergeant). Peter senior was born in 1867, his father before him, another Peter, was born in Pembrokeshire. By 1911 the family had settled in Maritime Street, Pontypridd; Peter worked for the Great Western Colliery.

Ian's grandfather, Peter James Dale, married Beatrice Sarah Jones in Pontypridd on Christmas Day 1912. Peter served in the Welsh Regiment in 1915, his eldest son, Albert Samuel, was born on 10 November that year. On 18 June 1917, Peter James Dale enlisted into the Royal Flying Corps a daughter followed in January 1918. By 1921 the family were back in Maritime Street, Pontypridd, with a new addition – son Alex.

Mervyn Raymond Dale was born in September 1930 in Pontypridd, the family continued to live in Maritime Street for some years. In those days, the choice was often to go into the mines or join the Forces, Mervyn chose the latter. He married Shirley Margaret Webb in 1954. Ian Anthony Dale was born on 13 March 1963 in Pontypridd, younger brother to Phillip.

Ian attended Hawthorn School, Pontypridd, growing into a big lad who stood 6ft 5ins tall, a wonderful stature for a Guards Uniform. Ian met his sweetheart Debbie when they were just teenagers. Following in his father's footsteps he joined the British Army, completing his training in 1981. His proud parents were to see him on Guard Duty at Windsor Castle; they also attended the Trooping of the Colour when he was escort to the Colour.

On 3 April 1982, just a day after the Falkland Islands were invaded, Ian and Debbie married in Pontypridd with their families wishing them well for their future. A little over a month later Ian set sail with the 1st Battalion Welsh Guards on the requisitioned cruise liner QE2. The ship was crammed with Welsh Guards, Ghurkhas, and Royal Marines.

Less than a month later Ian was dead, killed on the fateful day the *Sir Galahad* was mercilessly bombed. Debbie was widowed just two months after her wedding, still a teenager and pregnant with her first child. Gareth Ian Dale was born in September that year.

The year after the war, Mervyn and Shirley made a pilgrimage to the Falkland Islands with many other families. It was their plan to go again but Mervyn died in 1992 before they were able to return. After his death Shirley took his ashes back 'Down South', they were scattered over the sea where their son had perished. Mervyn, like many other parents, wished to be reunited with his lost child.

Who knows why some people survive and others do not; two generations of Dales had survived their service; Ian was one of the fated Guards who died on 8 June 1982.

Shirley remarried; she died in 2009. Debbie remarried in 1987, she had another son. Gareth wishes to visit the Falkland Islands but as of 2022, he had yet to make the trip. Like many children he feels he needs to see the place where his father lost his life. This is so often the way with no grave to visit, it can help with acceptance. Ian was the youngest soldier from Wales to be killed in the conflict.

In 2022, as part of the Falkland Islands 40th Anniversary Place Names Project, Ian was honoured with 'Dale Island', a tussac island in North West Arm at the head of the Bay of Harbours, East Falkland.

His name lives on…

24057552 Sidney Albert Ivor Davidson 22 SAS Regiment
18 November 1947 ~ 19 May 1982 Age 34

Sid was born Albert Sydney Ivor Watkins on 18 November 1947, in St Mary's Hospital, Portsmouth. He was the eldest child of Peggy Rosina Watkins of Camp Road, Chepstow, Monmouthshire.

Sid was named Albert after Peggy's father Albert Watkins, a builder born in Bargoed, Wales. Albert married Hannah Maria Roynon in Bedwelty, Monmouthshire, in early 1915. Maria was born in Bedwelty, the daughter of a coal miner. Peggy was born in August 1924 in Bedwelty; by 1939 the family were living in Chepstow.

It is unclear why Sid was born in Portsmouth, but Peggy, a factory worker, was registered as still living at the family home at the time. Peggy married Wallace Henry David Davidson in 1952, Sid was adopted into the Davidson family. Peggy and Wallace had two children, a brother, and a sister for Sid.

Sid attended school in Chepstow, initially joining The Parachute Regiment before being selected for service with the Special Air Service in 1973. He served with the SAS in South Arabia, in Dhofar during Operation Storm, and also in Northern Ireland.

Sid married Liz in 1975, in Monmouthshire.

Sid was present at the capture of South Georgia at the very start of the British campaign. He was also present during the important action at Pebble Island at the north of the Falkland Islands, where 'D' Squadron were deployed by helicopter to a position nearby to scout the Argentine land and air forces based at the strategic airstrip.

The operation was then superbly executed, as the SAS soldiers (with the support of shelling from HMS *Glamorgan*, HMS *Hermes*, and HMS *Broadsword*) successfully disabled the airstrip, radar station, fuel, and ammo dump, while also disabling or destroying six Argentine Pucara aircraft, four T-34C Mentors, and a Coast Guard Skyvan. Furthermore, they also forced the surrender of the Argentine garrison, thus taking control of the island.

One setback was the unfortunate discovery of a previously unknown minefield, a member of his unit accidentally set off an anti-personnel mine, sending him high into the air and leaving him dazed and lightly injured from shrapnel. In the aftermath, Sid Davidson helped to comfort him, he carried him to safety before extraction.

On 19 May 1982 Sid was tragically killed with fellow SAS troops in the Sea King disaster, the biggest SAS loss since the Second World War.

Sid's mother Peggy died in 2001.

In 2022, as part of the Falkland Islands 40th Anniversary Place Names Project, Sid was honoured with 'Davidson Island', a small tussac island southwest of the Becher Islands in Choiseul Sound, East Falkland.

His name lives on...

P037269B Lance Corporal Colin Davison Commando Logistic Regiment Royal Marines 9 October 1960 ~ 27 May 1982 Age 21

Colin Davison was born on 9 October 1960 in Isabella Street, Newcastle Upon Tyne, the youngest child and only son of William and Sheila Davison (née Hassan). The couple married in 1952, starting their family the following year. Colin had two sisters, Catherine and Maureen.

Colin's father William was the second son of Thomas and May Davison (née Laidlaw) born in September 1918. William served in the British Army, as did his brother Fred. Thomas and Mary had eight children altogether.

William's father Thomas was born in 1892, one of many children born to William and Isabella Thompson Davison (née Morgan). The Davison family has lived in the Newcastle area for generations.

Sheila Hassan was born in Newcastle in 1924, the youngest child and only daughter of Alexander and Mary Hassan (née Mulligan). The couple married in Newcastle in 1912, their first child, William, was born in 1914 just before the First World War. Alexander was born in Brunswick Road, Bangor, Northern Ireland on 21 March 1878, the second son of Alexander and Elizabeth Hassan (née Harrison).

Alexander's older brother, Harry Hassan, was Captain of the cargo ship SS *Belgian Prince* which left Liverpool with a cargo of blue clay on 26 July 1917, it was to sadly be her last voyage. The *Belgian Prince* was torpedoed by a U-Boat and sunk on 31 July 1917. All of the crew scrambled into three lifeboats and survived the U-55 attack.

In an act of cruelty, however, the Commander of the submarine (Werner) ordered all the men out of the lifeboats, which were then chopped up with axes. Most crew were left to stand on the sea-deck of the submarine, the vessel submerged leaving them to their fate in the icy waters. Just four men survived, having concealed their life belts; they were picked up after spending eleven hours in the icy Atlantic waters. Harry Hassan was one of those survivors, although his fate remains unknown; he is listed as a Prisoner of War but was never to be seen again.

In June 1919, Harry was officially declared dead. The *Belgian Prince* was not the only attack by Werner where the crew were left to die in a similar way and the Captain taken prisoner below, it was an eerily similar attack to the sinking of the SS *Torrington* earlier that year. Anthony Starkey, Captain of the *Torrington*, was also recorded as a Prisoner of War, but he survived and returned to live out his days in Somerset. Werner escaped War Crimes prosecution for the First World War by fleeing to Brazil. In the Second World War he became a senior officer for the SS; it is hard to say how many deaths he was responsible for.

Sheila's uncle, William Hassan, was born on 27 March 1889 at home at Brunswick Road in Bangor, Northern Ireland. He served with the 2nd Battalion, Royal Irish Rifles and was sadly killed in action on 9 August 1915, he is commemorated at Menin Gate.

Sheila Hassan served in the WRENS; she told her daughter that she came from a 'Naval family'. Records indicate that Alexander, her father, served in the Royal Navy as early as 1895. Sheila was based in Orkney while serving.

Colin Davison attended Moor Edge Primary School, followed by West Moor Middle School, he completed his education at Killingworth High School. After considering all services, Colin settled on the Royal Marines, he joined up in October 1977 just after he turned 17.

Colin met his fiancée Sally in Plymouth, the first time she saw him he had a broken arm, his friend a broken leg – a humorous sight while they were endeavouring to ride a motorcycle with their injuries. Sally was smitten with Colin, whom she met while on holiday, though initially living in London, weekend breaks soon morphed into a move to Plymouth.

The couple moved in together, setting the date for their wedding for Easter time 1983. A planned holiday to Scotland had to be cancelled as Colin was informed that he was being sent to the Falkland Islands. Sally waved Colin off, her last memory of him would remain the sight of him on his motorbike, his twinkling eyes, his lovely smile.

After starting out life with the Royal Marines in Arbroath, some time with 45 Commando and a move to Plymouth, Colin – known as 'George' to his Marine pals – was keen for promotion and intended to serve his full twenty-two years. His best friend Ronnie was with him when he died after Ajax Bay was bombed on 27 May 1982, something Ronnie will never forget.

Several Royal Marines were badly injured that day, and Colin was mortally wounded. In October 1982 the family planted 10,000 daffodils at Killingworth Lake. They chose daffodils as a living memory so that each year his memory would live on as they bloom. Colin liked to fish in the lake, making it a perfect location.

The original memorial plaque was damaged, it was rededicated by Tyneside Council in 2005 and relocated at the Jigsaw Memorial, White Swan Centre in Killingworth. It reads: 'In Memory of Colin Davison Royal Marines Killed in Action San Carlos Bay Falkland Islands May 27, 1982. "When all at once I saw a crowd, a host. of golden daffodils: Beside the lake, beneath the trees, fluttering and dancing in the breeze" (William Wordsworth 1807)'.

When someone is killed in action wide ripples of grief resonate through family, friends and comrades; as the years go by, we age but 'They shall not grow old'. Colin's final resting place is Blue Beach Cemetery, San Carlos, Falkland Islands.

In 2022, as part of the Falkland Islands 40th Anniversary Place Names Project, Colin was honoured with 'Davison Point', a point near the settlement on the north coast of Bleaker Island, East Falkland.

His name lives on…

D155633A Petty Officer Catering Accountant Stephen Roy Dawson in HMS *Coventry* 5 June 1959 ~ 25 May 1982 Age 22

Stephen Roy Dawson was born in Liverpool on 5 June 1959, the eldest son of Clarence and Joan Dawson (née Powell), who married at St Chard's Church, Kirkby, in June 1958. Joan was the daughter of George and Emily Powell, she lived in Southdene prior to her marriage. Joan's father George had been a window cleaner when he was just 14 years old, he later became a salesman. Joan was the youngest of three children.

The Dawson family had a very long history in West Butterwick, Lincolnshire. Clarence, an electrician, was the eldest child of Fred and Catherine Dawson (née Bateman). Grandfather Fred was the ninth child of William and Mahala Dawson (née Lindley). Sadly, Mahala was widowed by 1911, her youngest child also died that year. Fred was a Labourer in varying employments over the years, most of his siblings married and had children. Stephen therefore had many relatives.

After Stephen was born his family settled back in West Butterwick, Lincolnshire, he had a sister, Glenda, and younger brother, Ian. Stephen was a long way from home in May 1982, serving in the Royal Navy as a Petty Officer Catering Accountant in HMS *Coventry* – like many, headed for a great career.

Stephen was sadly killed in the Junior Rates dining hall when HMS *Coventry* was hit on 25 May 1982. Stephen is commemorated with a memorial stone in St Mary's Churchyard, Butterwick. St Mary the Virgin was the family's local church where other family members had married. The stone reads '*IN MEMORY OF PETTY OFFICER C.A STEPHEN ROY DAWSON RN DEARLY LOVED SON OF CLARENCE & JOAN DEAR BROTHER OF GLENDA & IAN KILLED IN ACTION 25 MAY 1982 AGED 22 ON HMS COVENTRY SOUTH ATLANTIC GREATER LOVE HATH NO MAN THAN THIS THAT A MAN LAYS DOWN HIS LIFE FOR HIS FRIENDS*'.

Many of Stephen's great-uncles and aunts outlived him, as did both his grandfathers.

West Butterwick Church of England Primary School present the Stephen Dawson Achievement Award each year to the pupil who shows the most progress.

In 2022, as part of the Falkland Islands 40th Anniversary Place Names Project, Stephen was honoured with 'Dawson Beach', a large sandy beach on mainland East Falkland on the west shore of Lively Sound, south of Seal Cove.

His name lives on…

24469565 Guardsman Derek James Denholm 2nd Battalion Scots Guards 10 May 1958 ~ 14 June 1982 Age 24

Derek James Denholm was born at 253 Duke Street, Glasgow, during the morning of 10 May 1958. Derek was the son of Fergus Daly and Elizabeth Kelly Denholm (née Travers), Fergus was a telephone engineer. The family lived at the time in Beechgrove Street, Glasgow. Fergus and Elizabeth married in Glasgow in September 1952.

Derek enlisted into the Scots Guards in January 1978. He saw service twice in Northern Ireland: first from 27 August 1978 until 26 December 1978, and his second tour 10 March 1980 until 10 November 1981. Operation Corporate, codename for the Falklands Conflict, was sadly to be his last.

During the war, Derek was serving with 2nd Battalion Scots Guards who fought on Tumbledown Mountain, where he was killed in the early hours of 14 June 1982. Derek suffered a blast injury and multiple shrapnel wounds. At the time of his death, he was serving with 14 Platoon, Left Flank Company.

Derek was repatriated and is buried in Sandymount Cemetery in Glasgow. His mother, Elizabeth, died in 1991, his father in 2017.

Derek was married to Grace, the couple had one son Andrew who was just 3 years old when his father died. Grace and her son visited the Falkland Islands for the 40th Anniversary.

In 2022, as part of the Falkland Islands 40th Anniversary Place Names Project, Derek was honoured with 'Denholm Bay', a small bay north of Fox Point, near Bertha's Beach, East Falkland.

His name lives on…

498255 Captain Christopher Dent 2nd Battalion Parachute Regiment 13 October 1947 ~ 28 May 1982 Age 34

Christopher Dent was born 13 October 1947, the eldest son of Arthur and Winifred Dent (née Merrick), the couple married in Northumberland in early 1946. Arthur was born in Hampstead Road, St Pancras, the only son of James and Lily Dent. grandfather James was born in New Zealand. Chris had one younger brother, two years his junior.

Chris attended Barnard Castle School, County Durham, known locally as 'Barney's', Chris was a student of Durham House, he attended the school from 1959–1966. A member of the Combined Cadet Force and the Police Cadets, Chris earned his full colours in swimming.

In 1974, Chris was commissioned into The Parachute Regiment. During the Falklands War, Chris was second in command of A Company, 2 Para. Prior to Operation Corporate, he had been a Platoon Commander with Junior Parachute Company.

Chris and Cathy married in Scotland in 1977. Cathy was also an Army Officer with the Royal Army Medical Corps. The couple had one son during their marriage, Robbie was born in 1981 while the family were based in Aldershot. Two months before the Falklands invasion, his wife and the couple's six-month-old son had flown to Australia where the family planned to live after Chris returned from the Falklands. Fate, sadly intervened.

Chris braved enemy fire to retrieve a vital radio from another soldier who had been killed. As the men came under renewed fire, their attack threatened to grind to a halt, and they were forced to take cover. Captain Dent was warned by a colleague that if he tried to proceed, he would be killed. However, he realised that if the momentum were lost, the lives of his men would be in even greater danger and that the battle might be lost. He stood up and sprinted towards the Argentine positions but was cut down by machine-gun fire.

Cathy made the decision to let Chris have his final resting place in the Falkland Islands. In an interview twenty-five years after the Falklands War, she described her horror at seeing her husband's first burial live on television. Cathy recounted how the funeral had come on the news without warning. She said she felt completely caught out. As she saw her husband's body, third to be named, Cathy sat and cried.

Many widows can relate to the emotional invasion of the media, it remains impossible to adequately describe the horror of seeing your loved one buried in a mass grave while the nation looks on.

Chris has a special tribute close to his parents' old home in Tyneside. The memorial was unveiled by Mrs Doreen Walker, Mayor of North Tyneside on 18 October 1982. A small bronze plaque placed on a stone plinth it reads 'In memory of Captain Christopher Dent, 2nd Battalion Parachute Regiment, Killed in action Goose Green, Falkland Islands 28 May 1982'. The plinth is set within a flowerbed and fifteen oak trees were planted close by at the time.

In 2022, as part of the Falkland Islands 40th Anniversary Place Names Project, Chris was honoured with 'Dent Harbour', the innermost basin at the west end of Port Purvis, West Falkland.

His name lives on…

24541964 Private Stephen Jeffrey Dixon 2nd Battalion Parachute Regiment 6 September 1963 ~ 28 May 1982 Age 18

Stephen Jeffrey Dixon was born in Commercial Road, Stepney, London, the eldest child and only son of John and Linda Dixon. The family lived in Stepney where Steve's younger sisters Wendy and Susan were also born, the three siblings were very close.

The Dixon family moved to Basildon where Steve attended Swan Mead Junior School, followed by Woodlands School. Steve had a lifelong friend David; the pair were inseparable as youngsters. Steve loved riding his motorbike but kept his adventures away from his parents because they did not like them. After his death his parents were brought photos of Steve from his biker friends, they were very proud to learn that he had won a few trophies for racing. Steve left his motorbike to Dave, which may have faded into memory over the years, but Dave kept the number plate.

Steve was very popular with the local children who would knock for him to help mend their toys. Steve and Dave once went to the local skip and put together a bike for a local boy who did not have one. His mother says he did not have a nasty bone in his body, he exuded kindness.

Steve had an aspiration to join the army from around 14 years of age, he initially joined the Army Cadets. When it came time for him to join up with the British Army, he brought home papers from Southend for his parents to sign. His parents were against the idea, a determined Steve just pestered them until they relented and signed the papers, to their cost.

Steve was 18 years old and serving with 11 Platoon D Coy 2 Para when he was killed by shellfire as D Coy began to take the school house at Goose Green.

Steve is buried in All Saints Church off Vange Hill Drive in Vange, Essex.

In 2022, as part of the Falkland Islands 40th Anniversary Place Names Project, Steve was honoured with 'Dixon Arm', a narrow arm off the upper reaches of Swan Inlet, East Falkland.

His name lives on...

Petty Officer 1 Bosun John Benjamin Dobson SS *Atlantic Conveyor* 24 February 1924 ~ 25 May 1982 Age 58

The Dobson family have a long history in Lincolnshire. John's father Harry was the eldest son of William and Louisa Dobson (née Harrison), married in Lincolnshire in 1875. Harry was born the following year in January 1876, and by 1881 the family lived in Castle Street, Lincoln St Nicholas. William was a general labourer; Harry already had a brother Bertie and sister Frances.

Ten years later the family living at Bardney Dairies where William was a farmer and the couple had gone on to have five more children: George, Mary, William, Ada and Benjamin (John Benjamin). It appears that William and Louisa had twelve children altogether, losing their second son William Godson Dobson.

The Dobson family mainly remained in farming, sadly Harry's sister ended up in Horncastle Workhouse, she died in 1932. John Benjamin, born in 1891 joined the Lincolnshire Regiment, he was killed in France and Flanders on 21 March 1918. He is honoured on the Wragby War Memorial and also on the CWGC Pozieres Memorial in France.

Selina Hewitt was born in Horncastle, Lincolnshire, on 10 April 1887; by the age of 13 she was working as a domestic servant in service at Bealey House, Horncastle, to a retired grocer and his family.

Harry Dobson married John's mother, Selina, in 1909. Selina and Harry Dobson started their family the year after their marriage and welcomed Hilda May into the world in February 1910. They went on to have a large family of twelve children. John Benjamin Dobson was their eighth child, born on 24 February 1924 in Rand, Lincolnshire.

John's younger brother, Charles Edwin Dobson, was born on 13 February 1927. Charles married Dorothy Stray in Boston, Lincolnshire, in 1952. They had just one child, Janet, who married in 1978 and had two children; one of them, a son, was born late in 1982 after his great-uncle had been killed. Interestingly John's great-nephew was a Cadet Engineering Officer in the Merchant Navy.

Whatever his reasons, whether it was the call of the ocean over that of the land or just a spirit for adventure, John Benjamin Dobson joined the Merchant Navy, sadly just like his namesake uncle, he was not to return from his last voyage.

At 19.40 hrs on 25 May 1982 'Emergency Stations' were sounded by the ship's alarm on the *Atlantic Conveyor*. Despite the counter measures of HMS *Alacrity* and other warships the missiles aimed at the ship found her and as they hit, they ripped through C Deck.

Despite some controversy as to whether both missiles hit the ship, a board of enquiry stated: 'ACO hit by two Exocet, port quarter level with after end superstructure, 10–12 feet above waterline. Missiles entered C cargo deck in vicinity of lift shaft. Ship in a port-turn passing through approximately 90 degrees at the time.'

The Bosun was one of twelve men killed. In June 2007 a memorial to the *Atlantic Conveyor* was unveiled at Cape Pembroke, which is the most easterly point on the Falkland Islands. Until then the *Atlantic Conveyor* had been the only vessel sunk during the war without a memorial. The memorial is a propeller shaft feature which is aligned on a magnetic bearing of 60 degrees to indicate the point ninety miles out to sea where *Atlantic Conveyor* met her fate. From 2008 she was finally included in the Protection of Military Remains Act of 1986.

At the time of his death John's home on land was Exmouth. John met his wife Mary in Falmouth at a guest house she ran, while home on leave he would stay there. Mary later moved to Exmouth; the couple married on 15 December 1973 at a Register Office in Devon. John's stepson Jim remembers him as a quiet man who loved the ocean and enjoyed a pint.

In 2022, as part of the Falkland Islands 40th Anniversary Place Names Project, John was honoured with 'Dobson Bluff', a high bluff near Cape Percival on the north-west coast of Beaver Island, West Falkland.

His name lives on....

D183607L Weapons Engineering Mechanic (Radio) John Keith Dobson HMS *Coventry* 9 December 1961 ~ 25 May 1982 Age 20

John Keith Dobson was born on 9 December 1961 in Plympton, Devon. His parents Quenilda Jennifer (known as Jennifer) and Peter Graham Dobson married in 1954 in Torquay, Devon. John was the youngest of five children born to the couple. Jane was the eldest, followed by Valerie, Trevor, Kay and lastly John.

John was schooled at Exmouth Comprehensive, after which he commenced his training with the Royal Navy at HMS *Raleigh*. John was on exercise aboard HMS *Coventry* around Gibraltar when the Falkland Islands were invaded. The ship was immediately sent to Ascension Islands and on to the Falklands.

During Operation Corporate, John was a Weapons Engineering Mechanic (Radio) on HMS *Coventry*. When setting sail 'Down South' he was about to become an uncle; his oldest sister was due to have her first child. Jane's son was born on 1 May 1982, sadly John was never to meet his nephew. He died on 25 May 1982 aboard HMS *Coventry*. The news is always devastating to any family but Jane was particularly emotional on hearing the news. For her it was compounded by the fact that her husband worked away, she says she was 'extremely tearful and the sun did not shine'.

HMS *Coventry* was a type 42 Destroyer originally laid down by Cammell Laird and Co Ltd in Birkenhead on 29 January 1973. She was commissioned on 10 November 1978 having been accepted into service at a cost of £37,900,000. HMS *Coventry* was attacked by Argentinian Air Force A-4 Skyhawks, she sank shortly after, leaving nineteen men dead and a further thirty injured. John was one of the casualties.

There were two John Dobsons killed during the Falklands War on the same day. In a twist of fate, John Keith Dobson's sister Jane heard on the news that John Dobson was missing presumed dead. Jane called her father who in turn called Naval welfare, they apologised advising that the family should not have heard that news. Later that day a Chaplain and a Naval Officer went to visit John's parents to inform them that their son had indeed been killed in action.

A few days later Jane's husband called Naval welfare to enquire about the news. It turned out that the John Dobson they had initially heard about on the news was John Benjamin Dobson the Bosun of *Atlantic Conveyor*. John Keith Dobson was single and had served approximately two years in the Royal Navy.

Jane says 'I don't think I feel anything about the conflict. I am sad that lives were lost on both sides. I feel for the men who are still suffering physically and emotionally and have probably died as a result.'

There is a memorial plaque in St Mary the Virgin Church, Ramsden Lane, Offwell, East Devon which reads 'IN LOVING MEMORY OF WEM JOHN KEITH DOBSON RN AGED 20 OF HMS COVENTRY KILLED IN ACTION 25 MAY 1982 OFF THE FALKLAND ISLANDS'.

In 2022, as part of the Falkland Islands 40th Anniversary Place Names Project, John was honoured with 'Dobson Passage', the passage into Rolons Cove (between Port Harriet and Bluff Cove), East Falkland.

His name lives on…

24355141 Private Mark Steven Dodsworth 3rd Battalion Parachute Regiment 5 April 1958 ~ 12 June 1982 Age 24

Mark Steven Dodsworth was born in Walsall on 5 April 1958, the eldest son of Bryan and Carole Dodsworth (née McKechnie), he had three younger brothers and a sister.

Mark grew up in Walsall attending Manor Farm School in Rushall before following in his father's footsteps to join The Parachute Regiment. Bryan Dodsworth had earned his Maroon Beret many years before, he was involved in the Suez Campaign in 1956.

Mark joined the Junior Leaders Regiment at Shorncliffe, straight from school, from there he was drafted to 3 Para at the tender age of 17. Mark was sent to Melton Mowbray to train with the Army Dog Unit, he was finally sent to Northern Ireland on his 18th birthday. Known as a quiet young man, unassuming and a gentle giant, he acquired the nickname of 'Doddy'.

Doddy was stationed in Palace Barracks Northern Ireland; he was part of 39 BDE Specialist Dog Unit. It was while there he met his wife-to-be, Caroline Bankhead. The couple were married for fourteen months before he died. Doddy was called back to his battalion in 1981 where he trained as a medic. The Falkland Islands were invaded just three days before Mark's 24th birthday, he was about to be deployed to a place where medics would be in great demand. The couple were living in Tidworth when the call to go 'Down South' came.

Doddy was killed during the Battle for Mount Longdon on 12 June 1982. He was shot while tending to an injured soldier just days before the end of the war. His battalion suffered heavy losses with twenty-three men killed during the bloody battle.

Mark's body was repatriated, he was laid to rest at St Peter's Church, Walsall in early December 1982. Mark's parents travelled to the Falkland Islands many years after his death when they were both in their seventies. Caroline eventually settled in Australia; she made the trip back to England for the 40th Anniversary. Doddy remains well remembered by friends and family alike.

In 2022, as part of the Falkland Islands 40th Anniversary Place Names Project, Mark was honoured with 'Dodsworth Beach', a beach on the north coast of East Falkland at the east end of Seal Bay.

His name lives on...

D155376N Cook Richard John Selwyn Dunkerley HMS *Ardent* 7 August 1959 ~ 21 May 1982 Age 22

Richard John Selwyn Dunkerley was born in Salisbury, Wiltshire on 7 August 1959. Richard was the eldest child and only son of John Nigel and Maureen Dunkerley (née McCracken) who married in Warminster. Richard's father was in the RAF, the couple went on to have three daughters, the youngest born in Scotland in 1963.

Richard's mother was no stranger to the upheaval of war or indeed forces life; in 1939 her mother was living with her parents in a village near Warminster. Maureen herself was born in Aldershot, the year before the Second World War commenced.

Richard's father John rode a motorbike and was tragically killed in a road traffic accident in September 1966, aged just 27 years. Maureen was widowed with four young children – Richard was the eldest at 7, and the youngest was just 3 years of age. Maureen remarried, the family settled in Stalham, Norfolk, by 1973 Richard had another brother and sister.

Richard attended Stalham Secondary Modern from 1970 to 1975 prior to joining the Royal Navy. 'Dunks', as he became known to his shipmates, joined up when he was 16 years old, like many young lads, fresh out of school.

Richard's naval journey began at HMS *Ganges*. Later he went on to HMS *Pembroke* in Chatham to train as a cook, his first ship was HMS *Leander*, after which he joined the crew of HMS *Ardent*.

When the Falkland Islands were invaded in April 1982 Richard's family were living in Windsor. Richard had left HMS *Ardent* to go to a shore-based establishment for some training but begged to return to his ship. He knew HMS *Ardent* inside and out and said it would be difficult for a new crew member to learn quickly, if anything happened, they would be at a disadvantage. He was allowed to go back to his ship for the long voyage south.

On 21 May 1982, Richard was killed when his ship was hit by waves of attack by Argentine aircraft. His family remain very close, they made the pilgrimage to the Islands in 1983. Several of his family members are still settled in Norfolk.

Richard is remembered as a very laid-back person, someone who seemed to handle whatever life threw his way. He was confident without being cocky, he was funny and loved a laugh. He loved music and always carried a stereo with two cases of cassettes wherever he went. His family miss him greatly.

Cook Dunkerley is honoured by a plaque in St Mary's Church, High Street, Stalham, Norfolk. The plaque is a circular slate tablet which bears a fouled anchor and incised inscription 'Remember Richard J Dunkerley RN', around the edges it says, 'KILLED IN THE FALKLANDS CONFLICT ABOARD HMS ARDENT 21 MAY 1982 AGED 22'.

In 2022, as part of the Falkland Islands 40th Anniversary Place Names Project, Richard was honoured with 'Dunkerley Bay', a bay on the east coast of Motley Island, in Lively Sound on East Falkland.

His name lives on…

24263842 Guardsman Michael Joseph Dunphy 1st Battalion Welsh Guards 20 June 1958 ~ 8 June 1982 Age 23

Michael Joseph Dunphy was born on 20 June 1958 at Selly Oak Hospital, Selly Oak, Birmingham. Mike was the son of Michael Joseph and Doreen Dunphy (née Griffiths). The couple married in Birmingham in 1957. Mike was one of three children, all boys. At the time of Mike's birth his father was a builder's labourer and the family lived at Belgrave Road in Raddlebarn, Birmingham.

The family later settled in Maesyderi, Llechryd, Cardigan, Wales, where Mike attended the local school. Mike is the only Falklands War casualty named on the Llechryd Council School War Memorial. Prior to joining the Welsh Guards, he was a cadet.

Mike is remembered as having a bit of a wild side and loving a party, but he was also likened to Shaggy in Scooby Doo by Simon Weston, a fellow Welsh Guard.

Mike was killed on 8 June 1982 when the *Sir Galahad* was bombed, his body was not recovered. His school held a memorial service for the former pupil just after he died.

In 2011 Mike's brother James received the Elizabeth Cross in a ceremony in Carmarthen. Mike's mother had died the year before.

Mike was unmarried when he died but left behind a daughter, born in December 1981.

In 2022, as part of the Falkland Islands 40th Anniversary Place Names Project, Mike was honoured with 'Dunphy Islet', a small tussac island between Button Bay and Archer Cove on the north shore of Choiseul Sound, East Falkland.

His name lives on…

D144844F Cook Brian Easton HMS *Glamorgan* 11 December 1957 ~ 12 June 1982 Age 24

Brian Easton was born on 11 December 1957 in Alyth, Scotland to Jim and Nellie Easton (née Fairweather). Brian had three sisters Maureen, Gladys and Shirley.

Brian was schooled at Alyth Primary and Secondary schools; he loved playing football and supported Glasgow Celtic. He loved speed walking and would make his family laugh with his speed walking 'wiggle'. Brian was a keen member of the Cubs and the Scouts for some years.

Like many youngsters Brian joined the Royal Navy when he was still 16 years old. A member of the Royal Navy Display Team, he performed at the Edinburgh Military Tattoo and the Remembrance Service as well as other events. He also performed in the Navy Field Gun competitions.

HMS *Glamorgan* was off Gibraltar about to take part in exercises when the Falkland Islands were invaded. The ship set off for the long journey 'Down South' as the flagship of the Royal Naval Task Force, headed by Admiral Sandy Woodward. On 15 April he transferred his flag to the Aircraft Carrier HMS *Hermes*. HMS *Glamorgan* had a very busy time 'Down South', engaging in her first action on 1 May 1982.

Brian was serving as a Cook in *Glamorgan*; he had been in the Navy approximately eight years by the time his ship went to war.

All families had in those days were letters home, they eagerly waited for the postman. His sister Shirley remembers, 'In one letter, Brian said that the ship had been under fire and that he was afraid but also chatting about everyday things and when he would be back in Scotland on his return.' Brian had married Julie in Portsmouth just two years previously, so as well as his family in Scotland, his wife was eagerly awaiting news.

Brian was killed on 12 June 1982 when his ship was hit by an Argentine missile, he was lost to the Atlantic Ocean. The family, consisting of his mother, father and widow, made the trip to the Falkland Islands for the families' pilgrimage in 1983.

Brian's surviving sisters Gladys and Shirley made their own trip to the Falkland Islands again in 2011 along with others, for the unveiling of the HMS *Glamorgan* Memorial. A truly beautiful memorial, it is situated at Hookers Point close to Surf Bay, a long white sandy beach to the east of Stanley.

Shirley says of her brother,

> Brian was a funny and caring son and brother. He made the most of the opportunities that the Royal Navy presented him, and in his short life, he saw much of the world. He is remembered not only by his family but by his friends in Alyth who still refer to him as Bumper or Biff.

Brian's parents lived out their days in Scotland, both died in their eighties. Gladys and Shirley both have fond memories of their brother.

In 2022, as part of the Falkland Islands 40th Anniversary Place Names Project, Brian was honoured with 'Easton Creek', an inlet running southwest at the head of West Arm in Adventure Sound, East Falkland.

His name lives on…

24584832 Guardsman Peter Edwards 1st Battalion Welsh Guards 3 September 1962 ~ 8 June 1982 Age 19

Peter Edwards was born in Denbigh on 3 September 1962, the third child and eldest son of Gordon and Evelyn Edwards (née Roberts). Peter had two older sisters, Barbara and Mandy, and a younger brother, Brian. He grew up in Llandyrnog, attending the local primary school, later he attended Denbigh High School.

Peter joined the Welsh Guards on 1 November 1980, his basic training was in Pirbright, Surrey, where his battalion was stationed at the time. Peter's father Gordon had served in the Royal Welch Fusiliers, his Uncle Thomas, a year younger than his father, served with the Welsh Guards. 22217659 Sergeant Thomas Edwards 1st Battalion Welsh Guards served in Aden in the early 1960s. Tommy, as he was known, was awarded the Radfan clasp for his General Service Medal, and was also awarded the Military Medal for his service in Aden.

Peter was in Prince of Wales company, 1st Battalion Welsh Guards, he was also a member of the Welsh Guards choir. Still a teenager, Peter lived at home when on leave.

Peter was killed on the *Sir Galahad* on 8 June 1982, a truly tragic day. Peter's mother Evelyn died in 2004, his father Gordon in 2005. Sister Barbara received the Elizabeth Cross on behalf of the family in 2010 in a ceremony at City Hall in Cardiff. The award was presented by the then Lord Lieutenant of Clwyd, Trefor Jones. Peter is remembered as being a quiet lad who loved cycling and was environmentally concerned from a young age; he was a member of the St John's Ambulance, and he loved a wide variety of music.

In 2022, as part of the Falkland Islands 40th Anniversary Place Names Project, Peter was honoured with 'Edwards Harbour', a sheltered harbour between Diddle Dee Island and Narrow Point on West Falkland.

His name lives on…

D076798T Chief Petty Officer Weapons Engineering Artificer Andrew Charles Eggington HMS *Sheffield* 29 November 1946 ~ 4 May 1982 Age 35

The name Francis was a running theme throughout the Eggington family.

Great-grandad Francis was a pupil–teacher at the Union Workhouse School, Kirkdale, West Derby, in 1881, he was 16 years old. Ten years later, in July 1891, he married Martha Selina Davies, their first child was born the following year in November 1892; in family tradition, they named him Francis. By 1901 the couple had two more children and still lived in Kirkdale.

By 1911, they had five boys and had moved to Disraeli Road, Forest Gate. Francis senior was a tramways chief clerk and Francis junior was an electrical engineer apprentice. The family had made the move down south sometime after 1902, all but their youngest son Cyril had been born up north. Cyril was the only child born in East London.

Francis Eggington worked for the West Ham Corporation Electricity Supply in 1921, the family still lived in Forest Gate. By the late '30s the Eggington family had moved to Airlie Gardens in Ilford, where three generations shared a home. Francis junior married Amelia Syrett in September 1917 at Stratford St John in East London. The following year their first child, Andy's father, Francis Charles was born. Francis died in 1950, Amelia remarried the following year.

By 1939 Francis Charles was a boiler fitter and within two years had met his bride. Francis Charles Eggington and Kate Eveline Bentley married in 1941 in Ilford, Essex. Their first child, a girl, was born a couple of years later; again, in family tradition, they called her Frances.

Two years later on 29 November 1946 their son Andrew Charles was born in Ilford. He was later known as Andy to his mates.

After joining the Royal Navy, Andy had become an instructor at HMS *Collingwood* in the early 1970s. He is remembered for taking great care of his appearance and being a whizz with electronics, which is hardly surprising considering his family history. He is remembered for being knowledgeable but modest about his abilities. He is also remembered for being kind.

Andy was killed when HMS *Sheffield* was hit by an Exocet missile on 4 May 1982. The 'Shiny Sheff' was the first ship to be sunk in the Falklands War, a great shock to many as the war became real for our Task Force.

At the time of his death Andy's home was in Purbrook, Hampshire. His father died in 1987, outliving his son by just five years. Andy's mother died in Southend, Essex in 1993.

There is a memorial to Andy in St Margaret of Antioch Church in Perth Rd, Ilford, Essex. The plaque reads 'IN MEMORY OF ANDREW CHARLES EGGINGTON WEA IST CLASS HMS SHEFFIELD BORN IN THIS PARISH 29 NOVEMBER 1946 DIED ON ACTIVE SERVICE 4TH MAY 1982 DURING THE FALKLANDS CONFLICT'.

In 2022, as part of the Falkland Islands 40th Anniversary Place Names Project, Andy was honoured with 'Eggington Bay', a large bay with a long sandy beach between Robinson Point and North Point on Keppel Island, West Falkland.

His name lives on…

24185183 Sergeant Clifford Noel Elley 1st Battalion Welsh Guards 15 December 1953 ~ 8 June 1982 Age 28

Clifford Noel Elley was born on 15 December 1953 in Pontypridd, Wales. Though some records show him with Nigel as his middle name, it was actually Noel, because he was born just ten days before Christmas.

The Elley name has a long association with Pontypridd though originally, Cliff's grandfather Albert Elley was born in Coleford, Gloucestershire, in 1875. The family were in the main miners of iron, and later coal. In the late 1800s the Elley family relocated from the Forest of Dean to Pontypridd.

Albert married his first wife, Alice, in March 1896 in Pontypridd; their first child, Annie May was born that year. Sadly, though they had four children together, Annie May died in 1899, she was 3 years old. The following year, on 16 May 1900, the couple had another daughter who they named Annie Mafeking. Annie Mafeking went on to marry and have four children; she lived into her eighties.

Alice Elley died in 1904, she was only 28 years of age, she left behind three young children. In 1910, Albert remarried Georgina Roberts and they had their first child, Trevor, while living in Birchgrove, Pontypridd.

Albert and Georgina went on to have nine children, their seventh child was Clifford Henry, Cliff's father. Another of their children, Ernest Edward Elley, served with the Welsh Guards in the Second World War; in a quirk of fate, he died on 2 April 1942 – exactly forty years to the day the Falkland Islands were invaded. He died as a result of an accident, the inscription on his CWGC headstone in Pontypridd cemetery reads 'TO LIVE ALWAYS IN THE MEMORY OF THOSE WHO LOVED HIM DEARLY IS NOT TO DIE'. He appears to be the first member of the Elley family to serve in the Welsh Guards.

Clifford Henry Elley married Edith Joyce O'Keefe in Pontypridd in 1946, the couple went on to have eight children, four girls and four boys. Three of their sons joined the services. Peter joined the Royal Marines, Cliff and Terry joined the Welsh Guards in 1971.

Cliff and Vivienne married in Pontypridd in 1978, the couple had two sons. Cliff is remembered as a lovely man. On 8 June 1982, Cliff was one of the casualties of the bombing of the *Sir Galahad*. Lost to the South Atlantic his family have no grave; he is, however, well remembered by family and fellow Welsh Guards alike.

In 2022, as part of the Falkland Islands 40th Anniversary Place Names Project, Cliff was honoured with 'Elley Bay', a bay on the north shore of Port Richard, West Falkland.

His name lives on…

C027074H Sub Lieutenant Richard Charles Emly HMS *Sheffield*
13 May 1946 ~ 4 May 1982 Age 35

Richard Charles Emly was born around 13 May 1946. He was adopted by Richard Walter Francis and Kathleen Emly (née Long), who married in 1940. There remains some mystery around Richard's actual birth, it is possible that he was a foundling but as the years went by, he choose not to investigate into his biological heritage. The Emly family were therefore the only family Richard knew until he formed his own.

Generations of Emlys before had hailed from Lewisham, Richard senior was the youngest son of John and Margaret Emly (née Gibbins), they married in 1907, their first son Jack was born two years later. According to records John had been an Able Seaman on HMS *Powerful* in 1899, when an incident occurred on 29 October which led to his leaving the Royal Navy for a life on land. John had served eight years; he had joined up at the age of 17.

Richard Walter Francis Emly was born on 22 May 1918 in Lewisham, he served as a Signalman in the Royal Signals in the Second World War. His service saw him earn the British Empire Medal while on duty in the Middle East.

Citation in the *London Gazette* 14 October 1943 reads:

> 'The KING has been graciously pleased to approve the award of the British Empire Medal (Military Division), in recognition of gallant and distinguished services in the Middle East, to the undermentioned: —
> No. 2332894 Signalman Richard Water Francis Emly. Royal Corps of Signals (Leeds 5).'

Prior to the Second World War, Richard Snr had been a travelling telephone engineer living in Mirfield, Yorkshire. After marrying Kathleen, the couple had been unable to have children, so Richard Charles was a welcome addition when he was adopted, it is thought via the church.

An only child, Richard Charles Emly joined the Royal Navy at just 16 years old. He met his wife-to-be, Mo Bigby, in the Zambezi Club in Earl's Court, and soon after he was drafted to Rosyth in Scotland. Mo was born and brought up in London and remembers, as do many women of that era, that all contact was confined to telephone landlines and letters. The couple married about a year after they met, the ceremony was in Chelsea, London, in 1970.

Richard and Mo had one son, Matthew Richard Emly who was born in 1976 in Chatham, Kent. Mo remembers Richard as a quiet man who was sociable but not brash at all. By the time the Falkland Islands were in invaded in April 1982, Richard was serving in HMS *Sheffield*, he had been serving in the Royal Navy for twenty years.

After twelve years of marriage Mo was to receive devastating news – surrounded by some confusion; she was first told that Richard was alive. Later it was confirmed that Richard had died on 4 May 1982 when HMS *Sheffield* was hit by an Exocet air-launched anti-ship missile from an Argentinian Super Étendard aircraft.

Seeking some refuge from the deluge of newspaper reporters, Mo left with her son to live in Gibraltar for eighteen months. It was a place she was familiar with, but with her son's future in mind she moved to Estepona, Spain, where they lived for twenty years. Matthew benefited from the environment in more ways than one, he was raised bilingual.

Mo says Matthew is very like his father and is particularly good at Maths. When Matthew was 14 years old, he and Mo were on a trip to London when they got talking to a group of Argentinians, made easy by Matthew's fluency in Spanish. They had a lovely lunch together, the group being quite anti-war. We forget sometimes that Argentina was under a dictatorship and had no choice in their participation in the Falklands War, many were young conscripts.

Mo finally returned to England in 2003 where she settled in the south. She still misses Richard and thinks of him often, but among the sadness are the great memories of a love that transcends death.

Richard is remembered on the Guisley War Memorial.

In 2022, as part of the Falkland Islands 40th Anniversary Place Names Project, Richard was honoured with 'Emly Cove', a small cove at Ruins Point on mainland West Falkland near Pirate Creek inside Tamar Pass.

His name lives on…

P024439G Sergeant Roger Enefer 45 Commando Royal Marines 1 July 1947 ~ 27 May 1982 Age 34

The Enefer family migrated to Lincolnshire from Essex; back in the mid-nineteenth century they lived in Little Baddow, Essex. Alfred Enefer was Roger's great-grandfather, born in Little Baddow in 1856 to George and Harriet Enefer (née Burr). Some of the family stayed in Essex, Alfred made his way to Lincolnshire where he became a blast furnaceman.

Alfred married Minna Goats Gray in Glanford Brigg in 1876. Much of the Enefer family lived within the Barrow, Glanford Brigg, New Brumby and Scunthorpe areas. The couple had six children: four boys and two girls. Roger's grandfather, Herbert, was born in October 1879.

Youngest son Talbot Enefer served with the 1/6th Northumberland Fusiliers in the First World War. Talbot was captured on 9 April 1918 and held as a Prisoner of War. Records indicate that a wounded Talbot was taken to Munster Laz, a hospital POW camp. He was captured in Frankeich Estaires, which suggests he may have escaped from his original captivity. Talbot had a baby daughter, just 1 year old at the time. He survived the First World War and returned to New Brumby, where he worked in the steelworks, his two sons were born in 1920 and 1922.

Roger's grandfather, Herbert, was born in New Brumby; he grew up in the area and later became a boiler maker in the steelworks. Herbert worked for some time in Yorkshire where he met Esther Womersley from Chapeltown; the couple married in Lincolnshire in 1907. Herbert and Esther had two sons, Adolphus was born in Yorkshire in 1911, named after his cricket-bat-making uncle. Youngest son, Herbert, was born in New Brumby in December 1916.

Herbert became a joiner and went on to marry Roslyn Green in 1946. Roslyn was one of five children; her mother had died when she was just 12 years old. Roger was their eldest child, born in Scunthorpe on 1 July 1947. Roger had a sister three years his junior.

Roger joined the Royal Marines; he married Sue in Plymouth in 1970. The couple had two children, one born in 1971 in Singapore, the other in 1974 in Plymouth, where the family settled. Roger's mother died when he was just 17 years old. Herbert died in the summer of 1996, outliving his son by fourteen years.

During the Falklands War Roger was serving with 45 Commando Royal Marines, he was killed on 27 May 1982; he died of his wounds after an enemy bombing attack while on operations at Ajax Bay. Roger was repatriated and laid to rest at Drake Cemetery, Plymouth.

Roger is remembered on the Roll of Honour at Scunthorpe War Memorial.

In 2022, as part of the Falkland Islands 40th Anniversary Place Names Project, Roger was honoured with 'Enefer Point', the tip of a long peninsular east of Wineglass Bay on Bleaker Island, East Falkland.

His name lives on...

PO25446U Sergeant Andrew Peter Evans MID 3 Commando Brigade Air Squadron Royal Marines 22 April 1949 ~ 21 May 1982 Age 33

Andrew ('Andy') Peter Evans was born in Plantation Road, Accrington, Lancashire, on 22 April 1949. Andy's father Andrew was a Leading Seaman in the Royal Navy when he married Mary McLean in 1944. Andrew Evans was home on leave when Andy was born.

Andy joined the Royal Marines in the 1970s, by 1979 he was serving with the Brigade Air Squadron as a Gazelle Pilot. He was still serving with 3 Commando Brigade Air Squadron during the Falklands War. The squadron was originally formed on 12 August 1968 at Sembawang Air Base, Singapore.

On 21 May 1982, Andy was flying a Gazelle with Sergeant Eddie Candlish as gunner. They were acting as an armed escort for a Sea King from 846 Squadron. Just as the aircraft passed Fanning Head and Port San Carlos settlement, the Sea King crew realised they were too far over enemy positions and diverted to the west. The Gazelle realised too late, unfortunately as events unfolded, it was shot at several times from the ground.

Andy was seriously wounded but managed to ditch the Gazelle into San Carlos water, where it sank and remained for several months. Eddie survived; Andy's body was never found. The helicopter was later recovered and returned to the UK for use as a battle-damage repair training air frame. Later it was acquired by the South Yorkshire Aircraft museum and restored by members of the AAC and REME. The original tail unit from the Gazelle is displayed at the Fleet Air Arm museum in Yeovilton.

Andy received a posthumous Mention In Dispatches for his bravery during Operation Corporate.

Andy was married, leaving behind a widow and two children. Andy was a very well-liked and respected NCO. At the time of his death, he was resident in the village of Landrake, near Saltash, Cornwall. Andy is honoured on the Landrake War Memorial, beside the Parish Church of St Michael, the inscription merely reads 'FALKLANDS 1982 ANDY EVANS', a simple but profound honour.

In 2022, as part of the Falkland Islands 40th Anniversary Place Names Project, Andy was honoured with 'Evans Beach', a sandy beach east of Little Creek and Smylies Black Point on the north coast of mainland East Falkland.

His name lives on…

P020436E Corporal Kenneth Evans 45 Commando Royal Marines 18 January 1946 ~ 27 May 1982 Age 36

Kenneth Evans was born on 18 January 1946 at 88 Stanton Street, New Houghton, Derbyshire, to Arnold and Kathleen Evans (née Barker). Arnold and Kathleen married in Pleasley St Michael in late 1940. Arnold was a coal miner for many years in the mining village of New Houghton, his mother came from a large mining family.

Ken Evans died during a bombing attack while on operations in Ajax Bay on 27 May 1982, he is buried in the San Carlos Military Cemetery in the Falkland Islands. The inscription on his grave reads '*DARLING YOU MUST HAVE BEEN A GOOD PENNY SAYA CHINTAKAN AWAK KEN*'.

A loving message indeed, which suggests that Ken was married to a Malaysian. The rule with Commonwealth War Graves is that the Next of Kin may leave a message via inscription on the headstone. At the time of writing, it is not known whether Ken had any children.

Ken's name was added to the War Memorial in New Houghton on 13 November 2016.

In 2022, as part of the Falkland Islands 40th Anniversary Place Names Project, Kenneth was honoured with 'Evans Bay', a bay at the south end of New Island, West Falkland.

His name lives on…

C016085B Lieutenant Commander John Edward Eyton-Jones 801 Squadron Fleet Air Arm HMS *Invincible* 24 April 1943 ~ 6 May 1982 Age 39

John Edward Eyton-Jones was born in Northampton on 24 April 1943 to John Arnold and Sarah Eyton-Jones (née Townley).

The Eyton-Jones family have a long association with Northampton, though prior to the move John's grandfather married in East London. Walter Edward Eyton-Jones was the youngest of three sons born to John Wynne and Julia Eyton-Jones (née Sisson).

Eldest son Hugh Wynne started his working life as a clerk, later he held a position in the First World War in the Royal Naval Reserve as an Assistant Paymaster. During the First World War he was also a commissioned officer in the Royal Flying Corps Hugh was stationed at Stannergate, Dundee, where he settled after the war, marrying in 1920. Hugh was a glove manufacturer, he died after an accident in 1932 leaving behind a widow and three children.

Second son John Bisset Eyton-Jones married in 1912 in London, his third son Sergeant Victor Eyton-Jones of 37 Squadron RAF Volunteer Reserve was also a pilot, he was killed in action 7 July 1943, lost without trace during a raid on Palermo, Italy. As he was based in Tunisia, he is commemorated on the Alamein Memorial, Egypt.

Youngest son Walter Edward (John's grandfather) married Annie Arnold in 1911 in East London, where their son John Arnold Eyton-Jones was born soon after. By 1939 the family had settled in Northampton. Walter was a company director for a wholesale boot and shoe company.

John Arnold Eyton-Jones married his bride Sarah Doris Townley in Northampton in 1936, and it appears he was soon working as assistant works manager in the family business. During the Second World War John served with the Royal Artillery, he appears in the *London Gazette* dated 29 January 1944. John also received the Queen's Silver Jubilee medal in 1977.

Records suggest that John Edward Eyton-Jones was one of five children, three boys and two girls, including one set of twins. John Edward became known as E-J. He attended Northampton Grammar School and joined the Royal Navy as a Fleet Air Arm pilot in 1964.

At the beginning of his career, E-J specialised in flying the all-weather Sea Vixen fighter from HMS *Eagle* and HMS *Hermes*. Moving on, he flew the F-4K Phantom of 892 Sqn in the Carrier Air Group of HMS *Ark Royal*. He had also become an Air Warfare Instructor (AWI) and completed a distinguished tour with the US Navy experimental squadron VX-4 at Point Mugu, California, where his record as an adversary in Air Combat Manoeuvring (ACM) was exceptional.

In the summer of 1966, E-J married Sally in Wellingborough, Northants. The couple had two daughters between 1969 and 1971. From the mid-70s E-J moved over to the Royal Air Force's Harrier GR.3; he joined No 1(F) Sqn at RAF Wittering. Later E-J returned to Royal Naval service, becoming an instructor with 899 Squadron Naval Air Command.

By now E-J was a Lieutenant Commander and after the invasion of the Falkland Islands he was seconded to 801 Squadron Fleet Air Arm departing to head 'Down South' aboard HMS *Invincible*. A pilot's life was certainly busy at that time, E-J was both an experienced pilot and instructor. It is not entirely certain what happened that night, but in the early hours of 6 May 1982, E-J and Lieutenant Al Curtis set off in two Sea Harriers to investigate some unusual radar activity near HMS *Sheffield*, abandoned two days earlier. History, it appears, was repeating itself.

The weather was appalling with rain, fog, and low cloud; though E-J was very experienced in these conditions he was never seen again. Neither pilot returned from the mission, it is a possibility there was a collision, though he is just recorded as 'Lost at Sea'.

E-J's mother died in 1981 but his grandparents outlived E-J, living into their nineties. E-J has many nieces and nephews to remember him. He also left behind a widow and two daughters.

In 2022, as part of the Falkland Islands 40th Anniversary Place Names Project, E-J was honoured with 'Eyton-Jones Cove', a sandy beach at the north end of Grand Jason Island in the Jason Islands group.

His name lives on…

D073064N Petty Officer Cook Robert Fagan HMS *Sheffield* 7 August 1947 ~ 4 May 1982 Age 34

Robert Fagan was born on 7 August 1947 in Canterbury, one of twin boys. Robert's father, Fred, was from Newfoundland, Canada; he married Lilian Maud Cheese in Lambeth, London, in 1943. Lilian was the youngest child of Richard John and Sarah Cheese (née Kately), who also had one set of twin boys.

Robert's great-grandfather, another Richard, married Sarah McQuire in Lambeth in 1882. A large family followed with three of their sons serving in the British Army during the First World War. Fourth son, Alfred William, served with the Royal Field Artillery, he was awarded the Military Medal for bravery. Alfred left the army a WO2 and later became a police officer with the Metropolitan Police. Unusual for the times, their daughter Annie served in the Royal Air Force before marrying in 1921.

Fred and Lilian had five sons altogether: eldest son John, followed by the twins Robert and David, Michael, and lastly Stephen. Robert Fagan was known as Bob; the family settled in Canterbury where he attended school. Bob loved sports, his favourite was football; he is remembered with the Bob Fagan Shield at Crofton Junior School; the shield represents the best all-round achiever in sports.

Bob joined the Royal Navy straight from school, at just 16 he joined HMS *Ganges* as a Junior Assistant Cook. HMS *Pembroke* and HMS *Osprey* followed as he continued learning, later he joined HMS *Whitby*, based in Portsmouth. Bob met his future wife while based in Portsmouth, they married in 1968 and went on to have a son, Bryan, and daughter, Karen. Both Bob's children married, there are now three grandchildren.

Over his years of service other ships followed, including HMS *London* when she was flagship for the Queen's Silver Jubilee. Bob joined HMS *Sheffield* in February 1980. Sadly, it was to be his last posting.

Bob was killed on 4 May 1982 in the attack on HMS *Sheffield*. He is remembered on a memorial in St Edmund's Church, Stubbington, Hampshire. The memorial is a wall-mounted tablet with black lettering, relief of anchor & rope at top centre, oak leaf next to one name, it lists four men lost on HMS *Sheffield*.

In 2022, as part of the Falkland Islands 40th Anniversary Place Names Project, Bob was honoured with 'Fagan Gulch', a narrow deep gulch that divides Split Island (King George Bay) West Falkland into two and gives the island its name.

His name lives on…

24410121 Lance Corporal Ian Raymond Farrell Royal Army Medical Corps 6 April 1960 ~ 8 June 1982 Age 22

Ian Raymond Farrell was born on the 6 April 1960 in Liverpool. Raymond Farrell and Iris Done married in 1958, they had their first child, a daughter, the following year. Ian was their second born.

Ian enlisted into the Royal Army Medical Corps as a Medical Assistant in October 1979 at Liverpool; he was in training until July 1980. Though he only served for just under three years before his death, every course Ian attended he passed. He was promoted to Lance Corporal in December 1981.

Prior to the Falklands War the only overseas service Ian had seen was two weeks in Denmark in September 1981. By March 1982 he had passed his Medical Assistant Class 1.

Ian was serving with 16 Field Ambulance Royal Army Medical Corps, Mons Barracks, Aldershot; he was single and lived at the barracks. The Falkland Islands were invaded in April 1982, just four days before Ian's 22nd birthday.

Ian was killed on 8 June 1982 when the RFA *Sir Galahad* was bombed at Fitzroy. He is remembered on many Falklands Memorials dotted about, but there is a special brass plaque on a wood base inscribed 'FALKLANDS 1982 LCpl IAN FARRELL AGE 22 HE DIED 8 JUNE 1982 THAT OTHERS MAY LIVE IN FREEDOM AND JUSTICE'. The plaque sits on a windowsill at St George's Church, Heyworth Street, Everton, in Liverpool.

In 2022, as part of the Falkland Islands 40th Anniversary Place Names Project, Ian was honoured with 'Farrell Bay', a bay in the southwest corner of Brett Harbour on Saunders Island, West Falkland.

His name lives on…

24070081 Colour Sergeant Gordon Petrie McIvor Findlay 2nd Battalion Parachute Regiment 14 May 1950 ~ 14 June 1982 Age 32

Historically there had been much moving around within the Findlay family. Gordon's father, Roderick MacIvor Findlay, was born in Montrose, Scotland, in 1915.

Rod served in the Royal Air Force for many years, but after his marriage to Gwen in 1939, the couple lived for a time in Upper Street, Islington, where Rod was a pharmacy dispenser.

Gwen's family were no strangers to moving around. Gwen was born in Essex in 1918, one of three girls born to Robert Frederick Henry and Beatrice Maud Wright (née Setchfield). Gwen's father was born in Canning Town, London, he was one of five children who were born between Suffolk and London. Gwen's grandfather served in the British Army in 1881, her cousin, Cyril John Brooke Wright, served in the Royal Artillery. Christmas had some significance in the family. Cyril died on Christmas Day in 1981, his sister Marie had died many years before on Christmas Eve in 1921.

Rod and Gwen had their first child, Robert, in 1941 in Downham. Three years later, twins Ian and Richard were born. Barry came next, the last of the children born in Downham; sister Fran was born in Cambridgeshire in 1949. Gordon Petrie MacIvor Findlay was born on 14 May 1950 in Biggleswade. MacIvor continued to be used with all the children, but for some reason it is spelt McIvor on some of Gordon's records.

The family were next stationed in Malta, where daughter Donna was born the year before Rod received the Coronation Medal. Caren completed their family. Eventually, the Findlay family settled in Grimsby, where Rod and Gwen ended their days.

Gordon enlisted into Junior Parachute Company in 1966. After passing P Coy he was sent to 2 Para in November 1967. He was soon to become known as 'Doc', not because of his medical training but because at the time there was a very popular TV programme called *Dr Finlay's Casebook*. The series ran until 1971, but the Parachute legend was to go on for a lot longer. As *Dr Finlay's Casebook* was coming to an end, much more significant things were going on in our Doc Findlay's life.

'Doc' met his wife Janet in 1969 while she was a WRAC attached to the Royal Corps of Transport. Married on 4 July 1970 in Newham Register Office, they started a family with daughter Pauline, born the following year in May. Three years later, on 27 November 1974, the couple welcomed another daughter, Denise, into the world. Sadly, tragedy struck; Denise died on Boxing Day, aged just 1 month. Another Christmas death in the family.

During his service between 1967 and 1977 Doc travelled a lot with his regiment. He travelled to Singapore, Hong Kong, Malta, Denmark, Germany and Malaya on various exercises and courses. He also served in Northern Ireland and went on tour in the USA with the gymnastics team. In May 1977, he was posted to Berlin with 2 Para for two years.

Prior to Operation Corporate he served as a Permanent Staff Instructor with B Company, 15th (Scottish Volunteer) Battalion. At the time of the trip 'Down South' he had been 2 Para (A Company) (CQMS) from September 1981.

Doc had survived Goose Green but was not to survive the next battle, when 2 Para engaged at Wireless Ridge. It is thought that Doc Findlay was injured on Wireless Ridge by 152mm enemy artillery fire during the advance to capture the first ridge. He died from his wounds on 14 June 1982. He is buried at Aldershot Military Cemetery in a beautiful corner of the cemetery with his Parachute Regiment brothers who also did not make it home from the Falklands War.

In July 1967, Doc had been invited back to Grimsby to act as a bearer for the dedication of the standard of the Grimsby Branch of The Parachute Regiment Association. It therefore seemed very fitting that in 2020, a bench was made for

Doc so that Grimsby had another reminder of this man who had given so much for his country.

The bench was placed at Pier Gardens, Alexandra Road, Cleethorpes on Thursday, 8 October 2020. It was installed free of charge by North East Lincolnshire council. The bench was organised by Falklands Veteran Ron Webster and paid for by donations from friends, family, Grimsby Cleethorpes PRA, and others who wished to contribute.

Gwen died in 1979, Rod just four years after Gordon.

In 2022, as part of the Falkland Islands 40th Anniversary Place Names Project, Doc was honoured with 'Findlay Cove', a sheltered cove on the west side of Purvis Narrows at the entrance to Port Purvis, West Falkland.

His name lives on…

P033189P Corporal Peter Ronald Fitton 45 Commando Royal Marines 10 March 1957 ~ 11 June 1982 Age 25

Historically the Fitton line went back to Lancashire. James Leach Fitton worked for Joshua Hoyle & Sons in the cotton mills. Many of the family worked in the same industry but son Harold was to change his path as industry moved forward in England, he became an iron moulder. The military was not to manifest in the Fitton family until Harold's son Ronald changed his path completely. Peter's father Ronald Fitton was one of two sons born to Harold and Alice Fitton (née Harrison).

Ronald was born in September 1929; his bride Sylvia Peers was born in Anglesey, Wales, in 1930; they married in Anglesey in 1951. Ronald carved himself an Army career in the REME. Their eldest son Stephen was born in Anglesey in 1953. Peter Ronald Fitton (known as Pete) was born on 10 March 1957 in Imtarfa, Malta. A daughter was born in Pembrokeshire, Wales, in 1961, and then in 1968 twins Karen and Sharron were born in Melton Mowbray.

At the time the youngest children were born Ronald was stationed at Old Dalby, originally selected as a site for a large army vehicle depot in 1940. In 1942 when the REME was formed, it became known as 35 Base Workshops where vehicles were not just stored, but also repaired. ABRO Old Dalby stayed open until 1996 but Ronald Fitton left in 1974, his family went to live in the farmhouse at Manor Farm, Goadby Marwood, Leicestershire, in November that year. Stephen had already left home but Pete and the girls all lived there until he left for his training.

Pete left home to train to be a Royal Marine. He saw service in Northern Ireland prior to the Falklands War and had seen promotion from Marine to Corporal. In April 1978, Pete married Linda at St Chad's Catholic Church in Sedgley, Midlands. In 1980, the couple had a son, Derek Peter, born in Arbroath where 45 Commando were stationed.

When the Falkland Islands were invaded, all leave was cancelled. 45 Commando were soon dispatched to Portsmouth to travel 'Down South' on RFA *Stromness*.

Pete was part of a returning patrol on 11 June 1982, he was killed prior to the attack on Two Sisters. Along with three other 45 Commando Royal Marines, Pete was mistaken for the enemy and killed in a 'blue-on-blue'.

Pete's final resting place is in the Western Cemetery, Arbroath. There is a plaque very fittingly dedicated to him in St Denys Church, Goadby Marwood in Leicestershire, which remained the family home. Pete's father Ronald died in 1999, Sylvia continued to live in the farmhouse until her death in 2004.

Linda Fitton, accompanied by her son Derek, was presented the Elizabeth Cross in 2013 by The Queen's Representative, Lord Lieutenant of Berkshire, The Hon. Mrs Bayliss JP. The presentation took place after the Annual Service of Remembrance and Thanksgiving on Sunday 16 June, at the Falkland Islands Memorial Chapel in Pangbourne.

In 2022, as part of the Falkland Islands 40th Anniversary Place Names Project, Pete was honoured with 'Fitton Bay', a bay west of Green Island in Port Salvador, East Falkland.

His name lives on…

D058206K Petty Officer Writer Edmund Flanagan SS *Atlantic Conveyor* 17 June 1944 ~ 25 May 1982 Age 37

Edmund Flanagan was born on 17 June 1944 at 129 Haslingden Road, Blackburn, Lancashire. Edmund's parents were Thomas Gerald Flanagan and Violet Elizabeth Fontana (née Herring). The couple lived in Commercial Street, Oswaldtwistle, at the time of his birth. Records suggest that Edmund was one of six children born to Violet, who made a new life in Lancashire.

Born in November 1910, Violet was originally from Bethnal Green; one of three children, she worked as a dressmaker prior to the Second World War. In 1939, she lived in the now famous Brick Lane in Stepney. Violet died in 1980.

Before joining the Royal Navy Edmund was a member of the Accrington Sea Cadets. He was fondly known as 'Ted the Red', having red hair with matching beard.

Ted married Anita Phillips in March 1972 at Chichester Register Office. At the time of their marriage Ted was with HMS *Excellent* based in Portsmouth. Anita was a State Registered Nurse working at St Richard's hospital in Chichester.

Ted and Anita had three children together Cassandra, Tarquin, and Jocasta while the family was based in Portsmouth. Ted also had a stepson, Grant.

Ted was killed when Argentine Super Étendard jets attacked his ship, the *Atlantic Conveyor*, after mistaking it for the carrier *Hermes*. The SS *Atlantic Conveyor* was carrying supplies for the British forces when it caught fire and sank. Edmund was 37 years old.

Anita died in 2002; it was her wish for her ashes to be scattered where her husband died. After an appeal by their daughter, former choirboy Aled Jones agreed to take the ashes to the Falkland Islands while travelling there to film an episode of 'Songs of Praise'.

In 2022, as part of the Falkland Islands 40th Anniversary Place Names Project, Ted was honoured with 'Flanagan Bay', a bay on the north shore of Ruggles Bay on the Falkland Sound side of East Falkland.

His name lives on...

24598563 Private Mark William Fletcher MID 2nd Battalion Parachute Regiment 11 February 1961 ~ 28 May 1982 Age 21

Mark William ('Fletch') Fletcher was born on 11 February 1961 in Stockport, Cheshire, to Brian and Alice Fletcher (née Adamson), who married in Stockport in 1958. Mark was the couple's second child; it appears he was one of five children.

Records indicate that Lewis William Fletcher, Mark's great-grandfather, served with the 10th Service Battalion, King's Royal Rifle Corps. Lewis married in 1910 and already had one son (Mark's grandfather) when he attested in 1914.

Fletch served with 10 Platoon, D Company 2 Para. Fletch travelled 'Down South' on the MV Norland, landing at San Carlos on 21 May 1982. Fletch was killed during the night advance towards Darwin Hill while attending to Lance Corporal Cork's wounds. He was found lying beside his corporal, a shell dressing opened in his hand.

Fletch was Mentioned in Despatches in the *London Gazette* supplement of 8 October 1982:

> *'The QUEEN has been graciously pleased to approve the following names of those Mentioned in Despatches in recognition of gallant and distinguished service during the operations in the South Atlantic: 24598563 Private Mark William FLETCHER, The Parachute Regiment (Posthumous)'*

Mark Fletcher is buried at Stockport Crematorium & Cemetery.

In 2022, as part of the Falkland Islands 40th Anniversary Place Names Project, Mark was honoured with 'Fletcher Bay', a bay in the south west corner of Danson Harbour, East Falkland.

His name lives on...

D150936G Leading Cook Michael Paul Foote HMS *Ardent* 8 September 1958 ~ 21 May 1982 Age 23

Michael was the eldest of seven children born to John William and Dorothy Ruby Foote (née Godding). John and Dorothy married at Portsmouth Register Office on 24 August 1957. At the time John was an Able Seaman serving in HMS *Torquay*, Portsmouth. Dorothy was a shorthand typist.

Michael attended Wakeford's Secondary School in West Leigh, Havant, excelling in maths. He joined the Royal Navy straight from school.

Michael commenced his basic training in 1975 at HMS *Ganges*, before joining HMS *Pembroke* for his chef training. After initial chef training Michael's first draft was HMS *Mercury*.

Seventeen months after signing up Michael got a draft to his first seagoing ship, HMS *Apollo*, which was present during the 1977 Silver Jubilee Royal Fleet review in the Solent, rising from acting cook to cook during his sixteen-month draft.

Michael then spent six months at HMS *Nelson* before his next draft saw a move to HMS *Blake*, where he spent the next two years. During this time, he did a nine-month deployment to the West Coast of the United States via the Panama Canal. While on this deployment, Michael was able to visit Las Vegas, where he saw his 'heartthrob', Donna Summer. He fed his love for music by buying several non-UK released albums and 12-inch singles, including coloured vinyl, (Donna Summer's *Bad Girls* in pink).

Music was Michael's passion, and while on his next deployment to HMS *Raleigh*, he was known to DJ for the Junior Rates Saturday night 'bop', in his familiar black woolly hat. Along with music on vinyl, Michael also fed his sense of humour by collecting vinyl recordings of several comedians, including Jasper Carrot, Max Boyce, and Billy Connelly.

Michael joined HMS *Ardent* in November 1981. Early in 1982 he transferred some of his vast selection of records onto audio cassette; he had his music with him until the end.

Michael is remembered at various memorials including St Francis Church in Leigh Park, where the wedding kneeling stool is dedicated to him. Also, St Faiths church in his home town Havant, the *Ardent* memorial on the Hoe at · Plymouth, HMS *Ardent*'s home port, and the Falkland's memorial at Sally Port, Portsmouth.

In 2022, as part of the Falkland Islands 40th Anniversary Place Names Project, Michael was honoured with 'Foote Creek', a creek at the head of Barrow Harbour in Adventure Sound, East Falkland.

His name lives on…

D189624P Marine Engineering Mechanic (Mechanical) 1 Stephen Nicholas Ford HMS *Ardent* 24 December 1963 ~ 21 May 1982 Age 18

Stephen Nicholas Ford was born on Christmas Eve 1963 to Charles Richard and Brenda Ford (née Gillett). Charles and Brenda married at Poole Register Office on 16 September 1960. Charles was a Leading Mechanical Engineer in the Royal Navy. Both the Ford and the Gillett families were from Branksome, Poole. Stephen was one of three boys; the couple's eldest child was a daughter.

Prior to joining the Navy, Stephen was in the Sea Cadets. The family lived at Constitution Hill Road in Poole, and Stephen completed his education at St Edwards School, he left in 1979. For the 40th Anniversary of the Falklands War the school held a special assembly for Stephen.

As a child Stephen would play at the Viewpoint, where there is also a memorial bench to his brother Andy who died in 1998 aged just 37.

Stephen had followed in his father's footsteps to join the Royal Navy, but his service was to be cut very short. Stephen was serving in HMS *Ardent*, being just 18, he was offered the choice to disembark when the Task Force set off. A brave young man, he decided to stay and stand shoulder to shoulder with his shipmates.

On 21 May 1982, while lying in Falkland Sound and supporting Operation Sutton by bombarding the Argentine airstrip at Goose Green, HMS *Ardent* was attacked by at least three waves of Argentine aircraft. *Ardent* stopped in the shallow waters of Grantham Sound, the fires in her stern out of control. With the ship listing heavily, Commander Alan West decided to abandon the ship.

HMS *Yarmouth* came alongside to take off survivors, the crew were transferred to the *Canberra*. By then it was known that twenty-two men had lost their lives. HMS *Ardent* continued to burn throughout the night, accompanied by the occasional explosion, until she sank at 06:30hrs the next day, with only her foremast remaining above the water.

There is a lovely freestanding memorial to Stephen in the Viewpoint park overlooking Poole Harbour. For the 30th Anniversary Stephen's father knelt at his son's memorial to place a wreath of red poppies in the shape of an anchor. It simply stated: 'In loving memory of my son and his 21 comrades.'

In 2022, as part of the Falkland Islands 40th Anniversary Place Names Project, Stephen was honoured with 'Ford Creek', a creek at the head of Flores Harbour, Falkland Sound side of East Falkland.

His name lives on…

468997 Major Michael Lancaster Forge Royal Signals 20 January 1942 ~ 6 June 1982 Age 40

Michael ('Mike') Forge was born on 20 January 1942, the eldest son of Edward Alexander and Mary Lilian Forge (née Davey). Edward and Mary married on 21 March 1940 at Woolwich Register Office. During the Blitz, Mike and his namesake-cousin were taken to live in Woolacombe, Devon.

The Forge family can be traced back to Bethnal Green in the 1850s where Mike's two times great-grandfather was in business as a fishmonger. His son, Charles Richard Alexander, was the eldest of eight children born to Charles Alexander and Louisa Ann Forge (née Smith). Charles junior went into the family manufacturing stationery and printer business, he married Susan Sarah Hinton in 1858, the couple went on to have eleven children, they settled in Surrey.

Mike's grandfather, Percy Hinton Forge, was born in 1871 and as a child he attended Hadleigh House School. Percy and Ellen Marie (née Gould) had two children, Edward Alexander Forge and a sister born three years earlier. Edward Alexander Forge attested into the Royal Artillery in 1936. At the time of his marriage to Mary he was a 2nd Lieutenant in the York & Lancaster Regiment. Later the same year Edward was promoted to temporary Captain.

Michael Forge was the eldest of three children, he had one brother and one sister. Their parents Edward and Mary divorced, and both subsequently remarried; Mary married Dr John Lambert Newton in London in 1976. Mary remained close to Mike, and at the time of his death Mike lived with his (by then widowed) mother in Syderstone, Norfolk.

Mike Forge attended Hereford Cathedral School between 1954–57, a Mace was later dedicated to Mike. Under the shields there is an inscription which says, '*dedicated to the memory of Michael Forge, Major, Royal Signals, O.H., killed in the Falklands, 1982*'.

Mike, as his father before him, joined the British Army as a 2nd Lieutenant, he commenced his service with the Royal Corps of Signals on 18 July 1961. His service saw him with 216 (Parachute) Signal Squadron, 204 Signal Squadron, 2nd Signal Regiment, School of Signals, 3rd Division HQ & Signal Regiment, 30th Signal Regiment and 24th Infantry Brigade HQ & Signal Squadron.

Mike is remembered as a keen sports parachutist; his career was varied, he was promoted to Lieutenant in January 1963, Captain in July 1967 and finally Major in July 1976. Mike joined the Sultan of Oman's Armed Forces for a year's secondment, he returned to the same in January 1979 until January 1982. Other tours included BAOR and Belize.

Early in 1982, Mike was selected to command 5 Infantry Brigade HQ & Signal Squadron, he set sail with his men in May that year on the QE2. Though not married himself, Mike was known for getting to know people well including being interested in their family life; for this he was well liked by his unit.

On the night of the 5 June 1982, the radio rebroadcast station was experiencing difficulty in communicating. Mike boarded the Gazelle helicopter with Staff Sergeant Joe Baker, Troop Sergeant of the station in question, and set off to sort out the problem. Sadly, the Gazelle they were travelling in was hit in a 'blue-on-blue' incident, Mike died along with Joe Baker, Simon Cockton, and the pilot Chris Griffin.

Mike is buried at Blue Beach Cemetery, San Carlos, he is honoured on the Syderstone War Memorial in Norfolk. Mike's mother died in 1991, his father in 2004. Edward's ashes were taken to the Falkland Islands by Mike's sister and scattered at the top of Mount Pleasant.

In 2022, as part of the Falkland Islands 40th Anniversary Place Names Project, Mike was honoured with 'Forge Island', a tussac island off the north coast of Philimore Island, East Falkland.

His name lives on…

Mechanic Frank Foulkes SS *Atlantic Conveyor* 9 December 1934 ~ 25 May 1982 Age 47

Frank Foulkes was from Great Plumpton, Lancashire, his close family originated in Rochdale, before that the family can be traced back to Holywell, Flintshire. The name Foulkes appears to have its origins in Denbighshire from as early as the ninth century.

Frank's great-grandfather, William, was born in Holywell, Flintshire in 1821. At some point in the 1800s the family moved to Manchester where a young William became an iron turner. People often moved around to find work in those days. William, it appears, married Harriet Wray in 1850; James Edwin Foulkes was the couple's youngest son. By 1891 William, by then 70 years old, appears to have still been working. William died aged 83 in 1904, by then the family were residing in Rochdale.

Frank's paternal grandfather, James Edwin Foulkes, was born on 29 December 1864. By the time James was 16 years old, he had followed in his father's footsteps to become an iron turner. In 1881 he was living with his mother and sister's family in Wardleworth, Rochdale.

James married Maria Mills in 1888 in Rochdale, the couple had at least six children. Frank's father, Herbert, was their youngest son; sadly, the couple lost a daughter, Nellie, when she was just 1 year old. Maria died in 1923, after which James stayed close to his youngest daughter Ada. By 1939 James was retired and living with Ada's family in Rathbone Street, Rochdale. Ada married Stanley, an aircraft inspector; James died in 1944.

For many years James and Maria lived in Arthington Street, Rochdale, by 1911 Herbert was an apprentice sheet metal worker. Herbert had an older brother, Frank, born in 1893. The children had grown up in Rochdale where some family remained but at some point, Herbert moved to Blackpool.

Frank's parents, Herbert Foulkes and Emily Baron, married in Rochdale in 1928. In a twist of fate, the family lived in Falkland Avenue, Blackpool, in 1939. Frank was their second son, born in Blackpool on 9 December 1934. His older brother was called Derek.

Frank was very young when his mother Emily died, she was just 39 years old. Herbert remarried after his wife's death; the couple had one son, Raymond, born in 1945. Frank spent some of his youth living with his Aunty Mary.

Frank's maternal grandmother, Margaret, was born in Norden, she was married to a carter. Margaret also sadly died in her late thirties when her youngest child was just 3 years old. Whether it was as a result of life experiences or his innate nature, Frank grew up to be a very caring man.

Frank married Elayne 'Dorothy' Reynolds in Blackpool in 1963. Dorothy was the daughter of Walter John Reynolds and Elizabeth ('Eliza') Darlow Sellers, who married in 1934. It is thought that Eliza was one of nine children; her line can be traced back to Northamptonshire where generations before, Joshua Darlow worked as a shoemaker, known in those days as a cobbler. Joshua Darlow married Mary Capel, sending the Capel name down through the next two generations.

Dorothy was born in Blackpool on 5 February 1935, she had one brother, Rodney Walter, who at one point served in the Royal Air Force.

Frank was a father to six children: Suzanne, Angela, David, Libby, Victoria and Charlotte. Frank and Dorothy were also foster parents; one long-term foster child, Alex, kept in touch with the family.

Frank served in the Royal Navy, joining as a teenager; in the early 1970s he joined the Merchant Navy where he continued his seafaring days. In his downtime Frank loved nature and touring Scotland. He shared a horse with his daughter Libby, he learned to ride, and they went on riding holidays.

Frank was a mechanic in the Merchant Navy in 1982; he was killed when the SS *Atlantic Conveyor* was hit on 25 May.

In one online article Dorothy is mistakenly called Frank's 'bereaved mother' in relation to the documentary made in 1986. Dorothy was also interviewed in 1987 when she is quoted as saying that Frank's South Atlantic Medal arrived in a jiffy bag.

There is a marble tablet dedicated to Frank in St Michael's Church, Weeton, Fylde in Lancashire. The inscription reads '*FRANK FOULKES OF GREAT PLUMPTON KILLED ON THE ATLANTIC CONVEYOR IN THE FALKLANDS 25 MAY 1982*'.

In 1983 some of the family went to the Falkland Islands on the families' pilgrimage of that year. Libby returned in 2022 for another trip 'Down South'.

In 2022, as part of the Falkland Islands 40th Anniversary Place Names Project, Frank was honoured with 'Foulkes Passage', a navigable passage connecting Lake Hammond to Port Edgar, West Falkland.

His name lives on…

D094740D Petty Officer (Sonar) Michael George Fowler HMS *Coventry* 21 May 1945 ~ 25 May 1982 Age 37

Michael George Fowler was born in Watford on 21 May 1945 to James and Irene Annie Jane Fowler (née King) who married in Watford in 1938. Michael was the youngest of two boys, his older brother was born in 1942. Mike's mother Irene was born in Bushey, Hertfordshire; the daughter of a gardener, she was one of six children. James was also from a large family; they were both born during the First World War.

Mike 'Foxy' Fowler married his wife Rose in Portsmouth in 1973. Rose was two years younger than Mike and hailed from Glamorganshire, Wales. Rose already had two children, Paul and Mary Rose, to whom Mike became a stepfather. The couple had no children together.

When the Falkland Islands were invaded Mike was a Petty Officer (Sonar) in HMS *Coventry*. He was killed in the Junior Rate's dining hall on 25 May 1982 when *Coventry* was hit. Mike died just four days after his 37th birthday. Had he returned he was due a promotion to Chief Petty Officer. His stepchildren were both teenagers at the time Mike crossed the bar, and his niece, Anita, was just 2 years old.

It appears from the records that Mike's parents, James and Irene, both died at the end of 1992, within a month of each other.

Mike was a Scout Leader in Southsea; he is remembered as a lovely man. He was a natural father figure to his colleagues as well as his stepchildren.

In 2022, as part of the Falkland Islands 40th Anniversary Place Names Project, Mike was honoured with 'Fowler Bay', a bay at the head of Adventure Harbour in Adventure Sound, East Falkland.

His name lives on…

N023442U Lieutenant Kenneth David Francis 3 Commando Brigade Air Squadron 24 September 1952 ~ 21 May 1982 Age 29

Kenneth ('Ken') David Francis was born on 24 September 1952 at the RAF hospital in Ely, Cambs.

Ken was the oldest son of Don Francis Olive Keays, who married in Ilford, Essex, in 1951. His younger brother made an entrance on Boxing Day 1956 in Louth, Lancs. Don was serving with the Royal Air Force, so the family moved around somewhat.

Ken attended many schools during his childhood, it did not deter him from study as it might some. After reading Law at Keene's College, University of Kent, he graduated with an Honours Degree in 1974. Travel and learning had become a huge part of Ken's life by then. After obtaining his degree he went off travelling and became a London Bus driver on his return, having passed his PSV licence. He later moved on to heavy commercial articulated vehicles.

By 1976 Ken had been accepted for officer training to join the Royal Marines and achieved the distinction of winning the Sword of Honour during his Young Officer training, he received his Green Beret on 1 April 1977. Ken first served with 41 Commando until 1981. During his time there, Ken was a rifle troop commander, anti-tank troop commander and finally a company second-in-command.

Ken met Jan in 1978, they married two years later in April 1980 in the New Forest, Hampshire.

After his time with 41 Commando Ken volunteered for flying training and gained his helicopter pilots wings at the Army Air Corps Centre in Middle Wallop. In February 1982 he joined 3 Commando Brigade, Air Squadron, in Plymouth, flying the Gazelle.

In April 1982, the couple should have been celebrating their second wedding anniversary and looking forward to the birth of their first child, instead Ken was leaving for the Falklands.

Sadly, on 21 May 1982, Ken was killed with his crewman as they flew support for the San Carlos landings. Shot down by groundfire from a heavy machine gun, they were killed instantly.

Both bodies were recovered to the SS *Canberra*, and when the ship was ordered to leave for South Georgia both men were buried at sea in a special ceremony.

Ken and Jan's son was born in October 1982.

Ken will always be remembered as a high achiever who put his heart and soul into whatever he chose to do in life. In St Nicholas's Church Fyfield, Essex, there is a brass plaque dedicated to Ken it reads: 'IN MEMORY OF LT KEN FRANCIS BA RM OF THIS PARISH WHO WAS KILLED IN ACTION IN THE FALKLANDS WAR 21 MAY 1982'.

In 2022, as part of the Falkland Islands 40th Anniversary Place Names Project, Ken was honoured with 'Francis Hill', a prominent low hill (350 ft elevation) on mainland East Falkland on the south side of Smylie Creek and east of Race Point.

His name lives on…

23860354 Warrant Officer Second Class Laurence Gallagher BEM 22 SAS Regiment 30 April 1945 ~ 19 May 1982 Age 37

Laurence Gallagher was born in Don Valley, Yorkshire, on 30 April 1945; he was proud to take on the name of Gallagher as many of his relatives had served their country.

Laurence's mother, Lily Gallagher, was born in August 1924 in Doncaster. Lily was part of a huge family, her parents, John and Elizabeth Gallagher (née Brice), married in 1904. John was born in Wigan, the Gallagher family had moved over from Ireland, later they settled in Thurnscoe, Yorkshire.

Laurence started out his Army career with the Royal Engineers in Old Park Barracks Junior Leaders Regiment, Royal Engineers. Although he was fondly referred to as 'Lofty' or the 'Yorkshire Pit Pony', he had decided that a life in mining was not for him.

Lofty's grandfather John served with the Royal Army Medical Corps in the First World War from 1914 until November 1918. Uncles James and John Thomas both joined the Royal Tank Corps within a week of each other in 1925. Uncles Michael and Edward Lawrence served with either the British Army or Navy in the Second World War, so it was for many families in those days as two world wars broke out so close together.

Lofty joined the SAS in 1968; he was awarded the British Empire Medal in April 1980 for 'meritorious service' on tour in Northern Ireland in 1979. In the early 1970s he was detached to the 10th Special Forces Group at Bad Tölz, Wolfratshausen, Upper, Bavaria, Germany. He also served with 9 Parachute Squadron, Royal Engineers.

In 1975 Lofty married Lynda, the couple went on to have three daughters. Lofty had one sister, Mary, who remains grateful to have seen him prior to his deployment to the Falklands.

Lofty was D Squadron (SSM) when tragedy struck on 19 May 1982. The Sea King helicopter crash claimed the lives of some great men as it was cross-decking members of D and G squadron from HMS *Hermes* to HMS *Intrepid*. The biggest single loss for the SAS since the Second World War.

There are many memorials dedicated to Lofty; a brass plaque is situated in Thurnscoe Working Men's Club. Lofty is also remembered in Bolton-Upon-Dearne Cemetery and St Martin's Churchyard, Hereford.

Lofty is included on a Falklands Memorial to his parent regiment the Royal Engineers, a bronze plaque in St Barbara's Church, Maxwell Road, Brompton, Gillingham, Kent, which is the Garrison Church of the Corps of Royal Engineers. There is a replica of the same brass memorial on Sappers Hill, Falkland Islands.

In 2022, as part of the Falkland Islands 40th Anniversary Place Names Project, Lofty was honoured with 'Gallagher Creek', a creek in Manybranch Harbour, West Falkland.

His name lives on…

24385786 Sapper Pradeep Kumar Gandhi 59 Commando Squadron Royal Engineers 24 February 1958 ~ 27 February 1982 Age 24

Pradeep was Hindu, and at the time of his death resided in Wembley, Middlesex. The house his family lived in is just off a vibrant and still thriving main road full of colour. In 2023 the streets still reflect a large Hindu community with shops and eateries in abundance and an array of coloured saris mixed with modern Western culture.

A local businessman remembers seeing an article in an Indian magazine just after he arrived in the United Kingdom, he speaks softly of the young soldier who gave his life some years before. The man thinks it must be at least twenty years and is surprised to learn it has been over forty. That is the illusion of this thing we call time which is so subjective.

Pradeep attested into the Royal Engineers as a Sapper in August 1975 when he was just 17 years old, like many young men fresh out of High School. Pradeep was born in Nairobi, Kenya, on 24 February 1958. During his service Pradeep served with 1 Training Regt, 3 Training Regt Royal Engineers, 24 Field Squadron and also served with 59 Independent Commando Squadron Royal Engineers in 1979.

To his comrades he was known as Goosey. Pradeep saw service in Cyprus, Northern Ireland, and Norway prior to the Falklands War. Pradeep passed several courses earning his Green Beret after Commando Training in February 1980, just in time for his 22nd Birthday. In 1981 Pradeep passed his Arctic Warfare training; in fact he passed every course, he was shining bright.

During the Falklands War, Pradeep was back with 59 Independent Commando Squadron based in Plymouth. According to a comrade, Pradeep was a big strong lad who was firing at Argentinian aircraft when a bomb landed near to his position, burying him in peat. By the time he was dug out after the event it was discovered he had been killed in the raid, he was 24 years old and single.

Pradeep's body was repatriated, he was cremated at Golders Green crematorium. His ashes were collected on 26 November 1982 by the funeral director, he does not appear in the Book of Remembrance at the Crematorium. His ashes, in true Hindu tradition, were later scattered in the Ganges.

Pradeep was very close to his mother, he was one of eleven children, eight girls and three boys. Pradeep is remembered fondly by his sister Kamni as a man who loved his elders and would always help them. A kind spirit still missed greatly.

In 2022, as part of the Falkland Islands 40th Anniversary Place Names Project, Pradeep was honoured with 'Gandhi Cove', a cove on the West Falkland shore of Falkland Sound south of Port Howard.

His name lives on…

24598683 Guardsman Mark Gibby 1st Battalion Welsh Guards 15 April 1960 ~ 8 June 1982 Age 22

The Rhondda Valley comprises of two valleys, the Rhondda Fawr, and the Rhondda Fach. Traditionally it was known for coal mining, which was at its peak between 1840 and 1925, but there was much more than coal that came out of the Rhondda.

Fred Gibby was a miner who married Margaret Davies in 1959, the following year their first child, Mark, was born on 15 April 1960. Mark was born in his grandmother's house in Porth, though the family home was in Pontygwaith. Mark continued to spend a lot of time with his Grandparents in Porth and was very close to them. Fred and Margaret went on to have two more children, Nicholas in 1962 and Kathryn in 1964.

Mark went to Pontygwaith Infants followed by Hendrefadog Secondary School. After leaving Maerdy Comprehensive School in 1976, Mark went down the mines as many of his family had before him. He worked at Ty Mawr Colliery first, and then at Lewis Merthyr Colliery with his granddad. Mark had seen his father-in-law Haydn, suffer from pneumoconiosis – as did many miners of that time, it was one of the reasons Mark left the mines.

Mark was a keen horseman and owned a horse called Captain; at one time there was talk of him transferring to the Household Cavalry. In his school days he had enjoyed being in the Scouts, and also practised Judo in his youth. Mark was a cheeky, mischievous and happy little boy and you never knew quite what he would do next. He is remembered by people with a great deal of fondness.

It is often the oldest brother that goes off to find his way in the world, but it was Mark's younger brother that joined the army first. Nicholas was in the 1st Battalion, Welsh Fusiliers. Like all young men he had many a tale to tell and share with his brother when home on leave. Nicholas had been in the army for two years when Mark became sold on the idea. He joined the Welsh Guards in late 1980, wishing to build a better future for his family than the pits could offer.

After completing his training, Mark joined the 1st Battalion Welsh Guards. Mark met his wife-to-be, Teresa Morgan, through family, she was best friends with

Mark's cousin. They married in August 1981 at St Anne's Church, Ynyshir. The month before, Mark had been on duty lining the route for the wedding of Lady Diana Spencer and Prince Charles. As a Guardsman there were many public duties to perform. During his brief service he also went to Kenya for six weeks with his unit.

The following year was to be a momentous one for the Gibby family. On 17 January 1982, daughter Katie was born in the Church Village Hospital in Pontypridd. By April that year Argentina had invaded the Falkland Islands, and the Welsh Guards were among those to be sent as part of the Task Force. Teresa's father Haydn sadly died on 3 May 1982; just ten days later, on 13 May 1982, the QE2 set sail from Southampton. Teresa waved Mark goodbye as she held 5-month-old Katie, accompanied by his sister. It was the last time they saw him.

Mark with his fellow Welsh Guards had transferred to the *Sir Galahad*, the men were preparing to go ashore to join the land war when the ship was hit at Fitzroy on 8 June 1982. It was one of the worst days of the war for British casualties. When Roll Call came Mark did not answer. Teresa had lost her father and her husband just a month apart.

Mark's daughter Katie lays a wreath for him every year at the Cenotaph in Ynyshir, she remembers with great pride the man she never had chance to get to know. His name is on various Falklands Memorials here and in the Falkland Islands, but it also has a place on the Memorial Stone in Ynysangharad Park, Pontypridd.

In 2022, as part of the Falkland Islands 40th Anniversary Place Names Project, Mark was honoured with 'Gibby Hill', a summit (945ft elevation) of South Jason in the Jason Islands group.

His name lives on…

P033537T Lance Corporal Brett Patrick Giffin 3 Commando Brigade Air Squadron Royal Marines 10 April 1958 ~ 21 May 1982 Age 24

The Giffin family can be traced back to Clapton, London, as far back as the early 1800s. William Giffin, a saddler and harness maker, married Elizabeth Steib in 1839 and Frank was their youngest son, born in 1860; the Steib name continued to be used within the Giffin family for many years.

Patrick's grandfather, Frank William Giffin, was born in Upper Clapton on 6 June 1887, the only son of Frank and Eliza Giffin (née Paul). Eliza was a baker's daughter, Frank a furrier. Frank William served in the Royal Naval Air Service in the First World War. Prior to his service Frank was a butcher, he married Minnie Hilda Wright in 1914 in Norfolk. Their eldest son, Frank Sylvester, was born in March 1915 in Cromer, Norfolk. Frank William died in 1937, his widow moved to Portsmouth; she died in 1972.

Frank Sylvester Giffin served in the Royal Marines; he married Eva Leonard in Portsmouth in 1941 and their eldest son was named Frank in family tradition. The family settled in Christchurch, Dorset. Brett Patrick Giffin was born in Christchurch on 10 April 1958. Their youngest son, he was one of seven children born to the couple. He became known as either Giff or Pat.

Pat attended The Grange school located in Somerford, Christchurch. He went to the same school as the girl he was to marry, though they had not spoken while pupils there. Pat joined the Royal Marines straight after leaving school, initially serving with 42 Commando. He is remembered as a wonderful combination of character, possessing a great sense of humour but also being professional while carrying out his duties.

Pat met his bride-to-be Susan in a pub, it was not a venue she had frequented before and the night they met she was there by a quirk of fate. Pat and Susan married in Christchurch in 1979, the couple had one son together, Nathan Patrick, born the following year.

When Pat was sent to the Falkland Islands, he was serving with 3 Commando Brigade Air Squadron, Royal Marines. On 21 May 1982, during the initial landings at Port San Carlos, Pat was acting as observer in a Gazelle flown by Lieutenant Kenneth Francis when they came under heavy fire. Sadly, both pilot and observer were killed as their Gazelle was shot down. Pat was later buried at sea.

Pat is remembered on a memorial at Christchurch Priory Memorial Chapel.

In 2022, as part of the Falkland Islands 40th Anniversary Place Names Project, Pat was honoured with 'Giffin Creek', a small creek on the north side of Port Sussex, East Falkland.

His name lives on…

D180188Q Cook Neil Andrew Goodall HMS *Sheffield*
27 September 1960 ~ 4 May 1982 Age 21

Allan Goodall and Joan Duffin married in Woolwich in 1957. Their first son was born the following year in 1958, by which time the family were living in Birmingham. Their second son, Neil Andrew, came along two years later on 27 September 1960 in Erdington, Birmingham.

Joan and Allan separated during the '60s and Joan moved to Enfield when the two boys were very young; she remarried, settled in the area and added to her young family. Neil had two half-brothers and a half-sister.

Neil first attended Chase side Primary school in Trinity Street, Enfield, and later Chase Boys, now known as Chace Community School. With an interest in motor studies Neil helped set up a technical workshop at the school.

The sea, however, was calling; Neil joined the Sea Cadets when he was just 11 years old and rose to the rank of Petty Officer Instructor. Neil joined the Royal Navy in 1979. He served on the frigate HMS *Ashanti* and the shore establishment HMS *Vernon* before joining HMS *Sheffield*.

HMS *Sheffield* sailed from Portsmouth on 19 November 1981, many of the ships that were to join the Falklands Task Force were on a huge exercise in the

Mediterranean prior to the islands being invaded. Instead of returning to 'Blighty' the ship found herself sailing 'Down South'. Neil had intended to announce his engagement to his girlfriend Pat on his return; instead, he was heading to a war zone.

Neil was a member of the Royal British Legion, the Royal Naval Association, and the RNLI. He was a likeable young man with a happy-go-lucky personality. Sadly, Neil was not to return home. HMS *Sheffield* was hit by an Exocet missile fired from an Argentine Naval Super Étendard aircraft on 4 May 1982. Neil was one of the twenty men killed that day.

Though Neil's body was not recovered; there is a memorial gravestone to him at Lavender Hill Cemetery in Enfield. Neil's sister gave a short radio interview on 6 May 1982 talking about the effect Neil's death had on their family.

In 2022, as part of the Falkland Islands 40th Anniversary Place Names Project, Neil was honoured with 'Goodall Islet', a small tussac island at the west end of Kelp Lagoon between Fitzroy and Mare Harbour, East Falkland.

His name lives on…

24511408 Guardsman Glenn Conrad Grace 1st Battalion Welsh Guards 12 December 1961 ~ 8 June 1982 Age 20

Glenn Conrad Grace was born on 12 December 1961 in Newport, Gwent. His father, Tom, was in the Armed Forces and served in the Royal Welch Fusiliers; Tom married Ursula Meyer in Gottingen, Germany, in 1951. Glenn was one of six children, his older siblings Herbert, Detlev, Allan and Jennifer, lastly younger sister Karen. When Glenn's two eldest brothers were born Tom was still a serving soldier.

The family have given a lot to our Armed Forces. By an uncanny coincidence Glenn's grandfather, Daniel Patrick, his father Tom and brother Allan were all Machine Gunners.

In November 1953, Tom was in Jamaica with his regiment when Queen Elizabeth II visited during her Commonwealth Tour. Tom's regiment were there to do the Guard of Honour and take the salute from Her Majesty. After this adventure the family returned to Wales where they settled in Newport.

Glenn attended St Gabriel's Roman Catholic Junior School and later Hartridge High School in Newport, where he enjoyed most sports. Glenn favoured football and played for his local pub team. He joined the Welsh Guards, his initial training was at Pirbright, Surrey, as many a Guardsman before him.

After starting out with the Prince of Wales Company he was transferred to the Mortar platoon. Glenn died on 8 June 1982 when the RFA *Sir Galahad* was bombed at Fitzroy, he was just 20 years old.

Glenn had followed his brothers into the Welsh Guards, he is remembered as an easy-going lad who took his job seriously. His father Tom died many years ago, Ursula passed away in 2001.

Karen also served in the British Army with the Royal Logistics Corps.

In 2022, as part of the Falkland Islands 40th Anniversary Place Names Project, Glenn was honoured with 'Grace Point', a prominent point on mainland north west of Blind Island.

His name lives on…

24520370 Guardsman Paul Green 1st Battalion Welsh Guards 21 January 1961 ~ 8 June 1982 Age 21

Paul Green was born on 21 January 1961 at Chatsworth House, Prestatyn, Wales. Paul was the second-born son of Michael John Vernon and Ann Green (née Garner). The couple had five children, three boys and two girls, the youngest children were fraternal twins.

Paul's father was a builder's labourer, as had been his father before him. At the time of Paul's birth his family lived at Elwy Drive in Rhyl.

Paul attended Rhyl High School; he is remembered on their War Memorial.

Both Paul and his older brother Mike joined the Welsh Guards, however Mike was seconded to the Scots Guards; he fought at the battle for Mount Tumbledown. Mike survived the war.

Paul was killed on 8 June 1982 when the RFA *Sir Galahad* was attacked by Argentine Skyhawks along with his fellow Welsh Guards, Paul's body was lost to the South Atlantic Ocean.

During a visit to the Falkland Islands in 1983, Paul's mother Ann fell in love with the Islands, she later moved there with three of her children.

In 2022, as part of the Falkland Islands 40th Anniversary Place Names Project, Paul was honoured with 'Green Bay', a bay south of the Old Fitzroy Bridge in Port Fitzroy, East Falkland.

His name lives on…

24399753 Private Anthony David Greenwood 3rd Battalion Parachute Regiment 31 October 1959 ~ 12 June 1982 Age 22

Anthony David Greenwood was born on the 31 October 1959 in Manchester, the eldest child and only son of Gordon and Catherine Greenwood (née Jones). During the next three years the couple had two daughters, Sharan and Lesley. Anthony was known as Tony or 'Fester' to his comrades.

Tony attended four different schools, St Paul's Infants, Old Moat Junior, Chaigeley School, and lastly Yew Tree High School. Tony loved cross country running, he joined and trained at Stretford Running Club. Tony also loved the outdoors, spending many school holidays in Barmouth, Wales, where his maternal grandparents lived, a perfect place to practice for training on the Brecon Beacons.

Tony was a strong swimmer but decided to join the army after leaving school at 16. He joined Junior Leaders in Folkestone, after his training and the infamous P Coy, he passed out and was posted to 3 Para in Aldershot.

When the Falkland Islands were invaded, 3 Para was the 'Spearhead' battalion. Embarking on the long journey aboard the SS *Canberra*, which sailed on 9 April, Tony left behind a pregnant fiancée. Christine was yet another woman who was left to bring a child into the world after her man died. So many children who would never know their fathers.

Tony was killed during the Battle for Mount Longdon on 12 June 1982, his daughter was born in September. His daughter now has a family, a son, and a daughter. Tony's grandson was named after him.

Tony's body was repatriated, he is buried at Southern Cemetery, Barlow Moor Road, Chorlton-Cum-Hardy, Chorlton, Manchester.

In 2022, as part of the Falkland Islands 40th Anniversary Place Names Project, Tony was honoured with 'Greenwood Point', a prominent point on the north coast of East Falkland, east of the entrance to Port Salvador.

His name lives on…

24075845 Staff Sergeant Christopher Anthony Griffin
656 Squadron Army Air Corps 10 October 1949 ~ 6 June 1982
Age 32

Christopher Anthony Griffin was born into military life on 10 October 1949 in Colchester, Essex. His father, Reg Griffin, served originally in the Essex Regiment, followed by the Sussex Regiment and finally the Royal Anglian Regiment during his service over the years. Reg was married to Olive, they had two children. Chris was their only son; his only sibling was younger sister, Tina.

As the child of a Forces family, Chris was schooled in Wuppertal (Germany), then Cyprus and Berlin. Later, he attended a boarding school in Colchester, followed by Felixstowe, Aden, and a grammar school in Great Yarmouth. Moving around is part of Army life. Chris joined the British Army in 1967.

Chris started his military service with the Royal Army Veterinary Corps, where his love of dogs made him a natural at looking after guard dogs. After life in the RAVC he went to the Royal Corps of Transport as a Driver. Lastly, Chris put himself forward for Helicopter Pilot Training and was accepted. He commenced his training course in 1975, by 1976 he was a qualified pilot specialising in the 'Gazelle'.

Chris met Christine in 1970 while he was based with the RCT at Cherry Tree Camp, Colchester. The couple married on 25 March 1972 at Holy Trinity Church in Caister on Sea, Norfolk. Their only son, Paul, was born on 14 September 1979.

Outside of his family Chris had two passions in life, one was Jensen cars and the other Labradors. Two of the family dogs were named after Jensen cars, one called Sceptre after the Interceptor, and CV after the CV8.

In 1982 the family were based in Aldershot as Chris was stationed at RAE Farnborough, Hampshire. Chris travelled 'Down South' on the MV *Nordic Ferry*, which was requisitioned by the British Armed Forces on 3 May 1982. In less than a week it was modified ready to depart, complete with a helicopter pad, able to carry troops, stores, and ammunition for the long journey to the Falkland Islands.

His widow Christine says:

> Chris was to be posted to Netheravon, Wiltshire, on his return from the Falklands. I had to pack and clean the quarter in Aldershot ready to hand over at the beginning of June 1982. So, in retrospect it was good I was kept busy as I didn't have the luxury of wondering how Chris was. We wrote to each other every day to share our thoughts.

Chris had to make a choice to go or to stay as his widow explains:

> We honestly believed that a peace broker deal would be negotiated, and it was mooted that the troops would be stationed down in the Falklands for a year in a peacekeeping role. Chris was given the opportunity to stay behind in the UK as our son was to be admitted into Great Ormond Street Hospital (GOSH) on the 5 June 1982 for open heart surgery. Chris and I discussed this line, but both came to the same conclusion that there was nothing we could do for our son as his life was totally in the hands of the clinicians, whereas Chris could possibly make a difference to the lives of his colleagues during this terrible episode.

Christine is indeed a strong woman; the day she was informed her husband had been killed, she was given the information just as their son was about to go into theatre for his heart surgery. Unlike many widows of that time who were hounded by the press, Christine was thankfully shielded. She stayed at GOSH and could venture outside without fear as they did not know what she looked like. The staff were very protective about the media and would turn the television off should news of the Falklands come on the screen.

Once Paul was discharged from hospital they went to live with Christine's parents in Norfolk. People often forget that you do not just lose your husband when there is this kind of tragedy, the home goes with the job, widows often have no choice but to move.

Christine made the decision to leave her husband in the Falklands.

Christine went on to remarry, considering herself lucky that she found a kind gentleman who was trustworthy. They went on to have a daughter who has kept Paul on his toes. Christine knows only too well how lonely life was as a Forces widow in the early '80s. With no internet or mobile phones, once you had moved away from your married quarter there was no support either.

With the help of two RAF widows and like-minded Army widows Christine helped set up the Army Widows Association in 2004. She was dismayed at the lack of support she received after Chris died and hated the idea that other widows might feel so alone. As a Forces widow it was indeed a lonely club, when your partner dies so young, often parents were still alive. We do not always understand that which we have not experienced, that is part of our unique experience as human beings. Empathy is often born from experience.

Christine has been to the Falklands twice so far, once in 1983 and again in 2002 for the 20th anniversary. Originally, Christine was told that Chris had died because he flew into a hill. She knew this could not be true because as a pilot he was too diligent to have made such a mistake. Later she was informed that Chris had died as a result of 'enemy action'. Five years later she was finally given the news that his helicopter crash was a 'blue-on-blue', that it had been shot down by a Royal Naval vessel. This came to light at the inquest of Simon Cockton.

Chris served a total of fifteen years in the British Army before his death.

In 2022, as part of the Falkland Islands 40th Anniversary Place Names Project, Chris was honoured with 'Griffin Creek', a creek at the north end of Port Edgar between Seal Rookery Creek and Malo Creek.

His name lives on…

P035633L Marine Robert Don Griffin 3 Commando Royal Marines HMS *Fearless* 9 February 1960 ~ 8 June 1982 Age 22

Donald Griffin and Pamela Croft married in Sheffield at the end of 1957. Don served in the Royal Navy; he saw service in the Korean War at just 16 years old. Don was born in Cheltenham, the eldest of seven children, and Pamela was born in Sheffield. Don and Pamela became pen pals, and the rest is history.

Robert Don Griffin, the couple's eldest son, was born on 9 February 1960 in Southampton. Over the next eleven years his parents went on to have three more children: Mandy, Joanne and Lee. Robert's two sisters were born in Southampton, but then the family moved back to Sheffield, where his younger brother was born.

Robert attended the King Edward VII school in Sheffield; while at school he joined the Sea Cadets, becoming a Petty Officer and Drum Major. Robert later joined the Royal Marines and passed his training at Lympstone.

Robert boarded at HMS *Indefatigable* School in Anglesey, North Wales, from 1974–76. Though names change over time, the Indefatigable Old Boys Association are proud to offer the 'Robert Griffin Award' and remember this brave young man with pride. On joining the Royal Marines, Robert successfully completed his initial training. Before his untimely death he had time for some adventure, Northern Ireland and Norway being just two places he saw service.

During the Falklands War Robert was serving with 3 Commando Royal Marines, he was attached to Task Force Landing Craft Squadron RM, Landing Craft Utility F4 (Foxtrot Four) from HMS *Fearless*. On 8 June 1982, the landing craft was bombed by Argentine Skyhawks, all but two of its crew were killed. Robert was one of the men who died. The landing craft was taken in tow but sank before reaching shore therefore Robert was lost to the ocean.

Foxtrot Four is often referred to as the Forgotten Falklands Wreck.

2022 saw Robert remembered during a service at St James Church, Carver Street, Sheffield. Members of his family presented his former unit with a mace engraved with his name.

In 2022, as part of the Falkland Islands 40th Anniversary Place Names Project, Robert was honoured with 'Griffin Islet', a tussac island east of Middle Island in Choiseul Sound, East Falkland.

His name lives on...

23929722 Guardsman Gareth Melvyn Griffiths 1st Battalion Welsh Guards 13 March 1951 ~ 8 June 1982 Age 31

Gareth Melvyn Griffiths was born 13 March 1951 in Llandeilo, Carmarthenshire, Wales. Gareth's father John married Hannah Davies in 1940. Gareth was the second to youngest of six children.

Large families were prevalent in the Griffiths family, as was premature death. Gareth's great-grandfather was a stonemason. The family have a long history in Brynamman, Llandeilo, Carmarthenshire. Gareth's grandfather was one of possibly eleven children, many became miners as the mining industry flourished in Wales. His father, John Melvyn Griffiths, was born in 1921, both his grandfather and father also died in their thirties.

Upon leaving school Gareth joined the Welsh Guards, after he finished his initial training, he joined the Corps of Drums where he played the flute. Postings to Northern Ireland and Munster followed, it was while he was in Germany that he met his wife to be. With no internet, life was very different back in the 1970s, there was a scheme that provided pen pals and kept the Welsh Guards in touch with the outside world. Janice, who lived in Cardiff, became Gareth's pen pal.

Gareth and Janice married in 1972, their first son John Melvyn was born the following year in 1973, both events taking place in Cardiff. Gareth by then was on a posting in Surrey, a tour of Cyprus followed. A longer tour for the Welsh Guards was next, 1977/79 they were stationed at Wavell Barracks in Spandau, Berlin. After the Berlin tour the family moved back to the Guards home of Pirbright; their second son Gary was born in early 1980.

Fate was to play a hand in Gareth's life; first, his son Gary was born the day he returned from his third Northern Ireland tour. Second was how he came to be deployed to the Falklands. Gareth was with the MT platoon as a Staff Car Driver, but in 1982 he returned to the battalion as they were training to leave for the Falklands. Instead of staying in the UK with the rear party, Gareth was sent to meet the QE2 at Ascension Island owing to a shortage of lorry drivers.

On 8 June 1982, Gareth was one of the men declared 'missing presumed dead' when the RFA *Sir Galahad* was bombed in Fitzroy.

He is remembered very fondly by his family as a man with a great sense of humour and one who loved rugby.

The family relocated to Ross on Wye in 1983; Janice and Gary went to the Falklands not long after Gareth died, though Gary was still quite young. Both boys eventually got to say goodbye to their father close to where he died. Gary's daughter was named Myah Liberty after the freedom our men fought for, and John's son Gareth was named after his grandad.

In 2022, as part of the Falkland Islands 40th Anniversary Place Names Project, Gareth was honoured with 'Griffiths Bay', a bay at Bluff Head on the west side of Low Bay, East Falkland.

His name lives on…

24576855 Private Neil Grose 3rd Battalion Parachute Regiment 11 June 1964 ~ 12 June 1982 Age 18

Neil was born on 11 June 1964 in Stanbridge, Bedfordshire, to David and Ann Grose (née Chick), who married in Taunton, Somerset, in 1961. Neil was the middle child of three children, he had two siblings Mark and Debbie. Neil's father, David, was a Major in the Medical Corps of the Territorial Army.

The family moved back to the West Country in 1966. Neil started his school years at West Monkton Infant School.

Neil was a Cub Scout and enjoyed the outdoors. His family moved to Hampshire in 1972. Neil attended Leesland Junior School, followed by St Vincent Senior School. Like many young men he liked sports and followed Leeds United. By the age of 13, Neil decided he wanted to become a gamekeeper, he loved animals and outdoor pursuits, but he was always told that gamekeepers are born, not made. That ended that career path.

Instead, Neil joined the army and became a Junior Sergeant and Junior Platoon Commander . His reports deemed him to be excellent material for The Parachute Regiment after P Coy he was posted to 3 Para.

'Grose', as he was called by mates, is described by one friend as a 'dark-haired, quiet, dependable lad and a talented marksman'.

On 9 April 1982, aged just 17, 'Grose' set sail with the rest of 3 Para. While most young lads prepare to enjoy their 18th birthday party, he was preparing for war. On 21 May 1982, just weeks later, 3 Para landed unchallenged on Green Two Beach at San Carlos Water on East Falkland.

After tabbing more than seventy-five miles across country, the infamous Battle for Mount Longdon was ahead of them. Twenty-three men were to lose their lives, and for 'Grose' it was certainly not the birthday he had ever envisaged.

As the night sky lit up and chaos ensued, the Paras came into their own while the loud thumping sound of a .50 calibre anti-aircraft machine gun could be heard sporadically. One young man already down, one of four friends, 'Grose' was wounded in the chest when he still had two young friends with him. Sadly, another of the four was to lose his life before they could get 'Grose' to safety. A tragic and unforgettable 'coming of age'.

'Grose' died of his injuries, he had just turned eighteen, he passed to Valhalla on 12 June 1982.

In 2022, as part of the Falkland Islands 40th Anniversary Place Names Project, Grose was honoured with 'Grose Beach', a small sandy beach west of Diamond Cove on the north shore of Berkeley Sound, East Falkland.

His name lives on…

3rd Engineering Officer Christopher Francis Hailwood Royal Fleet Auxiliary *Sir Galahad* 5 August 1955 ~ 8 June 1982 Age 26

Christopher Francis Hailwood was born in Altrincham, Cheshire on 5 August 1955, the oldest child of Cyril and Rita Hailwood (née Delaney), who married the year before in 1954. The couple went on to have a daughter, Barbara, and two more sons, Paul, and Terry.

Historically, going back just a couple of generations, the Hailwood family were bakers. Chris's grandfather married the daughter of a jeweller in 1901, sadly he was widowed just six years later. He remarried in 1908, the couple had three children; Chris's father Cyril was born in 1919, the family lived for a short while in Rhyl, later returning to Cheshire before the onset of the Second World War.

Chris finished his education at the Blessed John Sherd RC School in Crewe where he was Head Boy. Chris joined the Royal Fleet Auxiliary via Riversdale College, Liverpool, starting out as a Cadet.

Chris married Caroline in Weymouth in 1980, they were living in Farnborough as the Islands were invaded. The couple had one son, James, born early in 1982. During the Falklands War Chris served as 3rd Engineering Officer on RFA *Sir Galahad*.

Chris was killed on 8 June 1982 during the bombing of the *Sir Galahad* in Fitzroy. He is honoured on all of the usual Falklands memorials, but also on a very special one at St John's Church in Marchwood. It is dedicated to the memory of the men of the Royal Fleet Auxiliary who lost their lives in action in the South Atlantic in 1982 in defence of the freedom of the Falkland Islands and dependencies. The memorial was re-dedicated in 2016 and is well tended.

James got to present Her Majesty Queen Elizabeth II with a stone at another memorial for the 25th Anniversary of the war. Our late Queen placed a stone on a traditional Scottish cairn in the grounds of Pangbourne College, in Berkshire, completing the memorial to the 255 British Service Personnel killed in the Falkland Islands.

Chris is also mentioned on the Crewe War Memorial.

In 2022, as part of the Falkland Islands 40th Anniversary Place Names Project, Chris was honoured with 'Hailwood Bay', a bay with a sand beach west of Robinson Point on Keppel Island, West Falkland.

His name lives on…

D170776F Weapons Engineering Mechanic (Ordnance) 1 Ian Peter Hall HMS *Coventry* 1 March 1960 ~ 25 May 1982 Age 22

Ian Peter Hall was born a fraternal twin; his parents Peter William Hall and Iris May Lyndsey married in Portsmouth in 1953. The couple's first child, a daughter, was born in 1955. On 1 March 1960, Ian and his twin sister Alison were born in Oxford at the Radcliffe Infirmary.

Ian attended Church Cowley Primary School in Oxford, followed by Temple Cowley and Oxford Boys. He joined the Royal Navy in 1978, following in his father's footsteps.

Ian served in HMS *London* prior to joining HMS *Coventry*. Ian was in Gibraltar on operations until April 1982 when his ship was diverted 'Down South' instead of returning home. The family received a telegram to say that HMS *Coventry* was headed south, like many families all they could then do is wait for news. Ian was not married but left behind a girlfriend, Jane.

Ian was known as 'Nobby' to his shipmate; by the time of the Falklands War, he had served approximately four years in the Royal Navy.

HMS *Coventry* had carried out several operations around the Falkland Islands already. On 22 May she was tasked, along with HMS *Broadsword*, to operate as a 'missile trap' to the north of Pebble Island in defence of the San Carlos bridgehead. Having shot down several enemy aircraft, they were attacked and bombed on 25 May 1982.

Ian was one of the young men who died, just 22 years old. The family received news that he was 'missing in action'. As many a sailor before him, 'Nobby' went down with his ship. His twin sister said that she still felt numb thirty-eight years later, she also felt it was 'a dreadful waste'.

Alison travelled to the Falkland Islands in 1983, on a 'pilgrimage' arranged for families by the British Government:

> We travelled via Heathrow to Montevideo, Uruguay, where we then boarded HM Cruise Ship. We were escorted by police guards through Uruguay. It is all a bit of a blur; I remember we had to observe blackout. There was a huge florist set up in the depths of the ship for our floral wreaths. I remember an emergency evacuation drill with life jackets.
>
> We visited Islanders' homes where I ate mutton. I flew in a Chinook helicopter to Pebble Island where we had a small service and I collected some of the rock nearby. I remember our parents throwing our wreath of poppies into the ocean.

Alison says her memories of her brother are mainly from when they were young. They had some fantastic family holidays in Devon and Cornwall, sharing joint birthday parties as twins. Alison also remembers that Ian loved making Airfix models and riding his Suzuki. Ian and his twin sister shared the same dark curly hair.

From wars across the years, many a young serviceman has gone 'missing in action', and many a young matelot has gone down with their ship. It leaves a hole in the lives of loved ones that nothing can fill. Ships at the bottom of the ocean become timeless as our own lives move forward.

Ian's father, Peter, died in January 1985, his mother Iris on 26 April 2014.

In 2022, as part of the Falkland Islands 40th Anniversary Place Names Project, Ian was honoured with 'Hall Lagoon', a large tidal lagoon at the northwest end of Golding Island, West Falkland.

His name lives on…

499793 Captain Gavin John Hamilton MC 22 SAS Regiment
15 May 1953 ~ 10 June 1982 Age 29

Gavin John Hamilton was born on 15 May 1953 in Harrogate, North Yorkshire, to his parents Gavin and Betty Hamilton (née Smith). Known as John, he had one older half-sister, Jackie, one full sibling, Jane, and a younger half-brother, Julian. John's father was a civil servant, his mother an auxiliary nurse.

John attended Grosvenor Prep School in Harrogate followed by the Royal Masonic School for Boys in Bushey, Hertfordshire.

John joined the British Army in 1975. After graduating from the Royal Military Academy Sandhurst, he was commissioned as a subaltern with the Green Howards. He saw service in Cyprus, Belize and South Armagh in Ulster during Operation Banner. John married Vikki in Germany in 1977 while serving with the British Army of the Rhine, the couple had no children.

John transferred into the Special Air Service in 1981, being attached initially to D Squadron, 19 (Mountain) Troop, at the time the Falkland Islands were invaded he was their OC.

Between 19 April and 10 June 1982, when he was killed in action, Captain Hamilton and his SAS troop were responsible for some of the most successful SAS operations carried out during Operation Corporate.

Having survived two helicopter crashes in adverse weather conditions on the Fortuna Glacier in South Georgia during Operation Paraquet, two days later John led the advance elements of the forces that captured the main Argentine positions in Grytkyven. This action resulted in the surrender of an Argentinian garrison occupying South Georgia. Shortly after, he led the Raid on Pebble Island, which resulted in the destruction of eleven Pucarra and T-34 Mentor Argentinian aircraft on the ground.

Once British ground forces landed at San Carlos, Hamilton deployed with his SAS men forty miles behind the enemy lines to observe the main enemy defensive positions at Port Stanley. His leadership proved instrumental in seizing this ground, from which the final attack on Port Stanley would be launched to bring the war to a victory.

On 27 May 1982 he identified an Argentine probe into the squadron's position and during the ensuing fight captured an Argentinian POW. The next night his troop held off another enemy attack, in doing so enabling 42 Commando Royal Marines to fly in to reinforce the position on 31 May 1982, which was a key stage in Operation Corporate. The next day his troop ambushed another Argentinian patrol, capturing five members of it, three of whom were wounded.

On 5 June 1982, Hamilton was deployed in command of a four-man observation patrol into positions behind enemy lines on West Falkland to observe Argentinian activity at Port Howard. Establishing himself in an observation post only 2,500 metres from the Argentine positions, radio reports were successfully dispatched.

Just after dawn on 10 June 1982, John and a radio operator, Corporal Roy Fonseka, were discovered by an Argentinian patrol from the 1st Section of the 601 Commando

Coy operating out of Port Howard. Fonseka engaged the enemy force, followed by John. As the small arms firefight continued with grenades being exchanged, John was hit in the arm by a rifle bullet. He ordered that they both attempt to fight their way out. The only withdrawal route available was to the rear, which was exposed to enemy observation on the up slope of the ridge for fifty yards to the summit.

John maintained automatic covering fire at the Argentinian commandos to allow Fonseka to withdraw first, it was a coordinated fall-back manoeuvre. John then attempted to follow, in the process he was struck by Argentinian rifle fire and killed; Fonseka was taken prisoner of war.

John was killed by First Lieutenant Jose Martiniano Duarte. Nearly twenty years later, his widow Vikki Hamilton met with the man who killed her husband, at the Argentine military attaché in London.

John was buried with military honours by the Argentinian garrison on West Falkland, the grave lying in the small cemetery at Port Howard. He was awarded the Military Cross for his bravery – up to that time the only one granted posthumously.

Colonel Juan Ramon Mabragaña, was interrogated after the Argentine surrender, he asked that 'the SAS Captain' be decorated for his actions, as he was the most courageous man he had ever seen.

In 2022, as part of the Falkland Islands 40th Anniversary Place Names Project, John was honoured with 'Hamilton Point', a point at the exit of Double Stream into Port Howard, West Falkland.

His name lives on...

D191828F Steward Shaun Hanson HMS *Ardent* 15 January 1962 ~ 21 May 1982 Age 20

Shaun was born in Sheffield on 15 January 1962 to Peter and Rene Hanson (née Bramhall). Shaun had two sisters, Carol and Lisa.

Shaun went to Ecclesfield Grammar School, where he was a very popular pupil. Shaun has a school cup, a swimming trophy, a memorial tree, and a portrait that keeps his name both honoured and remembered. A plaque at Ecclesfield Grammar School reads 'WAR IN THE FALKLANDS IN MEMORY OF SHAUN HANSON 1972-1978 KILLED IN ACTION MAY 21ST 1982 ON BOARD HMS ARDENT'.

Summer holidays were spent at Filey. Shaun loved splashing in the waves as well as playing cricket and football on the sand. He also had a passion for ships and the sea.

When Shaun left school, he initially started an apprenticeship at a local firm, C I Jenkinson Ltd; being a toolmaker was not for Shaun, his heart lay elsewhere. With the sea beckoning, Shaun applied to join the Royal Navy in October 1980. Application successful, he was off to HMS *Raleigh* for his basic training in March 1981.

Training completed, Shaun took specialist courses at HMS *Pembroke* and HMS *Nelson*, before joining HMS *Ardent* in February 1982. He sailed with the ship to Norway, and Shaun enjoyed runs-ashore in Stavanger and Narvik.

With the Falkland Islands invaded on 2 April 1982, Shaun was soon off on HMS *Ardent* as it joined the Task Force to sail 'Down South'. HMS *Ardent* was launched on 9 May 1975, her motto 'Through fire and water' was sadly to come true. On 9 May 1982, exactly seven years later while 700 miles south west of Ascension, HMS *Ardent* closed to within 200 yards of the starboard side of the troopship *Canberra* and provided a gun power demonstration to the troops sailing south.

On 21 May 1982, while lying in Falkland Sound, supporting Operation Sutton by bombarding the Argentine airstrip at Goose Green, HMS *Ardent* was attacked by at least three waves of Argentine aircraft. The air strikes caused her to sink the next day. Shaun was seen fighting a fire in the helicopter hangar with great resolve and determination. He was giving First Aid to an injured colleague when the second attack came in. Shaun and his patient were both killed instantly.

The anchor from HMS *Ardent* was lost in Portland Harbour in 1980 when the ship was taking shelter from a storm. After the ship was sunk, the Queen's Harbour Master at Portland, a former First Lieutenant of HMS *Ardent*, Commander Nick Crewes, started a search for the anchor. After its recovery it was offered to the HMS *Ardent* Association, they decided it should become a permanent memorial to those who were lost with the ship. Originally it was placed at the China Fleet Club near Saltash in Cornwall.

Relocation to the National Memorial Arboretum came about thirty-three years after the ship sank. The memorial was unveiled by Admiral Lord West, Commander of HMS *Ardent* in 1982, and the Duchess of Gloucester.

In 2022, as part of the Falkland Islands 40th Anniversary Place Names Project, Shaun was honoured with 'Hanson Bay', a main landing bay at Second Passage in the Passage Islands group, West Falkland.

His name lives on…

24399337 Corporal David Hardman MID 2nd Battalion Parachute Regiment 22 December 1959 ~ 28 May 1982 Age 22

David 'Chuck' Hardman was born in Hamilton, Scotland, on 22 December 1959 to Thomas Arthur and Agnes Hardman. He was the youngest child, with three older siblings: sisters Ann and Barbara, and brother Frank. Dave's father, Thomas, was a Ravenscraig worker.

Dave spent his early years on the Beechfield smallholding in Meikle Earnock Road. Sadly, Thomas was electrocuted in an accident at the small holding when Dave was just a baby, he died in 1960, aged 39.

Dave went to Low Waters Primary and then St John's Grammar school. Young Dave played football for his school teams and had also been in the Boys Brigade.

Dave enlisted into the army on his 16th birthday in 1975, joining the Junior Parachute Company as a boy soldier at Aldershot. His nicknames included Dave, Mad Dog and Jock, but he was mainly known as Chuck.

When he finished his training, Dave was drafted to 2 Para, he did a tour of Berlin from 77–79. Sadly, his mother Agnes also died in 1977 at the age of 53.

Dave was on tour in Northern Ireland from July 1979 – March 1981. Dave was the senior corporal of 2 Platoon, A Company, 2 PARA from 1980 to 1982 when the Falklands were invaded. During the Northern Ireland tour, it was A Coy who were hit hard at Warrenpoint, but it did not deter him. Dave was a 'career soldier', having originally signed on for three years, he then signed on for another nine.

2 Para were first ashore on 21 May 1982, they dug in on Sussex Mountain above San Carlos, with a bird's eye view of the continuous bombing attacks on the ships below. They attacked on the morning of 28 May 1982, having been ordered to take Darwin and Goose Green.

By dawn, A Company had become pinned down in a gorse gully below Darwin Hill by very strong Argentine defences. Dave was killed by small arms fire having previously taken part in the casualty evacuation of both Corporal Prior and Private Worrall. He died on 28 May 1982 alongside Captains Dave Wood and Chris Dent.

The supplement to the *London Gazette* of 8 October 1982 saw Chuck Mentioned in Dispatches: '24399337 Corporal David HARDMAN, The Parachute Regiment (Posthumous).'

Dave is buried at Wellhall Cemetery, Hamilton, where a service is held each year in memory of him and two other Paras who died on active service, also interred there.

In 2022, as part of the Falkland Islands 40th Anniversary Place Names Project, David was honoured with 'Hardman Creek', a creek at the entrance to Bodie Creek, south side of Choiseul Sound, East Falkland.

His name lives on…

24154752 Trooper William Clark Hatton QGM 22 SAS Regiment 4 August 1950 ~ 19 May 1982 Age 31

'Willie' was born William Clark McAra Hatton on 4 August 1950, in the Maternity Hospital, Bellshill, North Lanarkshire, in Scotland. Willie was the son of James Hatton and Annie Shaw McConnell Sharp, who married on 23 July 1943 at Craigneuk. At the time of Willie's birth, the family lived in Argyle Street, Motherwell, and James was an engineer (turner).

At the time of the invasion 'Willie' Hatton of 23 Troop G Squadron 22 SAS, was in the vanguard of the operation in the Falklands. Willie served alongside 2 Special Boat Section and took part in the mission that led to the sinking of the Argentine spy ship, *Narwhal*.

On 19 May 1982 the Royal Navy Sea King HC4 *ZA294* of 846 Naval Air Squadron was transferring SAS troops from HMS *Hermes* to HMS *Intrepid* when it ditched in the sea following what was thought to be a bird strike. Sadly, Willie was one of the casualties that day.

Willie had previously received the Queen's Gallantry Medal for his work in Northern Ireland. His parent unit was The Parachute Regiment.

Willie was 31 years old when he died. He left behind a wife and a daughter. He is remembered in St Martins Churchyard in Hereford, as well as on all the Falklands Memorials worldwide.

In 2022, as part of the Falkland Islands 40th Anniversary Place Names Project, Willie was honoured with 'Hatton Cove', a cove north of Death's Head on mainland West Falkland.

His name lives on…

Steward David Reginald Stuart Hawkins SS *Atlantic Conveyor* Merchant Navy 9 February 1939 ~ 25 May 1982 Age 43

David Reginald Stuart Hawkins was born on 9 February 1939 at 39 St Thomas Street, Penryn, in Cornwall to Roy Currie and Louvain Beatrice Ann Hawkins (née Burt).

Roy Currie Hawkins was a Merchant Seaman born in Ellesmere, Shropshire. Louvain was the eldest daughter of Ernest Tildren Alfred Burt, a 'horse driver'. Ernest had served as a Sapper in the Royal Engineers in the First World War. Before that the family had been Mariners.

Ernest's grandfather William Burt was a Mariner, born in St Columb Minor, Cornwall. William married Maria Moyses in 1838, the couple went on to have a large family. Albert John Burt was their seventh child, born in 1853, he in turn went on to become a Master Mariner.

Ernest Tildren Alfred Burt was born in 1892, by 1911 he was an apprentice blacksmith, he attested into the Royal Engineers in Newquay on 11 January 1915, by which time he was a husband and father. In 1916, the father of two was sent to serve with the British Expeditionary Force on the Western Front. Ernest survived the First World War and a third daughter, born in 1921, completed the family.

By 1939, Ernest was back to working as a blacksmith but as times had changed, he was also a motor fitter; the family lived latterly in Newquay. Ernest died in 1962.

It appears that Roy Currie Hawkins was the grandson of a baker in Ellesmere, Shropshire his mother was unmarried. Roy, it seems, joined the British Army in 1933 at just 16 years old. In the same year he transferred to the Royal Welch Fusiliers and possibly left in 1936. For Roy the call of the sea came, and he settled in Penryn. David Reginald Stuart Hawkins, it seems, was the eldest of four children born to Roy and Louvain.

Generations before him had served in one way or another, sadly David, a steward on the SS *Atlantic Conveyor*, died on 25 May 1982, his body was not recovered. Though his father had died in 1979, his mother Louvain continued to live in Cornwall until her death in 2005.

In 2022, as part of the Falkland Islands 40th Anniversary Place Names Project, David was honoured with 'Hawkins Bay', a shallow bay on the west side of the entrance to Port Salvador protected by nearby Centre Island, East Falkland.

His name lives on…

4232387 Flight Lieutenant Garth Walter Hawkins Royal Air Force
17 June 1942 ~ 19 May 1982 Age 39

Garth Walter Hawkins was born in Maidenhead, Berkshire on 17 June 1942, the only son of Stuart and Kitty Hawkins (née Hughes). The Hawkins family had lived in Berkshire for many years, Garth's great-grandfather, Fred, attested into the Grenadier Regiment of Foot Guards in November 1854.

Brought up in Binfield, Garth attended the Junior School in the village, followed by Ranelagh in Bracknell. Ranelagh is over 300 years old, the school founded by the Earl of Ranelagh, Richard Jones, in 1709.

Garth was known as an outstanding sportsman. In football he played goalkeeper, playing originally with Bracknell Minors. He played for Binfield FC while still at school, followed by Oxford City, which was one of the top amateur teams of the time. Garth also played cricket and was known as a fearsome fast bowler for the village team in Binfield.

Garth joined the Royal Air Force when he was 22 years old, he travelled the world during his service.

In 1965, Garth married his first wife Sandra in Windsor, Berkshire. The couple had two sons: Gary, born the following year, and Robert Garth, born in 1971. Garth's sons are particularly proud of their father, but also their maternal grandpops, who was in the Royal Air Force in the Second World War. 'Jack' Wait is featured in the book *Royal Air Force Stradishall 1938-1970*, with a picture of him standing with crew in front of the Lancaster Bomber 'Champagne Charlie.'

Garth married his second wife Tina in 1979, the couple had no children.

Garth's specialist talents were soon noticed by the SAS, he first worked with them in Canada in 1979. By 1982, he had worked with all SAS squadrons both in the UK and worldwide. It is said that his favourite place was Belize.

On 19 May 1982, the 846 Squadron RAF Sea King 4 was transferring SAS troops from HMS *Hermes* to HMS *Intrepid* when it ditched in the sea. Garth was an expert in directing air strikes to support special operations and regarded by the Special Air Service as one of their own. Twenty-one men died that day, nineteen of them SAS. Though eight men survived, Garth, who was forward observer, did not. He was just one month short of his 40th birthday.

As Garth was attached to D Squadron, 22 SAS, he is remembered at St Martins Church in Hereford.

Garth was fondly called 'Gunner', he was known to love his job, and as an absolute professional. At the time of his death, he lived in Wokingham, Berkshire. Though his job had taken him all over the world, at home he had stayed close to his roots.

Garth was the only Royal Air Force death during the Falklands War.

In 2022, as part of the Falkland Islands 40th Anniversary Place Names Project, Garth was honoured with 'Hawkins Point', the north west point of Kidney Island in Lively Sound, East Falkland.

His name lives on…

D190628Y Able Seaman (Sonar) Sean Keith Hayward HMS *Ardent* 15 July 1963 ~ 21 May 1982 Age 18

Carole Ethel Knight was born on 19 December 1937 in Portsmouth. The Knight family lived in Norman Road, Portsmouth, for many years, sometimes with three generations under the same roof. Her parents, Eileen Broadbridge and Henry Knight, married in 1932.

Elsewhere in Portsmouth, Albert 'John' Hayward was born on 29 August 1936, the son of Albert and Louisa Hayward (née Sexton), who married in 1923. Albert served with the Royal Hampshire Regiment.

Carole Knight and 'John' Hayward married in Portsmouth in 1956; their first child, Beverley, was born in 1958. The couple went on to have three sons, the youngest two were a set of identical twins. Sean Keith Hayward and his twin were born in Portsmouth on 15 July 1963.

The family moved to Barrow-in-Furness in 1972, where John worked in the shipyard. After Sean was killed, John was no longer able to work on the ships and changed to working security until he retired through ill health.

Sean attended Alfred Barrow School for boys, he was just eleven years old when his sister Beverley left home to get married. Beverley moved back to Portsmouth. During his time at HMS Vernon, Sean lived with his sister in Gosport.

Sean loved music and loved to DJ with his brothers Jeff and Barry.

By 1982, Sean was serving in HMS *Ardent*, he was one of the men who were killed on 21 May 1982 when HMS *Ardent* was sunk by Argentinian aircraft in Falkland Sound. Just 18 years old, he died just two months short of his 19th birthday. A life over, almost before it had begun.

The following year in 1983, his older brother named his first son after Sean.

Carole died in 1995 and John in 2002 before the Elizabeth Cross was granted to Next of Kin for their loss. It therefore fell to Sean's sister Beverley to be presented with the Elizabeth Cross in a ceremony on 30 September 2012. Media reports claimed that Sean's twin brother felt it was an enormous honour to receive the medal. He was pleased to meet Sean's Commanding Officer, feeling that Sean would have been proud having died in service to Queen and Country.

At the time of Sean's death his family were living in Ramsden Street, Barrow-in-Furness where his father continued to live until he died.

In 2022, as part of the Falkland Islands 40th Anniversary Place Names Project, Sean was honoured with 'Hayward Creek', the inner part of West Cove in Port Philomel, West Falkland.

His name lives on…

C025065S Lieutenant Rodney Ritchie Heath HMS *Coventry* 23 January 1948 ~ 25 May 1982 Age 34

Rodney's parents, Trevor Heath and Gina Ritchie, married in Newcastle in 1946. Rod was their eldest child and only son, born on 23 January 1948 in Brighton, Sussex. A daughter, Barbara, was born three years later.

Historically there had been service in the Royal Navy during the First World War. Though many records are missing, great-uncle Sidney Victor Duck (brother to Rod's grandmother, Ethel) was just 16 years old when he joined the Royal Navy in November 1913, starting out in HMS *Powerful*. Sidney served until December 1922, surviving the First World War. One of ten children, he was born in Battersea; the family later settled in Hastings.

Ethel married Ernest Heath in 1921 in Sussex. Rod's father Trevor was the couple's eldest child, born in Surrey, apparently one of four boys, the family initially lived in Croydon. Ernest worked for the London and Brighton South Coast Railway. By the early 1930s the Heath family were settled in Sussex.

Rod attended Brighton and Hove Grammar School. Upon leaving school, the sea beckoned and on 4 January 1965, just short of his 17th Birthday, Rod joined the Royal Navy, spending some of his time at Collingwood.

Over the next seventeen years Rod saw service in more than one ship. Rod served on HMS *Ulster* for a year from 1968–69, HMS *Gurkha* from June 1970 – January 1973, HMS *Sheffield* from October 1975 – May 1978. Rod also spent some time at DWSP(N] Portsdown in 1975; lastly, in 1979, he joined HMS *Coventry*.

His widow Jan says:

> He specialised in Surface Weapons and spent five years of his career learning, instructing, and writing operating instructions for, and maintaining at sea the Sea Dart system. which was used successfully in the Falklands War.

Rodney Ritchie Heath married Janet Wake on 30 August 1975, the couple had no children. Jan was a civil servant working at HMS *Centurion*.

Prior to the invasion of the Falkland Islands Rod had undertaken a seven-month deployment to the Far East in 1980, when the ship visited Shanghai and many other places. HMS *Coventry* had already been at sea for five weeks when she was diverted 'Down South'.

Rod is described by fellow shipmates as 'A true gent. a Top Bloke, Brilliant Officer, Brilliant Shipmate'. Rod, or 'Rodders' as he was known, also had an affectionate nickname of 'Black Rod', he was a very popular and well-liked officer.

At the time of the Falklands War Rod Heath was a serving Lieutenant, the officer responsible for the missile system on HMS *Coventry*. On 25 May 1982, the *Coventry* had already survived two air raids and shot down three aircraft according to an account by its Captain, David Hart-Dyke.

Hart-Dyke states that there was another warning, and he went below feeling more fearful than before. As he did so he spoke briefly to Rod Heath, it was to be the last time he saw him.

Rod's widow Jan says:

> He liked sport and was a good squash player. He also played football, enjoyed cycling, and running. He loved cars and was never happier

than when he was tinkering under a bonnet. He owned an E-type Jaguar which he stripped down and rebuilt, and with a respray it was virtually a new car.

In 2022, as part of the Falkland Islands 40th Anniversary Place Names Project, Rod was honoured with 'Heath Passage', a passage between Jason Islet and Grand Jason in the Jason Islands Group, West Falkland.

His name lives on...

24581588 Private Peter John Hedicker 3rd Battalion Parachute Regiment 25 May 1960 ~ 12 June 1982 Age 22

Army service within the Hedicker family went back generations, prior to that there was service with the Royal Navy.

Robert Hedicker was a widower serving in HMS *Vincent* when he married his second wife, Mary Ann Topp, in June 1857. The couple's eldest son, Robert, was serving in HMS *Iris* in 1888. It was their youngest son, William Richard John Hedicker, who first brought the British Army into the family. In 1881 he was a Bugler at Browndown Camp, Hampshire. One of the Hedicker family also served in the Hampshire Regiment with the Red Cross at Clayton Court Auxiliary Hospital.

William and Laura Hedicker (née Peirson) had four sons; Reginald Walter Hedicker also served with the Hampshire Regiment during the First World War. Youngest son William Gordon Hedicker was Peter's grandfather, he also served in the British Army. William junior married Muriel Irene Hart in London in 1926. After the First World War he worked as a gardener, it is thought he served with the Guards. William and Muriel had two sons; their youngest, 'Bill', was born at a military hospital in June 1931, his birth registered in Woolwich.

'Bill' Hedicker also became a serving soldier, he completed twenty-seven years between the Royal Service Army Corps and the Royal Corps of Transport before he retired from the British Army. Bill Hedicker and Rita Rodgers married in Hatfield, Hertfordshire, in 1956.

Bill and Rita had their first son, Stephen, in 1957; Peter arrived on 25 May 1960, born in a military hospital in Aldershot. Daughter Nicola came along five years later.

Oldest son Steve followed in the family footsteps; he served in the Royal Signals for just under twenty-four years.

Being part of an Army family meant Peter went to a total of eight schools, ending up at Heron Wood in Aldershot. After Peter left school, he worked at the Royal Exchange pub where he got to know some young 'maroon berets' who inspired him to join up, which he did in September 1980.

When Peter finished his training, he was posted to 3 Para who were stationed in Tidworth. He became part of a Milan ATGM (Anti-Tank Guided Missile) fire team.

Landing on Green Beach on 21 May 1982, 3 Para tabbed their way from Port San Carlos to Estancia House and then on to the battle for Mount Longdon. During the night of 12 June 1982, Peter was killed by a direct hit from an Argentine 106mm recoilless weapon.

Peter was temporarily interred at Teal Inlet and then later repatriated in November 1982 and laid to rest in Aldershot Military Cemetery. Bill died ten years after his son in 1992.

Rita later settled in Yeovil, Somerset.

In 2022, as part of the Falkland Islands 40th Anniversary Place Names Project, Peter was honoured with 'Hedicker Bay', a bay on the south coast of Steeple Jason, in the Jason Islands Group, West Falkland.

His name lives on...

D175642S Air Engineering Mechanic (Mechanical) 1 Mark Henderson HMS *Glamorgan* 16 September 1961 ~ 12 June 1982 Aged 20

Mark Henderson was born in Greenwood Avenue, Westburn, Cambuslang, Lanarkshire, to Paul Echenberger (Ecbenberger) and Anna Henderson (née Green). The couple married in July 1960, and at the time of Mark's birth, the family lived in Main Street in Cambuslang. Paul was a steel worker.

Mark attended old Busheyhill Primary School and later Cathkin High in Cambuslang. Mark was well known in the area as a paperboy and member of the local Boys' Brigade company before joining the Royal Navy.

When the Falkland Islands were invaded in April 1982 Mark was serving on HMS *Glamorgan*, the ship was near Gibraltar involved in a large exercise involving several ships that went on to form the Task Force.

HMS *Glamorgan* was hit in the early hours of 12 June 1982, the third Exocet missile hit its mark.

Mark was among those who perished. Mark was 20 years old; he was buried at sea in Naval tradition with a memorial service being held for him at a later date in his home town.

Many years later a plaque was finally placed in the Cambuslang Parish Church. The problem many families had with inclusion on memorials was that the Falklands was classed as a 'conflict', because war was not officially declared. To everyone who fought there or perished during those seventy-four days, it absolutely was a war. Mark's mother, Anna, managed to visit the Falkland Islands to see where her son was laid to rest.

In 2022, as part of the Falkland Islands 40th Anniversary Place Names Project, Mark was honoured with 'Henderson Cove', a cove northeast of Crow Point on the northeast shore of the Bay of Harbours, East Falkland.

His name lives on...

2nd Engineering Officer Paul Anderson Henry GM, Royal Fleet Auxiliary RFA *Sir Galahad* 27 July 1948 ~ 8 June 1982 Age 33

Paul's father Ronald Johnstone Henry was born in Berwick in September 1915, his mother Barbara Joan Hammond in Croydon, Surrey, in the same year. Barbara gave birth to her son Paul the day after her own birthday. Ronald died on 12 August 1970, but Barbara lived on for many years after her son's tragic death. She died in Berwick on 28 November 2004, aged 89 years.

Ronald was the son of George Johnston Henry, born in 1881 in Duns, Scotland. The Henry family lived just over the Scottish Border until they settled in Berwick-Upon-Tweed. Great-grandfather Thomas Henry was an engine driver with the North British Railway Company, his wife Agnes ran a boarding house in Railway Street. George was the youngest of four children, all born before the family moved over the border.

George and Elizabeth, it appears, had only one son. George was also a train driver with the same company as his father. Ronald Johnstone Henry served with the Royal Northumberland Fusiliers in the Second World War. Records indicate that he was a prisoner of war at Stalag IXC Bad Sulza. After the Second World War ended and Ronald married Barbara, the couple returned up north to Ronald's home town.

Paul Anderson Henry was born at Castle Hills Maternity Home, Berwick-Upon-Tweed, on 27 July 1948. Paul had one brother, Graeme, four years his junior. Paul is well remembered in the Berwick area; he was set for adventure joining the Royal Fleet Auxiliary.

In 1978, Paul was 3rd Engineering Officer in RFA *Regent*. He is remembered as a 'gentleman through and through'. His actions were to prove that just four years later.

In 1982, during the Falklands War, Paul was 2nd Engineering Officer in the RFA *Sir Galahad*. When the ship was hit on 8 June 1982, he committed a huge act of bravery. RFA *Sir Galahad* was at anchor in Port Pleasant, about three cables from RFA *Sir Tristram* and about a mile from Fitzroy, preparing to disembark elements of the Welsh Guards. The Sky Hawk attack by the Argentinians that day was devastating.

The third bomb burst in the engine room, killing 3rd Engineer Officer Andrew Morris. The bomb produced thick clouds of choking smoke, trapping 3rd Engineer Officer Christopher Hailwood and Junior Engineer Officer Neil Bagnall in the Machinery Control Room. Bagnall attempted to escape from the engine room but was driven back by the smoke. 2nd Engineering Officer Paul Henry gave the only set of breathing apparatus to Junior Engineer Bagnall and ordered him to try again, thereby saving Bagnall's life and sacrificing his own.

His citation

> *MONDAY, 11th OCTOBER 1982*
> *The QUEEN has been graciously pleased to approve the Posthumous award of the George Medal to the undermentioned in recognition of gallant and distinguished service during the operations in the South Atlantic:*

> *Second Engineer Officer Paul Anderson Henry, Royal Fleet Auxiliary*
>
> *On 8th June 1982, after RFA Sir Galahad had been bombed by Argentine aircraft during troop disembarkation in Fitzroy Creek, the Engine Room compartments quickly filled with thick black smoke. Second Engineer Officer Henry and Third Engineer Officer Hailwood were present in the Main Control Room. A junior Engineer Officer was at the after end of the Engine Room and had to fight his way back through thick smoke to the Main Control Room area.*
>
> *Second Engineer Officer Henry then told the Junior Engineer Officer to take the breathing apparatus and get out of the Engine Room when they would follow. By this unselfish and courageous act, he saved the Junior Officer's life, at the same time sacrificing his own. The Junior Officer managed to reach safety, but both Second Engineer Officer Henry and Third Engineer Officer Hailwood perished.*

Paul is remembered on many different memorials. There is a bench in Edinburgh dedicated to him by the Scott Monument in Princes Street Gardens. He is also remembered on the Scottish National War Memorial.

In Tweedmouth there is a beautiful War Memorial. On top of the granite memorial is a female figure, with closed eyes she rests her head in her one hand and holds a floral wreath in the other. Paul's name has been added to those who gave their lives in the First World War and the Second World War.

There is also a plaque in honour to Paul in the Amateur Rowing club in Berwick-upon-Tweed. It reads, 'In memory of 2nd Engineering Officer Paul A. Henry GM, a member of Berwick Amateur Rowing Club who died in action on the RFA Sir Galahad in the Falklands Campaign in 1982'.

As Paul's father had died years previously, it was Graeme and his mother Barbara who were presented with his George Medal, granted posthumously. At the time of his death he lived in Osborne Road, Berwick-Upon-Tweed.

In 2022, as part of the Falkland Islands 40th Anniversary Place Names Project, Paul was honoured with 'Henry Island', a small tussac island at the entrance to Bodie Creek, Choiseul Sound, East Falkland.

His name lives on…

D166439B Weapons Engineering Mechanic Stephen Heyes HMS *Ardent* 10 October 1960 ~ 21 May 1982 Age 21

James Heyes and his bride Elizabeth Molyneux married at the beginning of 1960 in Wigan.

Stephen was the couple's first-born, arriving on 10 October 1960. Sadly his brother David, born two years later, died as a young baby. The couple's family flourished from 1964. Anthony arrived followed by Josephine, Angela and lastly Caroline, who arrived in 1978, after Stephen had already joined the Royal Navy.

Steve was schooled at St Cuthbert's Junior school, followed by St Thomas More Roman Catholic High School in Wigan; he is remembered as having a wonderful smile and being good at table tennis. Steve and his best friend joined the Royal Navy in January 1977. Steve completed basic training in Electronic Warfare at HMS *Raleigh* after which he joined his first ship HMS *Cleopatra*.

HMS *Cleopatra* was granted the Freedom of Harrogate in 1979, which led to the meeting of his wife. Steve met Christina Nelson at a Ministry of Defence dance in the town. Christina worked for the Ministry Of Defence at the time, the last thing she expected was to meet a sailor in Harrogate. Steve was immediately smitten, he proposed in a matter of weeks.

The couple were married on 28 March 1981 at Christ Church in Harrogate, and moved into married quarters in St Budeaux, Plymouth. They had moved into their own house in Plymouth on 17 April 1982, just two days before Steve set sail for the Falkland Islands.

Steve was killed on 21 May 1982 when HMS *Ardent* was bombed in Falkland Sound. He is honoured on all the Falkland Island memorials but also at his school and with a wedding cope kept at the church where he married Christina.

In 2017, Petty Officer Electronic Warfare (POEW) David Bell from POEW Qualifying Course 1603 received the AB(EW) Steve Heyes Award for Best Student of the training year. He was the first graduate from HMS *Collingwood's* Maritime War School to receive the award which was sponsored by Cobham Aviation.

Steve Heyes was already commemorated at the base by a tree, and a classroom within Lewin building named after him. It is important that we remember these men who brought freedom from the sea, who gave their lives for others.

In 2022, as part of the Falkland Islands 40th Anniversary Place Names Project, Steve was honoured with 'Heyes Bay', a bay at Round Point south of North West Bay in Port Philomel, West Falkland.

His name lives on…

24405614 Lance Corporal Peter David Higgs 3rd Battalion Parachute Regiment 7 October 1958 ~ 12 June 1982 Age 23

The Higgs family have a long history between Berkshire, Oxfordshire and Wiltshire.

In the late 1930s Ernest Higgs, Pete's grandfather, was a Farm Carter in Highworth, Swindon. He was born in Farringdon, Berkshire. Ernest Higgs and Mary Isabella Alice Jackson married in 1928 in Wantage, Berkshire. Kenneth George Higgs was their younger son, born in Swindon on 31 May 1933.

Pete's grandmother was also born in Farringdon, she was the eldest daughter of Frank and Fanny Jackson and was known to the family as Alice. They lived at Hill Barn Cottages, Knighton, where some of her siblings were born.

Kenneth George Higgs married Patricia Irene Burfitt in March 1955 at Newbury Register Office, Berkshire. Kenneth was a farm labourer at Maddle Farm, Upper Lambourn, when the couple married. Patricia was the daughter of Frank Burfitt, a licensed victualler.

Peter David Higgs was born on 7 October 1958. Pete was the middle child with an older brother and a younger sister. The family moved to Ashbury, near Oxford, where at one time Pete's father, Ken 'Stump' Higgs worked at Manor Farm.

Pete served in the Army Cadet Force at Shrivenham Detachment No 4 Area, Berkshire, he is remembered by his former Sergeant Major Instructor as a 'serious minded cadet' who was born to be a soldier.

According to official records Pete was in the 1st Division Regiment, Royal Corps of Transport, prior to joining The Parachute Regiment. After passing his training and earning the coveted Maroon Beret, Lance Corporal Peter David Higgs served with D/Patrol Company during the Falklands War. He was sadly killed during the battle for Mount Longdon on 12 June 1982.

Pete is remembered on the War Memorial in Ashbury, Oxfordshire, at the centre of the village.

Pete is now buried in Tidworth Military Cemetery in Wiltshire where 3 Para were stationed before they deployed 'Down South' on the *Canberra*.

Pete's dad Ken died on 27 June 1998 at the Age of 65, he is remembered alongside his son in Tidworth.

In 2022, as part of the Falkland Islands 40th Anniversary Place Names Project, Pete was honoured with 'Higgs Creek', a shallow enclosed creek at the shallow end of Grantham Sound between Port Sussex and Brenton Loch, East Falkland.

His name lives on…

D146866M Air Engineering Mechanic (Radio) 1 Brian Peter Hinge HMS *Glamorgan* 23 January 1958 ~ 12 June 1982 Age 24

Brian Peter Hinge senior was born in Bath in 1933, many years later he settled close by in Bristol with his wife Catherine.

Going back generations the family hailed from Bath. Brian's grandfather, William Edwin Hinge, began his service life as a Boy Sailor on 21 August 1913, serving with HMS *Impregnable* until June 1914. William then joined the British Army; he served for many years in India.

William served with the Indian Army Ordnance Corps; he married his wife Evelyn Maria in India in 1924. William stayed in India for some years, although son Brian Peter was born in England. He is mentioned in the *London Gazette* with a promotion in November 1941.

Brian Peter Hinge was named after his father, literally. He was born on 23 January 1958 in Warrington, Cheshire. Catherine and Brian went on to have two more daughters born at different locations as the family moved around during Brian senior's service in the army. The family eventually settled close to the Hinge family roots.

Brian junior joined the Cadet unit TS *Endeavour* in Bristol and was a regular there until he left school. After attending Saint Bernadette's Secondary School from 1969 to 1974, Brian joined the Royal Navy in 1974.

Brian started out at HMS *Ganges*, where he passed out as JEM(A)2 in December 1974. Next came HMS *Daedalus* followed by HMS *Osprey* until April 1977. Brian then saw service in HMS *Ark Royal* as REM(A)1 seeing out her last commission. He was stationed at HMS *Osprey* and HMS *Daedalus*; he attained the grade of AEM(R)1.

Brian's last posting was HMS *Glamorgan*, he joined the ship in October 1981. Brian was sadly killed when an Exocet missile hit the ship on 12 June 1982.

Brian is remembered at Saint Bernadette's School where a memorial plaque, consisting of both school and *Glamorgan* crests, has been placed in the entrance hall. There are further memorial plaques at Saint Bernadette's R.C. Church and on the Quarter Deck of TS *Endeavour*.

There is a plaque in St Bartholomew's Church, Yeovilton where Brian is also remembered with nineteen other men killed in the Falklands. The inscription reads 'TO THE GLORY OF GOD AND IN MEMORY OF THE OFFICERS AND MEN OF THE FLEET AIR ARM OF THE ROYAL NAVY WHO GAVE THEIR LIVES IN THE CAUSE OF FREEDOM IN THE FALKLAND ISLANDS AND SOUTH ATLANTIC 1982', followed by their names, and ending 'ALL OF ONE COMPANY'.

In 2022, as part of the Falkland Islands 40th Anniversary Place Names Project, Brian was honoured with 'Hinge Bay', a bay between Blake Inlet and Cattle Point on the east shore of Bay of Harbours, East Falkland.

His name lives on…

24513050 Private Mark Holman-Smith 2nd Battalion Parachute Regiment 9 March 1963 ~ 28 May 1982 Age 19

Mark Holman-Smith was born in Manchester on 9 March 1963 to David and Carole Holman-Smith (née Morris). The family moved from Manchester to Bodmin when Mark was very small; his sister Jane was born when he was 3 years old. Mark's family remained settled in Cornwall.

Mark joined The Parachute Regiment when he was 16 via Junior Leaders, he became known from there on as either 'Smudge', or latterly as 'MHS' by comrades. Smudge was a character by all accounts, most men who pass P Coy and don a Maroon beret are. On 29 July 1981, as a young 18-year-old soldier, he was part of the Guard of Honour for Prince Charles and Diana's wedding.

Smudge was known for being a good laugh. He loved chicken, and would order sweet and sour chicken from the Chinese after a night out – but without the sauce. He loved fried chicken too, and thought he looked like Paul Newman. He told his friend Sparky when they met up at a friend's wedding in early 1982 to get his hair cut and join back up. They enjoyed many a night out together. He loved a good night out with his mates at the Queen Hotel or the Trafalgar Inn in Aldershot.

Smudge was in Sigs Platoon, HQ Coy, attached to C Company during Operation Corporate. He was one of many young men who came off the landing crafts into freezing water at San Carlos. From there 2 Para had a tough tab to Sussex Mountain over 'unforgiving terrain', making it slow progress with approximately 130lbs of gear on their backs. Then it was on to Camilla Creek House.

On 28 May 1982, Smudge was killed by Oerlikon fire from the airfield at Goose Green while moving forward to recover a GPMG from a wounded Recce Platoon soldier, Private Stevie Russell, as the company advanced down a forward slope towards the schoolhouse.

Sister Jane says:

> He loved fly fishing. He used to skip school to fish at Dunmere river. We had a large collie-cross Irish wolfhound called Mutley who he would take running when he was home on leave. Loved the Fonz and until he was recruited used to have a 'ducks ass' hairstyle that took ages to 'gel' into place.

Mark is buried at San Carlos Military Cemetery, Falkland Islands; he is also remembered on the Bodmin War Memorial.

In 2022, as part of the Falkland Islands 40th Anniversary Place Names Project, Mark was honoured with 'Holman-Smith Point', a prominent point between Cliff Point and East Point on the East Coast of Saunders Island, West Falkland.

His name lives on…

Radio Officer Ronald Hoole Royal Fleet Auxiliary SS *Atlantic Conveyor* 18 December 1944 ~ 25 May 1982 Age 37

The Hoole family had a long connection with the Mansfield area of Nottinghamshire, though it appears Thomas Hoole, Ron's paternal grandfather, moved there from Lincolnshire.

Thomas Hoole married Harriet Ashley in 1901; the Hoole family settled in Sutton in Ashfield, a mining community in Nottinghamshire. Sadly, by early 1911, after ten years of marriage, Thomas had died, leaving his widow Harriet with four young children, including one set of twins. Ron's father, John Thomas, was the youngest of their children born in 1906.

Ron's maternal grandfather, Joseph Bertie Swain, was also a miner who lived in Sutton in Ashfield. JB married his bride Sarah in 1899. Ron's mother Rebecca was their youngest daughter. JB died in 1924 which left Ron without both grandfathers.

Ron's parents John Thomas Hoole and Rebecca Swain married in 1928. Ron was the youngest of four children born on 18 December 1944. Ron had two surviving siblings John and Terry.

Ron attended Forest Glade Primary School in Sutton-in-Ashfield, finishing his secondary school education at Eastbourne School, formerly known as Sutton Girl's Grammar. Following on from his schooldays, Ron studied Radio and Radar at Hull Technical College, after which he became a lecturer at the Radio College in Colwyn Bay, Wales.

As a young man Ron helped run the local Church Youth Club in Sutton in Ashfield. He enjoyed football and rugby; he played rugby for Hull College. Ron's other interests were following Nottingham Forest FC and riding his motorbike.

When the Radio College closed Ron joined the Royal Fleet Auxiliary in 1970, training at HMS *Collingwood*. By 1982, when the Falklands War erupted, Ron was Radio Officer aboard the SS *Atlantic Conveyor*. On 25 May 1982, Ron died when the *Atlantic Conveyor* was hit by an Exocet missile.

At the time of his death Ron was unmarried and lived in North End, Wirksworth, Derbyshire. His father John had died in 1978, his mother Rebecca in 1972.

In 2022, as part of the Falkland Islands 40th Anniversary Place Names Project, Ron was honoured with 'Hoole Islet', a small tussac islet south of Whale Island in Port Edgar, West Falkland.

His name lives on…

24277543 Corporal Stephen Hope 3rd Battalion Parachute Regiment 15 September 1954 ~ 13 June 1982 Age 27

Stephen Hope was born on 15 September 1954 at Crumpsall Hospital in Manchester. Stevie was the second to youngest son of Robert and Nellie Hope (née Entwistle). Robert married Nellie, a widow, in 1946. Stevie had two older sisters Joan and Ann, one older brother, Robert, and a younger brother, Billy. Ann was known to the family as 'Queenie'. Both Stevie's brothers also served in the Armed Forces.

At the time of Stevie's birth, the family lived in Nicholson Street; Stevie's father Robert was a furnaceman at an iron foundry. The family later settled in nearby Heywood. Stevie attended Sutherland High School, now Heywood Community School.

In April 1982, Stevie was serving with Signals Platoon, 3 Para, and travelled 'Down South' on the *Canberra*. His nickname was 'Gripper'. Stevie was injured in the Battle for Mount Longdon and later died of his injuries on the SS *Uganda* Hospital Ship on 13 June 1982.

Stevie's niece Jakki says of her uncle:

> He was the most loving caring uncle ever. When he used to come home on leave, he always used to visit us and take us to the little toy shop near our house and buy us anything we wanted, we used to get so excited when we knew he was coming. I always say he's my hero. My daughter is 27 now, the age he died and it's absolutely tragic to think he died so young and on the eve of surrender.

Jakki was just 9 years old when Stevie died. Stevie was eventually added to the local Memorial in Heywood. Jakki and her family attend every year to lay a wreath and remember him.

Stevie was repatriated and is now buried in Aldershot Military Cemetery. At the time of his death Stevie was unmarried but like many others, he had a girlfriend.

In 2022, as part of the Falkland Islands 40th Anniversary Place Names Project, Stevie was honoured with 'Hope Islet', a tussac island east of Middle Island in Choiseul Sound, East Falkland.

His name lives on…

24555311 Guardsman Denis Neil Hughes 1st Battalion Welsh Guards 26 February 1960 ~ 8 June 1982 Age 22

Denis 'Neil' Hughes was born on 26 February 1960 in Wrexham, Denbighshire, to Raymond and Patricia Hughes (née Williscroft), who married in 1958. Known as Neil, he was the couple's eldest son and one of four boys.

On his maternal side Neil's mother was also an eldest child. Her parents, Thomas and Gwendoline Roberts, were married in Denbighshire in 1939. Patricia was the eldest of five children. It appears, going back another generation, the Williscroft family were from Lichfield, Staffordshire.

Neil grew up in Wales, attending Rhostyllen Primary School followed by Ysgol Bryn Offa. Neil joined the Welsh Guards when he was 20 years old, it is customary with the Guards that those with the same surname were known by the last two digits of their Army number ergo Neil was known as 11. Neil enjoyed weightlifting, was very fit and is remembered as being a good guy who was full of life.

When the RFA *Sir Galahad* was bombed at Fitzroy on 8 June 1982, out of four friends Neil, Gareth, Yorkie and Simon, only one of them survived that awful day.

Neil's mother received the Elizabeth Cross in 2010 in honour of the loss of her son.

One of his nephews, Shane Hughes, took part in the 'Walk on Wales', a team walked 870 miles along the coastal path of Wales carrying a silver baton, inscribed with the names of the fifty Welsh Guardsmen who have lost their lives in armed conflict since the Second World War. During the walk, the date of 7 September 2013 was dedicated to Neil.

Neil's father Raymond died in 1998, his mother Patricia in 2021.

In 2022, as part of the Falkland Islands 40th Anniversary Place Names Project, Neil was honoured with 'Hughes Bay', a bay on the west side of Chatham Harbour next to the site for Chatham House on Weddell Island, West Falkland.

His name lives on…

24400658 Guardsman Gareth Hughes 1st Battalion Welsh Guards 12 May 1960 ~ 8 June 1982 Age 22

Gareth Hughes was born on 12 May 1960 to Edwin and Morwenna Hughes (née Jones). His large Welsh speaking family lived in Llanfairfechan (Little St Mary's), a small village in North Wales. Gareth was the second born of six children, having an older brother, Stephen, and younger siblings Dafydd, Ceri, Emlyn and Geraint.

Gareth first attended Ysgol Babanod Infants School followed by Pant y Rhedyn School in Llanfairfechan, later he finished school at Ysgol Tryfan in Bangor. Gareth joined the Welsh Guards after leaving school in 1976, as a junior soldier. Gareth's father Edwin had served with the South Wales Borderers, and his brother Stephen served in the Royal Welsh Fusiliers. Gareth and his brothers loved a game of football.

Gareth is remembered as a very outgoing lad who brought his younger brothers gifts when he came home on leave, he also kept up his fitness by running around the mountains when at home.

Gareth served in Berlin 1977–79, he performed ceremonial duties in London and Windsor. His battalion went on training exercises to Canada and Kenya, he also served in Northern Ireland.

There were to be five men from the same village that would serve in the Falklands War and one of them was Gareth's childhood best friend David Jones, who was serving with the 2nd Battalion Parachute Regiment. Gareth's sister Ceri and his best friend went on to marry in 1983.

In May 1982, Gareth sailed from Southampton on the QE2. The Welsh Guards were part of the 5th Infantry Brigade, sent to reinforce 3 Commando Brigade in the Falklands War. On 8 June 1982, having been transferred to the RFA *Sir Galahad*, Gareth was killed when the ship was bombed at Fitzroy. He was lost to the sea with all his fellow Guards who died that day.

Sadly, Gareth's father Edwin died in 1985 at the age of 52.

In 2022, as part of the Falkland Islands 40th Anniversary Place Names Project, Gareth was honoured with 'Hughes Pass', a passage between Pebble Island and Pebble Islet, West Falkland.

His name lives on…

Mechanic James Hughes Merchant Navy SS *Atlantic Conveyor* 29 May 1934 ~ 25 May 1982 Age 47

James Hughes was born in Killyleagh, Co Down, Northern Ireland, on 29 May 1934. He was one of four children born to John and Ena Hughes. The children were named James, Karl, Joseph and Janet.

Valerie Evelyn Rosine Hayward was born in Portsmouth, the eldest daughter of Leslie and Lily Hayward (née Palmer), who married in 1935. The couple had a son also called Leslie, born in 1936. Tragedy struck when Leslie fell into the fountain in Victoria Park and drowned, he was just 6 years old.

Valerie was then left as the oldest of three girls, her sisters were Mary and Dorothy.

James Hughes grew up and was schooled in Killyleagh, and though he did not particularly excel at sport he did have an ambition to join the services. James was known as Jim; he joined the Royal Navy on 12 February 1957 and served until 16 January 1969.

Two years into his service he and Val married on 4 April 1959 in Gosport. The couple had five children, all girls. Debbie, their eldest, was born on 6 January 1960 in Blakes Maternity Home. She was followed closely by Tina, Mandy, Karen and Lucene; by 1969 the Hughes family was complete. All the children were born in Hampshire apart from Mandy, who was born in Gibraltar on 8 August 1962.

When Jim left the Royal Navy, he continued to serve in the Merchant Navy. Jim was a Chief Petty Officer 2nd class and a Mechanic on the SS *Atlantic Conveyor*.

Tragedy had already struck twice in the family, Jim's brother Karl also drowned. When Jim was killed aboard the *Atlantic Conveyor* and his body not recovered, it was something his mother Ena was unable to recover from.

The year before Jim died, Lucene was lucky enough to spend six months with her mother and father when he was working on the container ship *Act 6* travelling to America, Australia, New Zealand and many other places. Lucene and her mother got off in America before flying home, Jim joined them at Christmas that year. Dave Hawkins, who also died on the *Atlantic Conveyor*, was a steward in the Officers' Mess at the time and Lucene remembers him giving her left over biscuits as treats.

Jim died just four days short of his 48th birthday, he left behind a widow and his girls; Lucene was just 13 years old. During the time he was away she says she felt 'Panic, as every time a ship was hit you worried, then of course after the news it was sadness.'

Afterwards she says 'The war was needed to give the islanders their independence. I am proud my dad served for his country.'

Lucene says about Jim, 'Dad was a kind, caring, friendly person. He lived for his job and loved being at sea. He never said a bad word about anyone. He was a loving husband and father. He always put his family first.'

Lucene received the Elizabeth Cross in 2012 in a ceremony at Pangbourne, she saw out her days in Northern Ireland, not far from Belfast. She had one set of fraternal twins.

In November 2019, Lucene visited the Falkland Islands for the first time. For many that visit brings them full circle. Lucene buried two of her sisters and her mother; sadly, Lucene herself has since passed away on 15 September 2021.

Jim is remembered on the family grave in Killyleagh where his mother is buried. He is also included on the Killyleagh War Memorial.

In 2022, as part of the Falkland Islands 40th Anniversary Place Names Project, Jim was honoured with 'Hughes Point', a point at the west end of Brookfield Farm in Port Salvador, East Falkland on the south side of the entrance to Dan's Shanty Creek.

His name lives on…

24076141 Sergeant William John Hughes 22 SAS Regiment
23 August 1947 ~ 19 May 1982 Age 34

William John Hughes was born at the County Hospital in Bangor, North Wales, on 23 August 1947 to John Pritchard and Elizabeth Annie Hughes (née Cruickshank) who married in Pwllheli in 1946. At the time of his birth his parents lived in Fron Dirion, Llanbedrog. Taff, as he was known, had two brothers and one sister. Taff attended Bryncroes School followed by Ysgol Botwnog High School, both schools in Gwynedd.

Like many Welshmen before him, Taff joined the British Army, specifically the Welsh Guards. One of his brothers also served in the Welsh Guards.

Taff married in Pwllheli, Caernarvonshire, in 1971; he joined the elite SAS Regiment the following year in October 1972. By the time the Falkland Islands were invaded in 1982, Taff was the SQMS of G Squadron.

On the fateful day of 19 May 1982, the Sea King helicopter carrying many of our SAS men went down, Taff was one of the men killed that day.

Taff is remembered on all of the main memorials for the Falklands War and at St Martins Churchyard, Hereford. He is also commemorated by a plaque on the War Memorial in Pwllheli which reads simply:

'SOUTH ATLANTIC 1982

HUGHES W J SAS'

In Falklands Way, Allied Forces Memorial Grove, there is a bench with a beautiful plaque dedicated to Taff. It reads:

'William John "Taff" Hughes
  SQMS "G" Squadron 22 SAS Regiment & Welsh Guards
  1947~1982 Age 34
  Lost in the Sea King helicopter crash 19th May 1982
  Rest In Peace on this seat and remember those that helped bring
"Freedom from the Sea" for the people of the Falkland Islands
  Taff is not forgotten by his family Michael, Kathryn, and Kevin
~ 23 August 2015
  Falklands Memorial Way ~ Allied Special Forces Grove'

A beautiful tribute from his three siblings. Taff also left behind a widow and two children.

In 2022, as part of the Falkland Islands 40th Anniversary Place Names Project, Taff was honoured with 'Hughes Pond', a pond near the San Carlos Freshwater River, East Falkland.

His name lives on…

P030085W Sergeant Ian Nicholas Hunt Special Boat Service Royal Marines 1 December 1953 ~ 2 June 1982 Age 28

Ian Nicholas Hunt was born on 1 December 1953 in the Willesborough Hospital, Ashford, Kent. He appears to be the eldest son of Hutchinson Edward Dalby Hunt and Annie Emily Clara Bent, who married in Ashford Kent in 1947. Ian had a sister, born six years later. Hutchinson was a lorry driver for haulage contractors at the time of Ian's birth, the family lived in East Stour, Ashford.

The name Hutchinson goes back several generations within the Hunt family.

Hutchinson Dalby Hunt was born circa 1814, he married Matilda Ann Ashby in London in 1860, they lived for many years in the Uppingham area of Northamptonshire. Hutchinson was a farmer and landowner and lived to the ripe old age of 91, he died in February 1906. After Hutchinson's death, records indicate that Matilda went to live with her daughter Helen and family, she died in 1915, aged 88.

Hutchinson Edward Dalby Hunt was born in 1863, and was baptised in September 1865 in Caldecott. Hutchinson married Emma Ethel Evans in 1895, their eldest son, also Hutchinson, was born in August 1897. Hutchinson Junior was a driver with the Army Service Corps, enlisting in Mill Hill London on 11 September 1916.

Hutchinson Jr married Lilian May Lassetter in 1918, the couple's eldest son was Ian's father. In 1921, the family lived in Portslade-By-Sea.

Hutchinson remarried to Louie Justine Violet Grainger in 1939, the family later lived in Coventry. Hutchinson, known as Edward, died in 1977. Records suggest that Ian's father was one of six boys and after the remarriage he acquired four step-siblings. Ian's Uncle Vernon served in the Royal Air Force during the Second World War; he died in 1994.

The Hunt family settled in Ashford where Ian's father, also Hutchinson, died in 1971.

Ian is thought to have lived in New Zealand, and so acquired the nickname 'Kiwi', but at the time of his death his home on land was Poole, Dorset.

Ian was a member of the Special Boat Service during the Falklands War; he was sadly killed in a 'blue on blue' incident with an SAS Patrol. Ian married in 1977, it is thought he had one son. He is buried at St Michael's Parish Church, Hamworthy, Poole, Dorset. Every year there is a memorial service for this brave man.

In 2022, as part of the Falkland Islands 40th Anniversary Place Names Project, Ian, known as Kiwi, was honoured with 'Kiwi Creek', a long inlet south of Brasse Mar at the southeast end of Port Salvador, East Falkland. Kiwi Creek is at the place where Ian was killed.

His name lives on...

24579367 Private Stephen Illingsworth DCM 2nd Battalion Parachute Regiment 25 April 1962 ~ 28 May 1982 Age 20

Stephen ('Steve') Thomas Illingsworth was born on 25 April 1962 in Durham; historically, the family had connections with both Yorkshire and Tyneside.

Going back a few generations the family came from a mining background. In those days children often did not finish their education, needing to work from an early age. Steve's great-great-grandfather, Sam, was working in the mines at the tender age of 11. Sam married Mary in 1871 in Tynemouth, the couple had a large family, their oldest son, Philip, was born in 1873.

Philip married Isabella Gray in 1895, their eldest son, Thomas Gray Illingsworth, was born in late 1897. By the turn of the century the family were living at Ushaw Colliery in Durham, just a few years before the First World War. During the First World War, Thomas Gray Illingsworth served as a Private with the Northumberland Fusiliers, he is listed as wounded in 1918.

Thomas Gray Illingsworth married Margaret in 1922, the couple started a family the following year. Their son, Gordon Gray, was born on 3 April 1931. Thomas was back working at the colliery as the Second World War broke out.

Gordon Gray Illingsworth (Steve's father) married Joyce Kirtlan in Sunderland in 1960. The family subsequently settled in Doncaster. Joyce was born in Sunderland in 1935. Brought up in Doncaster, Steve attended Edlington Comprehensive school, a place that still honours his name yearly with the 'Stephen Illingsworth Memorial Cup' for those who have demonstrated exceptional achievement in sport.

Steve's mother is reported as saying that he wanted to become a paratrooper to be among the elite; even as a child he had wanted to jump out of an aeroplane. After he became a paratrooper, he would go to Bridlington to jump when he was home on leave. For sure these Sky Gods enjoy the thrill.

Illie, as he became known, joined the army at 18 and thrived with his new Elite Band of Brothers known as the Maroon Machines. When the Falklands were invaded, the 'Reg' sent two battalions 'Down South', at the time Steve was serving in 5 Platoon, B Company, 2 Para.

Steve's 20th birthday was celebrated just the day before 2 Para set sail on the MV *Norland* for the long voyage. Many had hoped for a diplomatic solution before they so much as set foot on land, but for those young men who had joined the Task Force, who had trained for it, many were excited. Illie was one of them, as his mother remembered him always wanting to be where the action was, a young man excited about going to war.

As dawn broke on 28 May 1982, B Company was pinned down on a forward slope by an Argentine position at Boca House – the same time that A Company was pinned down from Darwin Hill. Private Illingsworth reached safety but then returned to assist in dragging a wounded comrade, Private Hall, into dead ground.

As the Platoon began to run short of ammunition, Private Illingsworth went forward into enemy fire to attempt to retrieve ammunition left on the forward slope. As he crawled forward, he was killed by small arms fire.

Illie was posthumously awarded the Distinguished Conduct Medal, his citation reads:

> '*In these two acts of supreme courage Private Illingsworth showed a complete disregard for his own safety, and a total dedication to others. While his action in coming to the help of a wounded soldier may have been almost instinctive on seeing the plight of a comrade, his move forward to collect much needed ammunition for his beleaguered platoon was a display of coolly calculated courage and heroism of the very highest order.*'

Courage and dedication to his Brothers in Arms, desperate for that ammunition as they were so outnumbered, so up against it and yet won the Battle of Goose Green 'Against all Odds'.

Illie is buried in Aldershot Military Cemetery.

Steve is also remembered with a road in the Falklands called Illingworth Road dedicated to him. The novel *Close Quarter Battles*, by former paratrooper colleague and ex-SAS soldier, Mike Curtis, is also dedicated to the young Doncaster soldier.

Steve's mum Joyce remembered him quietly every year by lighting a candle for him.

Steve had one younger sister Julie. Gordon died in 2003.

In 2022, as part of the Falkland Islands 40th Anniversary Place Names Project, Steve was honoured with 'Illingsworth Rock', a prominent unvegetated offshore rock just west of McBride Head, East Falkland.

His name lives on…

D098624T Chief Petty Officer Marine Engineering Artificer (Propulsion) Alexander Stuart James HMS *Fearless* 23 November 1949 ~ 8 June 1982 Age 32

Alexander Stuart James was born in Exmouth, Devon, on 23 November 1949, the son of William Henry and Jean Stuart James (née McGahey), who married in Partick, Scotland, in 1947. By the time Alexander was born the family had settled in Exmouth, where they lived for many years in Salisbury Road. Alex had one sister, Anne.

Alex attended Exeter Road Infants and Junior School, followed by Exmouth Secondary School for Boys. Alex also joined the Sea Cadets when he was 11/12 years old.

Alex was known as Jesse; he married his wife Yvonne in Portsmouth in 1973. The couple had three children, two girls and a boy.

By April 1982, Jesse was a Chief Petty Officer on board HMS *Fearless*, having served for some years in the Royal Navy. Jesse is remembered by a former shipmate as a man who loved rugby, a great character, and a gentle giant.

Jesse was killed on 8 June 1982 when the landing craft Utility Foxtrot Four from HMS *Fearless* was attacked and sunk by Argentine aircraft in Choiseul Sound. All six crew were killed in the attack. The landing craft had been working hard to rescue others in the weeks prior to the attack.

Both Jesse's parents lived into old age, both dying in 2011. Jesse's mother Jean died in February 2011 aged 93, William died later that year in December, aged 90. Sadly, they did not live until the 30th Anniversary when Jesse's name was added to the Exmouth War Memorial in Strand Gardens. Jesse's widow Yvonne was in attendance for the service, two of his grandchildren laid a wreath during the dedication service. In Jesse's case it was said that he was left off the War Memorial because the MOD had stated that he was from Portsmouth.

In 2022, as part of the Falkland Islands 40th Anniversary Place Names Project, Jesse was honoured with 'James Bay', a bay north of Saturday Island near the head of Adventure Sound, East Falkland.

His name lives on…

24339321 Guardsman Brian Jasper 1st Battalion Welsh Guards 20 July 1955 ~ 8 June 1982 Age 26

According to some records Brian Jasper was born on 21 July 1955, but in fact his birth certificate states 20 July 1955. Brian was born in the East Glamorgan hospital, Church Village, near Pontypridd, to Gladys Edna Jasper. Edna lived in Popular Road, Rhydyfelin, and unusually for the times Edna was a single parent.

Edna was the middle child of five children born to Wyndham and Margaret Jasper (née Howells). Edna was born on 21 July 1923, perhaps that is why his birthday is listed so, to be the same day as his mother.

Brian joined the Welsh Guards in the 1970s, he married Andrea Ellis in Pontypridd in 1975, and the couple had two daughters. Their eldest daughter, Helen, was born in Pontypridd. During his time with the Welsh Guards Brian was stationed in Berlin for two years, where youngest daughter Cathy was born.

Brian was killed on the RFA *Sir Galahad* on 8 June 1982 when it was bombed in Fitzroy. Brian rests along with his ship, which was scuttled as a War Grave on 25 June 1982.

Brian's mother Edna Gladys Jasper died in 2004 at the age of 81, she was still living in the Rhondda.

Brian is remembered as funny and mischievous.

In 2022, as part of the Falkland Islands 40th Anniversary Place Names Project, Brian was honoured with 'Jasper Rocks', prominent rocks west of Mount Low, East Falkland.

His name lives on…

24579020 Private Timothy Richard Jenkins 3rd Battalion Parachute Regiment 10 December 1962 ~ 12 June 1982 Age 19

Timothy Richard Jenkins was born in Ross-on-Wye on 10 December 1962. Timmy, as he was known to his family, was the third child born to John and Irene Ann Jenkins (née Fluck). Irene was known as 'Queenie', the couple married in 1959. Eldest son Martin was followed by a daughter; Timmy was born three years later, he also had one younger sister.

Timmy loved football, at the age of 12 he was the youngest qualified football referee. He was a popular lad with friends who remembered him fondly from school, football and the cadets. Timmy was very proud of his Ross roots, where he had been born and raised; he was proud of his heritage.

Joining the British Army at the age of 17, he was following in his father's footsteps. John had also served in The Parachute Regiment in the 1950s. Timmy passed P Coy, he was sent to 2 Platoon A Coy 3 Para where he fitted in well, he was known as either Tim or 'Jenks' to his mates. He is remembered by a friend as a 'cheeky Chappy, who always had a smile and spoke with a strong Ross accent'.

Tim did one tour of Northern Ireland in his brief time with 3 Para, after that tour he made his dad promise to bring his body home should anything ever happen to him, a promise that was later fulfilled.

3 Para were tasked with taking Mount Longdon where Argentinian troops were firmly bedded in. Tim was one of the young lads who didn't survive the battle, he died on 12 June 1982. Just as the family were about to celebrate the ending of the war, they got that awful 'knock on the door'.

John, of course fought, with many of the bereaved, to have the right to repatriate his son's body. Some newspaper accounts are however inaccurate; no bodies were 'flown home', that is something that is available now because of the families who changed history in 1982. Our men that year were brought home by ship, in lead caskets.

Tim's coffin was taken by gun carriage back home to Tudorville, where he is buried in the Tudorville Cemetery in Ross-on-Wye. He was given a full military funeral, surrounded by his friends and family. Another tragedy followed when Tim's mother died on 27 June 1985.

In 2002, for the 20th Anniversary, a good friend of Tim's made a pilgrimage back to the Falklands with other veterans; while there he set up a memorial on the spot where Tim had been killed on the approach to Mount Longdon. His friend found the depression and some link cartridges as well as a bog, with these markers, he was able to identify where Tim had died. He gathered some rocks and placed lovingly the plaque he had brought to make a special memorial for his young friend.

Ten years after the first trip, the same friend who had made the memorial in 2002, went back to the Falklands in 2012 with Tim's father John, his second wife Jean, and three other veterans from 3 Para. They were able to take John to see where his son died, John died later that year in November.

In 2018 a metal bench was unveiled in Ross-on-Wye which pays tribute to Tim and two other men from the town who were killed in the Falklands War.

Tim is not the only family member who is remembered by the Commonwealth War Graves Commission. On his mother's side, Great-uncle Sidney George Fluck served with the Royal Navy prior to and during the First World War. In 1901, Sidney was serving with HMS *Jupiter*, a 1st Class Battleship in Gibraltar. Sidney died of disease while serving as an Able Seaman with HMS *Pembroke* in March 1915. Sidney was the son of Charles and Hannah Fluck of Ross, he left behind a widow Edith Mary of Middle Stoke, Rochester, Kent. Sidney is Commemorated at New Cemetery, Gillingham, Kent.

In 2022, as part of the Falkland Islands 40th Anniversary Place Names Project, Tim was honoured with 'Jenkins Point', a point on the south coast of Dyke Island, West Falkland.

His name lives on…

P023116X Colour Sergeant Brian Ronald Johnston QGM
3 Commando Brigade Royal Marines HMS *Fearless* 9 June 1948 ~
8 June 1982 Age 33

Brian Ronald Johnston was born in Carrickfergus on 9 June 1948. Brian grew up in the large seaside town near Belfast, joining the Royal Marines as a teenager.

During the Falklands War, Brian was an Acting Colour Sergeant with 3 Commando Brigade Royal Marines on HMS *Fearless*. He was coxswain of the Landing Craft Utility F4 and had been instrumental in saving over 100 survivors from HMS *Antelope*. For his actions that day he received a posthumous QGM.

On 8 June 1982, the British Army's 5 Brigade separated from their vital communications vehicles back at Goose Green. F4 under the command of Colour Sergeant Brian Johnston had been dispatched in poorly charted waters, under significant threat of air attack. In a remarkable feat of pilotage, in darkness and without modern navigational aids, Brian Johnston reached Goose Green and loaded the vehicles.

Shortly afterwards, the landing craft was bombed and sunk by Argentine Skyhawks in Choiseul Sound. During this action Brian was killed with most of his crew. He died the day before his 34th birthday.

Citation

MONDAY, 11th OCTOBER 1982

The QUEEN has been graciously pleased to approve the Posthumous award of the Queen's Gallantry Medal to the undermentioned in recognition of gallant and distinguished service during the operations in the South Atlantic:

Acting Colour Sergeant Brian JOHNSTON, Royal Marines, PO23116X

Colour Sergeant Johnston, coxswain of LCU F4 was working in the vicinity of HMS ANTELOPE when her unexploded bomb detonated, starting an immediate fire which caused her crew, already at emergency stations, to be ordered to abandon ship. Without hesitation Colour Sergeant Johnston laid his craft alongside the ANTELOPE and began to fight the fire and take off survivors. At approximately 2200Z he was ordered to stay clear of the ship because of the severity of the fire and the presence of a second unexploded bomb. Colour Sergeant Johnston remained alongside until his load was complete. In all LCU F4 rescued over 100 survivors from the ANTELOPE.

Brian was married to second wife Evelyn; his son Neil was 8 years old when his father died. Evelyn was presented with the Queens Gallantry Medal in a ceremony at Buckingham Palace on 23 November 1982. Earlier that year the family received a moving letter from the Captain of HMS *Fearless*, Jeremy Larkin.

Brian had previously served in both Northern Ireland and South Arabia.

Brian was one of five children; sister Patricia was the only one remaining in their native Northern Ireland. Brian's father John, his wife Esther, and siblings John, Quinr and Margaret had relocated to Canada by 1982.

In 2022, as part of the Falkland Islands 40th Anniversary Place Names Project, Brian was honoured with 'Johnston Islet', a small island 400 metres north east of Scott Island in Choiseul Sound, East Falkland.

His name lives on…

24484389 Sapper Christopher Alan Jones 59 Independent Commando Squadron Royal Engineers 21 August 1962 ~ 12 June 1982 Age 19

Christopher was the only son of Stanley and Evelyn Jones (née Jackson) who married in the Forest of Dean in 1959. Chris was born in Cinderford, Gloucestershire, on 21 August 1962, the middle of three children.

Historically within his family there had been service in the RAF, Army and Royal Marines through various relatives.

Chris attended St Anthony's School from 1966 to 1973, followed by the Double View Secondary until 1978. He was a Cub during his junior years, he was also a member of the Army Cadets. Chris represented his school at rugby, cricket and cross-country. His other interests included fishing and swimming, and he played cricket for a local club.

Chris joined the army in September 1978 at the Army Apprentices College, Chepstow. He then went to the Royal Engineers at Chatham and volunteered for Commando training with the Royal Marines. Commando training completed; he was posted to 59 Independent Commando Squadron in Plymouth.

Chris landed in the Falkland Islands on 21 May 1982, at Red Beach, San Carlos Water, having travelled 'Down South' attached to 45 Commando Royal Marines. After the long 'Yomp' across East Falkland he finally arrived at 45 Commando's objective, a feature called Two Sisters. Chris was killed with three other Royal Marines, dying of his wounds on 12 June 1982. He was temporarily interred at Teal Inlet. He is now buried at Yew Tree Brake Cemetery in Cinderford, Gloucestershire.

In 2022, as part of the Falkland Islands 40th Anniversary Place Names Project, Chris was honoured with 'Jones Point', the northern point of First Passage in the Passage Islands group, West Falkland.

His name lives on…

24496627 Private Craig Everard Jones 3rd Battalion Parachute Regiment 14 December 1961 ~ 13 June 1982 Age 20

Richard Jones and Pamela Wain married in Derbyshire in 1960. Craig Everard Jones was their eldest son, born on 14 December 1961 in Northampton. Younger son Gareth was born three years later.

Craig spent some of his childhood in Limassol, Cyprus. Back in England, Craig was schooled in Hanslope, Buckinghamshire, and the Northampton School for Boys. He then completed his education at The Campion School, Bugbrooke, Northants.

Craig first joined the Royal Anglian Regiment TA, based at the Drill Hall in Northampton when he was 17 years old. Craig loved rugby, he played for Campion School and the Bugbrooke Rugby Club. After finishing school, he applied to The Parachute Regiment, as with all young recruits he had to earn his wings and his maroon beret. Craig transferred to the Intelligence Section after further training.

In April 1982, he travelled 'Down South' on the *Canberra* with 3 Para. A monumental tab followed after their landing at Green Beach, San Carlos. Craig was injured on Mount Longdon, he died from his wounds on 13 June 1982.

Craig was temporarily interred at Teal Inlet; his body was repatriated, and he now rests in Aldershot Military Cemetery.

A very small island in the Falklands, formerly known as Little Rabbit, has been renamed Craig Island, thirty years after his death his father made a pilgrimage to see the Island for the first time. There is a plaque in Craig's honour there which had a dedication service with a Military Padre during their visit.

Craig Island is a small island at the entrance to Long Creek towards the west end of Port Salvador, East Falkland.

His name lives on...

465788 Lieutenant Colonel Herbert Jones VC OBE 2nd Battalion Parachute Regiment 14 May 1940 ~ 28 May 1982 Age 42

William 'Herbert' Jones and Olwen Pritchard married in Lewes, Sussex, in 1934. Initially the couple made their home in London. Herbert was an American artist and author, born on 16 May 1888. Olwen Pritchard was born in North Wales on 6 January 1902. Married life prior to the birth of their first son was a small apartment in Charing Cross.

Herbert Jr was born on 14 May 1940 in Putney, London, just prior to his parents move to Devon, where they would remain settled for the rest of their days. They bought 'The Grange' in Kingswear, Devon, and moved as the Second World War was in full swing. Herbert was an American citizen, therefore not called to do his duty for England. He was 51 years old when the war broke out, but he still participated in the war effort with the Home Guard.

In February 1942 the couple's second son, Tim, was born, and in February 1945 their third son, Bill, arrived. All three children were born during the Second World War. It is hard to imagine how difficult life was through those years. Herbert was granted British citizenship finally in 1947.

Herbert was a wealthy man; the children were initially schooled at Tower House School in Dartmouth. Their father wanted the best for his children's education. Herbert Jr was known simply as 'H' by family and friends alike.

From the age of 8, H attended St Peter's Preparatory School in Seaford, Sussex. In September 1953, he went to Eton College, finishing his schooling at DLD College London. H graduated from the Military Academy in Sandhurst on 23 July 1960, initially commissioned to the Devon and Dorset Regiment as a 2nd Lieutenant. Sadly his father had died in 1957 at the age of 69, so never got to see H's passing out.

H seemed to like the 23rd, his next promotion to Lieutenant was on 23 January 1962, and then Captain on 23 July 1966. On 20th June 1964, H married Sara de Uphaugh in the New Forest. Sara already understood Army life, as both her father and Uncle Richard had been officers during the First World War.

Sarah and H welcomed their first son, David Francis H Jones, into the world in 1966, born in Aldershot and named after both grandfathers. Second son, Rupert Timothy H Jones, was born in April 1969 in Dusseldorf, Germany. Both boys followed in their father's footsteps, joining the Devon and Dorset's.

When H was promoted to Brigade Major, he was based at HQ 3rd Infantry Brigade in Northern Ireland, he was friends with Captain Robert Nairac. Nairac was abducted by the Provisional IRA and subsequently killed on 15 May 1977. H was responsible for the efforts to find his friend; in November of that year a man was charged with his murder. Interestingly, Nairac's killer was the son of an Englishman married to a woman from County Meath, the same place that Sara's parents married in 1931. Nairac was subsequently awarded the George Cross, his body was not found.

H was promoted to Lieutenant Colonel in June 1979, transferring to The Parachute Regiment in December 1979. H received his OBE in the New Year's honours list of 1981. In 1982 when the Falkland Islands were invaded, H was Commanding Officer of 2 Para. Though 3 para were the 'Spearhead Battalion', H was determined his men were going to war as well.

By 28 May 1982 there had been many losses, morale was getting low, winning seemingly impossible. Hungry, tired and cold, the men needed something to boost them. The Battle for Goose Green and Darwin did just that, it might have been a different story had it gone the other way.

[Authors Note: in a cruel twist of fate, I heard about H's death on the afternoon of 29 May. One of the wives ran out of her house screaming 'They're dead, they're dead, they're all dead.' An officer's wife had relayed information that 'Sunray was down', the assumption she made was that the whole battalion was lost as the CO is never in the frontline.]

H was awarded the VC for his actions. He was not killed outright, he died later of his wounds, but not before Lieutenant Richard Nunn DFC was killed in an attempt to CASEVAC H.

H Jones Road was named after him in Port Stanley. H is buried in San Carlos Military Cemetery.

His name lives on…

24398540 Private Michael Anthony Jones Army Catering Corps
17 September 1959 ~ 8 June 1982 Age 22

Michael Anthony Jones was born 17 September 1959 in Carmarthen, Wales. Michael, it appears, grew up in Carmarthen and attended Carmarthen Grammar School.

Michael is one of three men from Carmarthen who died in the Falklands War, their names appear on the Carmarthen War Memorial, St Peter's Church, Carmarthen, Wales.

During the Falklands War Michael was serving with the Army Catering Corps attached to the Welsh Guards. He was killed on 8 June 1982 when the RFA *Sir Galahad* was bombed at Fitzroy, his body lost to the sea.

In 2022, as part of the Falkland Islands 40th Anniversary Place Names Project, Michael was honoured with 'Jones Bay', a bay between Tom Watson's Point and Urchin Point on mainland East Falkland, on the west side of Adventure Sound.

His name lives on…

24184150 Sergeant Philip Jones 22 SAS Regiment 13 April 1954 ~ 19 May 1982 Age 28

Philip Jones was born on 13 April 1954 in Thrapston, Northamptonshire, the son of George Alfred and Megan Jones (née Richards). George and Megan married in Neath in 1942; prior to their marriage Megan was a hairdresser.

Phil joined the army originally at 1JLB Oswestry in 1969, he joined 1st Battalion Welsh Guards in 1971. Phil served with the Guards Parachute Company from 1973 until 1975 when he went for SAS selection. Successful in his selection, the Welsh Guards remained his parent unit.

His service included Operation Banner, Northern Ireland, Operation Storm, Oman and Operation Corporate, Falkland Islands. Phil also saw service with US Special Forces Delta Force on an exchange programme.

Phil, known also as 'Taff', married his wife Moira in 1975 in Lancashire.

In 1982 Phil was in 23 Troop G Squadron, SAS, he was a qualified parachutist and diver.

Over 100 people gathered for a service on the 30th Anniversary. Phil's widow laid a wreath with a touching message 'In loving memory of Philip "Taff" Jones, to have known and loved you, Always thankful.' Moira died just two years later in 2014 after a twenty-year battle with cancer.

Phil is honoured with all his SAS comrades included in the Regiment Plaque at St Martins Churchyard in Hereford.

Phil died in the Sea King helicopter tragedy of 19 May 1982; there still remains a question mark as to the cause of the crash.

In 2022, as part of the Falkland Islands 40th Anniversary Place Names Project, Phil was honoured with 'Jones Hill', a prominent hill 300ft elevation on Weddell Island west side of Quaker Harbour.

His name lives on…

24562019 Guardsman Anthony Keeble 1st Battalion Welsh Guards 8 October 1962 ~ 8 June 1982 Age 19

Anthony Keeble was born in Bridgend on the 8 October 1962 to Leslie and Audrey Keeble (née Richards), who married in 1961. The eldest child and first son, Anthony had a younger brother and sister.

Anthony's father Leslie was one of eight children. grandfather William Keeble was born in Glamorganshire, but his father Frederick was born elsewhere and moved to Wales. Frederick married Florence Page in Bridgend in 1911. William was the eldest of three boys, born in July 1913.

Anthony grew up in Llanharry, attending Llanharry Primary School followed by Cowbridge Comprehensive. The Keeble family do not seem to have a tradition of serving in the military. Anthony joined the Welsh Guards in April 1981, three months later he convinced his cousin Peter Thomas to follow him into service.

Peter had thought of joining The Parachute Regiment, but his cousin sold him on the idea of the Welsh Guards.

After initial training in Pirbright, the Falklands War followed hot on the footsteps of these young men. In 1982, Anthony was serving with Support Company, Mortars, and Peter in 3 Company, 1st Battalion Welsh Guards. The long voyage to the South Atlantic saw the cousins serve in their first war; sadly, only one of them returned.

Anthony died when the RFA *Sir Galahad* was bombed at Fitzroy on 8 June 1982. He was 19 years old and still lived in Llanharry, Rhondda Cynon Taf.

Peter says, 'he loved motorbikes, football. He had a wicked sense of humour and a good kind heart; we were very close. I miss him every day.'

In 2022, as part of the Falkland Islands 40th Anniversary Place Names Project, Anthony was honoured with 'Keeble Island', the westernmost of two small tussac islands in Shell Bay at the east entrance to Adventure Sound, East Falkland.

His name lives on...

24125031 Lance Sergeant Kevin Keoghane 1st Battalion Welsh Guards 13 January 1952 ~ 8 June 1982 Age 30

The Keoghane family originated from Ballymart, Cork, Ireland. Going back a few generations, Timothy Keoghane, born in 1773, was attested into the King's Own Scottish Borderers on 7 February 1800. Private Keoghane was with the 25th Regiment of foot, joining up at the age of 27. Timothy served in the Napoleonic War. After eighteen years and thirty-nine days' service, he was discharged in 1818 deemed 'Worn out after West India Service'.

Sometime in the 1800s the Keoghane family settled in Roath, Cardiff, though many records indicate a spelling of Keohane.

On 1 August 1899, Kevin's grandfather Timothy Keoghane was born in Cardiff to Timothy and Annie Keoghane (née Boutell), one of at least eight children. Timothy was a Private in the Royal Irish Rifles during the First World War; he was wounded in October 1918. Discharged in February 1919, he married Mabel Taylor in 1920, their oldest child, Phillip Timothy (Kevin's uncle), was born in February 1921. Phillip served in the Royal Artillery in the Second World War; he died in 2000.

Kevin's Great-uncle Denis, born in July 1897, also served in the Welsh Guards in the First World War. Denis was injured in November 1918; he is listed as being injured four times in total. Denis survived the First World War and went on to marry his first wife Emily in 1919 just after the war ended. Emily died in 1935 aged just 37, Denis remarried in 1938; he died in 1949.

It appears that Kevin's Uncle Fred was a Prisoner of War in Stalag 8b, Teschen, Poland, he was a Lance Corporal in the Welch Regiment. Fred went missing in the summer of 1944, believed to be a POW, which was not confirmed until October of that year. Ironically Fred was to outlive his nephew, he died in 1985.

Desmond Keoghane was born on 20 March 1929, he was a twin to sister Doreen, the youngest of Timothy and Mabel's children. Desmond joined the

Welsh Guards; he married Betty in 1949. The couple were living in Wuppertal, Germany, when their son Kevin Keoghane was born on 13 January 1952. Betty died in 1969.

Des went on to serve for a very long time, moving to Berkhamsted in 1973, he was Sergeant Major in the Combined Cadet Corps. Though he took some time out when his son Kevin was killed, he nevertheless did not miss a Yates Drill (a Combined Cadet Force competition), nor a General Inspection Day. Des returned to the CCF in 1992 in the same role as Sergeant Major, where he remained until 2002. He continued his involvement with the Yates Drill competition until illness prevented him in 2016.

Des, a huge fan of the Duke of Edinburgh Award Scheme, died in October 2016 when he lost his battle with cancer. His twin, Doreen, had died some years previously in 1995, Des was 87 years old.

Kevin Keoghane was the only son of Betty and Des Keoghane. Continuing a long line of tradition with the British Army, he joined Junior Leaders Oswestry in 1968. After his initial training, Kevin went to 1st Battalion Welsh Guards in 1969. Kevin was nicknamed Des after his dad; he married his wife Jane in 1976. Despite so many before him in the Keoghane family returning wounded, it was not to be the case for Kevin.

Kevin 'Des' Keoghane was tragically killed on 8 June 1982 in the incident with the *Sir Galahad*. His son Phillip Kevin was born later that year.

Phillip received the Elizabeth Cross in 2012 after a 30th anniversary service, the presentation taking place at the Barracks in Brecon.

In 2022, as part of the Falkland Islands 40th Anniversary Place Names Project, Kevin was honoured with 'Keoghane Stack', a prominent rock stack on the coastline south of Dunnose Head.

His name lives on…

Laundryman Lai Chi Keung HMS *Sheffield* 1 January 1951 ~ 4 May 1982 Age 31

Keung Lai-Chi was born on New Year's Day 1951, though the Chinese New Year in 1951 was on 6 February, making Keung the Chinese sign of the Metal Tiger.

The Task Force relied on the services of the Royal Fleet Auxiliary and the Merchant Navy for anything from supplies to laundry. Many Chinese served as laundrymen, a simple but essential task. The brave among them chose to stay at their posts as the Task Force headed towards the Total Exclusion Zone.

Keung was missing after HMS *Sheffield* was hit by an Exocet missile. His body remains unrecovered, it is thought to have been lost to the ocean.

In 2022, as part of the Falkland Islands 40th Anniversary Place Names Project, Keung was honoured with 'Keung Rocks', a prominent rock outcrop on the tussac slopes above the southwest coast of Hummock Island in King George Bay, West Falkland.

His name lives on…

D106285M Leading Marine Engineering Mechanic (Mechanical) Allan John Knowles HMS *Sheffield* 2 August 1950 ~ 4 May 1982 Age 31

Allan John Knowles was born 2 August 1950 in Fairfield General Hospital, Bury, Lancashire. Allan's parents, Edgar and Margaret Knowles (née Cornes), married at Stand Church, Whitefield, Manchester, in 1949, he was their first-born. The couple went on to have another son and two daughters over the next few years.

Edgar was a bricklayer, the family lived in High Bank Grove in Prestwich.

Allan joined the Royal Navy in 1967 aged 17. Three years later he married Sally Baker in Southend, Essex; their son Allan named after his father was born in Portsmouth in 1970.

On 19 November 1981, Allan set sail for patrol in the Arabian Gulf aboard HMS *Sheffield* for Operation Springtrain. Days before HMS *Sheffield* was due to head back home, she was instead diverted to the South Atlantic.

One month later, on Sunday 4 May 1982, disaster struck HMS *Sheffield* as she was struck by an Exocet missile fired from Argentine Naval Super Étendard aircraft. Though the warhead failed to explode, the 'Shiny Sheff' was soon raging with fires which quickly spread, causing the crew to abandon ship. Allan was among those who lost their lives.

Allan had married a second time to Carol Hadley in 1981, he also had stepchildren from that marriage.

In 2022, as part of the Falkland Islands 40th Anniversary Place Names Project, Allan was honoured with 'Knowles Bay', a bay on the south side of Gull Harbour on the east coast of Weddell Island, West Falkland.

His name lives on...

Laundryman Ben Kwo Kyu HMS *Coventry* 28 April 1932 ~ 25 May 1982 Age 50

Ben Kwo Kyu was born on 28 April 1932, he was from Shau Kei Wan, Hong Kong.

Known simply as Ben, he survived the attack on HMS *Coventry*. It is reported that he died of a heart attack in the water soon after leaving the ship. Ben joined HMS *Coventry* in 1978, the ship made a historic visit to Hong Kong with two other warships in 1980.

Ben was the only Chinese man to be buried in a temporary grave, later to be repatriated to Hong Kong. His body arrived in Hong Kong on a commercial flight in late November 1982, a special service was held in the restricted area of the airport. Ben's coffin, draped in a Union Jack, was received by members of his family and a Royal Naval party headed by Commander Beaumont representing the Captain-in-Charge, Hong Kong.

Ben was then taken to the Hong Kong Funeral Parlour, a Catholic burial service followed. Some reports incorrectly suggest that Ben was killed by a shell, it was fate that Ben's body was the only Chinese recovered.

Later Ben's daughter Miss Kuk, Yee-man was presented with a framed picture of HMS *Coventry* by Roy Jones, a Standard Bearer for the Royal Naval Association.

In 2022, as part of the Falkland Islands 40th Anniversary Place Names Project, Ben was honoured with 'Kyu Beach', a south-west facing beach on the west coast of Speedwell Island. East Falkland.

His name lives on…

24522393 Private Stewart Ian Laing 3rd Battalion Parachute Regiment 24 April 1962 ~ 12 June 1982 Age 20

Stewart Ian Laing was the youngest son of Andrew Linden and Joyce Ingrid Laing (née Hall) born 24 April 1962 in the county of Durham.

Andrew and Joyce married in the Parish Church at Newington, Kingston Upon Hull, in March 1955. Andrew was serving in the Royal Navy as a 'Seaman of Signals', his bride Joyce serving in the Women's Royal Naval Service. Andrew was from Gateshead, and Joyce from Hull.

Joyce was the daughter of George Robert and Annie Fall (née Taylor); in a quirk of fate George was lost at sea on 9 April 1932, fifty years to the day his grandson set sail for the Falkland Islands. George was serving on the *Lord Davidson*, off Iceland, at the time of his death.

George was born in Hull in 1899, the son of a fishing trawler captain, his family moved around between Hull, Scotland and Wales. Joyce was just a toddler when her father died, the sea had been with her for generations.

Stew's father was born in Gateshead in November 1931, it appears his grandfather, Andrew Smith Laing, served with the Durham light Infantry until the 1920s. In later life Andrew senior was a Maintenance Engineer. Stew's father, Andrew Linden Laing, was the eldest son of Andrew and Annie Laing (née Soulsby).

Called 'Geordie' because he hailed from Tyneside there are two locations for him online, Gateshead and Lanchester. Interestingly, there is a place called Stanley that lies between the two. Many years later another Stanley was to become important in his life.

Stew joined 459 platoon in 1979, suffering an injury while in another platoon. After training he was sent to A Coy 3 Para, seemingly a good fit with the maroon berets, brothers in arms. Stew stayed with A Coy until 1981 when he applied to do an Anti-Tank Cadre and subsequently joined Support Company. Stew saw service in Northern Ireland and Canada.

In April 1982, as 3 Para set sail on the *Canberra*. It was to be his last operation. Stew died as he lived, helping a friend during the battle for Mount Longdon. He was born and bred not far from one Stanley and died on his way to saving another Stanley, 8,000 miles away.

Stew is listed on the Lanchester War Memorial as the only death in the Falklands. Stew is buried in Lanchester Cemetery where he is well remembered.

Stew's father died in 1998.

In 2022, as part of the Falkland Islands 40th Anniversary Place Names Project, Stew was honoured with 'Laing Point', the northernmost tip of Sea Lion Easterly Island in the Sea Lion Islands group, East Falkland.

His name lives on…

D183357S Weapons Engineering Mechanic (Radio) Simon John Lawson HMS *Ardent* 3 January 1961 ~ 21 May 1982 Age 21

Simon John Lawson was born 3 January 1961 at the General Hospital Ramsgate to John and Audrey Lawson (née Everitt). Simon was one of three boys, he had two older brothers Geoffrey and Tony.

John was a catering manager for many years with Butlins, the family moved around a lot with his work until they eventually settled in Lincoln. At the time of Simon's birth, they lived in Cliftonville, Margate.

Simon attended City School, Lincoln, joining the Royal Navy in May 1980, first at HMS *Raleigh*. When the Falkland Islands were invaded in April 1982, Simon was aboard HMS *Ardent* as the Task Force travelled the long journey 'Down South'.

On 21 May 1982, HMS *Ardent* took a huge loss as she was attacked by Argentine Forces. Simon was single and at the time of his death he lived in Whitley Bay. Sadly, he was killed on his brother Geoffrey's birthday.

There are two memorial benches dedicated to Simon on the promenade in Whitley Bay. The benches were unveiled on 18 October 1982 by the Mayor of Tyneside. Made of wood with cast iron rests, one of them is inscribed '*In Memory of Simon John Lawson HMS Ardent Killed in Action San Carlos Bay Falkland Islands*', the other: '*Simon John Lawson 1961~1982*'.

Sometimes for families, these small memorials that are so personal are a special place of memory to those who gave their lives.

In 2022, as part of the Falkland Islands 40th Anniversary Place Names Project, Simon was honoured with 'Lawson Beach', a boulder beach on the north side of Whisky Island in the Sea Lion Islands group, East Falkland.

His name lives on…

D072303D Local Acting Chief Air Engineering Technician David Lee HMS *Glamorgan* 5 August 1946 ~ 12 June 1982 Age 35

David Lee was born in Leeds on 5 August 1946. Records suggest that he was the only son of Ernest and Annie Lee (née Harrold).

Ernest and Annie married on 3 July 1937, at St Peter's Church Burmantofts, Leeds. Ernest was a steel fitter, the son of the late James Lee, a 'showman'.

Annie was a machinist, the daughter of Arthur and Amy Harrold. Arthur was an engineer, the family lived for many years at Bread Street in Leeds. Arthur attested into the Royal Flying Corps in July 1916, exactly twenty years before his daughter Annie married. Records indicate that Arthur finished his service with the Labour Corps, he served until 1919. Annie was born in 1912, she was the couple's third child.

Dave joined the Royal Navy at quite a young age, it was a life he seemingly took well to. While in Scotland, Dave needed to see a nurse at the clinic, and there he met his wife. Dave Lee and Jeanie Glen Barbour were married in Airdrie in 1967. Jeanie was also serving in the Royal Navy.

Two years later the couple had a daughter, Elaine, born in Elgin, Scotland, where they were living in married quarters. The couple then moved to Weymouth where Elaine attended school.

Just before the Falklands War, Dave and Jeanie had bought a house in Roundhay, Leeds. Dave was taking classes in garden design; he had designed a fish pond for their garden which he sadly never got to see completed.

Dave, known as 'Grubber', was killed when HMS *Glamorgan* was hit by an Exocet missile. Dave was the Senior Maintenance Rating on the ship's flight (Wessex III), he died in the hangar.

After Dave's death, Jeanie moved back to Weymouth, Dorset, with her daughter.

It seems that there was a creative streak in the Lee family. Grandfather James had been a showman, Dave loved garden design, and later daughter Elaine settled in America where she runs a theatre company.

In 2022, as part of the Falkland Islands 40th Anniversary Place Names Project, Dave was honoured with 'Lee Bay', a sheltered bay on the east coast of Sea Lion Island in Choiseul Sound, East Falkland.

His name lives on...

P025875E Sergeant Robert Arthur Leeming 45 Commando Royal Marines 2 September 1949 ~ 11 June 1982 Age 32

Robert Arthur Leeming was born on 2 September 1949 in Tunbridge Wells, Kent. He was the youngest son of Edgar Taylor and Eileen Leeming (née Nuttall) who married in Yorkshire in 1937. Their daughter was born in 1942, after which the family settled in Kent. Oldest son Stuart was born in 1947, Robert completed their family.

Bob was schooled between Tonbridge and Erith; he joined the Royal Marines when he was 18 years old in September 1967. Bob began basic training in Deal, after which he went on to complete Commando Training, earning his Green Beret by 1968. He was posted to Singapore, where he joined 45 Commando.

Following on from Singapore, Bob was based at HMS *Condor* in Arbroath, Scotland. 45 Commando were nicknamed the 'Frozen Chosen' for their Corps Arctic Warfare specialist ability. Bob took to the cold well, and after passing the Arctic Warfare course in Norway he became a Military Ski Instructor, enjoying both downhill and cross-country. Bob also saw service in Belfast with 45 Commando.

During his time in Arbroath, Bob met Margaret who already had two children. After the children's father died, Bob adopted both Colin and Tracey, the couple went on to have a child of their own, a son, Mark. Bob was known by colleagues as a loving family man.

Here it appears history was repeating itself, as Bob's grandfather, Arthur Leeming, also took on three step-children after their father died. Edgar was the middle child of Arthur and Sarah Hannah Leeming (née Gould), who had three children together.

Bob saw promotion to Sergeant in 1980, in August that year his mother died in Yorkshire, by then Bob was a Heavy Weapons specialist First Class.

Tragedy struck twice in a short space of time for 45 Commando. In March 1982, several members of 45 Commando Mortar Troop were killed in a live training exercise.

45 Commando were soon to hear of deployment 'Down South', they set sail on RFA *Stromness*. She carried around 400 troops of 45 Commando, landing at Red Beach on 21 May 1982. Bob and his fellow Marines then made the Yomp via Teal Inlet towards their final objective, Two Sisters.

Bob was killed on 11 June 1982 alongside three other men when they were mistaken for the enemy and killed in the subsequent firefight, which occurred just before the main assault on Two Sisters. He was 32 years old.

After a temporary burial he was moved to his final resting place in the Blue Beach Cemetery, Port San Carlos. Bob's widow Margaret died in Arbroath in 2015.

In 2022, as part of the Falkland Islands 40th Anniversary Place Names Project, Bob was honoured with 'Leeming Creek', an inlet running west at the entrance to Pasa Grande Creek, towards the southeast end of Post Salvador, East Falkland.

His name lives on…

D187927E Marine Engineering Mechanic (Mechanical) 2 Alistair Roy Leighton HMS *Ardent* 14 January 1963 ~ 21 May 1982 Age 19

Roy Desmond Leighton married Evelyn Ginn in Windsor, Berkshire, in 1955. The couple welcomed their first child, Glenda, the following year. Two more daughters followed over the next few years as their family expanded. On 14 January 1963, their first son was born in West Moseley, Surrey. Alistair affectionately became known as Ali to his family. Ali also had two younger brothers.

The Leighton family moved to Windsor in Berkshire where Ali attended Clever Hill Infants when he was 5 years old. In 1972, the family moved again to Margate, where Ali attended Salmestone Primary School. Ali joined his first football team at Salmestone Primary, a team that came runner up in the Les Riggs Cup. Ali continued his schooling at Hartsdown Secondary School, where he also played football for the school team.

When Ali left school, he initially worked for Dalgety Freezer Centre, but the Royal Navy beckoned as he aspired to be a Marine Engineer Mechanic. On

13 October 1980, Ali was accepted at HMS *Raleigh* in Cornwall as a trainee MEM, he was 17 years old.

Ali's first ship was HMS *Ardent*, when the Falkland Islands were invaded in 1982, this young man set sail for the long trip 'Down South'. On 21 May 1982 tragedy struck as HMS *Ardent* was bombed in Falkland Sound. Ali was killed while firefighting; he was one of twenty-two young sailors who died that day. Ali remains 'at sea' with his comrades, he was just 19 years old.

Ali is remembered by his family as a kind and loving brother who always had time for others, he is also remembered on the Margate War Memorial.

In 2022, as part of the Falkland Islands 40th Anniversary Place Names Project, Ali was honoured with 'Leighton Pond', a large freshwater pond 10km east of the Fox Bay Road on West Falkland.

His name lives on…

Electrical Fitter Chau Leung RFA *Sir Galahad* 11 February 1921 ~ 8 June 1982 Age 61

Leung, Chau was born on 11 February 1921 near Shanghai, China, in the province of Shandong. Leung spoke more than one dialect; his daughter remembers him speaking to her in Cantonese.

Leung was a Seaman for many years, often away for two years at a time. He joined the Royal Fleet Auxilliary in 1958.

Leung married Dorothy, the couple had two children a first-born son and a daughter named Yi-Wah Leung, born in Hong Kong in August 1950. Yi-Wah was brought up in an orphanage from the age of seven months. Sister Cecilia Marie from the Maryknoll convent school would check on Yi-Wah while her father was overseas.

Dorothy had given her daughter the name of Margaret but elders in the community could not pronounce the name, so they called her by her Chinese name. At the age of 7 she was taken out of the orphanage system. Many children in China during these times were adopted by Americans but that was not to be Margaret's fate. Leung paid for her care with people in the community.

Though she only saw her father when he was home, they were very close. Sadly, the money Leung sent for Margaret's care was not always utilised for her benefit, so she worked from a young age.

Sister Cecilia Marie continued to visit Margaret and during an organised doctors check-up it was discovered that Margaret had a hole in her heart which needed surgery.

Margaret moved to Australia when she was 19 years old, first living in Killarney Heights with her mother. She soon moved to Nambucca Heads to work in a family motel in Macksville. Margaret settled in Sydney where she married and had two sons.

Leung's home was Kowloon, Hong Kong at the time of his death. He was reported 'Missing presumed dead'. He died on 8 June 1982 when the RFA *Sir Galahad* was attacked by Argentine Skyhawks.

After receiving the news of her father's death Margaret took her children, Daniel and Roger, to the Falkland Islands in 1983. With many other families they visited the islands on board the *Cunard Countess* for a pilgrimage that many feel they need to repeat.

Leung's grandson, Roger, remembers the trip as a young 5-year-old, he has fond memories of comedian Bob Carolgees, who entertained the children.

In 2022, as part of the Falkland Islands 40th Anniversary Place Names Project, Leung was honoured with 'Leung Beach', a sandy beach on mainland West Falkland south west of Hill Gap Island on the western side of Falkland Sound.

His name lives on...

24442111 Lance Corporal Paul Neville Lightfoot 264 SAS Signals Squadron 14 January 1961 ~ 19 May 1982 Age 21

Paul Neville Lightfoot was born on 14 January 1961 in Iserlohn, Germany, the eldest child and only son of Charles Neville and Vivianne Lightfoot (née Stubbs). The couple married in Norwich in 1960. Paul had a younger sister, Caroline, three years his junior.

Charles, known as 'Terry', was serving with the 1st Battalion Royal Ulster Rifles at the time of Paul's birth. Paul attended the Duke of York's Military School in Kent from 1972–77, he was in Wolfe House. Paul was in the swimming team and the gym squad while at school. Those who attend the school are forever remembered as 'Dukie's'.

After leaving school Paul went to the Signals Apprentice College in Harrogate and 11 Royal Signals. From there he went straight from training to 264 Signals Squadron (SAS attached) therefore he was never officially SAS 'badged'.

Paul was married to Julia in early 1982, sadly their marriage was to be short lived. Paul was killed on 19 May 1982 in the Sea King helicopter crash.

Paul's parents each remarried in 1987, his father Terry went back to his roots and lived out his days in Carrickfergus, Northern Ireland. Terry went to the Falkland Islands for the 25th Anniversary of the Falklands War as part of a pilgrimage organised by the South Atlantic Medal Association. Terry had struggled to come to terms with his son's untimely death and found acceptance with his visit. Terry died in October 2016.

In 2022, as part of the Falkland Islands 40th Anniversary Place Names Project, Paul was honoured with 'Lightfoot Beach', a sandy beach at Pond Point on the east coast of Weddell Island, West Falkland.

His name lives on...

21161666 Lance Corporal Buddhaprasad Limbu 1st Battalion 7th Duke of Edinburgh's Own Gurkha Rifles 27 October 1958 ~ 24 June 1982 Age 23

Buddhaprasad was born in Nepal on 27 October 1958 to Deoman and Chandramaya Limbu. The family lived in the village of Sakhewa, north-east of Dhankuta in the eastern hills of Nepal. He followed his father Deoman into the 1/7 Gurkha Rifles, enlisting as a recruit in 1976. Buddhaprasad was sworn in as a Rifleman in the 7th Duke of Edinburgh's Own Gurkha Rifles in August 1977.

Buddhaprasad, a well-educated young man, was in the Signals Platoon, he soon achieved his Class II Signallers qualification with a promotion to Lance Corporal. Like his father he was destined to be a career soldier. By the time of the Falklands War, he had served almost six years, seen service in Hong Kong, Belize, Brunei and the United Kingdom.

There are many stories surrounding the Gurkhas in the Falklands War and many were fabricated in war stories by the Argentinians, claiming that thirty were killed. When the facts, and their names, are checked, it becomes clear that these were just that – 'stories'. Sadly, sometimes stories are either made up or events become embellished for a variety of reasons.

The cut-off date for the Falklands Fallen is 12 July 1982. One Gurkha died before the cut-off date for the Falklands Fallen; although it was after the war had ended, he was killed in the line of duty. He was not the only Gurkha who died as a result of carrying out battlefield clearance though; those who went to 'clean up' after that date were to wait many years for their campaign medals. Ironically, another Gurkha from the Gurkha Engineers was killed on Remembrance Day 1982. He is buried in Manchester.

On 24 June 1982, Buddhaprasad Limbu of HQ/Sigs (D Coy Sig det) as part of D Coy was filling in trenches near Burntside House. His shovel hit what is thought to be and unexploded N79 grenade causing it to detonate. Buddhaprasad was killed instantly, two of his comrades Corporal Tamang Chandrabahadur and Rifleman Rai Dipmani were wounded.

There have been many Limbu's who have given service to the Gurkhas. The Limbu people are indigenous and native people of the Limbuwan region of Nepal. Their original tribal names can be translated as 'heroes of the hills'. Limbu's traditionally follow the Mundham which means 'the power of great strength' in Limbu language. Traditionally, Limbus bury their dead and hold death ceremonies.

At the time of his death Buddhaprasad was buried with full military honours in the civilian cemetery outside Goose Green. Of course, the islanders would have tended his grave with love, but his father wished his body to be repatriated, and on 18 March 1983 he was re-interred in the Military Cemetery in Aldershot.

On some records he is listed as Budhaparsad but on others Budhaprasad. The plaque at his graveside reads:

'IN LOVING MEMORY OF OUR BELOVED SON LATE LCPL BUDDHAPRASAD LIMBU [21161666] 1/7 GR WHO ACHIEVED MARTYRDOM IN FALKLAND WAR ON 24/06/82

WE ALL FAMILY WANT TO PRAY TO THE GOD THAT MAY HIS SOUL REST IN PEACE FOREVER'.

In this memorial, his parents' spelling of his name is honoured.

Buddhaprasad was unmarried at the time of his death. His father, WO1 D.M. Limbu, received his South Atlantic Medal, granted posthumously.

Call it synchronicity or fate, but it is certainly strange that his last three digits were 666 which just happened to be the BFPO number for Operation Corporate.

In 2022, as part of the Falkland Islands 40th Anniversary Place Names Project, Buddhi, as he was fondly known by comrades, was honoured with 'Limbu Point', the north entrance point to Chaffers Gullet on the West Falkland side of Falkland Sound.

His name lives on…

P035079S Corporal Michael David Love DSM 846 Squadron Fleet Air Arm Royal Marines HMS *Hermes* 22 August 1959 ~ 19 May 1982 Age 22

Michael David Love was born on 22 August 1959 in Preston, Lancashire. Michael was the eldest son of David and Elsie Love (née Roach), the couple had one other son Peter.

Michael attended Brownedge St Mary's School in Preston, followed by Preston Catholic College. At the time of his death Michael's home was in Walton-Le-Dale, Preston.

In 1976 there was a song by the band Kiss, *Calling Dr Love*; consequently, after Michael Love joined the Royal Marines, he was affectionately known as 'Doc'. Doc was serving with 846 Naval Air Squadron in the Falklands in 1982.

On the fateful day of his death, Doc was onboard the Sea King Mk 4 of 846 Squadron moving SAS troops between HMS *Hermes* and HMS *Intrepid*. Though the aircraft was a little overloaded the flight was short, and the pilot had apparently adjusted his fuel load to compensate.

The SAS suffered a huge loss that day, Doc was also one of the casualties of the crash. Amazingly, nine men did survive, able to describe the crash in the aftermath. Doc was the only body recovered from the crash. He was buried at sea from the *Canberra* alongside Ken Francis, Andrew Evans and Brett Giffin at 1600hrs on 22 May 1982.

Doc was posthumously awarded the DSM for his service his citation reads:

'MONDAY, 11th OCTOBER 1982.

The QUEEN has been graciously pleased to approve the Posthumous award of the Distinguished Service Medal to the undermentioned in recognition of gallant and distinguished service during the operations in the South Atlantic:

Acting Corporal Aircrewman Michael David LOVE, Royal Marines, P035079S

Corporal Love, 846 Naval Air Squadron, completed seven operational sorties in very hazardous conditions. He played a vital part in the success of these missions and displayed remarkable skill, bravery, and resilience during periods of intense activity. Sadly, he was later killed in a flying accident but his great contribution to the success of the Squadron's operations will always remain a source of inspiration.'

Seven operational sorties in hazardous conditions; everything about the Falklands was hazardous, from the unforgiving terrain to the unforgiving weather to unforeseen hazards.

In memory of Doc, 848 Naval Air Squadron at RNAS Yeovilton present the 'Doc Love Trophy' to the best aircrewman. The staff aircrewman instructors on the squadron vote for the winner, exemplifying the best student on the course, a wonderful legacy from one Jungly to another.

Jake Husker who served with Doc says, 'Doc was an outgoing fun guy, very proud to be a Royal Marine and also to be one of the first Royal Marine Aircrewmen.'

In 2022, as part of the Falkland Islands 40th Anniversary Place Names Project, Doc was honoured with 'Love Point', headland off Strike Off Point on the south shore of Berkeley Sound, East Falkland.

His name lives on…

24355078 Lance Corporal Christopher Keith Lovett MID 3rd Battalion Parachute Regiment 3 April 1958 ~ 12 June 1982 Age 24

Clifford George Lovett married Florence Mitchell-Charman in Worthing, Sussex, in 1955 and their daughter was born the following year. Christopher Keith Lovett was born in Worthing on 3 April 1958, he was the couple's eldest son. Altogether, they had two girls and two boys.

The family have a long association with the Sussex area, many were from a farming background. Chris, however, was not the first Lance Corporal in the family to lose his life in action. His maternal great-uncle, Samuel Ernest Mitchell Charman, enlisted in Worthing during the First World War and served with the 13th Battalion, Sussex Regiment. Samuel was killed in action on 30 June 1916 aged 23. He is included on the Loos Memorial.

Chris's maternal grandfather, Allen George Mitchell-Charman, married Gertrude Alice Ifould in 1928. The couple had four children; their youngest child, Florence, was Chris's mother.

Chris married his wife Michelle in Worthing in 1978. The couple had two sons together, at the time of his deployment they were living in Tidworth. Chris turned 24 years old the day after the Falkland Islands were invaded. He set sail on the *Canberra* with the rest of his battalion less than a week later.

Chris, a medic, was killed during the Battle for Mount Longdon on 12 June 1982. He was posthumously Mentioned in Dispatches, in the *London Gazette* 8 October 1982.

Chris is buried in Worthing Cemetery, Findon Valley, Worthing.

In 1987 Lovett Court, a sheltered housing scheme, was opened in Worthing, it was named after Chris. Lovett Court is situated in Maybridge Square, Goring-by-sea, Worthing. A permanent reminder of a brave man and his long family ties to the area.

In 2022, as part of the Falkland Islands 40th Anniversary Place Names Project, Chris was honoured with 'Lovett Bay', a bay on the west side of Shallow Bay, West Falkland.

His name lives on…

P035645L Marine Stephen Graham McAndrews 40 Commando Royal Marines 2 February 1960 ~ 27 May 1982 Age 22

Stephen Graham McAndrews was born on 2 February 1960 in Wythenshawe, Manchester. Graham was the eldest child and only son of Graham and Ann McAndrews (née Rostron), who married in Manchester in 1959. The couple went on to have three daughters: Jacqueline, Beverley and Nicola. Stephen also had an adopted sister, Lyndsey.

Like many young men Stephen aspired to wear a uniform – in his case, he wanted to be a Royal Marine; he joined up when just 16 years old.

During the Falklands War Stephen was serving with 40 Commando Royal Marines. On 27 May 1982, Stephen was killed during operations at San Carlos. Two Argentinian Sky Hawks had bombed allied forces at Ajax Bay, Stephen was killed by the explosion of a bomb.

When Stephen was killed his girlfriend Dawn was pregnant with their daughter Sarah, who was born in September 1982. Like many children from the Falklands War, Sarah was never to meet her father. Sarah was presented with the Elizabeth Cross in 2011.

Stephen's body was repatriated; a service took place in late 1982 at Manchester Crematorium.

On 30 May 2002 the Marines at Norton Fitzwarren, Somerset, paid tribute to Stephen when they laid a wreath in front of a plaque at the main gates. Members of 40 Commando also held a two-minute silence for all those who fell in the Falklands War.

In 2022, as part of the Falkland Islands 40th Anniversary Place Names Project, Stephen was honoured with 'McAndrews Bay', a sheltered anchorage on the east side of Burnt Island off the south coast of Saunders Island, West Falkland.

His name lives on…

D065361N Air Engineering Mechanician (1) Allan McAulay HMS *Ardent* 25 August 1946 ~ 21 May 1982 Age 35

Allan McAulay was born in the Provan area of Glasgow on 25 August 1946, to John and Peggy McAulay, who married the year before. Growing up later in Droitwich, Worcestershire, Allan attended St Peter's and Droitwich High School. After Allan left school, he joined the Royal Navy in the autumn of 1961, enabling him to indulge his love of travel. His father had served with the Royal Naval Defence Corps.

Allan was known as Mac, though on some sources he was known as Allan Joseph. Mac first had contact with his future wife through letters which started three years before they married. Allan married Barbara Hammond on the Isle of Sheppey in 1969. Their daughter was born in 1970 in Sheppey. A son arrived three years later, born in Weymouth, Dorset.

At the time of the Falkland Islands invasion Mac had served for over twenty years in the Royal Navy. He was serving with the Flight Crew on HMS *Ardent* as a Chief Petty Officer on the fateful day she was hit.

On 21 May 1982, HMS *Ardent* had been providing Naval Gun Fire towards Argentine Troops located around Darwin and Goose Green, a decoy away from the main landings at San Carlos water. Having survived sixteen air raids *Ardent*'s luck ran out. The next air raid consisted of four A-4 Skyhawks, hoping to sink the ship that had caused so much trouble for Argentina.

Two 500lb bombs hit their target and exploded in the dining room below the flight deck, the force of the explosion blowing the Sea Cat launcher on the hanger 80ft in the air. Three men were killed instantly, Mac was one of them.

Mac is commemorated on the Droitwich Spa Memorial and on the Old Portsmouth Sea Forces Memorial in Portsmouth.

Mac is also remembered with all the other Glasgow servicemen in Glasgow Cathedral inscribed; 'TO THE MEMORY OF SERVICEMEN OF THE CITY OF GLASGOW WHO GAVE THEIR LIVES IN THE FALKLAND ISLANDS CAMPAIGN.' Under the seven names the inscription reads 'WHOEVER SEEKS TO SAVE HIS LIFE WILL LOSE IT' St Luke 17.33

At RNAS Yeovilton there is an avenue of twelve Hornbeam trees planted by Mrs Betty Williams on behalf of the Captain, Officers and Ship's Company of HMS *Heron* on 23 February 1983, as a living memory for those who were of their ships company and died in the South Atlantic, twelve Sailors and Royal Marines. Each of the twelve men have a block of Portland stone and a nameplate by their tree.

During the Falklands War, Barbara's brother Peter was serving with 846 NAS, thankfully he returned home.

In 2022, as part of the Falkland Islands 40th Anniversary Place Names Project, Mac was honoured with 'McAulay Bay', a bay on the east side of the Channel Islands off Beaver Island, West Falkland.

His name lives on…

D121589B Petty Officer Air Engineering Artificer (Mechanical) 2 Kelvin Ian McCallum HMS *Glamorgan* 28 July 1954 ~ 12 June 1982 Age 27

Kelvin Ian McCallum was born in St Mary's Hospital, Kingston, Portsmouth, on 28 July 1954, the only son of Roy Dugald and Sheila Joyce McCallum (née Cottrell).

Sheila Joyce Cottrell was born in July 1931 in Portsmouth, Hampshire. At the time of Kelvin's birth, Roy was a painter and decorator, and the couple lived in Washington Road, Buckland, Portsmouth. Roy and Sheila had married the year before Kelvin's birth.

Kelvin's maternal grandparents, Henry Elliott Cottrell and Nellie Millicent Hannaford, married in Portsmouth in 1926, Sheila was their second daughter. The couple had five children together, their youngest born early in 1941. Sadly, Henry died on 29 April 1941, killed at Portsmouth Harbour, he is listed as Civilian War dead. He left a widow with a young family; Nellie remarried in 1943 and died in 1976.

Kelvin grew up in Portsmouth, he later joined the Royal Navy.

Kelvin married Angela in Southampton in 1977. The couple had one daughter, Gemma, who was born in 1982, sadly after her father's death.

Kelvin's father, Roy, died in 1998; his mother Sheila continued to live in Portsmouth until her death in June 2011.

On the way to the Falkland Islands Kelvin bought a bottle of rum, he planned to drink it with his father on his return to Portsmouth. Many years later some of his shipmates were to return to Hookers Point and hold a toast to their fallen comrade.

Kelvin died on 12 June 1982 when HMS *Glamorgan* was hit by an Exocet Missile. Unlike some of the other Naval ships lost from the Task Force, HMS *Glamorgan* herself was not sunk, but thirteen lives were lost that day.

In 2022, as part of the Falkland Islands 40th Anniversary Place Names Project, Kelvin was honoured with 'McCallum Rock', a low rock islet east of Elephant Point at the northwest end of Saunders Island, West Falkland.

His name lives on…

24373108 Corporal Keith John McCarthy 3rd Battalion Parachute Regiment 23 January 1955 ~ 12 June 1982 Age 27

Keith John McCarthy was born in Cardiff on 23 January 1955, the eldest child and only son of William and Jean McCarthy (née Petrie) who married in 1950. Keith's father was in the Royal Air Force, so the couple moved around somewhat over the years.

In March of 1957, toddler Keith travelled from Southampton to Singapore on board the P&O ship *Asturias*, he seemed destined for adventure from a young age.

Though Keith was born in Cardiff, his two sisters were born in Episkopi, Cyprus, and Shropshire. The family eventually settled in Frome, Somerset, where Keith attended Frome Grammar School, where he enjoyed sports.

Keith joined The Parachute Regiment in 1971 as a teenager. After successfully completing his training, he was posted to A Company, 3rd Battalion Parachute Regiment. Known as a reliable and capable soldier, his love of sports came to fruition once more on the rugby pitch. Keith's nickname was 'Ginge', a name often bestowed on men of a certain colouring…

Keith later transferred to Support Company and the Anti-Tank platoon. During his time with The Parachute Regiment Keith saw service in Northern Ireland, Canada and Osnabruck, his last posting was to Tidworth in Wiltshire.

Keith married Linda in March 1982; her sister was already married to Corporal Scott Wilson, who also died in the Falklands War. During the night of 11/12 June 1982, Keith had deployed to a forward position near the summit of Mount Longdon with a MILAN missile team consisting of himself and Privates West and Hedicker. They had an excellent view along the Longdon ridge and had already engaged a few targets with the MILAN. Their position was then hit with a round from a 106mm Recoilless AT gun, all were seriously wounded and died from their injuries.

Keith was buried at Beckington Church Cemetery in Frome, Somerset on 21 December 1982. His mother Jean died in December 2020 aged 93.

In 2022, as part of the Falkland Islands 40th Anniversary Place Names Project, Keith was honoured with 'McCarthy Islet', a low sparsely vegetated islet to the south of Box Island.

His name lives on…

24195687 Corporal Douglas Frank McCormack Royal Signals (attached 22 SAS) 14 June 1955 ~ 19 May 1982 Age 26

Douglas Frank McCormack was born on 14 June 1955 at the Eastern General Hospital in Leith, Midlothian, Scotland. Dougie, as he was known, was the son of Francis Frank McCormack and Mary Ellen Martin who married in St Giles, Edinburgh, in November 1953. Dougie's father was a rubber moulder, and at the time the family lived in Gilmore Place in Edinburgh.

Dougie enlisted into the Royal Corps of Signals in August 1970, attending the Army Apprentices College Harrogate. Dougie later married Karin Busch in Germany in 1977. During his service, he served with 6Q2 Sig Troop, 4 Armoured Div, 22 Sig Regt and 7 Sig Regt. At the time of his death, he was with 603 (TACP) FAC, he had been with the squadron since February 1981.

During the Falklands War, Dougie was Flight Lieutenant Hawkins's signaller; he was attached to 22 SAS Regiment. Prior to this deployment Dougie was based at Goojerat Barracks, Colchester, Essex.

The Sea King helicopter was used in the Falklands as a troop carrier and to move equipment. Another significant role was deployment in an anti-submarine role and the insertion and extraction of Special Forces. Each Sea King was capable of carrying up to twenty-seven troops over a distance of anything up to 400 miles.

On 19 May 1982 tragedy struck as the Sea King crashed into the sea while trying to land troops on HMS *Intrepid*. Of the twenty-two deaths that day, five were Royal Signals. Dougie was sadly one of the men who died, just one month short of his 27th birthday, which was coincidently the day the war ended.

Dougie is remembered with a plaque at St Martins Church in Hereford, along with the other SAS men who died that day.

In 2022, as part of the Falkland Islands 40th Anniversary Place Names Project, Dougie was honoured with 'McCormack Islet', a small tussac islet to the south of East Island.

His name lives on...

24398223 Lance Corporal Michael Vincent HcHugh 264 SAS Signal Squadron 3 February 1960 ~ 19 May 1982 Age 22

The McHugh family it appears were originally from Ireland though they have lived in the Stockport area for some time. It appears that Michael's great-great-grandfather, another Michael, was born in Ireland in the mid-1850s. By the late 1800s the family were living in Lancashire.

Michael 'Mick' Vincent McHugh was born on 3 February 1960 in Stockport, Cheshire. He was the eldest son of Vincent and Marian McHugh, who went on to have two more sons.

Mick joined the Royal Signals, at the time of Operation Corporate he was with 264 SAS Signal Squadron. Like many young men who served, he is remembered for having a lovely smile and not being easily fazed.

Sadly, Mick was one of those who perished on 19 May 1982 in the Sea King disaster.

Mick is remembered on all the Falklands Memorials and with a memorial plaque at the SAS Regimental Plot in Hereford (St Martin's) Churchyard, Herefordshire.

In 2022, as part of the Falkland Islands 40th Anniversary Place Names Project, Mick was honoured with 'McHugh Point', the western point of Sege Island.

His name lives on...

24209183 Corporal Andrew George McIlvenny 9 Independent Parachute Squadron Royal Engineers 2 October 1954 ~ 8 June 1982 Age 27

Andrew George McIlvenny served in the British Army as had his father before him. Andrew senior served in the Korean War.

Andrew McIlvenny was born on 22 July 1931; he joined the army serving with the 12th School of Mechanical Engineering in Chatham, Kent. Meanwhile, the Clark family had settled in Gillingham, Kent; their daughter Edith went on to marry Andrew in November 1953 in the Garrison Church in Chatham. Andrew George McIlvenny was born in Gillingham. The couple later had a daughter, Dawn.

Andrew George McIlvenny was known as 'Mac' or 'Andy', he joined the British Army and served with the Royal Engineers. Mac was with 3 Troop, 20 Field Squadron, 36 Engineer Regiment, Royal Engineers.

Mac married his wife, Heather, in Kent in 1977.

During the Falklands War Mac was temporarily attached to 9 Independent Parachute Squadron, Royal Engineers, he had seen service with the squadron previously in Northern Ireland.

When the call came in 1982, Mac was in Bravo Section 4 Troop 9 Para Sqn. Sadly, he was one of two casualties from 9 Para Sqn on the *Sir Galahad* on 8 June 1982. He was killed during the air attack on the ship by Argentine Skyhawks at Fitzroy Cove. Mac was being transported on *Sir Galahad* to provide engineering support following the upcoming landings.

Mac is remembered by a memorial tree at the Holy Trinity Church in Gillingham, Kent. A bronze plaque at St Barbara's Church, Maxwell Road, Brompton, Gillingham, is a memorial to all nine of the men of the Royal Engineers who died in the Falklands War. The memorial has a replica on Sapper's Hill in the Falkland Islands.

On Friday 25 June 1982 the RFA *Sir Galahad* was towed out to sea and declared a War Grave.

In 2022, as part of the Falkland Islands 40th Anniversary Place Names Project, Andrew was honoured with 'McIlvenny Creek', a creek on the east side of Fox Bay between Fox Bay East and East Head Street name in Stanley.

His name lives on…

24210031 Sergeant Ian John McKay VC 3rd Battalion Parachute Regiment 7 May 1953 ~ 12 June 1982 Age 29

The McKay name has Scottish roots; it appears that Ian's family on his father's side originated from the Govan area of Glasgow. Records suggest Ian's grandfather was Angus McKay, a fifth child and second son, born in Partick.

Angus married Sabina Jackson in Sheffield in 1923, the couple went on to have twelve children. Ian's father, Kenneth John McKay, born in October 1929, was the couple's fourth child. By 1939, the family were living in Owler Lane, Sheffield. Angus was a contractor in transport; the couple's youngest daughter was born in 1944.

Kenneth John McKay married Freda Doreen Hargreaves in 1952. Ian John McKay was their eldest son, born on 7 May 1953 in Wortley. The couple went on to have two more children, Graham in February 1956 and Neal in March 1957.

Ian attended Rotherham Grammar School, he left at the age of 17. Ian joined the army in August 1970, signing up to become a Paratrooper. He was posted to 1 Para in 1971 after which he saw service in Northern Ireland, Germany, and various postings throughout the United Kingdom. Next stop was Depot where, between 1976 and 1978, Ian became a Corporal Instructor. After Depot he joined 3 Para on a two-year posting, attaining the rank of Sergeant by 1978.

Depot Para and Aldershot brought love into Ian's life when he met his wife-to-be, Marica. Marica had been a dental nurse with the Queen Alexandra's Nursing Corps, her father was also in the military, so it was a life she knew well. Ian and

Marica married in late 1976, their only child, a daughter, was born the following year. Ian also inherited a stepson when they married.

In 1980, during his next posting to Depot, Ian was in the Weapons Training Wing, then with Recruit Company. Later he returned to 3 Para where he took on the role of Platoon Sergeant of 4 Platoon, B Company in February 1982.

3 Para as the 'Spearhead' Battalion in 1982 were soon off 'Down South' as part of the huge Task Force sent to reclaim the Falkland Islands. They deployed just a week after the Islands were invaded.

After the long journey Ian, like many men, wrote home of life on board ship and the wonderful sights they saw along the way. 3 Para faced a long hard tab across East Falkland. The Battle for Mount Longdon was vicious and bloody. Ian showed exemplary bravery in the field which earned him the Victoria Cross, his bravery spelled out in detail in his citation.

Exerts from citation in *London Gazette*:

During the night of 11th/12th June 1982, 3rd Battalion The Parachute Regiment mounted a silent night attack on an enemy battalion position on Mount Longdon, an important objective in the battle for Port Stanley in the Falkland Islands.

Sergeant McKay was platoon sergeant of 4 Platoon, B Company, which, after the initial objective had been secured, was ordered to clear the Northern side of the long East/West ridge feature, held by the enemy in depth, with strong, mutually-supporting positions. By now the enemy were fully alert, and resisting fiercely. As 4 Platoon's advance continued it came under increasingly heavy fire from a number of well-sited enemy machine gun positions on the ridge, and received casualties. Realising that no further advance was possible the Platoon Commander ordered the Platoon to move from its exposed position to seek shelter among the rocks of the ridge itself. Here it met up with part of 5 Platoon.

The enemy fire was still both heavy and accurate, and the position of the platoons was becoming increasingly hazardous. Taking Sergeant McKay, a Corporal and a few others, and covered by supporting machine gun fire, the Platoon Commander moved forward to reconnoitre the enemy positions but was hit by a bullet in the leg, and command devolved upon Sergeant McKay.

The assault was met by a hail of fire. The Corporal was seriously wounded, a Private killed and another wounded. Despite these losses Sergeant McKay, with complete disregard for his own safety, continued to charge the enemy position alone. On reaching it he despatched the enemy with grenades, thereby relieving the position of beleaguered 4 and 5 Platoons, who were now able to redeploy with relative safety. Sergeant McKay, however, was killed at the moment of victory, his body falling on the bunker.

> *Without doubt Sergeant McKay's action retrieved a most dangerous situation and was instrumental in ensuring the success of the attack. His was a coolly calculated act, the dangers of which must have been all too apparent to him beforehand. Undeterred he performed with outstanding selflessness, perseverance and courage.*
>
> *With a complete disregard for his own safety, he displayed courage and leadership of the highest order, and was an inspiration to all those around him.*

Ian was killed in action on 12 June 1982, leaving behind yet another broken family; the brutal, the often unseen, cost of war.

Sadly, of the three brothers, Ian had been the only one born healthy; both his siblings were born with an incurable disease, their futures precarious from birth. Neal died in June 1989, Graham in 1995.

Ian's parents attended a service in June 1998 and proudly helped unveil the memorial to all the Paratroopers who were killed in action in the South Atlantic. It is hard to imagine the grief for parents who, within sixteen years of the Falklands War, had lost all three of their sons. Kenneth lived only a short time after the service and died in November 1998.

Ian is buried in Aldershot Military Cemetery. The plot lies in a beautiful part of the cemetery where the birds sing, the sun often shines. There is often a stone on top of the headstones, a mark of respect from many a visitor.

In 1999, Ian's mother Freda finally made a trip to the Falkland Islands; a year later she went to live there for three months, it was time for healing, finally. Despite a series of health issues and deep grief from her losses, Freda lived to the age of 84, she died in 2018.

Ian's Victoria Cross is now on display in the Lord Ashcroft Gallery at the Imperial War Museum.

'McKay VC Barracks' is at the Territorial Army centre in Rotherham. An accommodation block at the Defence Academy, Shrivenham, was named 'McKay House'. In 2011, the Sergeant and Warrant Officers' bar at Mount Pleasant in the Falkland Islands was renamed 'Ian McKay VC Bar'. At Vimy Barracks in Catterick Garrison there is the 'McKay VC Gymnasium' – a gym facility and sports hall.

In 2006, Ian was featured in a Channel 5 docudrama *Victoria Cross Heroes*.

McKay Close is a street name in Stanley, Falkland Islands.

His name lives on…

P039338Q Lance Corporal Peter Burke McKay 45 Commando Royal Marines 4 October 1962 ~ 27 May 1982 Age 19

Peter Burke McKay was born at Chalmers hospital in Banff, Scotland, on 4 October 1962. Peter was the third son of Suzie and Jimmers McKay. The couple had two older sons, James and Stewart, and a younger son, Gordon, born a year after Peter.

Peter attended three schools in Macduff, Scotland; first, Fife Street and Shand Street Primary Schools, followed by Transition School (the school between primary and secondary, as the name would suggest). Macduff is a small coastal town off Banff Bay which looks out onto the Moray Firth in one direction and across at its neighbour, Banff, in the other. They are just a mile apart and joined by the seven-arch Deveron Bridge. Banff is well known for its fishing industry heritage; Macduff is a Burgh where the last deep-water fishing boats were built in the United Kingdom.

Peter was at Transition School for a year before entering Banff Academy. While at school, Peter took part in most sports without having an ambition to be a sportsman, his ambitions lay elsewhere. The sea was obviously no stranger to Peter; fishing, however, was not to be his destiny as he joined the Royal Marines.

Brother Gordon says:

> Peter always had an eye on the forces, feeling it would help him develop and mature. He joined the forces at 17, picking the Royal Marines, knowing how tough the challenge would be but that's what attracted him. He was hoping at some stage to progress into the SAS, again for the greater challenge.

In April 1982, Peter was serving with 45 Commando in Arbroath. 45 Commando, under the command of Lieutenant Colonel Andrew Francis Whitehead, formed part of 3 Commando Brigade sent to recapture the Islands. The Marines travelled the long journey on a variety of Royal Naval vessels. Peter started his journey on HMS *Hermes*, transferring to HMS *Invincible*, then finally to HMS *Fearless* for the landings at San Carlos.

Gordon says, 'It was a very difficult time for all the family, information and updates mainly came via TV news'.

Peter's young life ended abruptly just two years after joining the Royal Marines. On 27 May 1982, when the Argentinians bombed Ajax Bay, Peter of Recce Troop was badly injured; he died from his wounds.

After a temporary interment in the Falkland Islands Peter was repatriated to Macduff in November 1982. He is buried at Myrus Cemetery, Macduff, in Aberdeenshire, the family's decision to bring him home brought them some closure.

Gordon says,

> Since Peter's death, a number of his fellow comrades have been to his graveside, leaving messages of thanks. In 2020 there were around thirty ex-service men and women visited Peter's grave on motorbikes as part of a six-day commemorative bike run for all Falklands' fallen service personnel, Peter's mum took great comfort from the visit and continued support, she even managed a wee run on the back of one of the motor bikes....

When asked how he would like Peter to be remembered Gordon says, 'Peter was trustworthy, a solid family member and a great friend to many.'

Peter was still a teenager when he died; yet to marry or have children. He is greatly missed by his family. Peter's father died in March 2015.

In 2022, as part of the Falkland Islands 40th Anniversary Place Names Project, Peter was honoured with 'McKay Pond', a small pond close to New House Farm settlement on mainland East Falkland.

His name lives on…

24277023 Corporal Stewart Peter Frank McLaughlin 3rd Battalion Parachute Regiment 12 October 1954 ~ 12 June 1982 Age 27

Stewart Peter Frank McLaughlin was born in Wallasey on 12 October 1954, the eldest son of Edmund and Elizabeth McLaughlin (née Taylor). The couple went on to have a large family of boys between 1954 and 1965. The McLaughlin name originated from Ireland; Edmund's father settled in Wallasey where he married in 1926, Edmund was also one of a large family.

All Paratroopers must show courage and steel to pass P Coy, once they have earned the right to wear their Maroon Beret and the Wings, they don them with pride and a whole world of excitement opens up for them. For Stewart he was to go on to become part of an exclusive club, the 'Class of 82'.

Stewart was known simply as 'Scouse' to his comrades. Scouse was an experienced soldier having served for several years already. 3 Para deployed to Osnabruck, the newly formed 5th Field Force in BAOR Germany in the late 1970s. In 1980, they returned to the United Kingdom as part of 8th Field Force. As the 'Spearhead' battalion they were ready to deploy should trouble occur.

Stewart and Ruth married in Hereford in 1981, their son Stewart Kurt McLaughlin was born in early 1982 in Wiltshire, another child who has grown up without knowing his father.

Scouse deployed 'Down South' on board the *Canberra*; the men kept up their training in readiness for war. Friday 21 May 1982 was a busy day in San Carlos water as British Troops engaged in the landings.

3 Para tabbed across East Falkland to Teal Inlet prior to their forward approach to Mount Longdon and the fierce battle that ensued. Corporal Scouse McLaughlin was Section Commander of 5 Platoon, B Coy, 3 Para, as the men began the Battle for Mount Longdon.

During the next three days it was just pure old-fashioned war as assaults took place on Mount Longdon, Mount Tumbledown, Mount Harriet, Two Sisters and Wireless Ridge. Men literally fixed bayonets as they went into action with the knowledge that all objectives were significant in the pathway to take back Port Stanley.

The night assault in the Battle for Mount Longdon was fierce. The platoon sergeant of 4 platoon, was killed, his section commander injured. Scouse as the platoon commander of 5 platoon did not hesitate. He led his men forward; it is said he uttered the words 'I'm bulletproof'. The battle was fierce, the battalion were under heavy fire. Having survived the initial assault with horrendous wounds he continued on until mortar fire killed him.

Scouse is buried in Rake Lane Cemetery, Wallasey, Merseyside. Since his death there has been an ongoing campaign to try and get him recognised with a bravery award. So far, the campaign has been unsuccessful.

In 2022, as part of the Falkland Islands 40th Anniversary Place Names Project, Scouse was honoured with 'McLaughlin Bay', a small bay at the east entrance to Estancia Creek at the southeast head of Port Salvador, East Falkland.

His name lives on...

P041923R Marine Gordon Cameron MacPherson 45 Commando Royal Marines 27 June 1961 ~ 12 June 1982 Age 20

Gordon Cameron MacPherson was born in Oban on 27 June 1961 to Gordon and Dorothy MacPherson who married in 1959. Gordon had one younger brother David, two years his junior.

Gordon grew up in Oban, to this day he is remembered at the Dunbeg and Rock Primary Schools where Royal Marines from 45 Commando still visit annually in his memory. After Dunbeg Primary School, Gordon finished his education at Oban High School. Upon leaving school he started an apprenticeship with a painting firm but decided on a different career path.

Training in Lympstone was successful, Gordon passed out with 160 Troop in 1981. He found himself in 45 Commando based at HMS *Condor* in Arbroath. Like many, his Easter leave was interrupted as the business of war began. Deployed with Operation Corporate, Gordon was in Zulu Company, 45 Commando. He was sadly killed alongside Frank Spencer during the Battle for Two Sisters.

Gordon is remembered at Oban High School with a plaque which reads: 'MARINE GORDON CAMERON MACPHERSON 45 COMMANDO ROYAL MARINES FALKLANDS 12 06 82.'

In 2012, his brother David went to the Falkland Islands completing a retrace of 45 Commandos original Yomp, along with Mike Cole who was Zulu Company Commander in 1982. The idea was originally that of Simon Spencer, but he and his brother Gareth were unable to make the journey. The seventy-five miles from Port San Carlos to Stanley via Two Sisters was to honour their fathers and their journey in what was a short but brutal war. The men were raising money as they did so for the Royal Marines Charitable Trust Fund.

After he died a Gaelic song was written for Gordon called *Nam Anna Le Mo Smaointe* meaning 'Alone with my thoughts', the song was penned by family friends Erik Spence and the Reverend John MacLeod.

David revisited the Islands again in 2018.

In 2022, as part of the Falkland Islands 40th Anniversary Place Names Project, Gordon was honoured with 'MacPherson Island', a small tussac island west of the entrance to Double Creek, West Falkland.

His name lives on…

D173685W Cook Brian George Malcolm HMS *Glamorgan* 11 February 1960 ~ 12 June 1982 Age 22

Brian George Malcolm was born on 11 February 1960 at Tor Nursing Home, Corstorphine Road, Edinburgh. He was the eldest son of Derek Munro Malcolm and Julia Davidson Shields, who married in 1957. Brian had one younger brother, Gwyn, who also served in the Royal Navy.

Derek served in the Royal Air Force during his National Service, after which he went into the nursing profession, through which he met Julia. Working in the area of Mental Health, Derek was a warden, as such in charge of nurses and wards. Derek was in the frontline of mental health when 'Care in the Community' was in its infancy.

Brian grew up in the Newhaven area of Edinburgh. Brian attended Victoria Primary School, Broughton High School and finally Telford College where he trained as a chef before joining the Royal Navy in 1978.

His brother remembers him as a tall gentle giant who loved a drink with his shipmates. Brian would buy his mother a clock each year for her birthday; like many young men he loved his mum. Gwyn looked up to his older brother and so after Brian was killed, Gwyn followed his footsteps into the Royal Navy where he worked mainly on submarines over the years. Gwyn was just 15 when the Falkland Islands were invaded, he joined the Navy as soon as he turned 18.

Brian married Gill in 1981 in Yeovil, Somerset, the couple had no children. Like many, Gill was heartbroken when her husband was killed.

In 2022, as part of the Falkland Islands 40th Anniversary Place Names Project, Brian was honoured with 'Malcolm Creek,' a creek between Bluff Head and Guardian Point in the northwest corner of Low Bay, East Falkland.

His name lives on…

24503466 Guardsman David Malcolmson 2nd Battalion Scots Guards 15 July 1961 ~ 14 June 1982 Age 20

David Malcolmson was born on 15 July 1961 in Irvine, Ayrshire, Scotland. David was named after his father. He was the eldest of four children born to Margaret and David Malcolmson. Younger brothers Andrew and Gordon were followed by a sister, Christine. David's family nickname was Malky.

Malky attended Bank Street Primary School, Irvine, followed by Greenwood Academy, Dreghorn, Irvine. He enjoyed both football and golf at school. Late in

1979, Malky joined the Scots Guards. His sister Christine says that he had 'an interest', but like many young men mainly joined because of the high levels of unemployment.

In April 1982, Malky was on ceremonial duties in London, based at Chelsea Barracks. He travelled 'Down South' first on the QE2, then transferred over to the *Canberra* at Ascension Island.

Christine was just 14 years old at the time, she was at home looking after their disabled mother. She says, 'The whole time it was a terrible anxiety-ridden experience. Like everyone else, we just wanted it to be over and for David to be safe.'

She also says, 'I absolutely do think that the Falklands War was completely justified as Britain had to defend its citizens and subjects.'

David volunteered to be a stretcher bearer for wounded comrades; tragically he was killed just thirty minutes before the war ended on 14 June 1982. His body was later repatriated and is buried in Knadgerhill Cemetery in Irvine next to his comrade, Jim Reynolds.

His sister says, 'David was a 'home bird' and he would very much have wanted to return to his beloved family and hometown.'

David had served just two years when he died. His brother Andrew has visited the Falkland Islands twice since. Christine says, 'David was kind, happy-go-lucky, loved life, liked to laugh and was full of fun.'

In 2022, as part of the Falkland Islands 40th Anniversary Place Names Project, David was honoured with 'Malcolmson Point', a point on mainland East Falkland at the north entrance to *Eagle* Passage.

His name lives on…

24578382 Guardsman Michael John Marks 1st Battalion Welsh Guards 14 June 1964 ~ 8 June 1982 Age 17

Michael John Marks was born on 14 June 1964 at 47 Mistley Path in Basildon to Arnold Dennis and Josephine Agnes Marks (née Stephens). The couple married in the Register Office in Hackney in September 1962; at the time they lived in Evering Road in Stoke Newington where Arnold was a Bus Driver.

Every family has a story, the name Marks came from Michael's great-grandfather Marks Bretholtz, who was born in Austria in the 1870s. Marks was a confectioner who settled with his wife Fanny and family in the ancient borough of St George-in-the-East, in East London.

The Census states that Marks was born in Austria, the family for many years lived in Ship Alley which suggests that they may well have been Jewish Immigrants escaping persecution. Many families moved into Ship Alley because it was close to the ships that disembarked during the period 1870 to 1914.

Marks and Fanny had five children; they had just one son. Reuben Bretholtz was born in East London in 1908. Reuben became a taxi driver, he married Gladys

Ponting in 1933 – just as Hitler was coming to power to bring a different kind of evil to the world.

Arnold Dennis Bretholtz was born in 1934 in Stepney, somewhere between his birth and 1939 the family changed their name to Marks, a fitting tribute to Marks Bretholtz who died in 1938. It appears that by 1939, Reuben was using the name Harry Marks.

Michael's parents were both on second marriages when he was born, they had settled in Basildon, Essex. Michael joined the Welsh Guards; he was serving with the 1st Battalion during the Falklands War.

Michael died on 8 June 1982 when RFA *Sir Galahad* was bombed in Fitzroy. He was killed just a week short of his 18th birthday – ironically the day the war ended. At the time of his death, home was Stanford-Le-Hope, Essex.

Michael is honoured on the Tilbury War Memorial, Civic Square, Tilbury, Essex. It seems his family later settled in Somerset.

In 2022, as part of the Falkland Islands 40th Anniversary Place Names Project, Michael was honoured with 'Marks Point', the eastern point of Sedge Island.

His name lives on...

D176786Q Naval Airman Aircraft Handler Brian Marsden HMS *Invincible* 7 December 1962 ~ 16 June 1982 Age 19

Brian Marsden was born on 7 December 1962 at Rosendale General Hospital in Rawtenstall, Lancashire. Brian's parents, Jack Marsden and Joan Kirk, married in 1958. The couple had their first child, daughter Jacqueline, the following year in 1959. Brian was their third child, the middle of three brothers, Gary, Brian and David.

The family had their roots in Lancashire. Brian's maternal grandfather, John Kirk, and his wife Lilian were married in Blackburn in 1938. Joan was their eldest child; her brother John was born four years later. Uncle John served in the Royal Navy, he inspired Brian and his two brothers with his stories.

Before joining the Royal Navy, Brian had been a member of the Sea Cadets, which he loved. Brian went to Moorhead High School; he was described by his mother as a really happy-go-lucky lad. During his two years of training his service included HMS *Seahawk*, Culdrose, HMS *Heron*, Yeovilton and HMS *Bulwark*. Brian joined HMS *Invincible* as an Aircraft Handler after his training. Brian's nickname was Budgie. He was home on leave when the Falkland Islands were invaded.

During the Falklands War, while onboard HMS *Invincible*, he kept diaries about his experiences as a young 19-year-old. As Brian started to write about his adventure 'Down South', he wrote about the Total Exclusion Zone, explaining its meaning. He wrote an entry the day before the San Carlos landings, his expectation that hundreds of people would be killed that day thankfully turned out to be wrong.

Brian made another entry on 12 June 1982 about HMS *Glamorgan*, the event itself and the casualties. His last entries were happy ones about the surrender, the relief, the celebrations finally that the Islands were back with the British.

The war had ended with the Argentine surrender on 14 June 1982, an excited Brian made his last entries in his diaries. Brian was killed in a tragic accident two days after the war ended. Brian was using a vehicle to tow an aircraft when it crashed, he was crushed.

Twenty-five years later a television documentary aired, bringing Brian's diary entries to life. After he died Brian was buried at sea in Naval tradition, which may be expected but nevertheless leaves families with no grave to visit, no real goodbyes. His diaries were returned to his mother Joan.

Brian's brother Gary served in the Royal Marines; younger brother David followed him into the Royal Navy.

In 2022, as part of the Falkland Islands 40th Anniversary Place Names Project, Brian was honoured with 'Marsden Cove', a sheltered cove on the east coast of Adventure Sound, East Falkland.

His name lives on…

D101325D Leading Cook Tony Marshall HMS *Sheffield* 3 January 1951 ~ 4 May 1982 Age 31

Tony Marshall was born on 3 January 1951; records suggest he may have been a twin but there is nothing to suggest that he was named Anthony as some sources suggest. He appeared to marry in Liverpool in 1971.

During the Falklands War Tony was a Leading Cook on HMS *Sheffield*, sadly the first British ship to be sunk in action since the Second World War. A Type 42 Missile destroyer HMS *Sheffield* was the second ship to be named after the city of *Sheffield*.

Tony was working in the galley the day HMS *Sheffield* was hit by an Exocet missile on 4 May 1982, he died during the attack.

At the time of his death Tony's home on land was in Gosport, married with one daughter; his son was born in June 1982, just after the war ended.

Tony is remembered in St Columba's Church, Anfield, Liverpool. The memorial, a single stained glass window with a figure of St Aidan holding a crook in his left hand with a horned animal at his feet, a stylised cross with fouled anchor superimposed on it in the bottom centre of the window with two flowers either side of it. The inscription reads 'ST AIDAN OF LINDISFARNE IN LOVING MEMORY OF TONY MARSHALL KILLED IN ACTION FALKLANDS 1982'.

Remembrance 2021 saw Tony remembered at Blenheim Lodge by his brother Ray, who laid a wreath in his memory.

In 2022, as part of the Falkland Islands 40th Anniversary Place Names Project, Tony was honoured with 'Marshall Point', the south entrance point to Long Creek on the south coast of Weddell Island, West Falkland.

His name lives on…

24372545 Private Thomas Mechan 2nd Battalion Parachute Regiment 13 April 1957 ~ 28 May 1982 Age 25

Thomas 'Tam' 'Wee man' Mechan was born on 13 April 1957 in the Springburn area of Glasgow, the son of James Mechan. He had one sister. Tam enlisted into The Parachute Regiment in 1979 and passed out of P Coy with 456 Platoon on 2 November 1979. Tam was posted to 2 Para, the battalion was in Ballykinler, Northern Ireland, at the time. In August that year 2 Para had suffered terrible losses at Warrenpoint, a personality such as Tam's was welcome in the aftermath of such a tragedy.

Bill Bentley MM remembered Tam from the Northern Ireland tour as a man who could break the ice with humour in desperate moments. He likened it to the sun rising in the middle of the night. Tam broke both desperation and boredom while the battalion was dealing with awful circumstances in the wake of the heinous bombings of August that year, and the gruelling tour they endured.

When the Falkland Islands were invaded in April 1982, Tam travelled 'Down South' with his mates on the MV *Norland*. Tam was Company HQ, D Coy, 2 Para, he died on 28 May 1982, apparently killed by a stray bullet.

Like many families in 1982, Tam's father was reportedly very upset that his son had initially been buried in a mass grave. During the aftermath of the Falklands War, suddenly the Government found themselves for the first time under immense pressure to repatriate the bodies of the 'Fallen'. Tam's remains were repatriated, he is buried in the Military Cemetery in Aldershot.

Tam is also one of fourteen men who are honoured on a brass plaque in Glasgow Cathedral.

In 2022, as part of the Falkland Islands 40th Anniversary Place Names Project, Tam was honoured with 'Mechan Inlet', the northwest arm of Chaffers Gullet, Falkland Sound side of West Falkland.

His name lives on…

24196164 Corporal Michael Melia 59 Independent Commando Squadron Royal Engineers 21 September 1951 ~ 28 May 1982 Age 30

William Melia and Catherine Mannion married in 1933, starting their family the following year with eldest son William, named after his father. Known as Bill and Kitty, they went on to have nine children. Over the next nineteen years Jim, Jack, Maureen, Tony, Kathleen, Jacqueline, Mick and Terry arrived. Mick was the second to youngest of the large Oldham-based family.

Bill had been a Sapper in the Second World War, owing to the war there was a gap with the children between 1941 and 1948, thankfully Bill survived.

Mick attended St Anselm's Secondary Modern School where he did not excel academically but was very good at sport, especially football. After leaving school, he initially trained as a welder but joined the British Army in 1971 as a Sapper with the Royal Engineers. Three of his brothers had served in the Forces, Bill in the East Lancashire Regiment, Jim in the Royal Air Force and Tony in the Fleet Air Arm of the Royal Navy.

Prior to joining up Mick had been a member of the Territorial Army serving with 75 Engineer Regiment (202 Field Squadron (V) TAVR).

Once basic training with the Royal Engineers was completed, Parachute Training followed. Mick served with 9 Parachute Squadron Royal Engineers in both Aldershot and Belize. Next, he undertook Commando Training for service with 59 Independent Commando Squadron based in Plymouth. His physical ability then led to selection as one of the Training Team preparing Army Volunteers for the famous Royal Marines 'All Arms' Commando Course. He had earned the right to wear both Green and Maroon Berets.

In 1982 Mick travelled 'Down South' with 59 Commando Royal Engineers attached to A Coy, 2 Para for the initial landings and the assault on Goose Green. Mick was killed on 28th May 1982, alongside of his Parachute Regiment comrades.

Mick married Gill in Plymouth in October of 1978; the couple had no children.

After his temporary interment at Ajax Bay, Mick's body was repatriated, and a full Military funeral followed. He is now buried at the Weston Park cemetery in Plymouth. He lies surrounded by three football pitches, which seems quite fitting considering his love of football.

In 2022, as part of the Falkland Islands 40th Anniversary Place Names Project, Mick was honoured with 'Melia Creek', a creek at the head of New Haven on the Falkland Sound side of East Falkland.

His name lives on…

24442460 Private Richard William Middlewick Army Catering Corps 10 June 1961 ~ 8 June 1982 Age 20

Service was no stranger to the Middlewick family. Records indicate that great-great-grandfather Thomas Middlewick was a marine fireman in Plymouth while living in Southampton with his family in the early 1900s. Prior to that Thomas had been a ship's stoker. Thomas married Flora in 1878, their son Norman Walter was born in Southampton in October 1897. The Middlewick family had lived for generations in the West Country, gradually moving along the coast into Devon and Hampshire.

Norman Walter Middlewick was one of seven children born to Thomas and Flora, Thomas continued to work on the ships in one capacity or another. Norman was in the Gordon Boys' Brigade as a teenager. Most of the boys survived the First World War, however oldest son William Thomas a 2nd Engineer on HMY *Zarefah* died on 8 May 1917 when the yacht struck a mine with the loss of sixteen crewmen. William was married with seven children, an experienced seaman who was part of the Mercantile Reserve. He is commemorated on the Plymouth Naval Memorial.

Norman Walter Middlewick, Rick's grandfather, married Bertha Matilda Shute in 1923 in Bristol. Norman, it appears, served in the Hampshire Regiment in the First World War, by 1916 he had attained the rank of corporal. Bertha was born in June 1898 in Somerset. Seemingly their only son, Raymond was born in 1929, the family had by then settled in Bristol.

Raymond went on to marry Cynthia Hall in 1952. The couple had four children between 1954 and 1964, three boys and one girl. Richard ('Rick') William Middlewick was their third son born in Bristol on 10 June 1961.

By the time Raymond and Cynthia's only daughter was born in 1964, the family had relocated to Sussex. Rick finished his education at the Brighton Hove and Sussex Grammar School, he was a keen golfer. After leaving school Rick joined the army in 1977, he attended the Army Catering Corps College.

In 1982, Rick was attached to the 1st Battalion Welsh Guards. After arrival in the Falklands the troops transferred to the RFA *Sir Galahad* for the last slog of their journey to Fitzroy.

On 8 June 1982, the *Sir Galahad* was attacked by Argentinian A-4 Skyhawks and in the ensuing explosions there were the heaviest losses of any day during the whole war. Rick died just two days short of his 21st birthday. At the time of Rick's death his land address was Elizabeth Barracks in Pirbright.

In 2022, as part of the Falkland Islands 40th Anniversary Place Names Project, Rick was honoured with 'Middlewick Arm', the western arm of Double Creek East Arm, West Falkland.

His name lives on…

D158683V Acting Leading Marine Engineering Mechanic (Mechanical) David Miller HMS Fearless 31 December 1959 ~ 8 June 1982 Age 22

Harry Miller and Ann Gamble-Thompson married in Cleveland, Yorkshire, in 1958. They went on to have three children, their first child was a girl, Mandy; on the 31 December 1959 she was joined by a brother, David. The family have lived in Thornaby, Cleveland, for many years. Second son Bryan arrived two years later.

Though the family have a long history in Thornaby, they were originally on David's maternal side from Yorkshire. Herbert Gamble Thompson was born in August 1907. Herbert, it appears, was David's grandfather.

Herbert joined the Royal Artillery; he married Sarah Jane Newton in 1929. The couple had four children, Gladys, Herbert, Ann and Marion. Herbert senior was gassed during his service which led to cancer later in life. In 1939, he was working as a general labourer but died in April 1957.

Sydney Miller was born in November 1901, the son of a miner. Sydney married Elizabeth Jones in 1924, the couple's first child, Frank, it appears was born in 1925. Next came Billy, and their third son, Harry, was born in March 1928. Two girls, Betty and Elsie, came later. In 1939 the family lived at Briar Road, Thornaby, just as the Second World War was about to break. Later still came brothers Eric and Dennis.

When Harry and Ann married, he was a steel worker at Head Wrightson in Thornaby. David was born at his Nana Thompson's house in Beechwood Road, Thornaby.

David joined Stockton Sea Cadets T.S. *Fortitude* when he was 13 years old; he excelled. For the next three years he won Cadet of the Year until, on 8 June 1976, he joined the Royal Navy at 16 years of age. David's first ship was HMS *Fearless*, then The *Ark Royal* in 1978. In 1982, he was back in HMS *Fearless*.

David met Andrea Newman in Chichester; the couple married in Chichester in October 1980. At the time of David's death, they lived in Bognor Regis, they had no children.

David Miller was part of the crew of the Landing Craft Utility F4 from HMS *Fearless* when they were bombed by Argentinian Skyhawks in Choiseul Sound. David died with the majority of the crew on 8 June 1982, exactly six years to the day that he had joined the Royal Navy.

Thirty years later David's mother was presented with the Elizabeth Cross on the anniversary of his death. Normally it would have gone to his widow Andrea, but it was agreed that Ann would receive the medal so that it could stay with the family in Thornaby.

A new plaque in David's memory was also unveiled at the Irene Jessop Funeral Service home on Lanehouse Road, Thornaby, the old one retrieved by David's sister.

Sister Mandy says, 'We miss you so much David (Dusty) you are always in our thoughts, love from Mam, Mandy, Ronnie, Bryan, Sue, Ron, David Great nephews, and nieces Xxxxx'.

Dusty is remembered as a kind, loving, giving person and 'very lovable'.

In 2022, as part of the Falkland Islands 40th Anniversary Place Names Project, David was honoured with 'Miller Islet', a tussac island lying east of Big Samuel Island, Choiseul Sound, previously referred to as Big Samuel east islet.

His name lives on…

24185774 Lance Sergeant Clark Mitchell MID 2nd Battalion Scots Guards 17 February 1956 ~ 14 June 1982 Age 26

Clark Mitchell was born 17 February 1956 at Charleston Maternity Home in Montrose, Scotland. His parents, Robert and Fan, married in 1952 in Laurencekirk; they had six children altogether including a set of twin boys. Clark was Fan's maiden name.

Clark was brought up in Laurencekirk, a small town in Aberdeenshire known as 'The Lang Toun' or 'The Kirk' by locals. Clark was educated firstly at Laurencekirk Primary School followed by Laurencekirk Secondary School. As a youngster he had joined the Army Cadets. After leaving school Clark joined the British Army in

1972 aged just 16. He began his journey at the Guards Depot, Pirbright in Surrey, as a junior soldier.

Clark married Theresa Julie Manning on 5 September 1975 at St Theresa's Roman Catholic Church in Glasgow.

Clark was a well thought of young man who had risen through the ranks during his career, he held the rank of Lance Sergeant. His service included Northern Ireland, Belize, Germany, London, Kenya and Edinburgh. By the time the Falkland Islands were invaded in 1982, Clark was an experienced soldier with the 2nd Battalion Scots Guards.

Apparently, he was a quiet, shy man until you got to know him. He was also brave, which showed in his actions during the Battle for Mount Tumbledown. The enemy was well dug in, the mission not an easy one. During the assault he located and killed several snipers who were a danger to the Scots Guards. He was courageously at the front of the assault. Clark was killed on 14 June 1982, one of eight men from his battalion who perished that night. Clark's actions earned him a posthumous Mention In Dispatches.

Though Clark's siblings and their families mainly live in the same area of Scotland, his father Robert never quite got over his death and passed away after a long illness. Clark is remembered with much love by his comrades, friends, family and widow.

In 2022, as part of the Falkland Islands 40th Anniversary Place Names Project, Clark was honoured with 'Mitchell Stream', a north flowing stream rising between Mt Donald and Mt Adam on West Falkland.

His name lives on...

24608405 Guardsman Christopher Mordecai 1st Battalion Welsh Guards 21 July 1963 ~ 8 June 1982 Age 18

The Mordecai family has long standing roots, both in the Bridgend/Maesteg area and the British Army. Historically, in many parts of Wales young men had the choice to work in the coal mines or join up.

Christopher's grandfather, Harold Mordecai, was born in June 1915 in Bridgend, one of twins. It appears that Harold's older brother Richard joined the Royal Regiment of Artillery in 1919. Records also indicate that youngest brother, Trevor, born in 1918, was a Stoker 1st Class in the Second World War, he died on 19 December 1941 on HMS *Stanley*. The ship was hit by torpedoes and though there were some survivors Trevor was not one of them. Trevor is commemorated on the Plymouth Naval Memorial.

Harold married Louisa Barnes in 1936; they had a large family by the time war broke out in 1939, and he was working as a colliery hewer.

Christopher's father, Gary Mordecai, was born in Bridgend, he was Harold and Louisa's fourth son. Gary Mordecai and Heather Joynson married in Bridgend where eldest child and only son Christopher was born on 21 July 1963. The couple went on to have two daughters.

Christopher was brought up in Maesteg, attending Plasnewydd Primary School followed by Llangwynwydd Comprehensive. Christopher played rugby for his school. When he discovered a talent for woodwork he went on to the Technical College in Bridgend where he studied Art and Technical Drawing.

Many of the Mordecai family had served in the British Army, including Christopher's father; many of his relatives had been in the Welsh Guards.

Christopher worked for both the Forestry Commission and the Local Market in the tween time and school rugby was replaced by football. Thanks to his goal-scoring skills, he became known as 'Striker' when he played for the Maesteg Park Rangers team.

Six months after entering Pirbright, Christopher passed out just as the Falkland Islands were invaded. He went straight to Sennybridge for pre-deployment training with No 3 Company, 1st Battalion Welsh Guards.

The QE2 set sail from Southampton on 13 May 1982 with 3,500 military on board. Christopher, a young 18-year-old, barely out of training, was off to war.

On 7 June 1982, the Welsh Guards boarded the RFA *Sir Galahad* in San Carlos Water, for the journey round to Fitzroy settlement. They thought they were to disembark and go into battle, instead a huge tragedy occurred. The Argentinian air strike the following day was catastrophic. Christopher was not among the survivors; he died just over a month short of his 19th birthday.

On 21 June 1982, still smouldering, the remains of the *Galahad* were towed out to sea and sunk by HMS *Onyx*.

There is a Memorial at Fitzroy Cove and Christopher's name has also been inscribed on the cenotaph in the centre of Maesteg. The council took a bit of persuading, but eventually his name was added.

In 2022, as part of the Falkland Islands 40th Anniversary Place Names Project, Christopher was honoured with 'Mordecai Bay', a bay to the east of Hill Cove on West Falkland.

His name lives on…

3rd Engineering Officer Andrew John Morris RFA *Sir Galahad*
21 February 1957 ~ 8 June 1982 Age 25

Andrew's father, Douglas Osmond Morris, was born in the district of St Thomas, Devon, in April 1917. Douglas was an estate agent; Andrew's grandfather, Walter Morris, had been an auctioneer and estate agent.

Walter Osmond Morris was born in Monmouthshire in May 1885, the eldest son of Walter and Dorothy Mary Morris (née Towill). The family had settled in the Isle of Wight by the late 1800s. Walter Osmond Morris was a chemist's apprentice by the time he was 15, he went on to become a pharmacist and optician.

Walter Osmond was the eldest of three boys, brother Douglas died in 1911 aged just 23. Younger brother Malcolm attested into the Royal Flying Corps in 1916, records indicate he was an Aircraftsman, Naval Air Squadron, by 1918. Malcolm survived the First World War, he married in 1927, he became a consulting optician.

Carolie Madge Warrand de Montmorency was born in Dublin in August 1920. Douglas and Carolie married in Hampshire in 1947, their first child, a daughter, was born a few years later. Andrew John Morris was born on 21 February 1957, by which time the couple had settled in Poole, Dorset, where they were to live out their long lives.

Andrew was born at home at Danebury Hill, Greenwood Avenue, Lilliput, Poole, Dorset. It is likely Andrew would have attended the nearby Lilliput Infant School.

Known as Andy, he had served on a number of RFA ships before he was appointed to RFA *Sir Galahad* in April 1981, he was a respected Engineering Officer with a potentially bright career ahead of him.

The *Sir Galahad* had endured many attacks while in 'Bomb Alley' and had previously been hit by a 1000lb bomb that failed to detonate. The ship was damaged, and she had been evacuated once. Andy and his shipmates were tasked to make repairs to enable the *Galahad* to continue to give vital support to the troops ashore. Andy was known for a positive and pragmatic approach with a great sense of humour – qualities so needed at times of such great stress.

On 8 June 1982, the *Sir Galahad* was at anchor at Port Pleasant, close to Fitzroy. She was preparing to disembark the Welsh Guards when she was attacked by three Argentinian Skyhawks. The ship was hit by three bombs, the third of which exploded in the engine room killing Andy. Five members of the Royal Fleet Auxiliary were killed in the attack.

In 2009, it was announced that the next of kin would receive the Elizabeth Cross and Memorial Scroll from a grateful nation in recognition of their tragic loss.

Andy's mother had died in May 2004, his father in 2005 aged 83 and 88 respectively; it left his sister Diana entitled to claim the award on behalf of the family. By then Diana had settled in South Africa with her family. She was presented the award in September 2010 by Dr Nicola Brewer, the British High Commissioner to South Africa, in a ceremony in Cape Town.

In 2022, as part of the Falkland Islands 40th Anniversary Place Names Project, Andy was honoured with 'Morris Bay', a sheltered bay at the entrance to Arrow Harbour on the south side of Choiseul Sound, East Falkland.

His name lives on…

D140637W Leading Seaman (Radar) Michael Stephen Mullen HMS *Ardent* 24 August 1957 ~ 21 May 1982 Age 24

Michael Stephen Mullen was born on 24 August 1957 at the Princess Mary's RAF Hospital, Halton Camp, Wendover, Buckinghamshire. Michael, it appears, was the only son of James and Marjorie Mullen (née Derbyshire). James was a Flight Sergeant with the Royal Air Force, the family lived at The Old Kiln, Moor Common, Lane End, Buckinghamshire.

James was the only son of James and Annie Mullen (née McCarthy), records state that he joined the Royal Air Force between September 1939 and February 1940 aged just 17. Both his father and grandfather were also named James, it seems his grandfather was originally from Ireland.

Born in Kirkdale in June 1923, Marjorie was one of seven children to Joseph and Elizabeth Derbyshire (née Hopkins). Marjorie's grandmother was also born in Ireland. Her father Joseph and Uncle William were at one time marine firemen.

James and Marjorie married on 17 December 1949 at the Register Office in Prescot. James was by then a Sergeant, Marjorie a clerk for a government contractor. Marjorie's home was in Roby, a 1930s three-bedroom semi-detached house within walking distance of the Roby Park Primary school. It seems the couple returned at some point to Marjorie's roots, Michael's home became the area where the Derbyshire family had lived for many years.

The Royal Navy was Michael's service of choice. Deployed to the South Atlantic on HMS *Ardent* as part of the Task Force in 1982, Michael was one of twenty-two crew members on his ship that did not make it home.

Michael was killed on 21 May 1982; he was 24 years old.

James died in 1996, Marjorie on 3 April 1999, seventeen years after the invasion of the Falkland Islands.

In 2022, as part of the Falkland Islands 40th Anniversary Place Names Project, Stephen was honoured with 'Mullen Cove', a cove between Island Point and Knob Point on the Walker Creek side of Choiseul Sound, East Falkland.

His name lives on…

24282774 Lance Corporal James Hamilton Murdoch 3rd Battalion Parachute Regiment 21 May 1957 ~ 12 June 1982 Age 25

James Hamilton ('Doc') Murdoch was born in the Provan district of Glasgow on 21 May 1957, the son of Jim and Jean Murdoch. Jim had one brother, John, and three sisters: Phyllis, Jean and Anne.

Jim's sister Jean married a Paratrooper in 1983, the couple named their son James Murdoch after his hero uncle.

Jim joined Junior Parachute Company in September 1972 at Malta Barracks in Aldershot.

Chad Hulme joined up at the same time as Jim, he remembers leaves spent in Aldershot having fun and says, 'listening to Rod Stewart in a room we weren't supposed to be'. After their training Doc went to 3 Para and Chad to 1 Para, Chad however still pays his respects at Doc's grave regularly.

Tom Herring says:

> Doc Murdoch joined my section in B Coy 3 Para in 1975. He was
> prone to injuring himself, from getting too much sun on his pale skin
> in Singapore, to getting a phosphorous burn in Italy. He did such

a good job of bandage and self-treatment I made him the section medic. Hence the nickname Doc I was also his platoon Sergeant later in Osnabruck. I used to invite him and my other junior NCOs over for Sunday lunch at my married quarter regularly.

One of the most widely available photos of Doc is with his wrist in plaster.

Doc was particularly remembered for his laugh which apparently was both unique and infectious. Paul Read says:

> Doc was a close friend in 3 Para. We met as Company drivers in Germany. I was C and he B Coy. He was a great character who always had a smile and an infectious laugh. We were both at the same Drill and Duties cadre to get promoted in Tidworth in 1981. Doc and I were by far the worst students in our group – however, it was memorable for the amount we laughed at each other during various lessons.
>
> Once that laugh of his started it was infectious – needless to say, we were both jailed and shell PT on several occasions!! But you could never change his spirit. I recall the morning after the battle hearing with great sadness that Doc had been killed on top of Longdon.
>
> In 2006 I returned with a load of guys from Doc's platoon – I needed to go, to finally say goodbye – which was good. Although gone, he will always be remembered with fondness and in our hearts in 3 Para. Never Forgotten – Paul Read 3 Para 'Class of 82'.

Paratroopers are not exactly light and fluffy, yet their spirit might be. During difficult times such as P Company, exercise, tours, and troubles, men like Doc lift the spirits of others.

Doc died as he lived, trying to help others, during the Battle for Mount Longdon he died trying to save two comrades, yet once injured, he could not be saved.

After the Falklands War, it was not automatic for men to be added to local war memorials. In Doc's case it took thirty years; finally, in 2012, the local council agreed to add names of those local men who died post the Second World War. Doc's name was added in June 2013.

Doc is buried at Arkleston Cemetery, Paisley, Scotland.

For those who knew him, a close of the eyes and a little imagination would bring back the memory of that laugh described as somewhere between a cackle and a shriek.

In 2022, as part of the Falkland Islands 40th Anniversary Place Names Project, Doc was honoured with 'Murdoch Bay', a west-facing bay at Brown Point at the entrance to Christmas Harbour on the north shore of King George Bay, West Falkland.

His name lives on…

C022353P Lieutenant Brian Murphy HMS *Ardent* 24 March 1952 ~ 21 May 1982 Age 30

Brian Murphy was born in Dundee on 24 March 1952; he was one of two children. Brian had one sister, Maureen.

Brian attended Eastern Primary school followed by Grove Academy, Broughty Ferry, Dundee. As a youngster Brian played cricket, golf and football, specifically as goalkeeper. While playing football for the Boys' Brigade, Brian decided his path forward would be with the Royal Navy.

Brian joined the Royal Navy as an Apprentice Aircraft Artificer in January 1968. His initial training was at HMS *Fisgard* followed by HMS *Condor* in his homeland of Scotland.

Almost five years later, in late 1972, Brian married Lynn in Hampshire.

After training as a Fleet Air Arm Aircrew Officer, Brian won the Wallrock Trophy for being the best Aviation Special Duties Officer Cadet. Brian excelled in the Royal Navy with further training and awards, winning the Devenish Trophy.

By 1976, Brian was joining HMS *Endurance* visiting the Falkland Islands for the first time as part of the Royal Navy's Antarctic patrol.

Brian and Lynn had been married for ten years when their daughter Elizabeth was born in Somerset at the very beginning of 1982. Simultaneously to becoming a father, Brian became Deputy Flight Commander of HMS *Ardent*. This new position and basking in the delight of parenthood was to be very short-lived. Brian was killed on 21 May 1982 when HMS *Ardent* came under attack from Argentine Forces.

Brian is remembered with a plaque in his old school, Grove Academy, which takes pride of place in the Assembly Hall. There is also a trophy in his name which is awarded annually to pupils, very apt as Brian had worked his way up from a teenage apprentice to the rank of Lieutenant during his service with the Royal Navy.

In 2022, as part of the Falkland Islands 40th Anniversary Place Names Project, Brian was honoured with 'Murphy Islet', a small tussac island next to Turn Island on the east side of the entrance to Adventure Sound, East Falkland.

His name lives on…

D141680P Leading Physical Training Instructor Gary Thomas Nelson HMS *Ardent* 18 May 1957 ~ 21 May 1982 Age 25

Gary Thomas Nelson was born at 171 Painswick Road, Gloucester on 18 May 1957 to Simeon and Betty Nelson (née Armstrong). Simeon was a Sergeant with the Royal Signals. The couple had a younger son, born four years later in Malta.

Simeon, it appears, was one of six children, and he had a long career with the Royal Signals. By 1972, Simeon was a Warrant Officer First Class, he was honoured in the New Year's Honours list that year with an MBE. Simeon was born in Barrow-In-Furness, where the family later returned. Simeon worked his way up through the ranks and by the time the boys were teenagers he had attained the rank of Captain.

Gary opted for a life on the seas; after joining the Royal Navy, Gary saw service on HMS *Amazon* in the late 1970s. Gary married his wife, Jane, in 1972, the couple had one daughter who was born in 1981.

The Nelson's home on land in 1982 was Saltash in Cornwall, where Gary was a well-liked member of the Rugby Club.

At the time of the Falklands War, Gary was a Leading Physical Training Instructor in HMS *Ardent*. On board ship men still have to keep their fitness up; the Falkland Islands was a long voyage for the Task Force.

Gary was known by many as 'Ginge'. On 21 May 1982, Gary was one of the twenty-two men who lost their lives when HMS *Ardent* was attacked by Argentine Forces.

After Gary's death, his widow presented a trophy to the Saltash Rugby Club. Until 1999, it was presented to the winners of the match between Saltash and the Royal Naval PTI's. As of 2023, it is now presented each year to a serving serviceman who is a member of the Rugby Club.

In 2022, as part of the Falkland Islands 40th Anniversary Place Names Project, Gary was honoured with 'Nelson Island', a small tussac island close to Goose Green on East Falkland.

His name lives on...

24220165 Lance Corporal Stephen John Newbury 1st Battalion Welsh Guards 8 November 1957 ~ 8 June 1982 Age 24

Stephen John Newbury was born on 8 November 1957. He was the only son of Alan and Yvonne Newbury (née Ropke) who married in Cardiff in 1955.

The Newburys had their oldest child Karen the year after they married. Stephen was their second child; he was born in Stillington Street, London. Alan was serving in the Welsh Guards; he served a total of twenty-four years.

As part of a military family Steve moved around a lot. Younger sister Dawn was born in Hubbelrath, Germany, Gail in Mill Hill. There was a frequent change of schools along the way. After leaving school, Steve followed his father's footsteps into the Welsh Guards when he was just 16 years old.

Steve saw service in Berlin during his time in the Welsh Guards but he married closer to home. After Berlin, the Welsh Guards were posted to Pirbright.

Steve married Angela Cadby in Wales; they had two children, Paul Stephen in 1980 and Sian Louise born two years later, just before her father was deployed for the last time.

Steve loved football and went to see Cardiff play whenever he was back home.

Stephen died on 8 June 1982 when the RFA *Sir Galahad* was bombed at Fitzroy. Almost fifty servicemen died, many more were injured. His heartbroken father Alan died in 1988.

In 2022, as part of the Falkland Islands 40th Anniversary Place Names Project, Steve was honoured with 'Newbury Cove', a main landing beach at Grand Jason in the Jason Islands group, West Falkland.

His name lives on…

24380988 Corporal John Newton 22 SAS Regiment 6 June 1959 ~ 19 May 1982 Age 22

John Newton was born 6 June 1959 at Greenbank Hospital Darlington, Co Durham, the youngest son of John Tinkler and Florence Elizabeth Newton (née Jones). John senior was a groundsman, as his father had been before him. John and Florence married in early 1941 at St John the Baptist, Ault Hucknall in Derbyshire.

The name Tinkler appears to have come from John's paternal great-grandmother Sarah Ann Tinkler, who married John Newton in 1870. John also died young, he was just 36 years old, leaving Sarah a widow with two children.

Our John had two older brothers; he joined the SAS in 1980, at the time of the Falklands War he was with HQ (Armourer) Unit. His parent unit was the Royal Electrical and Mechanical Engineers. Though he was many years younger than his older brothers, between the three of them they gave much to our country through service.

John was killed on 19 May 1982 in the Sea King crash as it was cross-decking men from HMS *Hermes* to HMS *Intrepid*.

John had attended Haughton Community School in Darlington. There is a plaque at the school dedicated to John. It was moved in April 2006 when the Education Village opened. Each year the school lays a wreath and remembers him.

Bill Clark, Senior Science Technician when the Village opened, remembered John as a great lad, the kind that you would love to have as a son. Steve Jackson, an Assistant Headteacher at the Education Village, described him as someone who knew where he was going. Apparently, he had always wanted to join the army. These are the kind of memories that can easily be lost in the ether.

In 2019 the Education Village in Darlington invited two very special guests to their Remembrance Service. John's brothers, retired SAS Officer Peter and former Medic David, were in attendance, they had not known their brother was honoured by the school each year. Peter was impressed that the school had hung a plaque so soon after John's death. David felt it was good for the younger generations to remember and appreciate the past. Lest we Forget in its essence.

John is also honoured in a Book of Remembrance originally held at the War Memorial Hospital Darlington.

In 2022, as part of the Falkland Islands 40th Anniversary Place Names Project, John was honoured with 'Newton Islet', a small tussac island in the Outer Triste Islands, East Falkland.

His name lives on…

Seaman Por Ng SS *Atlantic Conveyor* 11 June 1926 ~ 25 May 1982 Age 55

Por Ng was born on 11 June 1926; he was from Hong Kong.

On 3 April 1982, the United Nations passed Resolution 502. This demanded that Argentina withdraw their forces, cease hostilities and seek a political solution. Apparently, Argentina was surprised at this as they had expected the UN to support them.

After a meeting at the Ministry of Defence on 14 April 1982 the *Atlantic Conveyor* under the command of Captain Ian 'Harry' North was designated to carry a number of Harriers and helicopters 'Down South'.

During the Falklands War, Ng served with the Royal Fleet Auxilliary. He died when SS *Atlantic Conveyor* was attacked on 25 May 1982. Ng was listed as 'missing', he is among those who were lost to the South Atlantic, his body remained unrecovered. He died just 17 days short of his 56th birthday.

Every man born is someone's son, often also someone's husband and father, but little is known about Ng.

In 2022, as part of the Falkland Islands 40th Anniversary Place Names Project, Ng was honoured with Ng Islet, a small tussac island south of Tussac Point near Bull Point, East Falkland.

His name lives on…

24498671 Guardsman Gareth Duane Nicholson 1st Battalion Welsh Guards 15 August 1962 ~ 8 June 1982 Age 19

Gareth Duane Nicholson was born in Bridgend, South Wales, on 15 August 1962, the only son for his mother Beryl. In a poem written by Beryl, Gareth is described as 'a joy and trouble free'.

Gareth was brought up in Bridgend with John and Beryl Nicholson and his two sisters. He seemed to be a very likeable young man. Gareth attended Ysgol Gyfun Bryntirion Comprehensive School.

Gareth loved sports and the scouts; he was an adventurous young boy. He fell in love with Lorraine, the couple married when he was just 18 years of age. Gareth joined the Welsh Guards rather than become a carpenter. He played rugby and managed to see a bit of the world, including climbing Mount Kenya.

The 1st Battalion Welsh Guards were deployed to the Falkland Islands in 1982 as part of 5th Infantry Brigade under the command of Lieutenant Colonel John Rickett.

Gareth was killed when the RFA *Sir Galahad* was bombed at Fitzroy on 8 June 1982. He is remembered with a plaque in St David's Church, Laleston, Ogwr, Mid Glamorgan, Wales.

In 2022, as part of the Falkland Islands 40th Anniversary Place Names Project, Gareth was honoured with 'Nicholson Islet', a small tussac islet north of Whale Island in Port Edgar, West Falkland.

His name lives on…

D126569P Petty Officer Weapons Engineering Mechanic Anthony Richard Norman HMS *Sheffield* 22 November 1956 ~ 4 May 1982 Age 25

Anthony's family lived in Cranbrook, Kent, where his parents Roy and Evelyn married in 1950. The couple started a family the following year when they welcomed fraternal twins into the world. They were closely followed by a brother in 1952, a sister in 1955, and Anthony was their fifth child born at home on 22 November 1956. Their last child, another son, was born in 1961.

The small town of Cranbrook, not far from Maidstone in Kent is also where Anthony's grandmother was born. Anthony's father was one of three boys all born in Cranbrook.

Anthony was schooled initially at Cranbrook Primary school; he finished his education at Angley Comprehensive School.

Anthony joined the Royal Navy straight from school, following very much in family footsteps. Anthony's father, both grandfathers and four uncles had served in the Royal Navy ahead of him. From Kent, Anthony set off to HMS *Ganges* for his initial training. After training Anthony was sent to HMS *Collingwood* in Portsmouth.

Prior to joining HMS *Sheffield*, Anthony's other ships included HMS *Ark Royal* and HMS *Rhyl*, he had also spent two years in Hong Kong.

When the Falkland Islands were invaded in April 1982, Anthony was in HMS *Sheffield*. He was well liked and by then had earned himself the nickname of 'Speedy'. Sadly, Anthony was one of those young matelots who perished when the ship was attacked.

1984 saw a plaque dedicated to Anthony at St Dunstan's Church, Carriers Road, Cranbrook, Tunbridge Wells, Kent. It reads 'In Memory of a much-loved Son and Brother ANTHONY RICHARD NORMAN killed on HMS SHEFFIELD FALKLANDS 4th May 1982 aged 25'.

Evelyn, Anthony's mother, died on 17 April 2013, just six weeks after his youngest brother Sean got married. Roy Hubert Norman, Anthony's father died on 1 April 2014 the day before the 32nd Anniversary of the invasion of the Falkland Islands.

In 2022, as part of the Falkland Islands 40th Anniversary Place Names Project, Anthony was honoured with 'Norman Beach', a sand beach on the south shore of Byron Sound, West Falkland.

His name lives on…

Captain Ian Harry North DSC SS *Atlantic Conveyor* Merchant Navy 5 March 1925 ~ 25 May 1982 Age 57

'Harry' North's family had a long history in the Doncaster area, he was one of just three Doncaster casualties of the Falklands War.

Harry's maternal grandfather William was a plumber, as was his great-uncle, Arthur.

Henry North and Dorothy Mary Nettleship married on the 4 April 1923 at Doncaster St George. Ian Harry North was the couple's eldest child, born at 11 Stanley Grove, Dunscroft, Hatfield, Doncaster, on 5 March 1925. Harry was one of two boys; his younger brother, Joseph William, was born in July 1926.

Harry's father was a headmaster at an elementary school and the family later lived in St Anne's Road in Doncaster. From a very young age Harry took to life on the ocean, in fact both brothers did. Harry for the Merchant Navy, his brother Bill served with the Royal Navy. Bill left service prior to the Falklands War, having attained the rank of Lieutenant Commander.

Harry remained single all his life, it is said that he had over forty years of service when he died. Nicknamed 'Captain Birdseye' for his resemblance to a certain television character, Harry certainly was very experienced on the seas. His niece remembers that Harry was many times asked to take shore-based jobs; somehow, he winged his way through medicals to stay on the seas. He apparently designed and helped build his parents' house, a place he would decorate with quirky items from his travels.

When the Falkland Islands were invaded the SS *Atlantic Conveyor* left Liverpool on 15 April 1982 to play her part as a cargo ship. Captain Ian Harry North was her skipper, her first port of call was Devonport.

SS *Atlantic Conveyor* was originally meant to be an aircraft carrier, but over the following week it was decided to make use of the cargo spaces for valuable task force stores. As well as other equipment, 600 cluster bombs, rocket motors, anti-tank missiles, grenades and small arms ammunition were stored in normal containers. The ship set sail for Ascension Island on 25 April 1982 after an incredible conversion taking just ten days.

The MV *Europic Ferry* and the MV *Norland* joined her for the trip 'Down South'. By 21 May 1982, SS *Atlantic Conveyor* had achieved her main mission and the Harriers she was carrying had been de-bagged. She continued to provide Battle Cargo support.

Reputedly, on 25 May 1982, Captain North said, 'Well boys, it's May 25th something spectacular should happen today.'

At 1940 hrs, 'Emergency Stations' was sounded by the *Atlantic Conveyor*'s ship's alarm. Despite countermeasures the ship was hit by two missiles at C deck. It proved to be devastating and the decision to abandon ship was made twenty-five minutes after the attack.

Harry is said to have been a tower of strength to his men as the ship was abandoned in very difficult circumstances; 137 men survived and Captain North was the last to leave the ship, it is claimed, with huge dignity and calm. Twelve men died that day, three on board and the rest in the water. Captain North was one of the men who lost his life after leaving the ship.

Harry was 57 years old when he died, he was awarded the Distinguished Service Cross, posthumously.

Captain North is remembered in many places, there is a memorial to him in Doncaster Minster. The plain state plaque carries both the Merchant Navy and Cunard company badges.

It reads:

'THIS PLAQUE COMMEMORATES CAPTAIN IAN HARRY NORTH DSC WHO RECEIVED THE FOLLOWING CITATION ON 14 APRIL 1982, SS ATLANTIC CONVEYOR WAS LAID UP IN LIVERPOOL. ON 25 APRIL SHE DEPLOYED TO THE SOUTH ATLANTIC, CONVERTED TO OPERATE FIXED AND ROTARY WING AIRCRAFT AND LOADED WITH STORES AND EQUIPMENT FOR THE FALKLANDS TASK FORCE. THIS ASTONISHING FEAT WAS LARGELY DUE TO CAPTAIN NORTH'S INNOVATION, LEADERSHIP AND INEXHAUSTABLE ENERGY. SS ATLANTIC CONVEYOR JOINED THE CARRIER BATTLE GROUP ON 19TH MAY 1982 AND WAS IMMEDIATELY TREATED AS A WARSHIP IN MOST RESPECTS. ALMOST COMPARABLE IN MANOEUVERABILITY, FLEXIBILITY AND RESPONSE, CAPTAIN NORTH AND THE SHIP CAME THROUGH WITH FLYING COLOURS. WHEN THE SHIP WAS HIT ON 25TH MAY, CAPTAIN NORTH WAS A TOWER OF STRENGTH DURING THE DIFFICULT PERIOD OF DAMAGE ASSESSMENT LEADING UP TO THE DECISION TO ABANDON SHIP. HE LEFT THE SHIP LAST WITH ENORMOUS DIGNITY AND CALM AND HIS SUBSEQUENT DEATH WAS A BLOW TO ALL. A BRILLIANT SEAMAN, BRAVE IN WAR, IMMENSELY REVERED AND LOVED, HIS CONTRIBUTION TO THE CAMPAIGN WAS ENORMOUS AND EPITOMISED THE GREAT SPIRIT OF THE MERCHANT SERVICE.'

Captain North has another plaque at HMS *Wellington* in London. It reads 'THE SOUTH ATLANTIC TASK FORCE 1982 Liveryman Ian Harry North DSC 25th May 1982.'

Harry's father Henry died in November 1970 aged 78, but Dorothy outlived her son by two years and died in August 1984, Aged 92. Though Ian Harry North never married, he had one niece who remains extremely proud of her Uncle Harry.

In 2022, as part of the Falkland Islands 40th Anniversary Place Names Project, Harry was honoured with 'North Inlet', the inlet at the head of Ship Harbour on Pebble Island, West Falkland.

His name lives on…

P036098F Marine Michael John 'Blue' Nowak 45 Commando Royal Marines 16 December 1958 ~ 12 June 1982 Age 23

The Nowak name originates from Poland, its meaning 'new guy in town'. Michael Nowak senior was certainly a new guy in town when he settled in Derby from the Ukraine. Michael Nowak married Sheila Spencer in Derby Register Office in 1956.

Michael Nowak was the youngest of three children, sadly his parents died when he was a child and he was brought up by his sisters Rosa and Maria. Both Michael and Rosa settled in Derby.

Michael and Sheila's eldest child, Michael John Nowak, was born in Derby on 16 December 1958. The couple had one other child: a daughter, Maria, born two years later on 14 December 1960. Maria and John (as he was known) were extremely close as siblings, they also celebrated birthdays together each year.

John attended Homelands Comprehensive School in Derby. Aspiring to join the Royal Marines, it was his sister who asked his mother to sign the papers as he was under 18. John passed out on 31 March 1977 with his proud family looking on. From then on, he was known as 'Blue' by his comrades. Sadly, his father Michael had died the year before on 22 January 1976, following a short illness.

Blue was posted to 45 Commando, mainly based in Arbroath, Scotland. At the time of the Falklands invasion Blue was with Yankee Company. The Royal Marines became the centre of Blue's life. Ironically, he had always wanted to be posted to the Falkland Islands, his wish was to come true – with a tragic outcome, however.

45 Commando were involved in the Battle for Two Sisters as our troops fought their way to retake Stanley. Blue was the only Marine from Y Coy to die at Two Sisters, killed on 12 June 1982. The Y company flag now contains a small blue square in memory of their only company loss in the Falklands War. There were losses on both sides at Two sisters, forty-four Argentinian prisoners were also taken that day.

Though Blue was unmarried, he did have a girlfriend at the time of his death. Kristina gave birth to their son, Michael David Nowak Greig, in 1982 in Penicuik, Midlothian, Scotland. Like so many children born at that time he would never know his father, though Blue is immortalised forever as one of the 255 servicemen who died during a short but brutal war. Although Blue still officially lived in Derby when he died, his heart was in Scotland.

Blue is buried at St Mary's Cemetery in Derby. Blue's mother Sheila died on 3 April 2011.

In 2022, as part of the Falkland Islands 40th Anniversary Place Names Project, Blue was honoured with 'Blue Nowak Reach', a stretch of the Malo River between the North Camp Road culverts upstream to Hawk's Nest, East Falkland.

His name lives on…

NO23329F Lieutenant Richard James Nunn DFC HQ 3 Commando Brigade Air Squadron Royal Marines 15 December 1954 ~ 28 May 1982 Age 27

Richard James Nunn was born in Cambridgeshire on 15 December 1954, the younger son of Stanley George and Margaret Nunn (née Chadwick). Richard's father, Stan, was born in Southampton in July 1920. Educated at Taunton School in Southampton, Stan went on to have an amazing career with the Royal Air Force starting with the Volunteer Reserves in June 1939; by September he had been called up for regular service.

Interestingly, on 28 May 1941, Stan escorted the battleships HMS *King George V* and HMS *Rodney,* a date that was to be tragic for the Nunn family forty-one years later. Stan was a Battle of Britain Pilot; he was one of three brothers who served in the Second World War. Stan was the middle son of Ernest and Elsie Nunn (née Doman).

Their eldest son, John Doman Nunn, served with the Royal Navy, joining the Fleet Air Arm in 1939. John retired a Lieutenant Commander in the 1950s, he had seen service in the Second World War and the Korean War. Youngest son Barry was born in November 1922, he served with the Royal Air Force Volunteer Reserve. Reported missing on 13 June 1943, Barrie (as he was known) is commemorated on the Runnymede Memorial.

Stan had a long career and retired a Group Captain on his birthday in 1975. During his service he earned the Distinguished Flying Cross, one of two granted to the Nunn family.

Stan married his bride, WRAF Flight Officer Chadwick, in Habbaniya Iraq in June 1949, the couple honeymooned in Nicosia, Cyprus. The couple's eldest child was a son, Christopher John Nunn. Christopher served with the Royal Marines during Operation Corporate as Officer in Command of M Company 42 Commando.

Richard ('Dick') was the couple's youngest child; he also had a sister, Sarah, two years his senior. Dick joined the Royal Marines in 1974 as part of Y074 batch. Dick joined 40 Commando post-training ,where he served as a Troop Commander, including a short period as LO(G) to Brigadier Moore.

A tour as OCRM to HMS *Gurkha* followed after which he left for the Lieutenant's Greenwich Course, which of course he passed.

Dick qualified as a Helicopter Pilot in 1981 becoming the fifth member of the Nunn family to receive their 'Wings'. Initially he stayed in Middle Wallop, he became a Scout pilot, after which he joined 3 Commando Air Squadron.

January 1982 saw Dick in Norway for winter warfare training, after which he had two weeks leave over Easter. Dick took over as B Flight Commander, he was soon deployed to the Falklands as history repeated itself: brothers on active service in yet another war, sadly only one would return.

28 May 1982 was a day that would go down in history and was arguably the turning point of the war, men were cold and hungry, and morale was dipping. During the Battle of Goose Green, unusually, the Commanding Officer was in the thick of the fighting. Colonel H Jones was seriously wounded; a call was made for his evacuation. That call was to cause the man who made it untold anguish in the years to come.

Dick had been flying his Scout for hours in support of 2 Para, bringing much needed supplies to the men. Dick's aircraft was hit by an Argentine Pucara, he died of his wounds.

Initially buried in a mass grave at Ajax Bay, Dick was later buried at the San Carlos Military Cemetery, a decision made by his father. Stan travelled to the Falkland Islands in 1983, with his other son, on the family pilgrimage for those who chose not to repatriate. Stan died in 1993 in St Austell, Cornwall, where the family had settled. The following year his ashes were buried with his son.

Dick was a very well-liked single man, known for his dedication to work and his pleasant personality. He was awarded the Distinguished Flying Cross posthumously. So much bravery and spirit within one family with a dedication to service thrown in for good measure.

In 2022, as part of the Falkland Islands 40th Anniversary Place Names Project, Dick was honoured with 'Nunn Bay', a main landing bay on Natural Arch Island in the Arch Islands Group, West Falkland.

His name lives on…

483497 Major Roger Nutbeem Royal Army Medical Corps
25 April 1942 ~ 8 June 1982 Age 40

The Nutbeem family had roots in both Hampshire and Wiltshire going back a couple of generations. Roger's grandfather, Frederick Charles Nutbeem, was the second son of Robert and Mary Nutbeem. The couple had four sons together; sadly Robert died in 1895, just after their last child was born, he was just 34 years old. Left to raise her children alone Mary continued to live in Wiltshire. Frederick Charles was a coach finisher apprentice when he was 20 years old.

Frederick Charles Nutbeem married Ellen Mabel Maybin in 1912; in October of the following year their eldest child, Frederick Walter, was born. The couple went on to have three more sons and a daughter. By 1939, the family had moved to London where Frederick Charles ran an Off Licence. Though the records are not transparent it appears as though Roger's uncle also served with the RAMC.

Frederick Walter Nutbeem married Edith May Waldron in Swindon in 1937, their oldest son Stuart was born in Swindon the following year. By 1939, the couple had moved to Redditch, their second son, Trevor, was closely followed by youngest child Roger, born on 25 April 1942.

Roger Nutbeem attended Alcester Grammar School followed by Agricultural College. After some time working in Holland studying the Dutch way of Dairy Farming, Roger joined the British Army. He was commissioned into the Royal Army Medical Corps in 1967.

During his time with the RAMC Roger developed his adventure skills, becoming an expert canoeist and mountain expedition leader.

In 1970, Roger married Tricia in Aldershot, Hampshire. The couple had their first child, Martin in 1974, followed by Kathryn, born in Hanover in 1977. Kathryn possessed her father's love of music. Roger played the guitar and enjoyed folk music. Like many a serviceman he carried his music with him wherever he went, back in a day when troops often made their own entertainment before technology advanced.

When the Falkland Islands were invaded in April 1982, Roger was deployed with 16 Field Ambulance, of which he was second in command. They deployed on the QE2 on 12 May 1982 as part of 5 Brigade. He was admired by his men for his ability to motivate and keep up morale.

On 8 June 1982, Roger was aboard RFA *Sir Galahad* when the Argentinian air strike occurred. Roger was on the upper deck and killed instantly by a bomb fragment. While those who died on the *Galahad* were lost to the sea, Roger's body was the only one recovered.

Roger was initially buried in the Falklands but later repatriated, he is buried in Tidworth Military Cemetery in Wiltshire.

His old Spanish Guitar was also found and returned to his family. In time the guitar was passed on to his daughter, who loved to sing with her father as a small child. Kathryn later was partially funded by the Army Benevolent Fund to train at the Royal Academy of music. In 2004 Kathryn made her singing debut in front of an audience of 13,000 people at the Royal Military Academy, Sandhurst.

Tricia, left to bring up her two children alone, was awarded an MBE for her counselling and practical work with 16 Field Ambulance Wives Club.

Roger's mother died in 2000, his father in 2007.

In 2022, as part of the Falkland Islands 40th Anniversary Place Names Project, Roger was honoured with 'Nutbeem Brook', a large stream in a valley to Freshwater the east of Mount Usborne.

His name lives on…

24048957 Staff Sergeant Patrick O'Connor 22 SAS Regiment 4 May 1949 ~ 19 May 1982 Age 33

Patrick O'Connor was born in Eire on 4 May 1949. Originally, he joined the Irish Guards, and went on to join the SAS in 1966.

Known as Paddy his service included South Arabia/Aden, Northern Ireland, Belize, Dhofar, Norway and the USA. Paddy was a Specialist Signaller, free-fall parachutist and a Norwegian linguist.

Paddy married his wife Iris in 1973, the couple had one son.

When the Falklands were invaded Paddy was recalled from the United States as he was trained in the use of the Stinger surface-to-air missile. Paddy was 24 Troop G Squadron SAS; he was Acting Warrant Officer 2 at the time of his death.

On 19 May 1982, Paddy was one of a group of SAS men who were cross-decking from HMS *Hermes* to HMS *Intrepid* when tragedy struck.

Paddy is remembered on all the Falklands Memorials as well as at St Martin's Church, Hereford alongside his SAS comrades.

In 2022, as part of the Falkland Islands 40th Anniversary Place Names Project, Paddy was honoured with 'O'Connor Bay', a bay on the west side of Seal Island in Lively Sound, East Falkland.

His name lives on…

D158914V Cook David Ernest Osborne HMS *Sheffield* 8 July 1959 ~ 4 May 1982 Age 22

David Ernest Osborne was born at the Maternity Home, Nant-Y-Glyn, in Colwyn Bay, Denbighshire, Wales. David was the third child of Goronwy and Joyce Osborne who married in 1954. Family roots were in Wales for a couple of generations though it appears that David's grandfather was born in Lancashire and that Ernest was a family name going back in time.

It appears that great-grandfather Ernest Osborne was born at the end of 1855 in Ashton-under-Lyne and married originally in 1884. Ernest had five children with his first wife before she died.

Ernest remarried in 1895 to Prudence Westwood. Ernest Baden Osborne was born on 9 April 1900. Two more daughters followed. Ernest senior was a gas stoker, Prudence had been in service from the age of 15.

Ernest Baden Osborne married Muriel Alice Williams in Wales in late 1931. It appears that Ernest Baden served with the Royal Fusiliers. The couple's eldest son, Goronwy, was born in September 1932. In 1939, Ernest worked at a timber merchant, the family were settled in Colwyn Bay. The name Ernest was to skip a generation, but reappeared when David was born.

David Ernest Osborne was the fourth child of Goronwy and Joyce, born on 8 July 1959. David joined the Royal Navy; at the time of the Falklands War, he was a Cook on HMS *Sheffield*. David was also known as Ozzie or Taffy.

On 4 May 1982, Ozzie was killed when HMS *Sheffield* was hit by an Exocet Missile.

Finally, in 2015, Ozzie was honoured with a plaque on the Old Colwyn War Memorial, it reads 'The Falklands War 1982 Osborne D.E.'

Ozzie lived in Portsmouth at the time of his death, but it was wrongly assumed that he had been added to their memorial. It might have taken thirty-three years, but he is now honoured as he should be.

Ozzie is remembered by a mate as 'a genuine lad, full of life and energy, an average footballer'.

In 2022, as part of the Falkland Islands 40th Anniversary Place Names Project, David was honoured with 'Osborne Point', the eastern point of First Passage in the Passage Island Group, West Falkland.

His name lives on…

D088253K Weapons Engineering Mechanician 1 David John Arden Ozbirn HMS *Coventry* 3 July 1948 ~ 25 May 1982 Age 33

David John Arden Ozbirn was born in Hull on 3 July 1948. He was the only son of Bud Ozbirn and Patricia Ann Mulcahy who married in Hull on 22 November 1945. Bud was an American serviceman and the couple met while he was serving in the United Kingdom during the Second World War.

After their marriage, and the war over, the couple went to live in America. The marriage was not to last however. Patricia came back to England while she was carrying David and gave birth to him that summer.

Patricia remarried in the mid-1950s, her husband, Roy, was grandfather to David's children. Bud Ozbirn died in Cody, Wyoming in July 1999.

David married Pamela in 1970, over the next few years the couple had two sons, Steven and Dean.

David joined the Royal Navy when he was 16 years old in 1964. Over the years he served on various ships including HMS *Mohawk*, *Cavalier*, *Juno* and lastly HMS *Coventry*. A massive music buff, David had a huge collection of vinyl records which his son later inherited, of course there was a state-of-the-art Hi-Fi system to play them on with headphones to boot.

A great family man, he would go on long walks with the family and their dog, Brandy. A tot of Pussers Rum would be enjoyed with shipmates.

David was killed when HMS *Coventry* was attacked on 25 May 1982. His family made the pilgrimage to the Falkland Islands in 1983. There is a memorial to the crew who died on HMS *Coventry* in the Church of Holy Trinity in Coventry.

In 2022, as part of the Falkland Islands 40th Anniversary Place Names Project, David was honoured with 'Ozbirn Point', a prominent headland midway along the coast between White Rock Point and the entrance to Tamar Pass, West Falkland.

His name lives on...

D134200P Petty Officer Weapons Engineering Mechanic (Radio) Andrew Keith Palmer HMS *Ardent* 4 March 1956 ~ 21 May 1982 Age 26

Andrew Keith Palmer was born at home in Berry Lane, Bodmin, Cornwall on 4 March 1956, the son of George and Barbara Palmer (née Webber). George was in motor accessory sales at the time.

It appears that Andy was the eldest son of an eldest son. The family had moved to Cornwall from Tavistock, Devon, in the 1920s. Andy's grandfather was a scoutmaster.

Andy's parents, George and Barbara, had two children; a younger brother arrived when Andy was 3 years old.

Andy was known as 'Pedlar' to his comrades. In 1982 Andy was serving in HMS *Ardent*, he died on 21 May 1982.

Andy is remembered on all the main Falklands Memorials here and there; he is also on the War Memorial in Bodmin and Truro. Though from Bodmin, at the time of his death Andy's home on land was Truro.

His mate Dapper remembers him as 'a nice guy, a big guy, and a rugby player'.

In 2022, as part of the Falkland Islands 40th Anniversary Place Names Project, Andy was honoured with 'Palmer Pond', a large pond 5km east of Colorado Pond below Rocky Mountain on mainland East Falkland.

His name lives on...

24565283 Private David Allen Parr 2nd Battalion Parachute Regiment 17 September 1962 ~ 14 June 1982 Age 19

Families are steeped in history that is all too easy to lose along the way, especially in these fast-moving times. Names are often passed down from generation to generation and the Parr family is no exception. Though by the time of Dave Parr's death the family were settled in Suffolk, their history came previously from London and Germany.

Louisa Corbyn married Louis Schulz in Islington in 1862. Louis was born in Germany in 1841. As teenagers Louisa and her sister Ellen were milliners. Louis and Louisa's eldest son was name Conrad Robert, he and his sister were born in Islington; later the family moved to South London. It appears that the name Conrad was passed down from the Parrs' maternal line.

Conrad John Parr, born in 1891, was Dave's grandfather. His sister Eleanor had a son also called Conrad born in 1908, though he was known as Claude. Claude died the year after Dave in 1983.

Dave's grandfather, Conrad John Parr, married Dora Kathleen King in Mutford, Suffolk, in 1920, eldest son Conrad Walter William Parr was born the following year, on 5 April 1921. Known as Con, Dave's father married Joy Allen in 1948. Con was with the Royal Naval Patrol Service in the Second World War. Still just 18 years old when the Second World War broke out, Con was a marine engineers labourer at the time.

Con and Joy had their first son, Harmer, in 1949, followed by Christopher in 1958. David Allen Parr was their youngest son, born on 17 September 1962 in Suffolk.

Oulton Broad is known as the 'Gateway to the Broads', where Dave enjoyed growing up in an environment that set him up for life in the military. Dave attended Ormiston Dene's Academy; he joined The Parachute Regiment in April 1980. Dave was part of 465 Platoon in June 1980, after gruelling P Coy training, he passed out on 5 December 1980.

Having turned 18 years old in September that year, Dave was able to join 2 Para serving out the last part of their tour as part of Operation Banner. The battalion were then posted to Aldershot in the spring of 1981 for a two-year posting which would be interrupted in quite an extraordinary way just a year later.

On 2 April 1982, the Falkland Islands were invaded by Argentina. Dave sailed 'Down South' on the MV *Norland* as part of 3 Section, 11 Platoon, D Company, 2 Para. The men kept fit on board as they sailed the 8,000 miles. Dave had turned 19 years old by then, but like many he was still a teenager.

On 28 May 1982, during the Battle for Goose Green, Dave was injured by a bullet that lodged in his webbing. Luck was on his side that day as he suffered nothing more than a large burn to his stomach. The Field Hospital at Ajax Bay treated Dave for his wounds, he made the brave decision to be 'patched up' and sent back to advance with his comrades.

On 14 June 1982, during the last knockings of a fierce seventy-four-day war, Dave was killed in a 'friendly fire' incident by a stray 105 mm light gun. Three days later, on 17 June 1982, his mother Joy received the news of her son's death while at work.

Dave's brother Harmer was also at work, a French teacher at Hadleigh High School his lesson was interrupted with a call to return home, instinctively he knew the reason. Middle brother Chris was away on an adventure of his own, as Dave was posted to Aldershot in 1981, Chris had left to trek across Asia. Chris received the news of Dave's death while working in Australia.

Dave was repatriated and is buried in St Michael's Churchyard, Ouston Broad, Lowestoft. A full military funeral took place at St Michaels Church on 2 December 1982.

In 2022, as part of the Falkland Islands 40th Anniversary Place Names Project, Dave was honoured with 'Parr Creek', a creek on the west side of Brenton Loch, East Falkland.

His name lives on…

24513947 Guardsman Colin Charles Parsons 1st Battalion Welsh Guards 9 August 1963 ~ 8 June 1982 Age 18

The Parsons family had their roots in Cardiff for generations where the name Charles featured often. It appears that Colin's grandfather, Charles Philmoor Parsons, was the second son of Philip J. Parsons and his wife Louisa. Charles was born in September 1918, just before the end of the First World War. In 1939, Louisa was living with six of her sons, Charles was working at a builders; merchant just as the Second World War was about to break. Records suggest that Philip was an air raid warden.

Charles married Florence in 1940, their oldest son, Kenneth, was born the following year in late 1941. Kenneth grew up and in turn married Gillian Donovan in 1962. Colin Charles Parsons was their eldest child and only son, born at 4 Cumnock Terrace, Cardiff, on 9 August 1963. Kenneth worked at the steelworks.

Colin joined the 1st Battalion Welsh Guards; he was deployed to the Falkland Islands travelling with his comrades initially on the QE2. Colin died on 8 June 1982, when the RFA *Sir Galahad* was bombed at Fitzroy. He was just 18 years old, barely old enough to drink or vote.

On 1 July 2009, Queen Elizabeth II graciously gave her name to an award 'The Elizabeth Cross'. The decoration was an award designated to be given to the Next of Kin of service personnel killed during her reign as a recognition of their loss. On 15 April 2010, Colin's mother Gillian was awarded the Elizabeth Cross in a ceremony at The Palace in Hereford. Gillian by then was living in Leominster.

In 2022, as part of the Falkland Islands 40th Anniversary Place Names Project, Colin was honoured with 'Parsons Bay', a bay on the east side of Low Island in Byron Sound, West Falkland.

His name lives on…

24428063 Lance Corporal John Brown Pashley 9th Parachute Squadron Royal Engineers 5 November 1959 ~ 14 June 1982 Age 22

John Brown McGhie was born on 5 November 1959 at Hallamshire Maternity Home in Chapeltown to Jean McGhie. Jean lived in Welland Crescent, Elscar, Barnsley, at the time.

Jean married originally in 1961, she later met John's stepfather 'Jack' Pashley. John had one half-brother nine years his junior born in Sheffield to Jean and Jack Pashley. He also had a step-sister from Jack's previous marriage.

John's stepfather had been a Marine Commando, he also had a serving uncle. John's military journey started when he applied to join The Parachute Regiment in early 1976, prior to leaving school. John attended Abbeydale Grange School in Sheffield where he had always been known as Pashley, though it seems he was not formerly adopted.

As there was no space in Junior Leaders, John was accepted into Depot Para, Aldershot, attesting on 2 August 1976. From that day he officially declared his wish to be known as John Brown Pashley, known to comrades as Pash.

Prior to joining the army Pash had attended youth clubs and had begun Judo training. He played rugby, basketball and football and also enjoyed cross country and swimming.

Pash first served in Northern Ireland in 1978, receiving his GSM in May that year. After passing his Combat Engineer course he applied for a transfer to the Royal Engineers in January 1979. From then on, he served with 9 Parachute Squadron, Royal Engineers. He saw service in Belize in 1979 and Germany later that year. A second tour in Northern Ireland followed in 1980, he was promoted to Lance Corporal in February that year.

Pash passed every course he undertook including his HGV 3 in February 1982; he was set to be a career soldier.

Pash from Sharrow Lane, Sheffield, married Carmella on 19 April 1980 in St Peter & Paul Parish Church, Eckington, Derbyshire. The couple had originally met at school.

When Pash deployed to the Falklands he was attached to the 2nd Battalion Scots Guards. Out of the men who fell on Tumbledown Mountain during the night of 13/14 June 1982, Pash was the only Royal Engineer. Pash was killed instantaneously from a blast injury and multiple shrapnel wounds.

Though many records online state that Pash died on 13 June, the official records show 14 June 1982. He was cremated in Sheffield, and in true Airborne style his ashes were scattered from a Hercules over Hankley Common on a Squadron jump. John Brown Pashley is honoured at the Eckington War Memorial.

In 2022, as part of the Falkland Islands 40th Anniversary Place Names Project, Pash was honoured with 'Pashley Ridge', a razor-backed ridge running the length of the northeast peninsula on Big Arch Island in the Arch Islands Group, West Falkland.

His name lives on…

D180507J Marine Engineering Mechanic (Mechanical) 2 Terrence Wayne Perkins HMS *Glamorgan* 18 May 1963 ~ 12 June 1982 Age 19

Terrence Wayne Perkins was born at The Maternity Hospital, Glossop Terrace, Cardiff, on 18 May 1963. Records suggest that Terry was the only son of Alexander Clive and Ruby Jean Perkins (née Williams).

Alexander Clive Perkins was born in London in 1931, unfortunately there is no discernible record of Terry's grandfather. Alexander first married in 1953, Terry seems to have had one older half-sister from that marriage.

On 5 April 1960, Alexander married Ruby at Cardiff Register Office. Alexander was a Labourer living in Crwys Road in the Cathays area of Cardiff. Ruby was an 18-year-old waitress living in Corporation Road just a couple of miles away. Ruby was born in Newport. At the time of Terry's birth, Alexander was a window cleaner, the family lived in Whitchurch Road, Cardiff. It appears that Terry also had one older biological sister.

Terry was one of the unlucky men who died when HMS *Glamorgan* was hit by an Exocet missile early on 12 June 1982. His grave is the South Atlantic Ocean. Both Terry's parents remarried, at the time of his death his home address was still in Cathay, Cardiff. Yet another teenager taken too soon.

In 2022, as part of the Falkland Islands 40th Anniversary Place Names Project, Terry was honoured with 'Perkins Point', a prominent point on mainland East Falkland south of Lion Creek Island and at the southern entrance to *Eagle* Passage.

His name lives on...

24503713 Guardsman Eirwyn John Phillips 1st Battalion Welsh Guards 4 June 1962 ~ 8 June 1982 Age 20

Eirwyn John Phillips was born on 4 June 1962 at Pantyrodyn Cwmffrwd, Carmarthen, the son of William Gwynfor Phillips and Phoebe Violet Lewis. The couple married in Carmarthen in 1949, at the time of Eirwyn's birth his father was a lorry driver.

Phoebe was a farmer's daughter, the second daughter of David and Phoebe Lewis of Gwentha Farm.

Eirwyn joined the 1st Battalion Welsh Guards as a young man; he, like many other young men, was set for a life of adventure – sometimes adventure does not quite follow the path we expect.

Eirwyn was deployed to the Falkland Islands on the QE2. On 8 June 1982, the *Sir Galahad* was attacked by Argentinian Skyhawks, the resulting devastation cost many lives. Eirwyn was one of the men who died.

After many years of fundraising a memorial was unveiled in Llanelli as part of the West Wales War Memorial Project, to honour those lost since the Second World War. Eirwyn Phillips and Nicholas Thomas were added to the memorial, both Welsh Guards from the Falklands War who died on 8 June 1982.

There is also a memorial at St Peters Church, Priory Street, Carmarthen.

In 2022, as part of the Falkland Islands 40th Anniversary Place Names Project, Eirwyn was honoured with 'Phillips Hill', a conspicuous hill top (550ft elevation) on the peninsula between Sweeney Creek and Anchor Inlet in Port Stephens, West Falkland.

His name lives on...

P039185R Marine Keith Phillips 45 Commando Royal Marines 1 October 1962 ~ 11 June 1982 Age 19

Keith Phillips was born at the Russell-Stonham Hospital in Crayford, Kent on 1 October 1962, the eldest son of Keith and Ellen Phillips (née Lee), who married in Kent.

Keith attended Marvels Lane Junior School followed by South East London School. As a youngster Keith was an Army Cadet in Bexleyheath, he excelled as such, opting to join the Royal Marines when he was 18 years old. Keith liked motorbikes, music, and football, and was the eldest of three boys, his younger brothers were twins; Mark and Colin were born in South London in 1965.

Keith was killed on 11 June 1982, tragically as he was returning from a patrol with 45 Commando, he died with three other Marines in an incident where they were mistaken for the enemy. Keith died just before the main assault on Two Sisters. Keith's final resting place is in Blue Beach Military Cemetery in Port San Carlos, Falkland Islands; his parents made the decision not to repatriate.

Keith is remembered on all of the main Falkland Islands memorials, but he also has a very special plaque dedicated to him in St Paulinus' Church, Perry Street, Crayford in Kent. The inscription is on a clear diamond-paned window with the Royal Marine Crest inserted into stained glass, the inscription beneath reads: 'IN MEMORY OF KEITH JOHN PHILIPS KILLED IN ACTION IN THE FALKAND ISLANDS 11 JUNE 1982'.

Though he was born simply Keith Phillips, it is thought the John may have been added later as he had an Uncle John.

Simon Jack, a great-uncle on Keith's mother's side of the family, was born in Scotland, and was a Trooper in the 2nd Life Guards before moving with his family to Kent.

Keith's family visited the Falkland Islands in 1983 as part of the family pilgrimage. Keith's father died in 2005, his mother Ellen died in 2021. His family still attend services and will forever remember Keith.

In 2022, as part of the Falkland Islands 40th Anniversary Place Names Project, Keith was honoured with 'Keith Phillips Creek', the western arm of Teal Inlet in Port Salvador, East Falkland.

His name lives on…

24562309 Guardsman Gareth Wynne Poole 1st Battalion Welsh Guards 21 December 1961 ~ 8 June 1982 Age 20

Gareth Wynne Poole was born in Pontypridd on 21 December 1961 at the local East Glamorgan Hospital. He was born Gareth Wynne Jones, son of Anthony John and Janice Jones. Gareth had one older sister, Adrienne, born in Cardiff in 1959. Janice remarried in 1965, Gareth had two younger sisters, Jeanette and Alison. All four children were brought up by Ray and Jan Poole in Pontypridd.

Gareth initially attended Pont Sion Norton Junior School, followed by Rhydyfelin Welsh Comprehensive School. The family moved to Upper Church Village in 1974, Gareth finished his education at Bryn Celynog School.

As a teenager Gareth was interested in the Air Training Corps, motorbikes and his favourite band was Queen. Gareth aspired to join the Royal Air Force initially but was swayed by his maternal grandfather, Idris Williams, who had served with the Welsh Guards.

Idris was Batman to Lieutenant Reginald John 'Rex' Whistler, a Welsh Guards Officer in the Guards Armoured Division. The 2nd Battalion Welsh Guards saw action in North Western Europe during the Second World War. Idris, who served as a tank driver throughout the Second World War, was with Rex when he was killed on 18 July 1944 by a mortar bomb, he had left his tank to rush to the aid of other men in his unit. Idris made it home, Rex is buried in the Banneville-la-Campagne War Cemetery situated 10km east of Caen, France.

Gareth joined the Welsh Guards in June 1980, initially training at the Guards Depot at Pirbright. The following year Gareth took part in the presentation of the battalion's new colours at Windsor Castle as well as the Queen's Birthday parade, Trooping the Colour.

A good shot, Gareth received a Marksman medal; he also saw exercise in Kenya also prior to the invasion of the Falkland Islands. In 1982, Gareth was serving in the Support Company's Mortar Platoon, he sailed 'Down South' on the QE2. The Welsh Guards were transferred to the SS *Canberra* at South Georgia and finally arrived at San Carlos Water.

On 8 June, RFA *Sir Galahad* alongside *Sir Tristram* were waiting for the landings for hours, landings that for these men never came. During the long wait Gareth played cards with three friends to pass the time, only one survived to tell the story of those last few hours before all hell broke loose.

RFA *Sir Galahad* was attacked by air strikes and the rest, as they say, is history. The ship took huge losses as the fires raged; Gareth was one of the men who perished that day.

After the war, funds were raised for a lifeboat for the RNLI; named the 'RFA *Sir Galahad*', the lifeboat was stationed at Tenby in Pembrokeshire from September 1986. She was the namesake of the original *Sir Galahad*, but after the Falklands War a 2nd *Sir Galahad* launched in December 1986 and went into service with the Royal Fleet Auxiliary the following year.

In time, Ray and Jan gave up their jobs as an aircraft engineer and nursing sister, they moved to Tenby where they ran a hotel. Adrienne left home from Church Village in 1977 to join the Kent Police, she retired from the police as a Sergeant in 2008. Adrienne by then lived in Hereford where she worked as a licensing officer, after her second retirement she moved to North Devon in 2016, she moved back to Wales in 2020.

The family were to experience a few tragic years. After Gareth died in 1982, his grandfather Idris, also known as Bampa, passed in 1985. Gareth's sister Alison died in 1988, and two years later in 1990 Jan died. Gareth's grandmother Mary died in 2003, reaching an amazing 92 years of age.

Philip Roberts, Captain of the *Sir Galahad* in 1982, unveiled a memorial plaque commissioned by Ray, it hung alongside the lifebuoy from the original *Sir Galahad*. The 2nd *Sir Galahad* was decommissioned in 2006.

Gareth is also remembered with a wall-mounted brass plaque on a wooden mount situated at the Llandwit Fardre Community Centre, Llandwit Fadre, Taff-Ely in Mid *Glamorgan*. The plaque reads 'IN MEMORY OF GUARDSMAN GARETH WYNNE POOLE FALKLANDS CAMPAIGN 1982.'

In 2022, as part of the Falkland Islands 40th Anniversary Place Names Project, Gareth was honoured with 'Poole Island', a small tussac island south of Cross Island at the east entrance to Port Stephens, West Falkland.

His name lives on…

23834301 Staff Sergeant James Prescott CGM 49 Engineer (Explosives Disposal Squadron) 33 Engineer Regt Royal Engineers 24 February 1945 ~ 23 May 1982 Age 37

James Prescott was born on 24 February 1945, to Thomas and Janet Prescott (née Conn). The couple married in Lancashire in 1944, Jim was their first born. The family moved to Auchinleck in Scotland from whence his mother originated, Jim attended the local Primary School. Jim's father served in the Second World War; he was a miner in Auchinleck when Jim was a child.

Jim married his wife Theresa in 1970, they had two children, both girls.

Jim was in the Army Cadets, by the age of 15 he was at the Army Training College in Chepstow. He joined 37 Field Squadron, Royal Engineers in 1964, he joined 33 Engineer Regiment as a Corporal. Jim was then promoted to Sergeant in 1973; by 1980 he was a Staff Sergeant.

At the time of the Falklands War Jim was with 49 Engineer (Explosives Disposal Squadron), 33 Engineer Regt.

On 21 May 1982, they were set a task on HMS *Argonaut* (F56) a Leander-class frigate. There was an unexploded bomb in the boiler room. Despite cramped and difficult circumstances, Jim and his colleague John successfully rendered the bomb safe, it was later removed from the ship.

They were not so lucky on 23 May 1982 when they were called to task on another Type 21 Frigate, HMS *Antelope*. She had been hit with two unexploded bombs; it was their task to diffuse them. The first bomb examined could not be approached until there could be extensive clearance of debris, so they moved on to the second bomb which was situated near the centre of the ship. Because the bomb had been slightly damaged it was assessed as being in a dangerous condition.

Brave men, three times they tried to diffuse the bomb remotely without success, each time they had to approach the bomb to adjust the equipment. On the fourth attempt, which involved the use of a small charge, the bomb exploded. Jim was stood just 30ft away and was hit in the chest and killed instantly, he was 37 years old.

The explosion tore a huge hole in the ship's starboard side from the waterline to the funnel. Like an opened tin can, HMS *Antelope* was the third ship to be lost in 1982. Commander Tobin gave the order to abandon ship and miraculously only one seaman died.

His citation stated: *'Staff Sergeant Prescott displayed courage of the highest order in persevering with attempts to defuse the bomb in HMS Antelope, fully aware that the condition was particularly dangerous.'*

Jim received the Conspicuous Gallantry Medal awarded to British Armed Forces personnel below commissioned rank until 1993. Jim's was to be the last one awarded however, and the only one during the Falklands War. He was awarded a Naval award because during the war he served on board ship rather than on land.

In honour of his sacrifice his comrades in the Royal Engineers paid for a bronze plaque to be installed on a bridge built by the Regiment in Milngavie and later renamed after Jim. It was subsequently stolen and never recovered.

John Phillips, who was injured in the blast, contacted his regiment and organised the fundraising and the installation of a replacement. The new plaque, made of granite, was officially dedicated during a ceremony on the 32nd anniversary of Jim's death in May 2014. The service was attended by his daughters and members of his regiment.

Jim is also honoured with a plaque at All Saints Church, Hindley, Lancashire.

In 2022, as part of the Falkland Islands 40th Anniversary Place Names Project, Jim was honoured with 'Prescott Bay', a sandy bay between Southwest Horse Island and East Falkland, east side of Falkland Sound.

His name lives on…

24505227 Private Kenneth Preston Royal Army Medical Corps 15 September 1961 ~ 8 June 1982 Age 20

Kenneth Preston was born in Merseyside on 15 September 1961, the eldest son of Roy and Jean Preston (née Fenney). He was known mainly as Ken or Kenny to those who knew him. Ken had one younger brother, born eight years his junior.

Ken was educated first at the local Parish School, later at the Central High School where he enjoyed running and swimming. As a youngster Ken also joined the St John's Ambulance Brigade. On joining the British Army, he found himself drawn to the Royal Army Medical Corps.

After initial training in Keogh Barracks, Aldershot, Ken served with 3 Field Ambulance in Sennelager, Germany. In 1981, Ken's next posting was with 16th Field Ambulance Brigade. Ken was called to service on Operation Corporate in 1982 on deployment with the main dressing station. Ken was assigned to 1st Battalion Welsh Guards.

Ken was with B section who cross decked to the *Canberra* at Grytviken, South Georgia for the final leg to the Falkland Islands. The unit finally embarked onto the RFA *Sir Galahad* where the Field Ambulance equipment and stores were in situ.

Ken died on 8 June 1982 in the attack on the *Sir Galahad.*

He is remembered in Merseyside with a memorial at St Thomas Eccleston Church, Westfield Street, St Helens, Merseyside. It reads:

'THIS PLAQUE MARKS THE SACRIFICE MADE BY PRIVATE KEN PRESTON AGED 20 YEARS OF THE ROYAL ARMY MEDICAL CORPS A SON OF ST HELENS WHO TOGETHER WITH 48 OF HIS COMRADES WAS KILLED IN ACTION ABOARD RFA SIR GALAHAD IN THE WATERS OF FALKLAND SOUND ON 8TH JUNE 1982 HE HAS NO KNOWN GRAVE AND HIS STORY LIVES ON FAR AWAY WITHOUT VISIBLE SYMBOL WOVEN INTO THE STUFF OF OTHER MENS LIVES'

Ken is remembered as a well-liked, outgoing kind of guy.

Ken was the only St Helens man to lose his life in the Falklands War. In 2007, a service was held at the War Memorial in Victoria Square to mark the 25th Anniversary of the liberation of the islands. Ken's mother Jean gave a reading and laid a wreath. Ken's name is inscribed on the memorial, a forever reminder of his sacrifice.

In 2022, as part of the Falkland Islands 40th Anniversary Place Names Project, Ken was honoured with 'Preston Islet', a small tussac island at the east end of Kelp Lagoon between Fitzroy and Mare Harbour on East Falkland.

His name lives on…

24343972 Corporal Stephen Ronald Prior 2nd Battalion Parachute Regiment 10 September 1954 ~ 28 May 1982 Age 27

Corporal Stephen ('Stevie') Ronald Prior was born in Brighton on 10 September 1954. Ronald Prior and Rita Philbrick married in Brighton in late 1939. Their first son, Robert, was born the following year in 1940, they went on to have seven children altogether, five boys and two girls. Stevie was their fifth child and third son.

Rita Kathleen Philbrick was born in Brighton in January 1920; her parents, Thomas and Alice, married in 1916 during the First World War. The couple had two boys and two girls; Rita was their third child. The couple's oldest son, Sydney Thomas Philbrick, was an Aircraftman First Class in the Royal Air Force. Sydney died on 18 August 1940 aged 23 he is buried at Brighton City (Bear Road) Cemetery.

Stevie attended Lower Bevendean Infant and Junior schools followed by Westlain Grammar School. Stevie left school at the age of 16 years old having passed several 'O' levels, he was employed by WH Smith in a trainee manager role. Stevie was restless and without job satisfaction, so he joined The Parachute Regiment around 1973. With a penchant for adventure, Stevie had found his stride.

Some of Stevie's service with 2 Para saw him in Berlin 1977/1979 and Northern Ireland 1979 /1981. At the time of the Falkland Islands invasion Stevie was based in Aldershot serving with A Company. During the Battle for Goose Green, Stevie was killed by a sniper while trying to pull a badly injured colleague to safety.

The year after Stevie died his nephew from his brother Ian was born. Daniel Stephen Prior was born on 31 December 1983, he also joined The Parachute Regiment. After completing his basic training in 2008, Daniel was posted to the 2nd Battalion. Two years later in October 2010, Daniel deployed to Afghanistan. On 16 March 2011, Daniel was mortally wounded by an improvised explosive device. He died two days later at the Royal Centre for Defence Medicine, Queen Elizabeth NHS Hospital, Birmingham.

Tragically, Ian Prior lost his brother Stevie and his son while they both served with the same battalion of the same regiment, they were also the same age when they died.

Though Stevie lived for today and was single, Daniel was married and had a new-born baby when he died. In three generations, uncles were not to meet their nephews this side of life.

Stevie is buried with his comrades in Aldershot Military Cemetery.

In 2022, as part of the Falkland Islands 40th Anniversary Place Names Project, Stevie was honoured with 'Prior Creek', a creek on the east side of Shag Rookery Point.

His name lives on…

D137112E Leading Air Engineering Mechanic (Electrical) 1 845 Squadron Fleet Air Arm Donald Leonard Pryce 13 January 1956 ~ 25 May 1982 Age 26

Donald Leonard Pryce was born one of fraternal twins on 13 January 1956 at Oddstock Hospital in Salisbury, his sister was named Terry. The twins were christened at Salisbury Cathedral. Don was the son of Donald Charles and Marion Pryce (née York).

Don's family moved around as his father served with the Fleet Air Arm which meant that Don attended various schools over the years, ending his schooldays at Bridgemary Community School in Gosport.

Don's parents went on to have two more daughters, he remained their only son.

After leaving school Don followed in his father's footsteps, he joined the Fleet Air Arm. Don had a few hobbies, he liked birds, stamp collecting, art music and chess. He also enjoyed football and followed his local team of Portsmouth.

Remembered as a funny, warm guy with a wonderful sense of humour, he enjoyed life and home comforts.

Just two days before he died, he and his flight were transferred to SS *Atlantic Conveyor*. On 25 May 1982, she was hit by an Exocet missile. Though his body was recovered, all resuscitation attempts failed, Don was buried at sea from HMS *Alacrity* in true Naval tradition.

At RNAS *Yeovilton* there is an avenue of trees, each one has a stone block with a name plate, Don is one of twelve names honoured.

In 2022, as part of the Falkland Islands 40th Anniversary Place Names Project, Don was honoured with 'Pryce Island', a small tussac island south of Cross Island at the east entrance to Port Stephens, West Falkland.

His name lives on…

24539305 Guardsman James Boyle Curran Reynolds DCM 2nd Battalion Scots Guards 18 February 1963 ~ 14 June 1982 Age 19

Jim, as he was known, was born on 18 February 1963 just after 02.00 hrs at 253 Duke Street, Glasgow, Scotland, to John and Martha Reynolds (née Barrett). The couple had married in Shettleston in the East End of Glasgow on 31 July 1946. Records suggest that Jim's mother may well have been a young widow when she married John Reynolds. At the time of Jim's birth, John was a boilerman.

Jim didn't have the best start in life and spent some of his early years in a children's home, the Gryff Castle, Bridge of Weir. The home was for orphans and those from broken homes.

One thing seems to have been apparent, right from a young lad, he wanted to be a soldier. He is remembered as a cheerful lad with a good nature which made him popular among his comrades. He became a very good soldier, despite his youth.

The only family that Jim had ever known was his sister Eleanor. Possibly orphans, Eleanor had been brought up by adoptive parents, which was not to be Jim's path. An independent young man, he joined the Scots Guards. When the call to go 'Down South' came, Jim was an orderly to Lieutenant Alastair Bruce, just barely older than Jim himself.

The end of the war was nigh but as the Scots Guards made an advance on Tumbledown, the fighting was still fierce.

An exert from Jim's citation for the DCM.

> '*During the attack, Guardsman Reynold's Platoon came under fire from a group of enemy snipers. His Platoon Sergeant was killed instantly. A confused situation developed, and his Section became separated. Guardsman Reynolds immediately took command. Having located the enemy snipers, he silenced several of them himself.*
>
> *That done and showing a complete disregard for his own safety, he moved forward to render first aid to a wounded comrade. He himself was wounded in the hand by enemy sniper fire but continued to aid his colleague. While doing so, he was killed by enemy mortar fire.*'

Alastair Bruce was owner of an estate in Sallochy, Lairg, and he was struck by the similarity of the terrain to the Falkland Islands. Indeed, at the time of the invasion many people thought the Falklands were in Scotland. Alastair had a cairn made to honour his young orderly, Jim. It was unveiled in 1983 by his sister Eleanor, it has his name, rank and how he died painted on a plaque on the cairn. The cairn stands 5ft-high and is the traditional memorial to Scottish men who have died in battle. Alastair read Psalm 27; the same psalm read by the Chaplain at the dedication of the memorial at Tumbledown. As a salute, RAF Lossiemouth arranged a fly-past by five Jaguar jets.

Jim was a member of Pollockshields Parish Church in Glasgow. His body was repatriated, he is buried at Knadgerhill Cemetery in Irvine in a grave next to his fellow Guardsman, David Malcolmson, also killed that day.

In 2022, as part of the Falkland Islands 40th Anniversary Place Names Project, Jim was honoured with 'Reynolds Bay', a bay on the east coast of Great Island in Falkland Sound.

His name lives on...

D138481K Cook John Raymond Roberts HMS *Ardent* 29 December 1956 ~ 21 May 1982 Age 25

John Raymond Roberts was born on 29 December 1956 in Bangor, Caernarvonshire. His parents, Tom John Roberts and Eileen Evans, married in 1950. To his family he was known as Raymond.

Raymond attended school at Ysgol Brynrefail, he liked cooking at school, in fact he seemed to have found his niche. After leaving school Raymond joined the Royal Navy at just 16 years old. His initial service saw him with HMS *Trent* and HMS *Southampton*, he started off his Naval life in Portsmouth. Raymond had also been part of the team who worked on the wedding cake of Prince Charles and Princess Diana.

Raymond had been with HMS *Ardent* for just six weeks before the fateful day on 21 May 1982 when she was attacked.

Raymond was married and a father of one when he died. His son was born the year before his death. Raymond's son was just a toddler and another child who would grow up with no memories of his father.

Llanberis has its own war memorial on which Raymond's name is etched.

In 2022, as part of the Falkland Islands 40th Anniversary Place Names Project, Raymond was honoured with 'Roberts Island', the largest of two tussac islands in Cape Lagoon on the West Falkland side of Falkland Sound.

His name lives on...

C013530R Lieutenant Commander Glen Stuart Robinson-Moltke HMS *Coventry* 9 February 1944 ~ 25 May 1982 Age 38

Glen Stuart Robinson was born on 9 February 1944. Glen was from Mirfield near Dewsbury, Yorkshire, the eldest of five, all the Robinson children's names began with G.

Glen's brother Garth says,

> Lieutenant Commander Glen Stuart Robinson served as First Officer
> of HMS *Coventry* and lost his life when she was sunk on 25 May
> 1982. His surviving family believe he was the senior Royal Naval
> casualty of the Falklands Conflict.
>
> Glen was born in Dewsbury, West Yorkshire, on 9 February 1944,
> the second child of Commander Harry and Lydia Robinson. He had
> an older sister, two younger sisters and a younger brother.
>
> Glen was educated locally at Heckmondwike Grammar School
> where, in his final year, he was head boy. Following Officer training
> at Dartmouth he specialised in gunnery and served on HMS *Penelope*
> as well as a tour as naval attaché to the Royal Canadian Navy.
>
> His two daughters from his first marriage both served as naval
> officers on short term commissions. His marriage to a Danish
> National resulted in his name change to Robinson-Moltke and
> produced a son and a daughter.
>
> Memorial plaques exist at both the Parish Church in Mirfield
> where he was brought up and at the English Church in Copenhagen
> where he married his second wife.

On his father's side, Glen's family had a long history in the Mirfield area. His mother, Lydia, was born in Winnipeg on 28 February 1916. Lydia's family moved back to England when she was 19 years old. Harry and Lydia married in Huddersfield in 1940, their first two children were born during the Second World War.

Harry was the second son of Edward Robinson and Mary Purver Scales born in January 1911. Harry's older brother, Keogh, was born in 1904.

Mary's middle name of Purver came from her grandmother, Elizabeth Burgess Purver. Elizabeth was the daughter of a Parish Clerk, she married Frederick Anscombe, a goldsmith, in 1853, their daughter, Kate, was born in London the following year. Kate later married George Scales.

Harry went to Dartmouth as a Cadet, but as his parents were unable to support him he worked in sales prior to the Second World War. At the start of the Second World War, Harry volunteered for officer training and hence served with the Royal Navy for the duration, he continued afterwards as a Lieutenant Commander with the RNVR. The Naval tradition continued for the next couple of generations. Harry adopted Purver as his middle name, he died in 1995 aged 84. Lydia died in 2006 aged 90.

Glen first married in 1967, the marriage produced two daughters. Second marriage to Christine Moltke bore a son, born in Canada, and a daughter, named after her maternal grandmother.

Glen was a career naval officer who in the autumn of 1981 was appointed Executive Officer of HMS *Coventry*. In January 1982, Glen was on board ship on exercise, just three short months later life was about to change for many. After the invasion, Glen sent his wife a telegram which merely said, 'Going South'. Glen like so many had hoped there would be a diplomatic resolution.

When the HMS *Coventry* was hit initially, Glen it seems was concussed and helped to reach the upper deck. Glen hit his head again on the stabiliser fin jutting out of the hull, his body was not recovered.

In 2022, as part of the Falkland Islands 40th Anniversary Place Names Project, Glen was honoured with 'Robinson-Moltke Island', the smaller of two tussac islands.

His name lives on…

24565127 Craftsman Mark Warren Rollins Royal Electrical Mechanical Engineers 25 August 1962 ~ 8 June 1982 Age 19

Mark Warren Rollins was born in Birmingham on 25 August 1962 to Donald and Emily Rollins (née McGrory). Mark was their third son; he was one of four children. Historically the Rollins family go back to Staffordshire where Mark's great-grandfather was a miner, living in Hednesford, Cannock Chase.

Great-grandfather Ernest Rollins served with the Royal Engineers during the First World War. Ernest married Florence Rowley in June 1905 at Cannock Register Office. Ernest enlisted in May 1915, he served until July 1918. Harold was born in December 1907; the couple's youngest child was born during the First World War.

Mark's three times great-grandfather wore another uniform, Stephen Rollins was a police officer for many years.

Mark's grandfather Harold was a petroleum lorry driver. Harold married Ivy Hall in 1933, son Donald Harold Rollins was their eldest child.

Mark married Theresa in December 1980; the couple were living in Reading at the time. Mark was just 18 years old when they married, his bride a year older. Their only daughter, Ria, was born the following year.

Mark was a Craftsman with the Royal Electrical and Mechanical Engineers and was stationed at Havannah Barracks in Bordon, Hampshire. During the Falklands War he served in A Company.

Mark died on 8 June when the *Sir Galahad* was attacked by Argentinian Skyhawks, like many he was lost to the sea.

Mark's father died in 1993.

In 2022, as part of the Falkland Islands 40th Anniversary Place Names Project, Mark was honoured with 'Rollins Tarn', a high-altitude tarn east of Shingly Mountain and south of Mount Robinson on mainland West Falkland.

His name lives on…

P027686Q Sergeant Ronald James Rotheram Royal Marines HMS Fearless 23 February 1948 ~ 8 June 1982 Age 34

Ronald James Rotheram was the eldest son of Manfred Byrne and Lilian Rotheram (née Newby) who married in Liverpool in 1944. Their first child, a daughter, was born in 1945. Ronald was born on 23 February 1948 in Liverpool. He had one younger brother.

Records indicate that Manfred was the son of James Alexander Davies Rotheram and his second wife Elizabeth Byrne.

Ronald was known as 'Scouse' or Ron, he joined the Royal Marines in 1969 and passed his Commando training at Lympstone. He saw service in Northern Ireland, Singapore, Cyprus, also in HMS *Nubain*, *Plymouth* and *Malta*. When the Falkland Islands were invaded Sergeant Rotheram had just completed his training with the Landing Craft Branch of the Royal Marines at Poole and was due to join HMS *Fearless* in June. However, he volunteered to go to the Falkland Islands as relief for another Royal Marine.

Ron duly set off 'Down South' and became part of 3 Commando Brigade Royal Marines attached to Task Force Landing Craft Squadron RM, HMS *Fearless*. The team had already been involved in rescuing over 100 survivors on 23 May 1982 from HMS *Antelope*, which had been hit by two bombs in San Carlos water during an air attack.

On 8 June 1982, the landing craft was bombed and sunk by Argentine Skyhawks in Choiseul Sound and all but two of LCU F4's crew were killed; Ron was among the dead.

Ron married his bride Maureen in 1966, the couple had one daughter Dawn both events taking place in Liverpool. The couple later settled in Dorset.

In 2022, as part of the Falkland Islands 40th Anniversary Place Names Project, Ron was honoured with 'Rotheram Island', the larger of two tussac islands joined by a tidal spit west of Big Samuel Island in Choiseul Sound, East Falkland.

His name lives on…

24495304 Guardsman Nigel Arthur Rowberry 1st Battalion Welsh Guards 24 December 1961 ~ 8 June 1982 Age 20

Nigel Arthur Rowberry was born on Christmas Eve in 1961 at 143 Ninian Park Road, Cardiff, to Frederick and Pamela Rowberry. Nigel's father was a Private with the Royal Army Service Corps. Nigel was the couple's second son.

Frederick Arthur Rowberry was born in 1940, records indicate that Frederick's father served with the Royal Artillery during the Second World War. The name Arthur had been passed down through the generations. Nigel's grandparents had also lived in Ninian Park Road.

Nigel attended Ottershaw School from September 1974 to July 1978.

Nigel married Maria in 1981. The couple had been married less than a year when Nigel was deployed to the Falkland Islands with the Welsh Guards, leaving Maria pregnant with their first child.

Nigel died on 8 June 1982 when the RFA *Sir Galahad* was bombed by Argentinian Skyhawks. Named after her father, Nigella was born in South Glamorgan, later that year.

In 2022, as part of the Falkland Islands 40th Anniversary Place Names Project, Nigel was honoured with 'Rowberry Point', a point on the west coast of Weddell Island at the south entrance to Stick in the Mud Passage, West Falkland.

His name lives on…

PO29758D Marine Anthony John Rundle HMS Fearless
1 September 1955 ~ 8 June 1982 Age 26

Anthony John Rundle was born on 1 September 1955 in Hanover, Germany, the eldest son of Tom and Mary Rundle. Tom served with the Royal Electrical and Mechanical Engineers. Tom and Mary were originally from Cornwall where they married in 1953. Anthony had one younger brother.

Mary's father served with the Royal Flying Corps in the First World War. Records suggest that Tom's father served with the Royal Garrison Artillery in the First World War and that he was convalescing in Cornwall for some time post-war.

Anthony was known as 'Big Jim', he stood over 6ft tall and liked to play rugby. He was known as Jim because of his love of Jimmy Hendrix.

At the time of his death Jim had a girlfriend, Carol, who met him while he was based in Poole. The couple had been together two years when he died. Jim's home address was in Cheadle Hulme, Cheshire.

After his death Carol kept close to Jim's family, Tom and Mary both died in 2023.

Jim died on 8 June 1982 during the attack on the Landing Craft Foxtrot 4.

There is a plaque located at the Landing Craft Branch Museum in Poole. The memorial was presented by the family of Lieutenant R.J. McConnell, Royal Marine, who died while serving at ATURM. It is in memory of all ranks of the Landing Craft Branch of the Royal Marines who have died on duty since the end of the Second World War.

In 2022, as part of the Falkland Islands 40th Anniversary Place Names Project, Jim was honoured with 'Rundle Rocks', prominent rock outcrop north of Princess Street stone run, East Falkland.

His name lives on…

D122283S Leading Cook Mark Andrew Sambles HMS *Glamorgan*
26 December 1952 ~ 12 June 1982 Age 29

Mark Andrew Sambles was born to Clifford and Jean Sambles in Bridport, Dorset, in December 1952. Mark had one older sister, two younger sisters and three younger brothers. Although he was born in Bridport his father was born in Cardiff; before that the family hailed from Cornwall.

Known as 'Sam', Mark felt the call of the ocean, and with a love of cooking it seemed the perfect fit to join the Royal Navy and train to be a chef.

Mark enjoyed music and played the banjo, guitar and mandolin. He enjoyed a game of rugby too. He attended Colfox school in Bridport which was renamed the Sir John Colfox Academy in 2015.

Mark had one son from his first marriage, named Anthony, he was born in Liverpool.

In August 1980, Mark married Dawn in Govilon, Monmouthshire, where there sits a refectory table dedicated to Mark in the Chapel. Mark joined HMS *Glamorgan* in 1981 as Leading Cook, he had spent Christmas at home that year. The couple had been married just short of two years when Mark died on 12 June 1982 in HMS *Glamorgan*. Mark was buried at sea wearing his Portsmouth Field Gun Crew tracksuit.

Most of the Falklands Fallen are well remembered, some more than others when it comes to personal memorials. As well as the refectory table, a 'Man of the Match' cup resides in St Mary's Church in Swansea along with other ships memorabilia, Mark was a 'Man of the Match' himself. A plaque is also dedicated to Mark at the Field Gun 'Hole in the Wall' club at Whale Island, Mark represented Portsmouth Field Gun Crew not once but twice, in 1977 and 1980 at the Royal Tournaments in Earl's Court.

In the United Church in Bridport is another plaque dedicated to Mark it reads: 'IN ENDURING MEMORY OF A BELOVED HUSBAND SON AND BROTHER MARK ANDREW SAMBLES 1952~1982 KILLED IN ACTION ON HMS GLAMORGAN'.

For the 30th Anniversary a memorial service was held at the cenotaph in Bridport. The service was well attended by Mark's mother Jean and four of his siblings, sadly Mark's father had died in 2004. Jean visited the Falkland Islands on the 1983 families' pilgrimage.

In 2022, as part of the Falkland Islands 40th Anniversary Place Names Project, Mark was honoured with 'Sambles Bay', a bay between Phillips Point and Rookery Bay near Stanley, East Falkland.

His name lives on…

24331574 Lance Corporal David Edward Scott 3rd Battalion Parachute Regiment 27 September 1957 ~ 12 June 1982 Age 24

The Scott family have a long association with Winslow in Buckinghamshire as well as generations of service to our country.

Thomas Scott was Dave's grandfather. Born in December 1898, Thomas worked on the submarines in the Royal Navy during the First World War. Thomas married Florence Wilson in Portsmouth in 1920. Thomas and Florence had three children, twin girls Phyllis and Violet born in March 1921, and son Thomas Edward John born in 1922.

Thomas junior was always known as Jack. Jack was in the Royal Air Force during the Second World War; he married Gladys Evelyn Adams in 1946 just after the war. Jack and Gladys had four children together, their oldest, John, was born shortly after they married, followed by Barbara, Michael and lastly David.

David Edward Scott was born in Winslow on 27 September 1957. Dave, as he was known, went to Winslow Secondary school, he joined The Parachute Regiment when he was 16 years old, straight from school. Dave enjoyed playing football as a youngster.

Dave met his wife Gloria while they were both serving in the army, the couple married in Kilmarnock, Gloria's hometown, in 1979. When Dave was deployed to the Falkland Islands in 1982, the couple were living in married quarters in Tidworth.

Dave's brother Michael remembers him with both brotherly love and humour, he says:

> Last time I saw him was at Tidworth, went to a Chinese takeaway with him. Irish Rangers were also there so a fight started. I got arrested by the red caps and let go as I was a civvy, then by the police, and he walked away SCOTT free, loved that brother.

The memories we must hold dear, the funny ones that remind us of the character of the person who is in Valhalla seated at the great table.

Dave sailed 'Down South' with the 3rd Battalion Parachute Regiment on the *Canberra*. At the time his brother Michael remained positive that he would make it home. Dave was killed during the Battle for Mount Longdon on 12 June 1982.

Dave is remembered by Michael as a 'loving, crazy, great character, my brother'.

Dave's final resting place is Aldershot Military Cemetery, he and the men of The Parachute Regiment buried there are never short of visitors and the graves are tended with loving care.

Jack died in February 1990. Gladys passed away in hospital in Milton Keynes in 2007, she is buried in Winslow.

Dave is remembered on the War Memorial in Winslow. He was known to many of his comrades as 'Scotty'.

In 2022, as part of the Falkland Islands 40th Anniversary Place Names Project, Dave was honoured with 'Scott Neck', a narrow neck of land separating the two sections of Lake Sullivan on mainland West Falkland.

His name lives on…

24576023 Private Ian Patrick Scrivens 3rd Battalion Parachute Regiment 12 August 1964 ~ 12 June 1982 Age 17

Ian Patrick Scrivens was born on 12 August 1964 in Weymouth, Dorset. His parents Roy and Rosemary were married in Yeovil, Somerset, in 1962. Ian had one younger sister.

Before joining the British Army, Ian lived in Yeovil, attending Westfield School. Ian was a member of the Army Cadet Force as a teenager. 'Scrivs', as he became known, joined Junior Parachute Company in 1981, after passing the infamous P Coy he was sent to 3 Para. Four firm friends were made during their training. Only one of them was to make it home in 1982.

Unusually, all four friends who passed out were all sent to serve with the same battalion. 'Scrivs' was described by a friend as 'a 6ft skinhead who was hard as iron but would dance like John Travolta to his favourite Motown music'.

Though not allowed to serve in Northern Ireland, the business of war meant that 17-year-olds in 1982 were allowed to serve if they wished – and Scrivs wished, as did his new comrades.

On 11 June 1982 into the night of 12 June the men of 3 Para were given the task of taking the heavily defended summit of Mount Longdon, which lies four miles west of the Falklands capital of Port Stanley. It seemed an impossible task, but the Paras do not know the meaning of the word impossible, to them that would merely be a song title.

That night, 'Scrivs' was to become the youngest soldier to be killed in the war, exactly two months short of his 18th Birthday.

Mount Longdon went from being cold, dark and still, to alive with action and alight with tracers in the blink of an eye. Two other young men were shot ahead of 'Scrivs' while they were trying to take an Argentinian position. In his last moments, Scrivs was with one of them, Neil Grose. In true Para style he was joking with him about upsetting the neighbours with the noise of his birthday party. While figuring out how to get Neil back to safety, 'Scrivs' was shot by an Argentine sniper, he died instantly.

Scrivs is buried in Aldershot Military Cemetery along with the young friends he served and died with.

In 2022, as part of the Falkland Islands 40th Anniversary Place Names Project, Scrivs was honoured with 'Scrivens Beach', a sandy beach on the south side of Byron Sound, west of Hill Cove, West Falkland.

His name lives on…

C021253B Lieutenant Commander John Murray Sephton DSC
HMS *Ardent* 29 November 1946 ~ 21 May 1982 Age 35

John Murray Sephton was born in Southampton on 29 November 1946, the eldest son of Eric and Jean Murray Sephton (née Pott). The couple married at Hillhead Baptist Church, Glasgow, in November 1945. John was one of three children; he was born just after the couple's first wedding anniversary.

Eric Sephton was from Southampton, he was a solicitor's clerk in 1939 and a Sergeant in the Hampshire Regiment during the Second World War; Jean was a Leading Wren in the Women's Royal Naval Service. Service to their country had been consistent in both the Sephton and Pott family.

John's grandfather, Edwin Swain Sephton, enlisted into the Services in February 1916. Edwin was a shipbuilder's clerk; he was retained as a civilian after the end of the First World War. Edwin, born in London in 1891, was the son of Metropolitan

Police Sergeant, Harry Swain Sephton. The Sephton family found their way to Southampton via Lancashire, Northamptonshire, and London.

Edwin married Florence Heywood in 1913, just before the First World War. Eric was the couple's eldest son. Records indicate that Eric's brother Reginald was a prisoner of war in Fukuoka, Japan, during the Second World War. A Sergeant with the Royal Artillery, he was held captive from February 1942 until September 1945, Reginald was discharged in 1954. All three Sephton brothers served during the Second World War.

Jean Murray Pott was the daughter of George Murray and Jess Mary Pott (née Gibson). George had been a Radio Officer in the Merchant Navy and a Lieutenant in the Royal Naval Volunteer Reserve. George was born in Great Mongeham, Kent in 1890. George married Jess Mary Gibson in Glasgow in 1919, daughter Jean was born in 1924. George served his country during two world wars.

The Sephton family had settled in Southampton by 1921.

John Murray Sephton was a member of the 7th Southampton (Bassett) Scout Group prior to joining the Royal Navy. At the time of the Falklands War, John was a Lieutenant Commander on HMS *Ardent*, he had served with HMS *Hermes* during the 1970s.

According to the Victoria Cross website John was recommended for the Victoria Cross by the Task Force Commander but the Second Sea Lord (Admiral Sir Desmond Cassidi KCB) referred the case back, as it was not considered strong enough. John was instead posthumously awarded the Distinguished Service Cross.

Citation from The *London Gazette* 8 October 1982:

> *The Queen has been graciously pleased to approve the Posthumous award of the Distinguished Service Cross to the undermentioned in recognition of gallant and distinguished service during the operations in the South Atlantic:*
> *Distinguished Service Cross*
> *Lieutenant Commander John Murray SEPHTON, Royal Navy.*
> *On 21st May 1982, HMS ARDENT on station in San Carlos Water came under heavy attack from the Argentine Air Force and sustained many bomb hits, causing great damage and loss of life. After the loss of the Seacat missile system, Lieutenant Commander Sephton, the Flight Commander organised the use of small arms by the Flight as a last-ditch defence against the concentrated and severe enemy attacks. In a dangerous and desperate situation, he was last seen directing fire on the exposed Flight Deck, shooting a sub machine gun vertically up into an A4 Skyhawk the instant before it dropped the bombs that killed him. Three other Flight members were also killed. Lieutenant Commander Sephton's extreme valour and self-sacrifice was an example and inspiration to all the Ship's Company and undoubtedly deterred the enemy from making even more attacks.*

John married in Weymouth in 1978, he and his wife had one daughter born in 1980. John's daughter visited the Falkland Islands in 2017.

In 2022, as part of the Falkland Islands 40th Anniversary Place Names Project, John was honoured with 'Sephton Island', a small island on the east side of Lake Hammond, West Falkland.

His name lives on…

24599828 Craftsman Alexander Shaw REME (attached 3 Para) 16 May 1957 ~ 13 June 1982 Age 25

Alexander Shaw was born in Blythswood, Glasgow, on 16 May 1957 to Alex and Jeanie Shaw (née Hamilton) who married in 1954.

When Alex was 9 years old the family moved to Corby, Northamptonshire, as many Scottish families did during that time – Corby became known as Little Scotland. Alex was their only child for ten years until his sister Susan came along, she remained his only sibling.

Alex attended Lodge Park School in Corby where he loved basketball, he was the captain of the school team. His sister says 'Alex originally joined the Royal Marines 40 commando upon leaving school which he loved. He left to marry his girlfriend Ann Blair and settled down in Corby working as a postman. He soon decided civvy life was not for him and signed up again.'

Alex and Ann married in Corby in 1978, their son Craig was born early in 1982 and was just a baby the last time he saw his father.

Second time around Alex served in the Royal Electrical and Mechanical Engineers, during the Falklands War he was attached to 3 Para. Alex sailed 'Down South' on the *Canberra* where he saw some familiar faces.

During the Battle for Mount Longdon Alex was injured at the same time as Denzil Connick and Craig Jones. A chopper was on its way to pick them up, ironically Denzil was the only one who survived. Alex died of his injuries on 13 June 1982. He was temporarily interred with his comrades at Teal Inlet.

Alex was repatriated later that year and after a cremation his ashes were buried at Shire Lodge Cemetery in Corby.

Susan was just 15 years old when her brother died. She remembered listening for the news each day with her family. She says, 'I always remember Alex as a kind, fun loving brother who liked to play jokes. I loved him very much and always looked up to him. He was my hero!'

Lonnie Donoghue says 'I knew him briefly. When I was on my upgrader course in 1981, he was on his basics having left the Royal Marines and transferred to the army. He was a top Armourer student in 1981 and very well liked.'

Alex's ashes were exhumed in 2020 and re-interred in Bordon Military Cemetery. His widow visited the Falkland Islands for the first time forty years after he died.

In 2022, as part of the Falkland Islands 40th Anniversary Place Names Project, Alex was honoured with 'Shaw Point', a point on the west side of Kiwi Creek, Port Salvador, East Falkland.

His name lives on…

D135675L Leading Cook Anthony Elwyn Sillence HMS *Glamorgan* 30 May 1956 ~ 12 June 1982 Age 26

Anthony Elwyn Sillence was born in Edenthorpe, Doncaster on 30 May 1956. His parents Elwyn George Sillence and Coral Rosemary Allen were married in Doncaster in 1949. Tony had two younger sisters, Rosemary and Mary.

Tony attended Edenthorpe School where he excelled at Long Jump and football. He joined the Royal Navy straight from school as a J A/Ck 2 at HMS *Raleigh* on 10 October 1972. Just 16 years of age, his journey to becoming a Cook had begun, he was headed for a career with the Royal Navy.

Tony's service saw him next at HMS *Pembroke*, Chatham, on 20 November 1972 where he stayed until the following April receiving a promotion in the March of 1973. HMS *Collingwood* was his next stop in April 1973, by November of that year Tony had another promotion.

By August 1974, Tony held the rank of Acting Cook as he took up his next challenge at HMS *Bristol*, in November that year he was promoted to Cook. HMS *Jura* followed in 1975, HMS *Caledonia* in 1976. Finally, on 7 March 1977 Tony joined the crew of HMS *Juno* and by December 1978, he was an Acting Leading Cook.

In 1978 Tony and Linda were married in Rotherham, their only daughter was born the following year.

In 1979 Tony's next stop on his career ladder was HMS *Nelson* then back to HMS *Collingwood*. After another promotion he joined HMS *Glamorgan* on 10 February 1981 as Leading Cook.

Tony was not an overly tall young man, but he was fresh faced with light brown hair, green eyes, and a wide smile. His sister remembers him as 'Bright, funny, a tormentor, football fanatic and a great dad, brother and son.'

His mother and sister Rosemary were at home when the Falkland Islands were invaded, his sister Diane was working in Italy. Diane says she was, 'scared for him and the crew but proud that he was doing his duty and serving Queen & Country.' She also added 'I'm glad and proud of him that our country saved the Falklands from invading Argentinian Forces.'

Like many, Tony's mother has visited the Falkland Islands and laid a wreath where he died.

In 2022, as part of the Falkland Islands 40th Anniversary Place Names Project, Tony was honoured with 'Sillence Point', a prominent point midway along the north coast of Sea Lion Island in the Sea Lion Islands Group.

His name lives on…

24000417 Sergeant John Jamieson Simeon 2nd Battalion Scots Guards 24 March 1946 ~ 14 June 1982 Age 36

John Jamieson Simeon was born in Devon on 24 March 1946, the eldest son of Adam Jamieson and Pat Simeon (née Vickery). The couple moved back to Scotland

and went on to have three more children, all boys. Mick, Benny and Adam junior were all born in Scotland. Adam went on to serve in the Gordon Highlanders.

Pat had already seen tragedy when her family home in Vauxhall Street, Plymouth, was bombed on 23 April 1941. Her mother and several relatives were killed on the day. As families lost their homes, they often lost all possessions during the Blitz, Plymouth was often under attack. Pat survived; she was dug out of the rubble. Homeless with just the clothes on her back, she was taken in by a relative.

John's father, Adam, was born in Scotland. Jamieson is a family name passed down from generation to generation, though it is thought that the name Simeon originally came from the Lorraine District of France.

The family settled in Glasgow where John attended Knightswood Primary followed by Knightswood Secondary School, he joined the British Army in 1965. John was originally in the 1st Battalion Scots Guards until the mid-1970s, after which he served in the 2nd Battalion.

John saw service in Malaya, Borneo and did several Northern Ireland tours.

John married his first wife in 1968, the couple had one son, Jamieson, known as 'Jamie'. John went on to marry for a second time and had two more boys.

When the call came to go 'Down South', John travelled the long journey with his comrades on the QE2. John was a well-liked Platoon Sergeant who enjoyed boxing and football, he is remembered as a good instructor who had time for people.

John was killed by a sniper in the Battle for Mount Tumbledown on 14 June 1982. A young boy when his father died, Jamie Simeon later joined the Scots Guards and carved out a career in the Regiment. He has frequently made speeches and paid tributes to his father over the years, including a pilgrimage to the Falkland Islands. Jamie also served in the Falkland Islands as part of the Rouliment Infantry Regiment, F Company Scots Guards in 2008.

During the Battle for Mount Tumbledown the Scots Guards lost eight men, a further forty-three were wounded.

Pat Simeon died in 2019, she was 95 years young.

In 2022, as part of the Falkland Islands 40th Anniversary Place Names Project, John was honoured with 'Simeon Hill', the summit of Gid's Island in King George Bay, West Falkland.

His name lives on…

24507759 Private Francis Frederick Slough 2nd Battalion Parachute Regiment 18 April 1963 ~ 14 June 1982 Age 19

Dennis George Slough and Valerie Margaret Phillips married in Surrey early in 1959, they had met in London. Their eldest child, Stephanie Jane, was born in 1962 but sadly died a day later; by then the couple were living in Reading, Berkshire.

On 18 April 1963, son Francis Frederick Slough was born in Reading, his sister Maureen followed in 1966. From a very young age Francis was called Fred to everyone but his mother.

Fred was the second Frederick to serve in the Slough family, his great-grandfather Frederick James Slough served with the Royal Engineers in the First World War. Fred survived the war; he died in 1962.

Young Fred attended Sonning Common Primary School in Reading, and later at Chiltern Edge Secondary School. At school Fred excelled at sports, especially boxing, when he was at Chiltern Edge School, he belonged to the boxing team. Fred also attended the local youth club.

When Fred and his sister Maureen were very young their parents Dennis and Valerie divorced; both subsequently remarried. Dennis married Margaret Crouch in 1971 and Fred stayed with them in England. Valerie remarried to Patrick Barry in Dublin on 17 October 1970, it was her 35th birthday and Maureen's 4th birthday.

Margaret and Dennis went on to have three more children: Cliff, Phillip and Rachel, all half-siblings to Fred.

Valerie and Patrick went on to have three girls: Wendy, Hazel and Victoria. The couple had settled in Tallaght, Dublin, Ireland. Maureen grew up in Ireland with her mother while Fred continued his education in England with his father. In total Fred had one full sister, four half-sisters, two half-brothers and one step-brother, David.

Fred joined the army straight from school. Maureen says, 'Two years he served in the Forces. He went to Army Careers, Market Street, Reading and enlisted in the Junior Leaders regiment 1979–80. Later he was first badged to the royal military police and then badged to the parachute regiment.'

At the time of the Falklands War, Fred was in 12 Platoon D Coy, he first saw action at Goose Green, which he survived. Fred was mortally wounded in the final stages of the Battle for Wireless Ridge. Although he was taken to the Field Hospital, he died of his wounds just hours before the Falklands War ended on 14 June 1982.

Maureen continues, 'I was only 16 and I was in boarding school at the time. I only found out that Fred was in a war when I got a phone call from our mother Valerie to say that he was killed in action which was very devastating. Over all the war saddened me, and the loss of life.'

Fred's father chose to leave his son in the Falkland Islands, against the wishes of Fred's mother. Buried initially at Teal Inlet with his comrades, Fred was finally interred in the Military Cemetery at Blue Beach, Port San Carlos.

When families were offered a pilgrimage trip, Fred's biological mother was not included. Valerie did manage to visit her son's grave twice before her death on 10 January 2000. Fred's father died on 20 May 2018.

Fred is remembered by his old village Sonning Common, where there is a plaque in his name. The granite memorial and remembrance plaque to Private Slough was already in place at the village hall, but in November 2018 the Women's Institute made a Poppy Wreath consisting of wool and felt poppies numbering over 100. They placed the wreath over his plaque in a special coffee morning, a lovely gesture.

In 2022, as part of the Falkland Islands 40th Anniversary Place Names Project, Fred was honoured with 'Slough Islet', a small tussac between Scott Island and Arrow Islands in Choiseul Sound, East Falkland.

His name lives on…

P036299J Corporal Jeremy Smith 42 Commando 25 November 1958 ~ 11 June 1982 Age 23

Jeremy Smith was born at Torbay Hospital, Torquay, Devon, on 25 November 1958 to William Henry Thomas and Pamela Smith (née Brimacombe). Jeremy's father was a licenced bar manager, at the time the family lived in Shiphay, Torquay. Jeremy's parents married on 16 August 1946 at the Register Office in Newton Abbot. At the time of their marriage William was an Able Seaman with the Royal Navy, Pamela a hotel barmaid.

Pamela's grandfather had run the Half Moon Inn in Stoke Climsland, Cornwall, he married Jane Box in 1896. Pamela's father, Harold Box Brimacombe, was born in Cornwall. Harold, it appears, served in the Dorsetshire Regiment in the First World War.

Pamela had one brother, Leon Box Brimacombe, who served with the Scots Guards in the Second World War.

When Pamela and William married, they lived in Stokeinteignhead, Devon. Both Pamela's grandfather and her father died in 1945. It seems that Jeremy had one sister and one brother.

Jeremy spent much of his childhood in Torquay. Prior to joining the Royal Marines Jeremy was a member of 1528 (Torquay Boy's Grammar School) Squadron, where he attained the rank of Cadet Corporal. He left school aged 17 and immediately joined up.

As the British Forces made their way to retake Stanley, Mount Longdon, Mount Harriet, Wireless Ridge, Tumbledown, Mount Kent and Mount William were all strategic points. The Argentinian Troops were well dug in with a huge advantage. 42 Commando was making its way to take Mount Harriet. Jeremy was killed by shellfire while engaged in actions at Wall Mountain on 11 June 1982, a single loss for the British at Wall Mountain.

Jeremy is buried at Buckland Monachorum Cemetery, Horrabridge, Yelverton, Devon. A plaque bearing his name was added to the Torquay War Memorial in 2003.

In 2022, as part of the Falkland Islands 40th Anniversary Place Names Project, Jeremy was honoured with 'Smith Cove', a cove between Cape Terrible and Lion Point on the east coast of Westpoint Island, West Falkland.

His name lives on…

24428703 Lance Corporal Nigel Robert Smith 2nd Battalion Parachute Regiment 16 August 1960 ~ 28 May 1982 Age 21

Nigel Robert Smith was born in Cheltenham on 16 August 1960, the eldest son of Michael Robert and Joyce Smith (née Holtham). Nigel grew up in Cheltenham with his parents and two younger brothers.

In 1979, Nigel was serving in Ballykinler as part of 1 Platoon A Coy on an eighteen-month tour, many comrades were killed at Warrenpoint on 27 August that year. By 1981, the 2nd Battalion was based in Aldershot.

After Nigel met his sweetheart, he wished to combine a career with family life. Nigel and Wendy married on 3 April 1982 at St John's Church, Upper Hale in Farnham. Wendy was no stranger to Army life; her father Colin was a serving soldier. Having just married at the tender age of 16, nothing could prepare Wendy for the events that were about to unfold before her.

On 26 April 1982, Nigel set sail aboard the MV Norland as part of a huge Task Force designated to retake the Falkland Islands, invaded the day before his wedding. Barely moved into their married quarters, the young couple faced both their first and last separation.

Nigel was killed on 28 May 1982 by small arms fire alongside Corporal Sullivan and Lieutenant Barry. He died a week before his wife's 17th birthday, Wendy was married and widowed within less than two months. Wendy had broad shoulders for such a young woman, she gave birth to their daughter Natasha months later, another child bereaved from war. Despite her grief Wendy's wishes were carried out, Nigel was repatriated and now lies with his comrades in Aldershot Military Cemetery.

Wendy's father served in both The Parachute Regiment and REME for thirty-six years, he also saw service in the Falklands after the war. Wendy became the youngest Falklands widow. In his last letter Nigel wrote home promising Wendy the big family and the dog she craved. So many dreams were suddenly shattered.

Nigel was serving in D Coy. Remembered as a quiet man who was caring towards his family, he loved to ride his motorbike and listen the odd Smokey Robinson song. His mates called him either 'Smudge' or 'Meano'.

In 2022, as part of the Falkland Islands 40th Anniversary Place Names Project, Nigel was honoured with 'Smith Islet', a small islet with some tussac north of Jersey Harbour Islands in White Rock Bay at the north entrance to Falkland Sound, West Falkland.

His name lives on…

P032324V Corporal Ian 'Frank' Spencer 45 Commando Royal Marines 10 December 1955 ~ 12 June 1982 Age 26

Ian 'Frank' Spencer was born in Weston-super-Mare on 10 December 1955. With an interesting family background 'Frank' Spencer was so much more capable than his hapless TV namesake.

It appears that Frank's great-great-grandfather was the vicar of Daresbury. William Henry Spencer was born in 1818 in Hertfordshire. By 1851, he was the Chaplain of Christchurch, Oxford. Devoted to his profession William married late in life, marrying his bride Jane Walker in December 1860 at St Peter Ad Vincula in Stoke-on-Trent. The couple went on to have a large family; their youngest child; Septimus Alfred Spencer; was born in 1873. William Henry died in 1883, his youngest son was just 10 years old.

Septimus Spencer served in the Royal Naval Reserve; he was a stoker in the First World War by which time he was in his mid-forties. He married Mary Isherwood in 1893, prior to the First World War he was a tanner's labourer. The couple started their family with the birth of their eldest son William Lawton in March 1894.

William Lawton Spencer was Frank's grandfather, it was in his generation that we see the name Frank in the family. William's younger brother, Frank Isherwood Spencer, was born in 1904. William married Elizabeth Ann Jones in 1917, their eldest child, a daughter, was born the following year. The couple's second son, William Frank, arrived just before Christmas 1919. Youngest son Alan Peris Spencer was born in January 1922.

Alan married Muriel Dickman in Liverpool in 1951. Their oldest son, Ian 'Frank' Spencer was born on 10 December 1955 in Weston-super-Mare. Ian had a sister, Ann, born four years later.

Ian was educated at Price's Grammar School where he played cricket in the under 13s. Though he was a promising cricketer he also enjoyed swimming and judo at school.

Frank joined the Royal Marines; he later married Fiona in Arbroath. The couple had two sons together, Simon and Gareth.

Frank Spencer was a Corporal in Zulu Company, 45 Commando, Royal Marines in April 1982. He was admired for his professionalism and sense of humour. Frank was killed on 12 June 1982 during the night attack on Two Sisters North.

As the Marines took Two Sisters, 3 Para were heavily engaged in the Battle for Mount Longdon, the Scots Guards about to take Mount Tumbledown. 2 Para after their success at Goose Green were about to engage in their second battle for Wireless Ridge. All these concerted efforts during those four days in June were to see the British reclaim the Islands as the Argentinians admitted defeat.

Frank died alongside Gordon McPherson, also Zulu company; he is buried in the Western Cemetery in Arbroath, Scotland.

For the 30th anniversary Simon came up with the idea of a Yomp of the original Marines footsteps in honour of his father. Though the Spencer brothers were unable to travel to the Falkland Islands to complete the Yomp, David Macpherson made the trip with the former company commander of Zulu company.

In 2022, as part of the Falkland Islands 40th Anniversary Place Names Project, Frank was honoured with 'Spencer Bay', a bay on the west side of Carew Harbour, West Falkland.

His name lives on…

D184547G Steward Mark Royston Stephens HMS *Antelope*
6 October 1963 ~ 23 May 1982 Age 18

Mark Royston Stephens was born in Mansfield, Nottinghamshire on 6 October 1963 to Stanley Royston and Doreen Stephens (née Birkin). Mark was the eldest of four boys, his younger brothers Wayne, Glyn and Kelvin, were born over the next ten years.

Mark attended Robin Hood Junior School followed by Manor Comprehensive. He like to watch and play football, playing for Southwell Boys team.

His aspiration to become a sailor started when he was just 10 years old, he decided to join the Royal Navy after visiting HMS *Torquay* while on holiday.

During the Falklands War Mark was a Steward in HMS *Antelope*. A popular young man, he was well liked. HMS *Antelope* left Devonport on 5 April 1982, arriving in the Total Exclusion Zone on 22 May 1982.

While sat in San Carlos water HMS *Antelope* was bombed on 23 May 1982, hit by two 1,000lb bombs, neither initially exploded. Mark was killed as one of the bombs hit the senior rates' mess. Though a member of the First Aid party himself, he could not be saved. Mark died of his injuries in the arms of Bob Hutton, he was later buried at sea.

Later that day one of the bombs exploded, the ship subsequently sank and is now a War Grave.

In the Parish of Mansfield Woodhouse there is a war memorial, a small plaque underneath the Second World War memorial reads: 'IN LOVING MEMORY OF MARK ROYSTON STEPHENS AGED 18 YEARS KILLED IN ACTION ABOARD HMS ANTELOPE SAN CARLOS WATERS FALKLAND ISLANDS 23 MAY 1982 FOR COUNTRY AND FREEDOM'.

Mark's mother and brother went on the families' pilgrimage in 1983. Dor remembers her son as a happy lad, loving and caring. Brother Glyn sadly died in 2002.

In 2022, as part of the Falkland Islands 40th Anniversary Place Names Project, Mark was honoured with 'Stephens Island', an island in San Carlos River, East Falkland.

His name lives on...

D183504T Leading Seaman (Electronic Warfare) Bernard James Still HMS *Coventry* 30 December 1955 ~ 25 May 1982 Age 26

Bernard James Still was apparently from Co Laois in Eire. Loais is pronounced Leesh, the county was known as Queen's County between 1556 and 1922. Laois is taken from the name Loigis, a medieval kingdom.

Little is known about Bernie apart from the fact that he worked in Whitehall in the mid-1970s and possibly was in HMS *Kent* prior to HMS *Coventry*.

On 25 May 1982, Bernie was one of the men who died when HMS *Coventry* was bombed, his body lost to the sea.

In 2022, as part of the Falkland Islands 40th Anniversary Place Names Project, Bernie was honoured with 'Still Point', the southern point of Fox Island in Queen Charlotte Bay, West Falkland.

His name lives on...

24546294 Guardsman Archibald Graham Stirling 2nd Battalion Scots Guards 10 November 1960 ~ 14 June 1982 Age 21

Archibald Graham Stirling was born in Glasgow on 10 November 1960, he was known as Archie. Archie's parents William Hutchison Stirling and Alice Kincaid married in Glasgow in 1950. The couple had three children Catherine, Anne and young Archie; he was their only son.

William Hutchison Stirling was born in Paisley in 1917, one of eight children to William Miller Stirling and Jane Hutchison Rodger, who married in Paisley in 1915. William's brother Herbert was born in 1920 and his son, Archie's cousin, was also named William.

William and Jane's oldest son was also named Archibald Graham, siblings James Miller, William Hutchison, Herbert, David, Robert, Jean and Margaret followed. The family lived at McKerrel Street in Paisley.

It appears that Archie was named after his great-grandfather, Archibald Stirling, who was born in Alva in 1856, and also his Uncle Archibald. Archibald married Margaret Miller in 1879, the couple had four girls before William was born in 1890. The family moved to Paisley.

William ('Bill') did not see a lot of his cousin Archie when they were younger as his family had moved away from Scotland. Herbert served in the army during the Second World War and met his wife while in Belfast. The family moved back to Glasgow in 1974. Bill has fond memories of playing in parks and swimming pools in the Drumoyne and Govan areas with Archie when they were young lads. Bill joined the police and Archie the Scots Guards.

Archie was a quiet lad, in fact quite an introvert. He was 'rugged', a bit like the terrain where he later found himself some 8,000 miles from home. Initially when Argentina surrendered there were celebrations in the Stirling household, but the bubble soon burst as the family received that fateful 'knock on the door'. Archie had died in the Battle for Mount Tumbledown. Bill, his father, never quite got over the shock of the news and died the following year in 1983.

Archie is buried at Cardonald Cemetery, Mosspark Boulevard in Glasgow. His cousin Bill regularly visits his grave.

In 2022, as part of the Falkland Islands 40th Anniversary Place Names Project, Archie was honoured with 'Stirling Cove', a cove on the lower reaches of Swan Inlet, close to Mare Harbour, East Falkland.

His name lives on…

D154502T Petty Officer Marine Engineering Artificer 2 Geoffrey Leslie John Stockwell HMS *Coventry* 9 May 1957 ~ 25 May 1982 Age 25

Geoffrey Leslie John Stockwell was born in the borough of Lewisham on 9 May 1957. Geoffrey was the only son of Leslie John Claude Stockwell and Patricia

Seaton, who married in Kent in 1956. The couple had a daughter born a year after Geoff.

The family settled in Kent where Geoff grew up in Herne Bay, he attended Kent College.

Geoff joined the Royal Navy; he trained in Rosyth with HMS *Caledonia*. He was a great hockey player described as 'talented' which got him a place in the Combined Services Hockey Team. Geoff also liked a game of cricket and was known to amuse himself with makeshift bats and stumps at times.

By 1982, Geoff was a Petty Officer in HMS *Coventry*, he was killed by a bomb that tore through the engine room on 25 May 1982. At the time of his death, on land he still lived in Herne Bay.

Geoff's father Leslie was born in September 1913, he was a councillor and the local Sheriff of Canterbury. Many years previously he had been a civil servant in Bath, serving his country in a different way to his son.

It appears that Geoff's great-grandfather was Thomas Stockwell who was born in Gloucestershire; Thomas married Mary Ann Wilson in Surrey in 1859.

Herbert John Stockwell was the couple's second to youngest child; born in 1873 in Lee, Herbert was Geoff's grandfather. Herbert married Violet Rainer in 1912, the couple had two sons, and by 1921 they lived in Loampit Vale in Lewisham. Leslie John Claude Stockwell was their eldest son, younger son Kenneth was born in Kent in 1917.

At the grand age of 91 years young, Geoff's mother Patricia was one of the first people awarded the Elizabeth Cross. Her daughter received the award on her behalf in 2010 as by then Patricia was in a Nursing Home in Herne Bay. Senior officers from the Ministry of Defence later made a trip to present the award to Patricia, a lovely gesture.

Geoff's sister married in late 1980; her eldest son, born the year after Geoff died, was named after him. Geoff's father died in 1989.

Geoff is honoured on the Herne Bay War Memorial.

In 2022, as part of the Falkland Islands 40th Anniversary Place Names Project, Geoff was honoured with 'Stockwell Bay', a bay between Horse Island and Reef Point on the east coast of Saunders Island, West Falkland.

His name lives on…

24463538 Lance Corporal Anthony Roy Streatfield Royal Electrical and Mechanical Engineers 21 February 1960 ~ 8 June 1982 Age 22

Anthony Roy Streatfield, it appears, was born in Mill Hill, London, on 21 February 1960. Tony, as he was known, was the youngest son of Ernest and Rosina Streatfield (née Ginger). The couple married on 26 June 1948 at Hendon Register Office, both lived in Burnt Oak at the time.

The Streatfield family had a long history in North London, Ernest was born in Islington in February 1928. Records indicate that Ernest served in the Second World War with the Royal Artillery.

Ernest was one of eight children; by 1939 the family had moved from Islington to Edgware. Ernest worked as a baker's roundsman when he married Rosina Ginger, a 17-year-old factory hand. The granddaughter of a postman, Rosina was one of six children; the family lived for many years in Queens Park, London. It is hard to know, as so many the First World War records were destroyed during the Blitz, how many of the Ginger family served. Rosina's father was one of ten children.

Rosina's uncle, Lance Corporal Sidney Ginger, served with the 2nd Battalion Middlesex Regiment; he was killed in action on 28 June 1917, he is honoured on the Ypres Memorial at Menin Gate.

Tony was the youngest of three boys. Although Tony's father appears to have predeceased him, his mother Rosina lived into her eighties, she attended many services over the years to remember her son.

In April 1982, Tony was a Lance Corporal with the Royal Electrical and Mechanical Engineers. On 8 June 1982, Tony was on board the RFA *Sir Galahad*, he was one of the forty-eight men killed that day.

The *Sir Galahad* later sunk and is now an official War Grave, like his great-uncle, Tony has no known grave.

Tony married in 1981, the couple had one daughter at the time of his death.

In 2022, as part of the Falkland Islands 40th Anniversary Place Names Project, Tony was honoured with 'Streatfield Beach', a beach south of Sea Lion Point at the west entrance to Port Salvador, north coast of East Falkland.

His name lives on…

D138928M Chief Petty Officer Weapons Engineering Artificer David Anthony Strickland HMS *Coventry* 14 September 1952 ~ 25 May 1982 Age 29

Dave Strickland was born in Freckleton, Lancashire, in September 1952. The area of Amounderness was one of sixty-two settlements in the area; Freckleton itself appears in the Domesday book as 'Frecheltun', the name a mix of the Old English word 'Tun' and the Nordic name of Frecla. With a history of supplying water to a Roman Fort, later it became a port for the ship building industry with rope and sailcloth made locally.

Jack Strickland and Ruth Cooper married early in 1944 in Northumberland, though the Strickland family has a long history in the area of Longton, near Preston in Lancashire.

Jack and Ruth settled back in Lancashire where Dave was born, his younger brother Malcolm followed four years later. As Dave grew up, he became a Sea Cadet with aspirations to join the Royal Navy. Jack and Ruth were not keen on the idea so initially Dave took an apprenticeship with the Post Office. The sea, however, was still beckoning, so when he was around 20 years old, he finally joined the Royal Navy.

Cindy and Dave met in a wine bar in Portsmouth on 13 April 1979, which was Good Friday that year. In May 1981, Dave married Cindy in Harrow, Middlesex. Prior to the Falklands War, Dave had been shore based at HMS *Nelson* in Portsmouth. He joined HMS *Coventry* in March 1982, because his next posting would have meant a move to Rosyth, he wanted Portsmouth to remain his base. Dave swapped with another sailor to join HMS *Coventry*.

Cindy was a personal assistant and remembers being very stressed as Dave sailed with the Task Force. People constantly asked her what was going on, but in reality families had no more knowledge than anyone else. Cindy's employers gave her some time off and she left for a Greek Island in a bid to find some peace, away from the news. Ironically, she was due to leave for home on 25 May 1982.

She says:

> I was leaving to come home on 25 May, the day it was announced that two ships had been hit, HMS *Coventry* and *Atlantic Conveyer*. I saw this on the little TV in the hotel reception area while waiting for my transport to the airport and as it was all in Greek, I couldn't really understand what was happening – awful. I couldn't wait to get home and ring the contact number given to find out what was happening. I never got 'the knock on the door'. I found out when I rang up for the umpteenth time when the young lad on the other end of the phone went silent and the next voice that I heard was the Naval chaplain telling me the news.

Initially Cindy was very angry; she felt quite bitter about the war but that changed in 1986 when she visited the Falkland Islands:

> Meeting the lovely Falkland Islanders, who are probably more patriotic than most British people are, I realised that my husband had played his part in protecting these people. I accepted that when he signed up to the Navy, he, like anyone else doing so, would accept that at any given moment they may have to put their life on the line. Sadly, he paid the ultimate price, and I lost a much-loved husband & soulmate all too soon.

Dave was killed when HMS *Coventry* was hit, as with so many of our men, he was lost to the ocean.

Cindy, like many young Forces' wives, thought she had a lifetime ahead of her with Dave. He was cut down in his prime; the couple had no children when he died. For the next few years Cindy changed jobs a few times but in 1988 decided to take a new path starting a university course for a BSc in Speech Sciences so that she could become a speech and language therapist. Cindy enjoyed the role very much and continued her work in that field until her retirement in 2015.

After her pilgrimage in 1986, Cindy returned to the islands in 1990. She would like Dave remembered thus:

I can't really think of enough words to do him justice but certainly a wonderful, loyal, humorous, and clever man who always made me feel very loved and cherished. Our time together was all too short – so many questions I wish I asked him, but which didn't seem important at the time when you're young and think you have your whole life ahead of you.

Dave's parents, Jack and Ruth, had birthdays just one day apart. They both died in 1995, seven months apart, Jack in January, Ruth in August that year. The couple saw out their days in Preston. His brother Malcolm died in 2001.

David Anthony Strickland was mainly known as Dave, but sometimes DAZ because of his initials.

In 2022, as part of the Falkland Islands 40th Anniversary Place Names Project, Dave was honoured with 'Strickland Point', the western tip of Pebble Islet.

His name lives on…

D175899F Steward John David Stroud HMS *Glamorgan* 11 May 1962 ~ 12 June 1982 Age 20

John David Stroud was born on 11 May 1962 at Bolton District General Hospital to John Leslie and Sheila Grace Stroud (née Stamp). Sheila had been widowed at a young age. John senior was a dental technician, the family home was in Harwood. John had one sister.

John went to Parklands High School in Chorley Lancashire. He was a member of Chorley Sea Cadets and spent time at HMS *Indefatigable* in Anglesey in his last school year.

John initially joined the Merchant Navy, travelling to West Africa; he later joined the Royal Navy. He previously served in HMS *Invincible*.

John was just 18 when he met Jean, she was 26. The couple met in a bar in Southsea while John was out with his friend. John and Jean married on 2 February 1981; they had been going out together for just eight weeks. After the ceremony they went to a night club in Southsea.

Despite being an amazing dancer, John slipped on the dance floor and broke his leg on their wedding day. He ended up in hospital wearing a full leg cast, he was then in plaster for two months.

Once recovered, John joined HMS *Glamorgan*. Life revolves often around shore leave in the Navy, but John just happened to be home for son John Paul's birth when he arrived four weeks early, born on 10 October 1981.

HMS *Glamorgan* ran aground so he was also home unexpectedly again for Christmas. When they set sail again, *Glamorgan* was engaged in exercises off Gibraltar. Later she was diverted to join the main Royal Navy Task Force and served as flagship for Admiral Sandy Woodward during the voyage south until 15 April, when he transferred his flag to the Aircraft Carrier HMS *Hermes*.

On 12 June 1982, John was killed when an Exocet missile hit HMS *Glamorgan*. In the last days of the war Argentine navy technicians fired a land-based MM-38 Exocet missile which struck the ship, causing damage and killing thirteen sailors.

John did not have a nickname but always signed his cards to his wife John David. Their son was named Paul John, but it was changed to John Paul when his father died.

In 2022, as part of the Falkland Islands 40th Anniversary Place Names Project, John was honoured with 'Stroud Cove', a cove on the north side of Bulls Road near Bull Point, East Falkland.

His name lives on...

D187549X Seaman (Missile) Matthew James Stuart HMS *Argonaut* 21 May 1964 ~ 21 May 1982 Age 18

Matthew James Stuart was born in Lichfield on 21 May 1964, the second son of Ray and Janet Stuart. Married in Birmingham in 1960, the family lived in Lichfield. Ray worked in Sales, Janet in Admin within retail. Matthew had a younger sister, Alison, and a younger brother, Ronald.

Matthew grew up between Twyning, Forthampton and Bredon. Schooling was first at St Michael's Primary School in Lichfield followed by Twyning Primary and Tewksbury School.

Though not very sporty Matthew loved climbing trees and was very adventurous; he owned an air rifle and some hunting knives, and loved a story of 'derring-do'. He was a member of the Forthampton Youth Club, his sister remembers him either being in the middle of the action or leading it.

Matthew enjoyed the backstage side of drama, was really funny and loved to make people laugh. Halloween was a time to dress up as a ghost and jump out on people. Holidays were spent in Woolacombe, Devon, and later in the South of France where he enjoyed the water – whether on it or in it.

The family owned an old Cortina and would drive down and stay in Eurocamp-type places; being a chatty, friendly soul, Matthew loved meeting other kids along the way. He enjoyed making models, both aircraft and ships, and had an interest in all things military. His dream was to become a diver, which led him to join the Navy hoping to achieve his goal one day.

From the age of 13 he worked delivering newspapers, at the local petrol station or farm labouring to earn his own money. One of the local farmers wrote to the family for the 30th Anniversary remembering Matthew fondly.

In his teens his parents bought him a Suzuki 250cc which he loved, and while home he went everywhere on it.

Matthew joined the Royal Navy in 1980. While at HMS *Raleigh* he was back classed when he got a bad ear infection, but he persevered. Despite struggling with kit inspections, he never gave up.

Matthew was killed when HMS *Argonaut* was bombed on 21 May 1982. Tragically it was Matthew's 18th Birthday, his birthday cards were returned to his family unopened.

Matthews parents presented HMS *Raleigh* with the Stuart Cup; it is awarded to the student who shows the most endeavour.

Matthew is honoured on the Twyning War Memorial, he is also remembered on the Stuart Memorial, Bredon St Giles Church.

In 2022, as part of the Falkland Islands 40th Anniversary Place Names Project, Matthew was honoured with 'Stuart Cove', a sandy cove at the northwest end of Fanning Harbour in San Carlos Waters, East Falkland.

His name lives on…

D082300A Chief Petty Officer Weapons Electrical Artificer Kevin Richard Frederick Sullivan HMS *Sheffield* 16 February 1947 ~ 4 May 1982 Age 35

Kevin Richard Frederick Sullivan was the eldest child of Frederick William and Helen Sullivan (née Boyle). Kevin was born in Dormanstown, Cleveland, Yorkshire.

Frederick and Helen married on 5 June 1944 in Cleveland, Yorkshire. When the couple married Frederick was a motor vehicle fitter in the Royal Marines and Helen was serving in the Women's Land Army; Helen was from Dormanstown, Redcar.

Kevin was the eldest of four children; he had one brother Fred, sister Linda, and lastly Marie.

Kevin is described by his siblings as a good brother, he always looked out for and after his siblings. 'He was funny and brightened up the room. He was very sharp and very quick witted; he could tell a tale. He also liked to call family by nicknames and had a mischievous spirit.'

Later, Leamington Spa became Kevin's home; he first attended Whitnash Primary and later at Aylesford School which was near the old library in Leamington. Kevin was good at sports and excelled in every subject. He was very intelligent and could turn his hand to anything. Kevin particularly enjoyed wood and metalwork and was presented at school with many books for his achievements. With a thirst for knowledge, he loved to read about everything – from the pyramids to Greek mythology. He had shelves full of books and also a love for birds and nature.

In his spare time, Kevin would be in his 'mam's' kitchen stripping down his BSA bike and putting it back together. He once built himself a radio.

Kevin's ambition was to join the Royal Air Force, but his eyesight was a problem. He joined the Royal Navy at the age of 17 on 4 May 1964 at HMS *Fisgard* as an Artificer Apprentice.

Kevin's daughter Nikki says:

> Mum (Patricia Joyce) and dad met on a blind date, set up by my
> dad's best friend and wife in 1970. They got married on 23 April

1973 in Warwick. They moved into a naval hiring for two years before buying their own house in Portchester. First son Paul was born in March 1976. Daughter Nicola was born October 1978 and youngest son Michael was born in May 1981. He was a very proud family man.

During his service, he served a year at *Fisgard* followed by eighteen months at HMS *Collingwood*. HMS *Forth* followed in 1969. Kevin's service prior to joining HMS *Sheffield* on 19 March 1979 saw him in *Victory*, *Collingwood*, *Juno*, and *Leander* as he worked his way up the ranks.

Kevin deployed to the Gulf for six months in November 1981, he had stopped off in Gibraltar to meet close friends on his way home. Days away from a much-needed homecoming HMS *Sheffield* was diverted to join the Task Force.

Nikki continues:

> As mum was expecting dad home, she had been out and bought us all new clothes and everyone was excited. When the news came that dad was diverted as you can imagine we were so upset. So much so that mum took my eldest brother out of school for two weeks and we travelled up to Warwick to be with family (mum's parents). I was only 3 and my little brother just 1. This period of time was incredibly stressful and filled with worry. It was the second week when mum saw the news on the television about the *Sheffield* being hit. We stayed with my grandparents from then on.

A safe haven at a terrible time, Pat's neighbours told her that reporters were surrounding their house.

By the time of the Falklands War, Kevin was a Chief Petty Officer and the gyro system maintainer on HMS *Sheffield*. Kevin tragically died on the anniversary of his joining the Royal Navy, he had served eighteen years.

Nikki says:

> The war was in my opinion a requirement to protect our empire abroad, and the justification was understood. However, the loss of life, including that of my dad, is always a tragic result of war, and he will be forever missed. It was pleasing though to feel the sacrifices of many were not for nothing, and the Falkland's were liberated.

She would like him remembered as 'An outgoing person who loved life, and who had a large friendship group and a strong sense of patriotism and his role in society.'

Kevin has a memorial stone of his very own at St Mary's Church, Portchester Castle, Portchester, Fareham, Hampshire. The memorial stone is in the style of a headstone it reads 'SACRED TO THE MEMORIES OF ALL WHO FELL IN THE FALKLANDS CAMPAIGN AND ESPECIALLY OF CHIEF PETTY OFFICER

KEVIN SULLIVAN AGED 35 KILLED IN ACTION IN HMS SHEFFIELD ON 4TH MAY 1982 THIS MEMORIAL WAS ERECTED BY HIS FRIENDS'.

In 2022, as part of the Falkland Islands 40th Anniversary Place Names Project, Kevin was honoured with 'Sullivan Point', a point on the west side of the entrance to Port Salvador at the entrance to Brazo del Mar, East Falkland.

His name lives on…

24353770 Corporal Paul Steven Sullivan 2nd Battalion Parachute Regiment 15 June 1954 ~ 28 May 1982 Age 27

Paul Steven Sullivan was born in Northampton on 15 June 1954. Parents Beryl and Ray Sullivan had three younger children: Elaine, Glenn and Peter. Though Paul did not know his grandfathers, he was close to his maternal grandmother Margery, who looked after him often.

Paul joined 2 Para when he was 19 years old, prior to joining up he had worked in the building trade. It started with a train journey and a dream of being a 'sky god'. Lonnie Donoghue boarded the train at Birmingham in 1974, he found himself sat diagonally opposite to a young man, both men armed with holdalls. Engaging in conversation, they discovered they were both headed for Aldershot destined to become Paratroopers. Paul became known to his army mates as Sully, he was the first 'mukker' that Lonnie met on the road to earning the coveted Maroon Beret

Sully met Bette when she was doing her basic training in the Queen Alexander Royal Army Nursing Corps, she met Paul at the end of her first week. He proposed three weeks later. Bette says Paul was her soulmate, for all who experience that kind of love, time is irrelevant, feelings are as real as the ground beneath your feet, as deep as the ocean.

Bette and Paul married eleven months later in April 1977 at St Alphage Church, Burnt Oak. They were proud to be chosen as one of three couples to meet Prince Charles in Berlin for a cup of tea. Bette says, 'Paul got a teaching post after a year in Berlin at depot Para and enjoyed teaching the juniors and they respected him because he worked them hard but was also very fair.'

Bette and Paul had one daughter, Alesia, who was born in Aldershot in 1979.

Sully was in 12 Platoon D Company when he left for the Falklands. Bette continues:

> He died at Goose Green, during a mix up when 2 Para thought they were taking the Argentinian surrender, when mortar firing by us in the distance made them panic and shoot our men. He died just three weeks before his 28th birthday and before being made sergeant as a substantive post.
>
> Paul was father to Alesia, who is now called 'Sully' by her good friends, looks like him and has many mannerisms her dad had. He would be so proud of her being a school teacher.

Paul had a great career ahead of him, but like so many other families Bette and Alesia lost their future as they knew it, with just one 'knock on the door'.

Paul had the widest of grins and is remembered well among the 'Class of 82'.

Paul was later repatriated; his final resting place is the Military Cemetery in Aldershot.

In 2022, as part of the Falkland Islands 40th Anniversary Place Names Project, Paul was honoured with 'Sullivan Creek' a small creek on the north shore of Choiseul Sound between White Bluff and John Point, East Falkland.

His name lives on...

D187550T Able Seaman (Electronic Warfare) Adrian Derek Sunderland HMS *Coventry* 20 April 1963 ~ 25 May 1982 Age 19

Adrian Derek Sunderland was born in Dorchester on 20 April 1963. Adrian was the only son of Derek and Lilian Sunderland (née Denman) who married in Weymouth in 1960. Derek was born in Heptonstall, Yorkshire; he met Lilian while he was docked close to her hometown of Weymouth. The couple had four children, three girls and Adrian, who was known to the family as 'Adge'.

Historically the Sunderland family had a long association with the Heptonstall area in Yorkshire. If you are in the area many of the Sunderland family were buried in St Thomas a Becket church in Heptonstall, a ruined but still beautiful church.

Back through the generations there were cotton weavers, coal baggers, draymen, and a Wesleyan minister, a rich family history caught in a snapshot of time.

Willie Sunderland (Adge's grandfather) married Violet Parkinson in 1928; the couple had two sons: Norman, born on Boxing Day 1933, and Derek, who was the youngest and born in April 1940. The family lived in New Street, Hebden Bridge.

Derek Sunderland joined the Royal Navy in the late 1950s. Lilian Denman was born and raised in Weymouth. Derek is remembered as a hard worker, a protective man who would help anyone but did not suffer fools.

After Derek left the Royal Navy, he worked locally in Yorkshire before moving south where he became a herdsman. Adge was Derek and Lilian's second born, younger brother to Lin. Adge attended Sexeys School in Bruton, joining the Navy in September 1980. He played rugby and football and like many young lads, loved a laugh and a drink.

Adge was with Drake 39 at HMS *Raleigh*, he passed out in November 1980. Adge completed his Electronic Warfare in March 1981 at HMS *Dryad*, he joined HMS *Exeter*, on loan, shortly afterwards to get some sea time. Later he was posted to HMS *Coventry* as a junior rate he was given the option to leave the ship before she headed 'Down South' but chose to stay.

To his Naval mates he was known as 'Ade' or 'Sunny'. On 25 May 1982, Adge was killed when an explosion wrecked the Junior Rate's dining hall. Adge was just 19 years old. At the time of his death, the family home was in Charlton Horethorne, Dorset.

Adge's father Derek died in December 1988 in Milborne Port.

In 2022, as part of the Falkland Islands 40th Anniversary Place Names Project, Adge was honoured with 'Sunderland Islet', a small tussac island west of Middle Island in Choiseul Sound, East Falkland.

His Name lives on…

Butcher Yuk Fai Sung *Sir Galahad* 13 November 1930 ~ 8 June 1982 Age 51

There are so many components in a war. While incredible feats are achieved by our men on the ground, there are those who fly high in the skies and those who man the ships that get them there.

Most of the general public would remember the *Galahad* for the Welsh Guards we lost on that fateful day, but the ship was manned by many Chinese civilian crew, mainly from Hong Kong, and their British Commanding Officers.

Yuk-Fai Sung was born 13 November 1930, he was from Kowloon, Hong Kong. Sung joined the Royal Fleet Auxiliary in 1980.

Sung was a butcher on the RFA *Sir Galahad*, one of many Chinese who decided to remain at post as the ship headed towards the Total Exclusion Zone.

Sung was killed when the *Galahad* was attacked by A4-Skyhawks on 8 June 1982, his body lost to the South Atlantic.

In 2022, as part of the Falkland Islands 40th Anniversary Place Names Project, Sung was honoured with 'Sung Point', the northern tip of North Island near New Island, West Falkland.

His name lives on…

D178106E Cook Andrew Charles Swallow HMS *Sheffield* 8 May 1963 ~ 4 May 1982 Age 18

Andrew Charles Swallow was born in Cuckfield Hospital, Cuckfield, Sussex, on 8 May 1963. He was the middle son of three brothers born to Charles John Thurlby and Gillian Mary Swallow (née Broomhead) who married in 1959.

Andy's father was born November 1935 in Hendon, Middlesex; he appears to have been known as John. Grandfather Harry North Swallow married Janet Gray Thurlby in Nottinghamshire in 1932. Janet was a farmer's daughter, the third daughter of Francis John Thurlby and Eva Augusta Emma Gray, who married in Lincolnshire in 1897. Eva's father had farmed over 900 acres in Lincolnshire in the late 1800s.

Harry was the third son of Charles Robinson Swallow and Alice Maud North, who married in Grantham, Lincolnshire, in 1894. Harry was one of at least eight children.

Charles Robinson Swallow was born in 1870, he became a butcher.

Charles's younger brother, Alfred Bailey Swallow, was killed in action on 21 March 1918, he was a Company Sergeant Major, aged 37. Alfred had married Ethel Martha Keal in 1907. Alfred served with the Royal Engineers; he is remembered on the Grantham War Memorial.

Alfred Bailey Swallow joined the British Army around 1900, he had served in India and been awarded the Delhi Durbar in 1911. During the First World War he was sent to the Western Front. No one could have known that a great-nephew would also die some sixty-four years later, lost to the sea but with greater certainty that he had crossed the bar.

Sadly, the First World War claimed another Swallow life, Alfred Bailey's nephew, Lawrence Frederick Swallow, died on 1 July 1916 aged just 19. Lawrence was a Corporal in the 2nd Battalion Lincolnshire Regiment, he died during the opening day of the Battle for the Somme. Lawrence was the son of Lawrence Herbert Swallow and his wife Florence. The Swallow family were well known and respected in the area.

Many of the Swallow family were in corn or coal merchandising, much-needed resources in wartime. The Swallow family from Barrowby were well known operators of the Barrowby Mill, later the Spitalgate and Manthorpe Mill.

Andy's parents later moved from Cuckfield, settling on the Isle of Wight.

Andy was killed on the 4 May 1982 when HMS *Sheffield* was hit, he is remembered on the Bembridge War Memorial.

Although on some memorials and sources Andy is listed as being 19 years old, he was still 18; he died four days short of his birthday.

In 2022, as part of the Falkland Islands 40th Anniversary Place Names Project, Andy was honoured with 'Swallow Cove', a sandy cove on the south side of Saddle Island near New Island, West Falkland.

His name lives on…

24433054 Lance Corporal Phillip Anthony Sweet 1st Battalion Welsh Guards 7 May 1960 ~ 8 June 1982 Age 22

The Sweet family have roots in Aberdare in the Rhondda Valley. Phil was not the first in his family to serve in the British Army. Phil's maternal great-grandfather, Howell Moyle, served with the Welsh Regiment in the First World War; he enlisted into the 12th Battalion in January 1915. Howell later transferred to the Labour Corps; he was discharged during the Miners' strike in 1921. Phil's maternal grandfather, Idris, was just 12 years old at the time.

Idris Moyle enlisted into the Royal Artillery in November 1940, he served with the Royal Artillery until his discharge in 1954. In 1939, he was with the Militia Civilians in Winterbourne Dauncey, Wiltshire. Idris was married to Rosina; Phil's mother Vilma was the couple's eldest child.

Phil's parents, Cliff and Vilma, married in 1955; the couple had three children. Phil was their only son and middle child, born in the district of Pontypridd on 7 May 1960.

Phil attended primary school at Cwmbach, followed by Gadlys Comprehensive and Blaengwawr Comprehensive. Phil had always aspired to join the army which he did straight from school, his parents were very proud of him.

As a young boy Phil loved his bicycles which naturally progressed into motorbikes. He had a shed in the garden and loved to experiment with things.

After initial training Phil was posted to Prince of Wales Company in Berlin. While in Germany, Phil attended the NATO Weapons Trials in Hammelburg. It was there that Phil met Eva Emmert; the couple married in 1980. Their son was born in 1981, he was given Phillip as his middle name. At the time of his death Phil was stationed with the Welsh Guards in Pirbright.

Phil was killed on 8 June 1982 when tragically the *Sir Galahad* was hit by Argentinian Aircraft.

Phil's family visited the Falklands in the families' pilgrimage of 1983. It was his mother's wish to be with her son therefore when she died in 2002, her ashes were taken to the Falkland Islands to be scattered where he died.

Phil is remembered on a plaque added to the local cenotaph in Aberdare. It reads: 'IN MEMORY OF LCPL PHILLIP ANTHONY SWEET KILLED IN ACTION FALKLAND ISLANDS JUNE 8TH 1982 RIP'.

In 2022, as part of the Falkland Islands 40th Anniversary Place Names Project, Phil was honoured with 'Sweet Hill', a prominent hill (550ft elevation) south east of Isthmus Cove on the north shore of Port Philomel, West Falkland.

His name lives on…

24256419 Corporal Stephen John Godfrey Sykes 22 SAS Regiment 10 April 1957 ~ 19 May 1982 Age 25

The Sykes family had a long association with Huddersfield.

Steve's paternal grandfather, Arthur Sykes, lived in Huddersfield prior to World War Two. As a representative for a paint manufacturer, he travelled for work for many years.

Arthur married Marie Atkinson in 1923 in the district of Thanet, Kent. Steve's father, John Clifford Sykes, was the couple's eldest son born in April 1924; the family lived at Crosland Moor, Huddersfield.

John Clifford Sykes married Brenda Marie Godfrey at the Church of Our Lady of Lourdes, Harpenden, Hertfordshire, in July 1947. At the time John was a 3rd Officer in the Merchant Navy. Brenda was the daughter of Frederick James and Winifred Godfrey. Records indicate that Frederick was born in Canterbury, Kent in 1897, he served in the Bengal Sappers and Miners of the Indian Army during the First World War. Frederick married Winifred Hourahan in Kent in 1917. By 1921, Frederick was a Lance Sergeant with the Royal Engineers based in Roorkee, India.

After leaving the army Frederick worked as a telecommunications engineer, the family settled in Park Hill, Harpenden. At the time of Brenda's marriage Frederick was a Captain with the Royal Army Service Corps.

John and Brenda eventually settled in John's native Huddersfield. Stephen John Godfrey Sykes was born at the Princess Royal Maternity Home in Huddersfield on 10 April 1957. At the time of his birth Steve's father was an Assistant General Manager of an iron foundry, the family were living in Marsh, Huddersfield.

It is thought Steve joined the British Army in the mid-1970s. He joined the SAS Signals in February 1978. While serving with 264 Signal Squadron SAS, Steve was one of the unlucky men who died in the Sea King crash on 19 May 1982.

Steve is described as 'a good bloke who would have gone far', a phrase we hear too often with our fallen.

Tony Shaw says,

> Steve passed the SAS Signals Probation course in 1978 after serving in 604 Signal Troop which is where I first met him. He was a qualified military parachutist and had also recently qualified as a Class 1 radio telegraphist. While with 264 (SAS) Signal Squadron Steve saw operational service in Northern Ireland attached to G Squadron, 22 SAS Regiment. I am proud to have known Steve and have him as a friend.

In 2022, as part of the Falkland Islands 40th Anniversary Place Names Project, Steve was honoured with 'Sykes Islet', a small tussac island north of Rookery Island on the east side of Falkland Sound, East Falkland.

His name lives on…

24239030 Guardsman Ronald Tanbini 2nd Battalion Scots Guards 4 August 1956 ~ 14 June 1982 Age 25

Ronald Tanbini was born in Dundee on 4 August 1956, the eldest of five children born to Ronald and Laura Tanbini.

The Tanbini name is Italian and came from Ronald's grandfather, Alberto. Alberto, born in Palma, left Italy for a better life with his cousins and brother, had he had just £2 more for his fare, he would have continued to New York with them.

Alberto made a life in London running a fish & chip shop on Oxford Street; he later sold the corner building to Jewellers, H. Samuel. Alberto married Christina Scott in St Clements in 1923; the couple went on to have ten children. Ronald Tanbini was their sixth child, born in London, in October 1934. The couple later made a life in Scotland.

Ronald became a vehicle transporter, driving vehicles from southern ports to their destinations, through his work he met his future wife, Laura. Ronald and Laura married in the mid-fifties in Dundee, their eldest son Ronnie was born soon after their marriage.

Ronnie Tanbini grew up in Dundee, he attended Charleston Primary School and later Logie Secondary Modern. In 1972, he joined the British Army at the Guards

Depot as a Junior Guardsman. After passing out in 1974 he was posted to the 2nd Battalion Scots Guards in Münster, West Germany. During his service Ronnie saw exercises in Kenya, Belize, and Canada, as well as a tour in Londonderry in 1976.

Ronnie also spent two years in the battalion's Assault Pioneer Platoon, after which he was chosen by his Company Commander to be driver of his armoured personnel carrier. In 1978, he was selected for promotion to Lance Corporal, subsequently he was posted to the Guards Depot, later he returned to 2nd Battalion Scots Guards as second in command of a rifle platoon section. In 1979 he returned to the Guards Depot as an instructor.

During his last posting Ronnie returned to the 2nd Battalion at Chelsea Barracks in London in 1980. During this posting Ronnie took part in the 'Trooping the Colour' in front of Queen Elizabeth II. It was after partaking in the exercise in Kenya in 1981 that Ronnie moved from Right Flank to Left Flank Company, where he was a member of 13 Platoon.

Ronnie met Kathleen Quinn while posted in West Germany, Kathleen worked in the NAAFI. Friends for some time, they eventually began a romance and married in London in August 1980. Only daughter Danielle was born the following year, in August 1981.

Ronnie was known as a hardworking and cheerful man, an experienced soldier, a likeable character with a nature that was firm but fair. In the Falklands War his Platoon Sergeant John Simeon selected Ronnie as his bodyguard while siting an anti-tank weapon during the assault on Mount Tumbledown. It was during the Battle for Mount Tumbledown on the night of 13/14 June that both men lost their lives.

In 2022, as part of the Falkland Islands 40th Anniversary Place Names Project, Ronald was honoured with 'Tanbini Stack', a stack with a tussac covered summit south of Clump Island in the Arch Island group, West Falkland.

His name lives on…

24529017 Sapper Wayne David Tarbard 9th Independent Parachute Squadron Royal Engineers 6 January 1963 ~ 8 June 1982 Age 19

In 1959, David Tarbard married Aimee Jocelyn Potter in Marston on Dove, they went on to have five children over eleven years. Their first child, Sharon, was born in Greenwich in 1960. Wayne David was born on 6 January 1963 in Burton upon Trent, followed by Karl, Maxine and Kirsty.

The family settled in Derbyshire and have strong connections to the village of Marston on Dove in South Derbyshire, where there is a polished black granite tablet on a cremation burial plot to both Wayne and his mother Jocelyn, who died on 18 March 1988, aged 49.

Wayne attended primary school in Hilton, followed by secondary education at Hatton school. He was a 'people person', always interested in those around him;

he loved football, and played for a local team. Wayne was also a member of the Marston church choir, though word had it that he did not have the best voice, his talents lay elsewhere. Like many young boys he aspired to be a footballer, he supported Liverpool.

Wayne was just 16 years old when he joined The Royal Engineers Apprentice College in Chepstow with the idea of learning a trade. Wayne completed his training to become an Engineer, he was posted to Maidstone in Kent to 36 Royal Engineers Regiment. He made a lot of friends in the regiment and like many young soldiers he loved to take his mates home and partake of copious egg banjos.

When the Falklands were invaded in April 1982 Wayne was to travel 'Down South' as part of 9th Independent Parachute Squadron. On the 7 June 1982, Wayne's Squadron was aboard HMS *Fearless* alongside the Welsh Guards in order to undertake a frontal assault on Port Stanley. This mission was aborted due to bad weather conditions. The men were dropped off on land and picked up by the *Sir Galahad*.

On the 8 June 1982, the *Sir Galahad* was lying off Fitzroy Bay when she was bombed by Argentine Skyhawks . Wayne was listed as 'missing in action'.

This popular young man is remembered in several places. A Silver Birch Tree was planted in his memory on the 4 August 2014 in Roma's Garden, Hilton, Derbyshire. Roma's Garden is a piece of land restored by the Hilton Gardening Club in dedication of Roma Walton, who had given her time so freely to village causes. In a memorial service Wayne's father David and his sister Maxine unveiled the sundial and plaque.

The Tarbard family also funded a Rose Bowl which has been presented each year since 1983 to the top Sapper on the Cadre Course. Wayne's South Atlantic medal was put on display at the Royal Engineers museum in Chatham, Kent.

In 2022, as part of the Falkland Islands 40th Anniversary Place Names Project, Wayne was honoured with 'Tarbard Island', a tussac island in Port King on the East Falkland side of Falkland Sound.

His name lives on…

C020574N Lieutenant Nicholas Taylor 800 Squadron Fleet Air Arm 28 May 1949 ~ 4 May 1982 Age 32

Nicholas Taylor was born at the Cottage Hospital in Lynton, Devon, on 28 May 1949. Nick, as he was known, was the eldest of three children born to Harry and Edith Taylor who married in Sussex in 1947. Harry was the proprietor of a hotel in Lynton.

Nick always had a passion for flying, acquiring his license at the age of just 17. Born to be a pilot, he died as he lived. Initially, Nick joined the RAF when he was 18. After flying helicopters, he moved on to Harriers. Apparently, though he lived for flying, he was very aware of the dangers. An experienced pilot by the end of the 1970s, Nick completed Sea Harrier training, after which he joined 800 Squadron Fleet Air Arm.

In late 1980 Nick married Clare. At the time of her husband's death Clare was an officer in the WRENs serving at Yeovilton, the couple lived in a cottage in the village of Ryme Intrinsica, Dorset.

Most of the action during the Falklands War was on East Falkland. Nick was shot down over the Goose Green airfield on 4 May 1982, his body was recovered by residents of Goose Green, still in the ejector seat. Nick was buried under the supervision of the Argentinians close to where he came down. He was buried with full military honours.

The site of Nick's grave is now lovingly tended by Islanders who hold a memorial service each year for him. The grave now has a headstone and is surrounded by a fence. Traditionally, prior to the Falklands War, the 'Fallen' were not repatriated, they were buried where they fell and certainly not with full military honours. Nick's resting place is quite unique in that respect. Nick's brother Tony visited the grave in 2022.

In 2022, as part of the Falkland Islands 40th Anniversary Place Names Project, Nick was honoured with 'Nick Taylor Island', a tussac island south of Goose Green at the head of Choiseul Sound, East Falkland.

His name lives on…

24454603 Lance Corporal Christopher Charles Thomas 1st Battalion Welsh Guards 11 August 1959 ~ 13 June 1982 Age 22

Christopher Charles Thomas was born on 11 August 1959 in Cardiff, Wales. He was the only son of Terry and Paula Thomas who married in Cardiff in 1957. Terry and Paula also had three daughters together.

Terry was born in May 1934, one of four children of Charlie Thomas and Gwladys Mabel Wathen. Gwladys was born on New Year's day in 1909, she was baptised at Roath St Saviour in March 1909. Gwladys was the second child of Trevor Carlton Wathen and Amelia Hobbs, married in Cardiff in 1906.

The family on Gwladys's side moved from Newport to Sunderland, followed by Cardiff. Trevor was born in 1878, the family lived in Bishopwearmouth in the 1880s. Great-great-grandfather Edward William Wathen was a millers commercial traveller and moved about during his career. Born in Newport, he married Jane Francis in 1870 in Newport. The years following saw the family living in Bishopwearmouth, Hereford, and Pontypridd. By 1911, Edward was working as a colliery ostler.

On Terry's paternal side it appears that his grandmother was born in Wales, but the family were originally from Ireland.

Charlie Thomas was born in Cardiff on 12 December 1907, the son of William Thomas and Bridget Leahy. The couple had four children: Margaret, Bridget, Anthony and Terry.

Chris attended St Illtyd's School in Cardiff; he joined the British Army in 1977 when he was 18 years old.

During his service Chris did tours of Northern Ireland and Berlin with the Welsh Guards. Chris is described by his sister as 'friendly, extrovert, loud, the life and soul of the party but also generous to a fault and dependable'. A lovely way to remember your only brother.

Comrades knew Chris as 'Bowser'; his nickname came from the likeness to American Singer Jon 'Bowzer' Bauman. Bowser died from wounds, inflicted when he ran over a mine on a supply run, on 13 June 1982. As the only Welsh Guard who died on land in the Falklands War, Chris was able to be repatriated. Chris is buried at Brookwood Military Cemetery in Surrey.

In 2022, as part of the Falkland Islands 40th Anniversary Place Names Project, Chris was honoured with 'Thomas Cove', a small cove on the south side of Middle Island in the Golding Island group, West Falkland.

His name lives on…

24497060 Guardsman Glyn Kenneth Thomas 1st Battalion Welsh Guards 4 July 1961 ~ 8 June 1982 Age 20

Glyn Kenneth Thomas was born at home at 80 Shakespeare Street, Cardiff, on 4 July 1961 to Donald and Doreen Thomas (née Nelson). Glyn's parents married in Cardiff in 1956, records suggest that the couple had four children, all boys. Glyn was their youngest. At the time of Glyn's birth, Donald was a painter and decorator.

On 8 June 1982, Glyn, a Guardsman with the 1st Battalion Welsh Guards, was killed when the *Sir Galahad* was bombed by Argentinian aircraft.

Glyn died just a month short of his 21st birthday.

In 2022, as part of the Falkland Islands 40th Anniversary Place Names Project, Glyn was honoured with 'Thomas Point', a prominent narrow point on a sharp bend in the channel to Crooked Inlet (westernmost of the two Crooked Inlets) King George Bay, West Falkland.

His name lives on…

24436475 Lance Corporal Nicholas David 'Mark' Thomas 1st Battalion Welsh Guards 11 May 1957 ~ 8 June 1982 Age 25

Nicholas David 'Mark' Thomas was born on 11 May 1957 at the Morriston Emergency Hospital, Morriston, Swansea, to Frank and Glenys Thomas (née Hugh).

The Thomas family were from Llanelli in Carmarthenshire. To everyone he was known as Mark. Interestingly, Mark's maternal grandmother had the middle name of Malvina. Historically the family had worked in the tin and steelworks.

Mark's father Frank Esmor Thomas served with the Royal Air Force in the Second World War. Records show that Frank died in 1980.

Mark was a Lance Corporal with the 1st Battalion Welsh Guards based at Elizabeth Barracks, Pirbright, Surrey.

Tragically, Mark was killed on 8 June 1982 when the *Sir Galahad* came under heavy attack from Argentinian aircraft. He was 25 years old.

Mark is one of two Welsh Guards from the Falklands War remembered on the Llanelli War Memorial.

In 2022, as part of the Falkland Islands 40th Anniversary Place Names Project, Mark was honoured with 'Thomas Island', the easternmost of two small tussac islands in Shell Bay at the east entrance to Adventure Sound, East Falkland.

His name lives on…

24446382 Guardsman Raymond Gregory Thomas 1st Battalion Welsh Guards 29 September 1953 ~ 8 June 1982 Age 28

Raymond Gregory Thomas was born in Barry, South Wales on 29 September 1953. Greg (as he was known) was the fourth child of Raymond Percival and Ruth Thomas (née Ellett) who married in 1949. The couple had eight children, six girls and two boys. The Thomas family had a long history in the Barry area.

Robert Henry Ivor Thomas and Doris May Louise Edwards married in Cadoxton-Juxta, Barry, in August 1920. Robert was a carpenter; their son, Raymond Percival, was born in March 1925. Records indicate that Raymond joined the army in 1943, he saw service in Burma and was also attached to the Gurkhas during the Second World War. Raymond Percival Thomas died in early 1981.

Greg's mother Ruth served in the Land Army during the Second World War. Ruth was the daughter of William Ellett and Jane Lancastle, the fourth of five children born to the couple. Jane was the daughter of a dock worker and lived almost until her 90th birthday. As a teenager, Ruth had worked as a milliners shop assistant.

Greg attended Gladstone Primary School; he joined the army in 1976 after visiting an Army Recruitment Office. His journey with the 1st Battalion Welsh Guards had begun.

On 8 June 1982, Greg was one of the unlucky men to lose his life on the *Sir Galahad* when she was attacked. The family had a wedding that week, one of Greg's sisters was getting married. Despite hearing that Greg was 'Missing in Action' the wedding went ahead.

In 1983, Ruth and two of Greg's sisters went on the families' pilgrimage to the Falkland Islands. Ruth died in 2006.

In 2022, as part of the Falkland Islands 40th Anniversary Place Names Project, Greg was honoured with 'Thomas Rock', a large unvegetated rock east of Ten Shilling Bay Islands, near the entrance to Port Stephens, West Falkland.

His name lives on…

D099091A Acting Chief Weapons Engineering Mechanician (Radio) Michael Edward Gordon Till MID HMS *Sheffield* 4 February 1947 ~ 4 May 1982 Age 35

On Mike's mother's side, the family were miners from Houghton-le-Spring in Durham. His mother, Mary Gordon Laidler, was born in October 1919; her parents, James Laidler and Jane Stockport, were married in 1913. Both James and Jane's family were miners, though prior to their marriage Jane had been in service. The Laidler family may be traced back to the 1700s, working in the pits in the Houghton-le-Spring area. Prior to her marriage, Mary had worked in a drapery shop.

Jack Edward Frederick Till was born in Southampton in November 1920, to Edward and Elsie Till, who married in 1918. Jack had an older sister, Mary Elizabeth. Elsie's family, originally from Wiltshire, had settled in South Stoneham by the turn of the twentieth century.

Jack Till and Mary Laidler married in 1946 in Southampton, the year after the Second World War ended. Michael Edward Gordon Till, the couple's oldest son, was born on 4 February 1947 in Southampton. Mike had two brothers.

On 27 March 1957, Jack set sail from Liverpool on the *Empress of France* headed for New Brunswick, Canada, all set to make a new life. Jack travelled ahead of his family. Mary and the boys left Liverpool on 21 June 1957 on the *Empress of England*. Jack died less than five years later, so Mary and her children returned to England to be near her mother.

After leaving school, Mike initially studied communications in Durham, he joined the Royal Navy when he was 19 years old. Initially, Mike trained at HMS *Collingwood* and HMS *Rhyl*. On his travels as a young matelot Mike met and married Audrey; the couple had their first child in Weymouth in 1967. The couple's second daughter was born in 1970, Mike had started work on the submarines that year. The couple's third daughter was born in Scotland in 1971.

In April 1982 Mike was serving in HMS *Sheffield*, he was due to leave the ship that month but that was postponed as *Sheffield* joined the Task Force. Mike had written home often; he was very committed to his family life.

Mike loved cross country and middle-distance running, he had quite a collection of trophies. In March 1982, HMS *Sheffield* became the first to carry out a 100 x 1 mile relay while underway. In doing so they claimed the waterborne record, Mike was 4th in the event.

As a Senior Computer Chief, Mike was sadly to perish at his post when his ship was hit by an Exocet missile on 4 May 1982. Without their computer systems ships are unable to defend themselves and therefore it is these amazing service personnel who stay working in extremely difficult circumstances to try their best to get those vital systems back up.

Mike was described as kind, gentle, patient and tolerant.

For his bravery on 4 May 1982, he was Mentioned in Dispatches, therefore his medal contains a single bronze oakleaf to denote this.

The year after his death his family presented the fleet with the 'Mike Till Trophy', the trophy is of an albatross soaring over a breaking wave, it is sculpted in wood.

In 2022, as part of the Falkland Islands 40th Anniversary Place Names Project, Mike was honoured with 'Till Point', the east entrance point to Carcass Bay on the West Falkland side of Falkland Sound.

His name lives on…

C023934B Lieutenant David Hugh Russell Tinker HMS *Glamorgan* 14 March 1957 ~ 12 June 1982 Age 25

Hugh Tinker and Elisabeth Willis married in Wycombe, Buckinghamshire in 1947. Hugh was a writer and university professor. The couple had their first child, Michael, in Cambridge. The family had relocated to North London by the time they had second son Mark. David Hugh Russell Tinker was their youngest son, born in Barnet on 14 March 1957.

In 1954, university lecturer Hugh travelled to Rangoon, Burma, on the *Derbyshire*. The name Russell appears to come from David's grandmother, Gertrude Marian Russell, who was born in Wiltshire. This is the generation where teaching appears in the family. Gertrude was a school teacher, she married David's grandfather, Clement Hugh Tinker, in London in 1920.

Clement was the son of a clothier; his parents were born in Yorkshire, though Clement was born in Cardiff. The family later moved to Islington, London. Hugh Russell was born in Essex in 1921.

David attended Mill Hill School; he was Coxswain of the Royal Naval section of the School Combined Cadet Force. David went on to training at Dartmouth Naval College and to study at Birmingham University. While at university he met his wife, Christine. The couple married in 1980 in Lancashire, they bought a cottage in Clungunford, near Craven Arms, just before their wedding ceremony. David set off 'Down South' on HMS *Glamorgan* for what was to become his last voyage.

David loved writing and wanted to follow in his father's footsteps had he lived to see out his Naval service. He was killed when HMS *Glamorgan* was hit by an Exocet missile on 12 June 1982.

After David's death, his father collated letters and poems from David's life and had them printed in the book *A Message from the Falklands*, inside is a simple inscription 'For Christine'.

In one exert he talks about the trivia of life, the unimportance of material things and how value and ways of living are thought about by us all. These thoughts were penned aboard the *Glamorgan* on 22 May 1982.

Jane Anderson says:

> David was a pupil at Hendon Prep. I was the first ever female Headteacher from 1 April 2008 to 31 August 2013 when I took up position as Education Executive. I met his brother Mark at the first

Memorial Lecture held at Mill Hill School in June 2013. David was the first alumni I researched.

In 2022, as part of the Falkland Islands 40th Anniversary Place Names Project, David was honoured with 'Tinker Island', a small, vegetated island off Island Point on the west side of Bay of Harbours, East Falkland.

His name lives on…

D192370P Marine Engineering Mechanic (Mechanical) 2 Stephen Tonkin HMS *Coventry* 21 November 1961 ~ 25 May 1982 Age 20

Stephen Tonkin was from Eckington in Derbyshire. Born on the 21 November 1961, he was the eldest of three children born to Philip and Margaret Tonkin (née Smith). The couple married in St Peter and Paul, Eckington in early 1960.

The Tonkin family had roots in Cornwall in the 1800s, they later moved to Dalton on Furness in Lancashire where Stephen's great-grandfather was born in March 1881. Lionel Tonkin was the eldest of at least eleven children born to James and Mary Ann Tonkin (née Richards). James was originally from St Agnes in Cornwall.

Lionel was a shipyard worker in Dalton before joining the Royal Navy. Lionel Tonkin married a widow, Mary Reid, in 1907. The couple had two children before Mary died six years later. Second son Lionel, born in 1912, was Stephen's grandfather.

In late 1913, Lionel remarried Emma Whitehouse, the couple's second son was named Eric Soudan Tonkin after HMHS *Soudan*, the hospital ship on which Lionel had served during the First World War. Originally, she was named SS *Soudan*, but requisitioned as a hospital ship for use for the treatment and movement of casualties during the Gallipoli Campaign between 1915–16.

Interestingly, Eric Soudan Tonkin was born on 2 April 1915, exactly sixty-seven years before the invasion of the Falkland Islands. Eric was an Able Seaman on HMS *Niger* when she was struck by a mine on 6 July 1942; the ship sank with only eight crew surviving. Eric is remembered on the Chatham Naval Memorial.

Lionel survived the First World War, he and his family moved to Manchester where he worked in a gas works. He lived into his seventies.

Growing up, Steve attended local schools in Eckington followed by Westfield Comprehensive School, Mosborough.

Steve was part of the crew of HMS *Coventry* when she was attacked on 25 May 1982, he was one of the men who died, killed in the forward engine room.

HMS *Coventry* was Steve's first ship and sadly to be his last. Steve is remembered at Eckington War Memorial, one of two names from 1982. There is also a special rock there to remember him.

In 2022, as part of the Falkland Islands 40th Anniversary Place Names Project, Steve was honoured with 'Tonkin Rocks', a prominent rock outcrop west of Bluff Cove Peak, East Falkland.

His name lives on…

D189147F Cook Ian Edward Turnbull HMS *Coventry* 7 February 1964 ~ 25 May 1982 Age 18

Ian was born on 7 February 1964 in West Hartlepool, Durham. His parents, Edward Turnbull and Norma Williams, married in 1959. Ian was their only son.

Ian attended Brierton School, Hartlepool, the family lived in Lyndsay Road. Growing up Ian was a member of the Eighth Hartlepool Boys Brigade.

It appears that Ian joined the Royal Navy straight from school at HMS *Raleigh* and from there went to HMS *Dryad* as a young chef. His interests in cooking were complimentary to his interest in fishing. Ian was affectionately known as 'Tiny'. He seemed to be a very well liked, gentle giant.

Ian's sister Susan remembers that he broke his leg at his 18th birthday party on 7 February 1982, he went back to HMS *Dryad* in March because he was booked to start a submariners course in August that year. In a twist of fate, he was loaned to HMS *Coventry* for three weeks to do some 'sea time', he did not return as War intervened.

At the time of the Falklands War, Ian was a Cook on HMS *Coventry*, during the attacks on the ship he was one of nineteen men killed that day. The ship was badly damaged and sank, the crew lost to the ocean.

The loss of her only son hit Norma hard; she died just ten years after her boy gave his life for his country. Ian's nephew was named David Ian Edward in his memory.

In 2022, as part of the Falkland Islands 40th Anniversary Place Names Project, Ian was honoured with 'Turnbull Inlet', a sheltered inlet running southwest off North West Arm in Port Albemarle, West Falkland.

His name lives on…

P035194P Corporal Andrew Bryan Uren 45 Commando Royal Marines 27 December 1958 ~ 11 June 1982 Age 23

Andrew Bryan Uren was born on 27 December 1958 in Southend-on-Sea, Essex, the eldest son of Bryan and Patricia Uren (née Brown).

The Uren family name in the United Kingdom was first found in Cornwall where it can be traced back to ancient times. The Uren's held a family seat at Trewarevra, descended from Driff, in Cornwall. The original name was Trewen, Uren being an abbreviation. In the late 1800s almost 70 per cent of all Uren families resided in Cornwall. However, Andy's family had roots elsewhere.

It appears that William Richard Uren married Charlotte Barkshire in Pancras in 1891, their son, William Frederick Thomas Uren, was born in July 1897. William married Eva Hawtin in 1922, and their son Bryan Frederick Uren arrived in 1938. By then William was an estate agent and the family were living in Essex. The couple had an older daughter, Christine Eva, born in 1929. William Frederick died in Essex in February 1965.

Eva Hawtin, Andy's grandmother, was born in London in 1898; her brother, Frederick Charles Hawtin, a Rifleman with the 13th Battalion, King's Royal Rifle Corps, was killed in action on 23 April 1917 aged 35. He is commemorated on the Arras Memorial in France. Eva had already lost her other brother in 1909. Eva died in Southend in 1960.

Bryan and Patricia Uren had two sons; Andrew Bryan was their eldest. The family moved to Crediton, Devon, where many of Andy's family still reside. At the time of his death Andy lived in Lapford, a village in mid-Devon.

Corporal Andrew Bryan Uren was killed on 11 June 1982 in an incident when his patrol was mistaken for the enemy.

A memorial for him is situated in St Thomas of Canterbury Church, Church Close, Lapford. A wall-mounted wooden board in the form of a raised carved laurel wreath, which contains his name inside. The Royal Marines badge sits above the inscription which reads '1982 Andrew Bryan Uren Falklands'.

In 2022, as part of the Falkland Islands 40th Anniversary Place Names Project, Andy was honoured with 'Uren Bay', a bay east of Teal Inlet and southwest of High Island on the southside of Port Salvador, East Falkland.

His name lives on…

D083308A Petty Officer Aircrewman Colin Paul Vickers HMS *Glamorgan* 31 March 1949 ~ 12 June 1982 Age 33

Many of the Naval men had a few years of service behind them, Colin was one of those men.

Ernest Vickers and Edna Annie Donaldson married in 1929 in Selby, Yorkshire. Ernest was born in July 1909, the eldest son of Ernest Vickers and Annie Hirst. Ernest, it appears, had two older sisters and three younger brothers. Edna Annie was born in September 1908, the third child of Hector and Ellen Donaldson. Ernest Vickers Sr was a watchmaker and jeweller prior to the start of the First World War.

Some members of the family were born in Leeds, others in Grimsby, by 1911 they were settled in the Selby area of Yorkshire.

By the start of the Second World War, Ernest and Edna Annie had four children: Norman, Gordon, Anne and Kathleen. Colin Paul Vickers was their last child born in Selby on 31 March 1949. Two Vickers brothers went on to marry two sisters. Norman married Joyce Farmery in 1952, and Gordon married Maisie Farmery in 1954. Both Gordon and Colin served in the Royal Navy.

Colin started his journey with the Royal Navy at HMS *Ganges* when he was just a lad of 16 years old. Colin married Patricia in Selby in 1970. By the time of the Falklands invasion Colin had almost eighteen years of service behind him.

After HMS *Ganges*, Colin went to HMS *Vernon* and then on to HMS *Minerva*. He then did his Underwater/Control Helicopter training and qualified. He last served with his shipmate Buck Ryan on the *Ark Royal*, by which time Colin was 824 NAS.

HMS *Glamorgan* was built by the builder Vickers-Armstrong, she was launched on 9 July 1964, the same year that Colin joined the Royal Navy. HMS *Glamorgan* was delivered to the Royal Navy two years later. In April 1982, HMS *Glamorgan* was off Gibraltar on exercise with many other ships. She was immediately sent on divert to join the Task Force, by 1 May she joined HMS *Arrow* and HMS *Alacrity* as they sought to bombard the Argentine positions around Stanley.

Colin was a Petty Officer Aircrewman on HMS *Glamorgan* when, at 06.37 hrs on 12 June 1982, the ship was attacked with an Exocet missile fired from an improvised shore-based launcher. Despite evasive measures the missile hit the deck, the ship's Wessex helicopter exploded, causing a severe fire in the hangar. Colin was one of the thirteen men who died. He was buried at sea in Royal Naval tradition.

In 1983, Colin's widow and his brother Gordon made the pilgrimage to the Falkland Islands.

When Gordon died his ashes were taken 'Down South' and scattered at the burial site; brothers who served together, were again united in death.

In 2022, as part of the Falkland Islands 40th Anniversary Place Names Project, Colin was honoured with 'Vickers Point', a prominent point at the west entrance to Roy Cove Creek.

His name lives on…

Mechanic (Petty Officer 2) Ernest Norman Vickers Merchant Navy SS *Atlantic Conveyor* 30 July 1924 ~ 25 May 1982 Age 57

The Vickers family have a long history with the Middlesbrough area. Ernie was born at 108 Barritt Street, Middlesbrough on 30 July 1924 to William Henry and Olive Vickers (née Wilkin). Ernie was the youngest of four boys. William worked for the North East Railway, Middlesbrough Dock. William was born in 1883, the eldest of at least eleven children born to James and Emily Vickers.

According to the *Boxing News*, William was army sprint champion in 1910, paving the way for a sporty family. Records suggest William joined the Yorkshire Regiment in 1902. William and Olive married in Middlesborough in 1919, the year after the First World War ended. One of Ernest's brothers apparently became the Yorkshire champion for the quarter mile, another brother Jack boxed professionally between 1951 and 1956.

Ernie joined the Royal Navy serving on HMS *Ganges* towards the end of the Second World War.

Ernie became well known as a boxer; he fought as an amateur welterweight, winning eleven out of twelve fights. In 1949, Ernie turned professional, he was managed by Eric Munro. From his first twenty-seven contests he won twenty-six, often he would knock his opponent out.

During the '50s Ernie did well, he found his way to the Northern Area Welterweight Championships. Ernie continued to box until 1956, by which time he had won thirty-nine out of fifty-eight fights.

Before joining the Merchant Navy, Ernie had also worked as a docker. Ernie married Elaine Haggas in 1947. Several children were born to the couple over the next fifteen years, their eldest daughter, Elaine, was born in 1949.

When the Falkland Islands were invaded in April 1982, Ernie was a mechanic aboard SS *Atlantic Conveyor*. For the main part she had completed the important task of delivering the aircraft she carried. Unfortunately, when the ship was hit, the rest of her cargo contributed to uncontrollable fires.

Most of the crew escaped with their lives on 25 May 1982 when C deck was hit by Argentine missiles. Six of the twelve men who perished that day were Merchant Seamen. Ernie Vickers was killed in the Engine Room.

The last lifeboat was recovered by HMS *Alacrity* at 2300 hrs. There is never an easy time to lose your husband or father, but unlike many children who were bereaved as a result of the Falkland's War, Ernie's children were grown.

In 2022, as part of the Falkland Islands 40th Anniversary Place Names Project, Ernie was honoured with 'Vickers Ridge', a prominent rocky ridge above Bold Cove on West Falkland.

His name lives on...

24508985 Guardsman Andrew Walker 1st Battalion Welsh Guards 2 November 1961 ~ 8 June 1982 Age 20

Marjorie and John Walker had six children, all born in Yorkshire. Denise, John, Heather, Andrew, Brian and Fern. Andrew was born in York on 2 November 1961, he was very close to his slightly younger brother Brian.

Growing up in York, Andrew attended Lowfields Secondary Modern School. Andrew had a passion for rugby; a very good player, he was a member of the York Rugby Club. When Andrew joined the British Army, it was through his love of rugby that he joined the Welsh Guards. Andrew soon acquired the nickname 'Yorkie'; he became very good friends with Simon Weston, both men played rugby for the battalion team.

During his time in the Welsh Guards, Yorkie saw service in Northern Ireland, Kenya, and Germany. Yorkie scored the winning try in March 1982 when the Welsh Guards won the cup in Berlin.

Yorkie met Jocelyn Johnston in the NAAFI in Pirbright where she worked. By the time Yorkie left on the QE2 the couple were engaged and planned to marry that summer.

Yorkie was one of thirty-two Welsh Guards who lost their lives on the 8 June 1982. His fiancée gave birth to their son Andrew in Glasgow in December 1982.

In 1983, the family went to the Falkland Islands as part of the families' pilgrimage that took place that year. For all families the loss of their loved one in the war was deeply sad, but for many who still have no grave these trips are so important in the understanding and healing necessary to find acceptance.

Yorkie's brother Brian joined the Welsh Guards the year after Yorkie died. Brian and Yorkie's widow Jocelyn married in Glasgow in 1986, the couple went on to have a daughter Natalie together. For many children, growing up with either scattered memories, or none at all, is indeed so terribly hard. For some such as Andrew there are no direct memories of his father. With his stepfather, he was able to share so much more than most. He was able to gain an understanding of who his father was – the person behind the name.

Tragedy struck the family again when Brian was killed in a motorcycle accident when Andrew was 22 years old.

Andrew is married to Sharon; the couple have two sons, Ethan and Harrison.

Yorkie was the only serviceman from York to die in the Falklands War. Acomb is now swallowed up into York itself, but prior to becoming a suburb in the 1970s it was a village in its own right; because of this it has a village green where resides the Acomb War Memorial.

At Acomb Green there is a memorial plaque, the inscription reads 'IN LOVING MEMORY OF WELSH GUARDSMAN ANDREW WALKER, KILLED JUNE 8TH 1982 AT BLUFF COVE, FALKLAND ISLES. NEVER FORGOTTEN BY HIS LOVING FAMILY & FRIENDS'.

In 2022, as part of the Falkland Islands 40th Anniversary Place Names Project, Yorkie was honoured with 'Walker Stream', a tributary stream of the Warrah River, flowing north from a valley between Tent Mountain, Rocky Mountain and Poncho Hill above Port Howard, West Falkland.

His name lives on…

D135931G Weapons Engineering Mechanician 2 Barry James Wallis HMS *Sheffield* 11 January 1956 ~ 4 May 1982 Age 26

Barry James Wallis was born in Krugersdorp, South Africa, on 11 January 1956, to Frederick and Paula Wallis.

Barry's father, Frederick George Wallis, served in the Royal Navy between 1939 and 1945 as a Signalman. Frederick married Paula in 1946, the couple lived in North Road, Southend-on-Sea; their oldest child Brian was born in Southend.

Barry's grandfather, Reginald Wallis, served with the 1st Battalion Essex Regiment in India, he also served in the 2nd Boer War.

Frederick and Paula moved to East Ham and later emigrated to South Africa where Frederick died. Reginald and his wife Lilian also went to South Africa.

When Barry was about 12 years old the family returned to the United Kingdom. Barry had always wanted to join the Royal Navy; he joined up after attending Westcliff High School.

Barry married Jenny in Chatham, Kent, in 1978. Barry and Jenny had one son, Alan James Wallis, born in Portsmouth in 1981. Barry and Jenny lived in Portchester; Barry was serving in HMS *Sheffield*.

HMS *Sheffield* had been away for six months. Jenny was at home with a young baby, like most wives she would have been preparing for Barry's imminent return when the news came through that HMS *Sheffield* was heading 'Down South' without stopping at Blighty.

HMS *Sheffield* went on divert on 2 April 1982; a month later, on 4 May 1982, she was struck amidships by an Argentinian Exocet Missile fired by a Super Étendard aircraft. Thankfully the missiles warhead failed to explode, otherwise there would have been many more deaths. In many ways luck was on the side of the ship but nevertheless twenty men perished that day. Barry James Wallis was one of those men.

Barry is described as very laid back, until he was wound up. Barry's hobbies included fixing cars, shooting, and sailing, which he partook on behalf of the Navy. He was also on the social committee at HMS *Collingwood*. Alan is like so many children who grew up without knowing his father.

In 2012, Alan received the Elizabeth Cross. It was thirty years after his father Barry had died.

AFC Portchester always remembers the fallen each year from different conflicts, Barry is one of two men killed in the Falklands War who lived in the town.

In 2022, as part of the Falkland Islands 40th Anniversary Place Names Project, Barry was honoured with 'Wallis Island', the largest of four tussac islands northwest of Top Island in River Harbour, West Falkland.

His name lives on...

24110456 Corporal Edward Thomas Walpole 22 SAS Regiment
30 September 1945 ~ 19 May 1982 Age 36

Edward Thomas Walpole was born in Islington on 30 September 1945. His family had lived in London for generations. Grandfather John Walpole was born in Bethnal Green in late 1878. John was a coal porter, he married Johanna Lambourn in 1900. By 1911, the family were living in Newhall Street, Islington. George Edward Walpole was the middle child of five, born in May 1909.

Frances Blake was born in Islington in June 1912, to James and Florence Blake (née Brawn). Frances was one of at least eight children. Many the First World War records were destroyed in the Blitz during the Second World War, so it is difficult to know how many of Frances's brothers served. There is, however, one record of her brother William serving in the Royal Naval Division.

George Edward Walpole married Frances Blake in Islington in 1934, the couple had their first child, a daughter, the following year. In 1939, George worked on the railway, Frances was a dressmaker and they lived in Shepperton Road, North London.

Edward Thomas Walpole, like his father, was one of five children. Known as Ted to his family, living in Islington he became understandably a Gunners supporter. Ted had three older sisters and one half-brother three years his junior. Sadly, Ted's mother died in 1955, he was just 10 years old. Life was tough and much changed for the Walpole family when Ted's sister married later in 1955.

Ted joined the Royal Green Jackets intending to be a career soldier. He found himself with a new nickname of 'Wally'. With an enviable IQ, Ted was anything but a 'wally', but the name did compliment his surname of Walpole. Wally saw service in Germany, Norway, Brunei, Belize, Cyprus and Gibraltar. He also served on several tours of Northern Ireland.

It was in 1977 that he found his niche as the store man for D Squadron 22 SAS. By its nature the squadron headquarters is very compact, consisting of the Officer Commanding, a Sergeant Major, SQMS, Squadron Clerk and a store man. A great deal of responsibility rests on ensuring that all the specialist and general equipment, ammunition and rations are up to date and available for immediate deployment. Apart from fulfilling his role, Ted was a natural organizer and could always be relied upon to come up with whatever was needed in the field.

Prior to deploying to the Falkland Islands, Wally had supported the squadron in both Greece and Kenya. The three days prior to flying out to the Ascension Islands was a flurry of activity, arranging for ammunition and equipment that may be required and could not be supplied while in theatre. The difficulty in being involved in numerous ship-to-ship moves and keeping track of a mass of stores on a crowded war ship called for his specialist skills and a particular sense of humour.

Having finished yet another cross decking, he was on the final helicopter that crashed into the sea.

In 2022, as part of the Falkland Islands 40th Anniversary Place Names Project, Wally was honoured with 'Walpole Tarn', a tarn east of Clay Mountain above Port Howard, West Falkland.

His name lives on…

24433056 Lance Corporal Christopher Francis Ward 1st Battalion Welsh Guards 10 December 1959 ~ 8 June 1982 Age 22

Christopher Francis Ward was born on 10 December 1959 at 45 Raglan Street, Newport in Wales.

Frank, as he was known, was the eldest son of Francis Joseph and Madeline Mary Ward (née Borg). Frank was named after his father, while two of his siblings were named from the Borg side of the family. Records suggest that Frank's maternal grandfather, Leone, was born in Malta in 1903, it seems he was serving with the Merchant Navy until 1921.

Frank, it appears, was one of five children.

Frank's choice of service was the Welsh Guards. In early 1982, he married Diane in Berkshire before setting sail for the Falkland Islands on the QE2.

Frank died on 8 June 1982 when the RFA *Sir Galahad* came under attack from Argentinian aircraft.

In the Union Jack club in London there resides a wall-mounted marble tablet which reads: 'IN LOVING MEMORY OF OUR DEAR SON LANCE CORPORAL FRANCIS CHRISTOPHER WARD AND COMRADES OF THE WELSH GUARDS DIED IN ACTION IN RFA SIR GALAHAD JUNE 8TH 1982 FALKLANDS CAMPAIGN'.

Diane finally visited the place where her young husband died thirty years later armed with a wreath, she was able to attend a memorial service on board RFA *Gold Rover*.

In 2022, as part of the Falkland Islands 40th Anniversary Place Names Project, Frank was honoured with 'Ward Cove', a cove east of the entrance to Hill Gap on the West Falkland side of Falkland Sound.

His name lives on...

P032593N Corporal Laurence George Watts 42 Commando Royal Marines 12 February 1955 ~ 12 June 1982 Age 27

Laurence George Watts was born in Hertfordshire on 12 February 1955, he carried the name George, as did his father and two generations of Watts before him. Laurence was known as Larry, but mainly 'Lofty'.

George William Watts married Florence Violet Andrews in the district of Hendon in early 1915. George and Florence had three sons: Ronald Arthur, Percy Henry, and youngest son, Dennis George.

By 1921, the family were living in Pinner Hill Road, George William was a photographic emulsion mixer for Kodak Ltd. As the boys grew up, they went in different directions workwise. Ronald served in the British Army, Percy became an executive for Guinness, and Dennis was employed with Kodak as an engineer.

Dennis George Watts married Mary King in the district of Watford in 1951. Mary's parents had at one time been in service to the Duke and Duchess of Bedfordshire, in fact when their Banns were read in January 1925, they were both living at Chenies Manor House.

Dennis and Mary went on to have three sons; Lofty was their eldest, brothers Nigel and Richard followed. Richard also served in the Royal Marines.

Lofty attended primary school in Croxley Green, Rickmansworth. He passed his eleven-plus and later attended Rickmansworth Grammar School. Mr Harrison was the form tutor of RSH form where Lofty began his secondary education in 1966. His schoolfriend Jane Anderson remembers him, 'Larry was a gentle giant who I remember with fondness from school. He was kind to me when others weren't, and he stood up for what was right.'

Although Jane remembers him as Larry, she remembers how he gained his nickname 'Lofty', as he shot up in height, looking taller than many for his age.

Lofty joined the Royal Marines when he was still 17 years old, just six months shy of his coming of age. Stationed in Scotland he met Susan in a hotel in Arbroath. The couple dated for a couple of years prior to marrying on 9 April 1977, at Barry Church, Carnoustie.

Susan remembers Lofty as a man that was easy to talk to and who loved to dance. He excelled at PE and enjoyed both cricket and rugby. Susan was in the Naval Reserves when she met Lofty, continuing after their move to Exmouth, giving up only when she found out she was pregnant. Lofty was also a member of the Inshore Lifeboat crew.

In 1982, Lofty deployed to the Falklands with 42 Commando, he served with K Company. During the second week of June the attacks on Argentinian positions heated up as British Troops executed their plan to liberate the Islands. 42 Commando was tasked with taking Mount Harriet. Lofty, a corporal and section commander, was killed during the attack.

When Susan received the 'knock on the door' she was staying with her mother in Scotland. During the last trimester of her pregnancy with the couple's first child, she was one of many widows left to bring a child into the world alone.

Lofty and Susan's daughter was born in August 1982 in Scotland, named Laura after her father.

Lofty was repatriated and his funeral took place in November 1982; he is buried in the Western Cemetery, Arbroath.

In 2010, Susan and Laura made a trip to the Falkland Islands. During that visit Laura, amazingly, found her dad's foxhole.

In 2022, as part of the Falkland Islands 40th Anniversary Place Names Project, Lofty was honoured with 'Lofty Watts Hill', the summit (414ft elevation) of Middle Island in King George Bay, West Falkland.

His name lives on…

24516114 Guardsman James Francis Weaver 1st Battalion Welsh Guards 14 October 1961 ~ 8 June 1982 Age 20

James Francis Weaver was born on 14 October 1961 at the General Hospital in Neath, Glamorganshire. James was the eldest of four children born to Edward James Francis and Mary Weaver (née Camenzuli). At the time of his birth Ed and Mary lived in Ocean Way, Aberavon, Port Talbot. Ed was a Steel Erector.

James had two brothers and one sister. James went to St Joseph's Catholic Comprehensive School in Port Talbot; he is described as quite a character. James loved to fish.

James was killed on 8 June 1982 when the *Sir Galahad* came under attack from Argentinian aircraft.

Though unmarried himself at the time of his death, James has a nephew named after him, born in 1987. Many of the Weaver family still live in Port Talbot, which was his home.

In 2022, as part of the Falkland Islands 40th Anniversary Place Names Project, James was honoured with 'Weaver Islet', a small tussac islet inside Duperrey Harbour on the south side of Berkeley Sound, East Falkland.

His name lives on…

D134889L Leading Cook Adrian Kelvin Wellstead HMS *Sheffield* 13 April 1956 ~ 4 May 1982 Age 26

April was a significant month in the Wellstead family, Adrian's Uncle Harold, and his grandfather Reginald all had birthdays within a week of his own.

Adrian was born on 13 April 1956 in Blandford, Dorset, the son of Alan and Beryl Wellstead (née Barnes) who married in 1949. Wellstead is a well-established family name in the Dorset area.

Adrian's grandfather, Reginald Wellstead, was born in April 1893, one of twin boys. Reginald served with the Royal Army Medical Corps, attesting in 1915, serving as part of the Labour Corps. Records suggest that his twin brother William served with the Dorset Regiment, Somerset Light Infantry during the First World War.

Reginald married Daisy Elizabeth Stickley in 1920, it appears they had four children. Harold, Iris, Alan and Eric were born between 1921 and 1926. Daisy died in 1936 when her youngest son Eric was just 10 years old. Son Alan, Adrian's father, was born in June 1925. Alan died in 1994, outliving his son by twelve years.

Adrian's mother Beryl was the youngest daughter of Albert Edward Barnes and Ellen Diment, who married in 1910. Albert and Ellen had two children before the First World War broke out, their next child was born in 1919.

There appear to be a huge number of Wellsteads in the Dorset area, sometimes tracing back details draws a blank, for now it has only been possible to trace back to Adrian's great-great, great-grandfather, who was born in 1830. Though unable to trace a birth record there is a baptism record for Henry on 26 September 1830, where he is listed as 'son of Alice'. Interestingly, when he married his bride Ann Luther in 1859, he is recorded as Henry 'Alice' Wellstead. As far as can be ascertained, Alice died when Henry was just a boy.

Henry and Ann were both gardeners. They had at least seven children; the eldest, Henry, was Adrian's great-grandfather. Their second son was named Martin Luther who, unlike his famous namesake, was a painter.

Adrian attended Blandford school, where he is well remembered.

Adrian married his bride Coleen in 1979. The couple had one daughter, Sheree, who was born after Adrian died.

Adrian is honoured on a plaque at the Church of St Edmund, Lychgate Green, Stubbington, Fareham, along with three other shipmates from HMS *Sheffield*.

In 2022, as part of the Falkland Islands 40th Anniversary Place Names Project, Adrian was honoured with 'Wellstead Point', a point on the north shore of Christmas Harbour, West Falkland.

His name lives on…

D088134X Master at Arms Brian Welsh HMS *Sheffield* 13 March 1948 ~ 4 May 1982 Age 34

Brian Welsh was born at Bensham Hospital in Gateshead on 13 March 1948 to Robert and Wilhelmina Welsh (née Joyce). The Bensham Hospital had been a workhouse for many years, changing to a hospital circa 1938. Brian thankfully had a better start in life.

Brian was one of four children, he had two brothers, David and Bobby, and a sister, Joyce. Brian attended Elgin School in Gateshead. He liked to play rugby and continued to play after joining the Royal Navy.

Brian married Grace in 1969, the couple had one son, also named Brian, who was born in the mid-1970s. Brian was drafted to HMS *Sheffield* as Master At Arms in 1979, he still held the same position in 1982. The Master At Arms is a warrant officer appointed to carry out and supervise police duties on board a ship.

Brian was killed on 4 May 1982 when HMS *Sheffield* was hit by an Exocet missile.

There is a memorial for Brian at the Royal Military Police Church, Defence School of Policing and Guarding (DSPG), Southwick Park in Fareham. A rectangular stone tablet with inscribed black lettering reads: 'IN MEMORY OF MAA BRIAN WELSH D088134X KILLED IN ACTION ONBOARD HMS SHEFFIELD FALKLANDS CONFLICT 4 MAY 1982 "NE CEDE MALIS"'.

NE CEDE MALIS is the motto of the Royal Navy Police; it translates as 'Do not yield to malice'.

A brass plaque mounted on oak in St Albans Church, Windy Nook, Gateshead, Tyne and Wear reads: 'IN LOVING MEMORY OF BRIAN WELSH MASTER AT ARMS AND HIS CREW MATES OF HMS SHEFFIELD LOST IN ACTION OFF THE FALKLAND ISLANDS 4TH MAY 1982'.

Son Brian would like his father remembered as 'Beloved father, husband, brother, friend, and son. Highly respected member of the RN Regulating Branch taken far too young.'

In 2022, as part of the Falkland Islands 40th Anniversary Place Names Project, Brian was honoured with 'Welsh Hill', a prominent hill (700ft elevation) between Calm Head and Wood Cove, West Falkland.

His name lives on…

24507897 Private Philip Alexander West 3rd Battalion Parachute Regiment 8 February 1963 ~ 12 June 1982 Age 19

Alexander West and Marina Armstrong married in 1959; they welcomed their daughter Karen into the world the following year. Philip was born three years later, their youngest child and only son. Philip Alexander West was born on 8 February 1963 at home in a small, prefabricated house near Gosforth High Street, Newcastle-Upon-Tyne. He was known throughout his life as Westy.

Westy's first school was St Oswald's Primary in Gosforth. He spent a brief time at St Josephs before moving to Gosforth High School. Westy was a popular lad, friendly, cheeky with an inquisitive nature. He was appreciated by his peers and teachers alike.

Philip was an athletic lad at school, he loved to play football. When he was training for his recruitment, he would often be seen running around the streets with his dog Shona by his side. He joined Junior Para in August 1979, aged 16. His sister says, 'As long as I remember he wanted to join The Parachute Regiment. He was even more determined after a local boy Billy Snowden who was in The Parachute Regiment lost his life in Northern Ireland.' William 'Geordie' Snowden was A Coy 3 PARA, he was killed on the 1976 South Armagh tour by a CWIED (Command Wire Initiated Device).

Westy passed out in October 1980, he joined A Coy, 3 Para. A tour in Northern Ireland followed from December 1980 until April 1981; the remainder of 1981 saw travels with his battalion to Canada and France.

As a young paratrooper love was on the horizon for Philip, he met and fell in love with Sarah. The couple welcomed a daughter, Aimee, into the world in August 1981; he has two beautiful grandchildren.

In April 1982, Westy was stationed at Tidworth on the new Anti-Tank MILAN training. Like many young paratroopers he was on leave, his destination Bristol. Westy and his friend Kevin Johnson (Jono) were planning a visit to Jono's parents but the call back to barracks came.

Westy set off for the long voyage with the 3rd Battalion on the *Canberra*. As they travelled across the Atlantic Karen remembers:

> While he was on the ship correspondence was good with Philip, it was a comfort to receive his letters. We wrote and sent him photos of his daughter Aimee who was only a baby. The media was reporting daily about what had happened the night before, there was so much anxiety hearing things on the radio and TV. It was a rollercoaster of emotions, we missed him so much. We were devastated when he did not return.
>
> I feel sorry that it had to happen at all, but it did. Devastated by the loss but pleased for their victory. We feel incredibly proud of Philip. We feel the injustice of him losing his life so soon, He was only 19 years old, his career was cut short, and he has missed out on so much in life.'

Westy had a military funeral, he was laid to rest at Hollywood Avenue Cemetery in Gosforth.

Karen remembers her brother in her own words,

> Philip was a young lad, very loyal and a very good friend, always grounded and had a cheeky jovial personality, he loved comedy and had an infectious laugh. I think he was incredibly strong, honourable and I think that is how he would like to be remembered.
>
> It's very hard to think how a young lad would like to be remembered but he was always a best friend, protective and reasonable with everyone he was very quick to gauge a situation, and nothing phased him, he always had the right response.

Pause for a moment and imagine who Westy was, imagine him with his beret at an 'ally' angle, laughing with his mates, get a feel for a loving, cheeky chappie who was well liked all of his short life.

In 2022, as part of the Falkland Islands 40th Anniversary Place Names Project, Westy, was honoured with 'West Pond', a pond between Rodeo Mountain and Rabbit Mountain near the source of the San Carlos River and Fork of the Brooks, East Falkland.

His name lives on…

D154510D Acting Weapons Engineering Artificer 2 Philip Patrick White HMS *Coventry* 10 May 1956 ~ 25 May 1982 Age 26

Philip Patrick White it is thought grew up in Ballyshannon, Co Donegal, he was known as Paddy. Paddy joined the Royal Navy on 2 January 1976 at HMS *Fisgard*, Torpoint, Plymouth. He spent four weeks in basic training at *Fisgard* in Tribe Division. Paddy is remembered as a likeable lad who was easy to get on with.

With a smile like Tom Cruise and a certain Irish charm Paddy was young and full of fun. He enjoyed a trip to Amsterdam during his service where, apparently, he had to be dissuaded from racking up large bar bills.

During the Falklands War Paddy was serving on HMS *Coventry*. Paddy was the computer maintainer; he was killed by the blast that destroyed the computer room which was directly under the operations room. Like many sailors who died his grave is the sea.

In 2022, as part of the Falkland Islands 40th Anniversary Place Names Project, Paddy was honoured with 'White Hill', a hill in Round Hill Camp, West Falkland.

His name lives on…

D177273B Marine Engineering Mechanic (Mechanical) Stephen James White HMS *Ardent* 24 December 1960 ~ 21 May 1982 Age 21

Stephen James White was born on Christmas Eve in 1960 to James and Brenda White (née Dove), who married in 1957. The couple's first child was a daughter, Stephen was their eldest son, he also had a younger brother and sister.

Steve and his brother Ian both joined the Royal Navy, sisters Dawn and Mandy became nurses, there were a lot of uniforms in the White family.

According to his mother, Steve initially applied to join the Merchant Navy who wanted to send him for officer training, but instead he opted for the Royal Navy. After training at HMS *Raleigh*, he served on different ships before joining HMS *Ardent*.

Steve was also known as 'Snowy' to his Navy comrades. His friend Tom Capeling says, 'I joined with Stephen or 'Snowy' as we called him, I met him on the train from Sunderland on our way to Raleigh, he was a great lad, older than me and clearly focused on what he wanted. A clever happy man who loved life.'

Steve was one of the men who died on 21 May 1982 aboard HMS *Ardent*. The ship had been under brutal attack from air raids all day while she was in Falkland Sound. The last strike by the Argentine Air Force meant tragedy for twenty-two of the crew.

Steve has a bench located in Market Place, Stanhope, Wear Valley, Durham. The bench is a modern metal-framed bench, of plain design with wooden slatted seating and backrest. The plaque says: 'TO THE MEMORY OF STEPHEN WHITE WHO LOST HIS LIFE IN SERVICE TO HIS COUNTRY ABOARD HMS ARDENT IN SAN CARLOS WATER, FALKLAND ISLAND ON 21 MAY 1982'.

Steve's mother was reportedly up all night the night before she received the news of her son's death, like many, with a feeling of dread that something was wrong. Steve had been sent home for a couple of days prior to his deployment.

Steve's second name of James was after his father. He is remembered as a wonderful funny, mischievous character who, like many young lads, could shine a light on others.

In 2022, as part of the Falkland Islands 40th Anniversary Place Names Project, Steve was honoured with 'White Point' the northern tip of Staats Island and Weddell Island and Beaver Island, West Falkland.

His name lives on…

D152859L Acting Leading Marine Engineering Mechanic (Electrical) Garry Whitford HMS *Ardent* 2 February 1959 ~ 21 May 1982 Age 23

John Whitford and Teresa Bell married in 1951, their eldest son was born the following year. Garry Whitford was their youngest child, born in Blackburn on 2 February 1959, just four years after his sister.

Garry joined the Royal Navy at the age of 18, starting out at HMS *Devonport* followed by HMS *Lowestoft*. Easter 1982 saw him join the crew of HMS *Ardent* .

HMS *Ardent* was a Type 21 frigate. On 9 May 1982 she was 700 miles south of Ascension Island where she closed to within 200 yards of the *Canberra*. She provided a gun power demonstration to the troops on board the SS *Canberra*.

On 21 May 1982, HMS *Ardent* took part in Operation Sutton, the British landings at San Carlos. Lying in Falkland Sound she was tasked with bombarding the airstrip at Goose Green. *Ardent* herself, however, came under attack by at least three waves of Argentine aircraft.

The Sea Cat anti-aircraft missiles failed to lock on to their attackers and she was outmanoeuvred. HMS *Ardent* still had control of her engines and steering, she headed north but by this time the ship was virtually defenceless. As she headed to Port San Carlos she came under further attack. As she came to rest in the shallow waters of Grantham Sound the fires in the stern were out of control and the ship was listing. Garry was one of the men who died.

Garry Whitford is honoured in his home town by a bench at the local war memorial, Belthorn Corner, Blackburn. The plaque reads: 'IN MEMORY OF GARRY WHITFORD OF THE ROYAL NAVY. DIED 21 MAY 1982 AGE 23 YEARS WHILE SERVING ON HMS ARDENT DURING THE FALKLANDS WAR.'

After Garry's death, his mother Teresa continued to live in the family home for many years.

In 2022, as part of the Falkland Islands 40th Anniversary Place Names Project, Garry was honoured with 'Mount Whitford', a summit (550ft elevation) of a hill at the north entrance to Hoste Inlet in Port Stephens, West Falkland.

His name lives on…

23908198 WO2 Daniel Wight 2nd Battalion Scots Guards 28 April 1945 ~ 14 June 1982 Age 37

Daniel Wight was the eldest son of Glenville Wight and Mary Seath Macdonald, who married in Newington, Edinburgh, in 1944. Daniel was born on 28 April 1945, in the same area in which his parents had married. Daniel became known to everyone as Danny; he had one younger brother, Jim, two years his junior.

Danny attended James Clark School, Edinburgh, after leaving school he joined the British Army in 1962. Initially he trained at Pirbright, after which he went to 1st Battalion Scots Guards where he served for much of his service.

Danny was a tall man standing 6ft 4in tall, but he was also a big character, not easily forgotten. Danny met his wife, Shenia, in the Park Hotel in Edinburgh while home on leave. They both liked folk singing, which was featured at the hotel the night they met. Danny Wight and Shenia Brown Duffy married in St Giles in 1971.

Prior to meeting Shenia, Danny had played the big drum in the pipe band. Shenia says, 'Once he had a drink, he would get the sticks out. Many a Christmas, my decorations would be broken with him swinging them.' Danny, it seemed, loved music; he would sometimes drum on the coffee table as well as turn a song in the mess.

While in Honduras in 1971, he asked his wife to send him the words of 'Flower of Scotland', when Shenia returned to Scotland in 1982, she was surprised to find the song had become so popular. They were both fans of the Scottish folk duo The Corries. Danny was posted to the Guards Depot in the late '70s, he later transferred to the 2nd Battalion Scots Guards.

The couple had two children: Darren, born in Edinburgh in 1971, and Matthew born in London in 1976. Both boys attended the Queen Victoria School in Dunblane. Darren became a Major in the Army Air Corps and Matthew developed his own business, Discreet Scotland, which provides private tours.

Both Danny and Shenia's sons have married, Darren with two children, Daniel and Leah; Matthew with two girls, Gracie and Emeli.

Danny was killed on 14 June 1982 in the battle for Mount Tumbledown, alongside John Pashley.

In 2021, a plaque was unveiled to the fallen Scots Guards in Blackpool; Shenia was in attendance. The Tumbledown Veterans' and Families Association sought permission to add the plaque to the cenotaph in Blackpool where they meet each year.

Danny's mother Mary died in 2007. Danny was a big character in life and remains so in death.

In 2022, as part of the Falkland Islands 40th Anniversary Place Names Project, Danny was honoured with 'Wight Arm', the eastern arm of Double Creek West Arm, West Falkland.

His name lives on…

24090540 Sergeant Malcolm Wigley 1st Battalion Welsh Guards 23 December 1950 ~ 8 June 1982 Age 31

Malcolm Wigley was born in Chester Hospital on 23 December 1950, just in time for Christmas. The family have a long association with Connah's Quay and Hawarden along the River Dee in Flintshire, very close to the English border, just six miles west of Chester. Malcolm was the oldest child of Doug and Doreen Wigley who married in 1949, he had two siblings Janet and David.

Malcolm's father, Douglas Bryan Wigley, was the only son of John Wigley and Hannah Fletcher; Doug had three sisters. Doug married Doreen Povey in 1949. Doreen was the daughter of Robert and Gwendoline Povey, their family had been living in Connah's Quay for many years.

Malcolm attended junior school in Connah's Quay and later Shotton Central, he joined the cadets from the age of 13. He had gained the rank of Sergeant by the time he was 16. The Welsh Guards followed, commencing in Oswestry; owing to an outbreak of 'foot and mouth' in 1968, his nan bought him out of the army.

Malcolm met his wife Kath when he came out of Junior Leaders and started work at Courtaulds in Flint. In June 1971, Malcolm married Kath in Hawarden, after which he worked locally as a driver. The Guards beckoned once again; he re-joined in 1974, stationed initially in Caterham. Tours of Northern Ireland and Cyprus followed. In 1977 the 1st Battalion Welsh Guards were posted to Berlin, based at Wavell Barracks often guarding Spandau prison and Checkpoint Charlie.

Malcolm and Kath had one son, Bryan, born in 1978 while in Berlin. Their next posting was Pirbright prior to the Falklands War. Malcolm travelled 'Down South' on the QE2 with his battalion. Like many, Malcolm's family were very worried as they watched the news on the television.

Malcolm was one of the unlucky Welsh Guards who died on 8 June 1982 as the *Galahad* turned into an inferno. His grave may be 8,000 miles away, but he is remembered with a headstone at the plot at Connah's Quay Cemetery where his parents are also buried. Doreen died in February 1994; Doug died on 30 May 2012, just a week short of the 30th anniversary of his son's death.

Malcolm has a plaque at the Quaystone Chapel, High Street, Connah's Quay, it reads: 'IN MEMORY OF SGT MALCOLM WIGLEY AND ALL WELSH

GUARDS WHO DIED FOR FREEDOM 1982 FROM THE WREXHAM BRANCH RWF COMRADES'.

In 1983, the family travelled to the Falkland Islands as part of a pilgrimage that many families made that year. Bryan was also able to revisit the Islands with the South Atlantic Medal Association in November 2012. He now lives in Connah's Quay, Bryan is married with two children.

Malcolm served a total of ten years in the Welsh Guards. Bryan was just 4 years old when his father died.

In 2022, as part of the Falkland Islands 40th Anniversary Place Names Project, Malcolm was honoured with 'Wigley Lagoon', a tidal lagoon north of White Bluff on the north side of Choiseul Sound, East Falkland.

His name lives on...

24472259 Guardsman David Richard Williams 1st Battalion Welsh Guards 30 December 1961 ~ 8 June 1982 Age 20

The Williams family have a long history in North Wales. David Richard Williams was born 30 December 1961 in Bangor, the fourth child of John Owen and Eluned Williams (née Owen). A large Welsh-speaking family, their son Dei was in the company of siblings John, Eirlys, Nesta and Arwen.

John Owen Williams was born in July 1924, the son of Owen Henry Williams and Annie Roberts, who married in 1923. Owen was a cycle repairer and salesman, his side of the family were from Marianglas, Brynteg in Anglesey. It is said that both Dei and his father loved bikes, perhaps it came from their grandfather. Although John died in 1998, his sister Annie lived until 2005. John also served in the British Army, seeing service in Burma during the Second World War. After his service he worked on the railway.

Eluned is a common Welsh name meaning 'Image', it is the name of a fifth-century Welsh Saint. Eluned came from the farming village of Llanfechell.

Dei's oldest brother, John, served in the Royal Welch Fusiliers for thirteen years. John married in Salisbury in 1979 and had one son by the time his brother died. The couple went on to have two girls and settled in Salisbury. Eirlys married in 1990 and still lives in Wales. Nesta married in late 1982 and has two sons one named Dafydd in honour of his Uncle Dei.

Dei finished his schooling at Holyhead Secondary School; from a young age he wanted to join the army. After signing up at the recruiting office in Bangor he passed out in 1977 and joined the 1st Battalion Welsh Guards. Before the invasion in 1982, Dei had seen travel and service in Northern Ireland and Kenya.

Dei was killed on the *Sir Galahad* on 8 June 1982.

In 1983, Dei's parents were among many families travelling on the Falkland Islands pilgrimage. Like many, they had no grave to visit.

Dei has a memorial, a Cairn with a dedicated polished black stone placed on the front face. A smaller tablet is placed on the 3 o'clock face with incised inscription in gold paint lettering. The inscription on the 6 o'clock face reads:

'IN MEMORY OF GUARDSMAN DAVID RICHARD WILLIAMS WELSH GUARDS OF 9 MAES YR YSGOL HOLYHEAD KILLED IN ACTION AT BLUFF COVE FALKLAND ISLANDS SOUTH ATLANTIC 8TH JUNE 1982 AGED 20 YEARS ONE TIME YOUNG WARDEN AT THIS RESERVE FROM RESIDENTS OF MAES YR YSGOL AND NORAWELON HOLYHEAD AND FRIENDS OF THE PENRHOS NATURE RESERVE.'

On the 3 o'clock face:

'THE SLAIN IN THEIR TENS WITHOUT COFFIN WITHOUT SHROUD BUT THE DEEP THEIR HOUSELESS GRAVE BENEATH THE WAVES IS THE ATLANTIC FOREVER MORE W R P GEORGE.'

In 2022, as part of the Falkland Islands 40th Anniversary Place Names Project, Dei was honoured with 'Williams Inlet', the east arm of Chaffers Gullet, West Falkland.

His name lives on…

D169265K Marine Engineering Mechanic (Mechanical) Gilbert Stephen Williams HMS *Ardent* 26 April 1961 ~ 21 May 1982 Age 21

Gilbert Stephen Williams was born in Oxfordshire on 26 April 1961, the oldest son of Gordon Percival and Shirley Williams (née Allen), who married in Ploughley, early in 1960. The family has a long history in the Kidlington area, and many members are buried there. Gordon was one of twin boys, born in October 1927 to Arthur Williams and his wife Florence.

It appears that young Gilbert was named after his paternal uncle, Gilbert Henry, who died two years before he was born. Gilbert had two brothers, his mother Shirley as a young child was separated from her own mother due to illness.

Gilbert attended Gosford Hill, Kidlington, before joining the Royal Navy in 1979. Prior to 1982, Gilbert served on HMS *Hermes* between 1979 and 1981, before her refit. His next ship was HMS *Ardent*, where he lost his life on 21 May 1982.

Gilbert was known to his shipmates as 'Bungy' and is fondly remembered.

His Uncle Victor also died at the end of 1982, Uncle Sidney just two years later in 1984.

Though Gilbert's grave is the South Atlantic Ocean, he is remembered nearer to home. On the east wall of the Soldier's Chapel at St Mary the Virgin Church, Church Street, Kidlington in Oxfordshire, a painted plaster cartouche of St George and the Dragon is placed on a small shelf.

Below the brass plaque the inscription:

'IN MEMORY OF GILBERT STEPHEN WILLIAMS LOST IN HMS ARDENT ON 21 MAY 1982 WHILE SERVING IN THE FALKLAND ISLANDS "SAFE IN GOD'S KEEPING" THEY SHALL NOT GROW OLD AS WE THAT ARE LEFT GROW

OLD AGE SHALL NOT WEARY THEM NOR THE YEARS CONDEMN AT THE GOING DOWN OF THE SUN AND IN THE MORNING, WE SHALL REMEMBER THEM'.

In 2022, as part of the Falkland Islands 40th Anniversary Place Names Project, Gilbert was honoured with 'Williams Hill', a hill in Diamond Corner Camp.

His name lives on…

D178859U Weapons Engineering Artificer (Apprentice) Ian Robert Williams HMS *Coventry* 13 January 1961 ~ 25 May 1982 Age 21

Ian was born on 13 January 1961 at 82 Quarry Avenue, Bebington on the Wirral. Ian was the son of Joseph and Barbara Williams (née Podmore), who married in 1959.

Ian's mother was from Bebington, Barbara's father Harry was born in Port Sunlight, Cheshire. Grandfather Henry Colby Podmore was an accountant, the family lived in Bridge Street, Port Sunlight. Harry served with the Royal Naval Air Service as a Fitter in the First World War. Harry married Annie Marion Laing in 1929. Annie's family had settled in Bebington, though she was born in Surrey.

Annie's father, like many, worked for William Hesketh Lever's Soap Works, indeed many of the company employees lived in Port Sunlight, a village built by Levers for their workers. Both Harry and his brother Herbert worked for the company, established in 1888. Herbert also lived in Quarry Avenue, where Ian was born. Annie worked as an insurance clerk prior to her marriage.

Ian's family settled in Neston; he joined the Royal Navy on 7 September 1979 as an Artificer Apprentice at HMS *Fisgard* in Torpoint as part of 793 entry. After leaving school post-A levels, Ian already had some experience, having been a member of the Royal Naval Reserve at HMS *Eaglet*. A member of the volunteer band, he played the clarinet.

Despite breaking his ankle, he finished training complete with plaster cast and was selected to become a Weapons Training Artificer. Ian joined HMS *Collingwood* in May 1980, he loved rock music and his biker's jacket, which apparently became like a second skin.

Ian was drafted to HMS *Coventry* in May 1981. He shared many memories with his long-term girlfriend Lil, including a rock concert with Iron Maiden in Portsmouth in 1981. After his death Lil later regretted not accepting letters which had arrived for her; some of the hardest letters received by loved ones were those received after their death.

Ian's action station was part of the Weapons Engineering Repair Team, but nothing could have repaired HMS *Coventry* after the attack on 25 May 1982. Within twenty minutes of being hit by three 1,000 lb bombs, HMS *Coventry* sank, taking those who had perished in the attack with her.

Ian has a memorial at Neston Parish Church where a small sandstone plinth is placed on the ground before the cenotaph, it reads: 'IN MEMORY OF WEA APP IAN R WILLIAMS BORN 13.1.61 KILLED IN ACTION HMS COVENTRY 25.5.1982.'

In 2022, as part of the Falkland Islands 40th Anniversary Place Names Project, Ian was honoured with 'Williams Point', the westernmost point of North Fur in the Jason Islands Group, West Falkland.

His name lives on...

D176707S Cook Kevin Joseph Williams HMS *Sheffield* 16 April 1962 ~ 4 May 1982 Age 20

Kevin Joseph Davey was born on 16 April 1962 in Neath, Glamorganshire in Wales. Kevin's parents, Philip Davey and Ann Smith, married in 1961; Kevin was the couple's oldest son, closely followed by his sister Debbie the following year. Philip and Ann had two other children together, Paul and Karl.

In 1971, Kevin's mother Ann went on to have a second family with Lyndon Williams, so Kevin then became a Williams. Kevin had five half-siblings: Theresa, Heidi, Linzi, Mark and lastly Lyndon, who was born in 1981.

On 19 November 1981, HMS *Sheffield* set sail for patrol in the Arabian Gulf. The ship then took part in Exercise Spring Train, she was diverted to the South Atlantic on hearing of the invasion of the Falkland Islands.

On Sunday 4 May 1982, disaster struck HMS *Sheffield* as she was struck by an Exocet missile fired from Argentine Naval Super Étendard aircraft. Though the warhead failed to explode, the 'Shiny Sheff' was soon raging with fires which quickly spread, causing the crew to abandon ship. Kevin was among the twenty men who lost their lives.

Kevin's youngest brother Lyndon was just 1 year old when his brother died; he has no memories of him. Lyndon's mum later told him about his brother when he started secondary school. He remembers that his mum had pictures of his brother and would cry at times. Lyndon had seen documentaries and news articles about the Falklands, he is immensely proud of the big brother he had no opportunity to know.

Kevin had celebrated his 20th birthday on 16 April 1982, a life cut short by fate. Kevin's mother Ann died in February 2015.

In 2022, as part of the Falkland Islands 40th Anniversary Place Names Project, Kevin was honoured with 'Williams Islet', a small tussac islet on the north side of the entrance into Shallow Harbour at Lively Island, East Falkland.

His name lives on...

P037820V Marine David Wilson 45 Commando Royal Marines 15 March 1962 ~ 27 May 1982 Age 20

Marine David Wilson, it appears, was from Glenrothes in Scotland. Eerily, David was not the only David Wilson from 45 Commando to lose their life in action. His namesake was killed on 26 May 1964 in Aden.

Little is known about David, who it seems was adopted. In 1962 there were over sixty babies named David Wilson born in Scotland, perhaps this one is for *Long Lost Family*. He may well have been born under a different name. All that is remembered by comrades is that David had a mother and a sister, though it is not known whether his sibling was a full biological sister.

Comrades remember that David's mother was already in her seventies at the time of the Falklands War. Both his mother and sister are now deceased.

David, of 45 Commando, died on 27 May 1982 aged just 20, he was killed in an enemy bomb attack while on operations in Ajax Bay.

Another namesake, David Wilson Homes, later named a house design after David, calling it 'The Falkland'.

Marine Wilson is buried in the Blue Beach Military Cemetery at Port San Carlos.

In 2022, as part of the Falkland Islands 40th Anniversary Place Names Project, David was honoured with 'Wilson Cove', a bay on the southwest side of Governor Island.

His name lives on…

24317228 Corporal Scott Wilson 9th Independent Parachute Squadron Royal Engineers 3 March 1957 ~ 12 June 1982 Age 25

Scott Wilson was born in Abadan, Iran, to William Spence and Janet Wilson (née Melrose) who married in St Andrew's, Edinburgh, in 1954. Scott's father was serving in the British Army at the time. The family home was the Sighthill area of Edinburgh. After William left the army, he joined the prison service and the family relocated to Durham. The family returned to Sighthill following the death of Scott's father in 1981.

Scott, a popular member of 9 Parachute Squadron RE, was apparently always happy. He spent many years in 9 Squadron. A very good sportsman, he excelled at football, indeed he represented the Corps. Scott married Jean in Dumfries in 1980, she was also from a military family. Her father was in the Royal Electrical and Mechanical Engineers, she met Scott while her father was posted to Aldershot.

2 Troop, 9 Parachute Squadron Royal Engineers departed from Portsmouth with a reinforced troop of fifty-three men on board the MV *Norland* with 2 Para Group. Scott and John Ferry shared a bunk on the journey 'Down South' and had many conversations about upcoming tasks and training programmes.

2 Troop were cross decked on 19 May 1982 to the *Canberra* to join 3 Para. A few days later, on 20 May, they were cross decked again, this time to HMS *Intrepid*.

During the initial search of some buildings that had been used by Argentine Forces, Scott recovered a Royal Navy White Ensign which was believed to have been flown at Moody Brook Barracks in Stanley. Scott carried this across the island before passing it to his Section 2IC Paul Moore for safe keeping with strict instructions that it was to go in the Airborne Forces Museum should anything happen to Scott. The flag was placed in the care of the museum in late 1983 having been embroidered with great care by Paul's wife Lesley.

3 Para attacked Mount Longdon on the evening of 11 June 1982, Scott was killed by artillery fire on 12 June.

Scott was buried in Eastern Hills Cemetery, Edinburgh, on 2 December 1982, following a service at St Nicholas Parish Church, Sighthill. HQ Scotland provided a ceremonial Land Rover and Gun Carriage to carry his coffin with John Ferry in charge of the coffin bearer party.

In 2022, as part of the Falkland Islands 40th Anniversary Place Names Project, Scott was honoured with 'Wilson Point', the northern tip of Tea Island, West Falkland.

His name lives on…

502804 Captain David Alexander Wood 2nd Battalion Parachute Regiment 15 January 1953 ~ 28 May 1982 Age 29

David was born in Fife on 15 January 1953, the eldest son of Jean and Alastair. He was brought up in Kennoway and attended Buckhaven Grammar School, joining the Leaven Air Training Corps. The family moved to Gillingham in Kent where David attended Gillingham Grammar School and joined the Air Training Corps, attaining the rank of cadet warrant officer.

On leaving school he was commissioned into the RAF Regiment and posted to RAF Salalah, then under constant threat from guerrilla attack. He also saw operational duty in Northern Ireland. After three years he opted to transfer to The Parachute Regiment and convert to a Regular Commission by studying at the Royal Military Academy, Sandhurst. He took up free fall parachuting and would spend most weekends here at Netheravon. He was notified that he had passed the Staff College examination before departing with 2 PARA on the MV *Norland* to the South Atlantic, now Adjutant to Lieutenant Colonel H Jones, the Commanding Officer. He took his parachute with him 'just in case'.

The Battalion was first ashore on 21 May 1982 and dug in on Sussex Mountain above San Carlos, with a bird's eye view of the continuous bombing attacks on the ships below. 2 PARA was ordered to capture Darwin and Goose Green and set off on a beautiful clear evening. David looked up and sardonically remarked, 'Just take a look at that night sky – it just might be your last'. For him it was.

The Battalion attacked on the morning of 28 May, and by dawn both lead companies were pinned down by very strong Argentine defences. David was forward with the Commanding Officer's Tac

Party and joined A Company in the gorse gully below Darwin Hill. H Jones became increasingly frustrated at the lack of progress and attempted a lone assault on the enemy, some seventy-eight soldiers dug in on Darwin Hill, mortally wounded in so doing. David was crawling forward with the officers and soldiers of A Company when he raised his head to observe the enemy and was instantly killed. His body was repatriated to Scotland where he was buried alongside his ancestors.

Of him, one is reminded of the words of the philosopher, Erasmus: 'Live every day as if it might be your last study as if you might live forever'. ~ David Benest

Written by the late Colonel David Benest about the man he remembered as The Sardonic Scot.

In 2022, as part of the Falkland Islands 40th Anniversary Place Names Project, David was honoured with 'Wood Point', a prominent point at the west end of Philimore Island off Lively Island, West Falkland.

His name lives on…

C021908A Lieutenant Commander John Stuart Woodhead DSC HMS *Sheffield* 7 October 1941 ~ 4 May 1982 Age 40

John Stuart Woodhead was born in Nottingham on 7 October 1941, the son of Stuart and Kathleen Woodhead (née Ford). Stuart and Kathleen married at Bolsover Methodist Church, Chesterfield in 1939.

Stuart born in Eckington, Derbyshire, had also served in the Royal Navy. Sadly, Kathleen died on 18 November 1946 when John was just 5 years old.

John was named after both his great-grandfather and father. His grandmother Jessie had been in service from the age of 14, she later became a Salvation Army officer prior to her marriage to Moses Woodhead in 1907.

At school John excelled at sport, becoming the Nottingham pole vault champion. Starting out at St Vincent College, John soon found himself in the Fleet Air Arm as a junior radio mechanic. He served on HMS *Albion*, later at RNAS *Culdrose*. John transferred to the Royal Navy in 1961, the following year he married Anne in Cornwall. The couple had two daughters Denise and Linda.

Various courses followed and in 1980 John joined HMS *Sheffield*. By 1981, promotion saw him WEO. During the Falklands War, John was a Lieutenant Commander in HMS *Sheffield*. Two days after the sinking of the *Belgrano* the Argentine Forces struck back. HMS *Sheffield* was brutally attacked.

Fire started aboard the ship which spread rapidly. Unfortunately, as the ship lost her fire-fighting systems and power, those on board were left with the old-fashioned system of buckets of water to fight the fierce flames. The ship's Lynx helicopters started with evacuations, aided by other ships.

In the computer room sat John Woodhead, the lead of a six-man team, their job was to try to get the ship's weapons systems back online and restore power. Sadly, their efforts, though valiant, meant they became cut off from an escape route. All six were overcome by smoke and fumes.

During the attack twenty men died, twenty-four were injured and 242 men escaped without injury. Though a bad day at the office, it could have been so much worse.

For his valiant efforts John was posthumously awarded the Distinguished Service Cross.

John's father Stuart died just a year later in 1983. His children, inspired by their father, grew up to achieve their own aspirations. John remains missed by many who knew him, a man of substance who loved the ocean. He died as he lived, with bravery and honour.

In 2022, as part of the Falkland Islands 40th Anniversary Place Names Project, John was honoured with 'Woodhead Lagoon', a tidal lagoon on the north side of Christmas Harbour, West Falkland.

His name lives on…

Seaman Shui Kam Yeung Royal Fleet Auxiliary *Sir Tristram* 27 July 1938 ~ 8 June 1982 Age 43

Shui Kam Yeung was from Cheung Chan Island, New Territories, Hong Kong. During the Falklands War Yeung was a Seaman on board the RFA *Sir Tristram*. Civilian crew were called Seaman or Sailor.

Sir Tristram, a Landing Ship Logistics of the Round Table class, was sister ship to the RFA *Sir Galahad*. At the time of the Falklands War, she was under the command of Captain Robin Green.

On 2 April 1982, *Sir Tristram* was diverted from Belize to Ascension Island to join the Amphibious Landing Group for Operation Corporate. She left Ascension Island 29 April 1982 in the company of RFA ships, *Sir Galahad*, *Sir Geraint*, *Sir Lancelot*, *Sir Percival* and *Plumleaf*, and Royal Naval ships HMS *Fearless*, HMS *Intrepid* and HMS *Antelope*.

Sir Tristram entered the Total Exclusion Zone on 8 May 1982, arriving in San Carlos Water on 21 May 1982 with the rest of the Amphibious Landing Force. The attack on 8 June 1982 is often misquoted as happening at Bluff Cove, but the ship was anchored alongside her sister-ship the *Sir Galahad* at Port Pleasant, Fitzroy Creek, which is just south of Bluff Cove.

During an Argentinian Sky Hawk attack, *Sir Tristram* was hit by three bombs. One bomb entered the 25-tank starboard and passed through without detonation. Another bomb passed across the tank deck and entered the 25-tank port. This bomb partially detonated which blew out a large plate on the port quarter and also caused damage to the forward bulkhead. A third bomb exploded under 25 and 26 tanks, which ruptured the ship's hull. It is thought that this third bomb exacerbated the effects of the other two bombs. With fires breaking out under pallets of ammunition the order was given to abandon ship.

Sir Tristram's crew were evacuated to HMS *Fearless* and HMS *Intrepid*. Yeung was among the missing, his body never recovered.

In 2022, as part of the Falkland Islands 40th Anniversary Place Names Project, Yeung was honoured with 'Yeung Point', the easternmost point of the north half of North East Island off Lively Island, East Falkland.

His name lives on…

Bosun Sik Chee Yu RFA *Sir Tristram* 15 December 1921 ~ 8 June 1982 Age 60

Sik Chee Yu was born on 15 December 1921, he was from Kowloon in Hong Kong.

Yu was one of two Chinese service personnel killed when RFA *Sir Tristram* was attacked on 8 June 1982. Neither men were found, initially declared 'missing' their bodies were lost to the South Atlantic.

Everything that a Royal Naval vessel uses comes to it by special delivery from the Royal Fleet Auxiliary and Merchant Navy. Vital supplies along an 8,000-mile-long supply chain throughout the war and the months afterwards. Vital help with the same threat, putting their lives on the line, in the line of duty.

What may be less known is that John Nott's Defence White Paper 1981 had ordered cuts, and the Royal Fleet Auxiliary was to be hit hard in those cuts which would include 1,000 redundancies. The first of those redundancies started arriving in the post from 2 April 1982. Oh, what irony…

It shows the calibre of the seamen who were part of the Royal Fleet Auxiliary because not only did each and every one of them report back to their ships, but also men who were on leave and some who were retired were soon calling RFA HQ demanding to take part in Britain's war with Argentina. The call for the sea is strong once it is in your blood.

Yu was Bosun of the *Sir Tristram* and had served with the Royal Fleet Auxiliary for many years previously serving on the *Sir Galahad*.

In 2022, as part of the Falkland Islands 40th Anniversary Place Names Project, Yu was honoured with 'Yu Point', the easternmost point of East Island at the entrance to Port Fitzroy, East Falkland.

His name lives on…

THE CIVILIANS

In any war there are civilian casualties, in the Falklands War there were just three civilian deaths. Though all loss in war is tragic, it is a testament to the British Troops that the war was so well executed and swift in its conclusion.

Doreen Millian Bonner 24 December 1935 ~ 12 June 1982 Age 46

Doreen Millian ('Milly') Browning was born on 24 December 1935. One of five children, she had three sisters and one brother. When Milly was just 17 years old, she married Harry Bonner. Harry was one of five boys born to Henry Harry John and Christina Catherine Bonner (née McCaskill). The family have been Falkland Islanders for generations. Harry and Milly had two children, both girls, named Shirley and Cheryl. Shirley died in September 1959; she was just 6 years old.

Milly was a civilian, one of just three lost tragically towards the end of the war and even more tragically by British fire during the bombings of Stanley. The three civilians had taken refuge in a four-bedroom house in Ross Road West. Doreen was killed when a naval shell exploded overhead. She was killed instantly.

Harry was heartbroken after Doreen's death; he died not long after the war on New Year's Day 1983. Cheryl passed away on 30 June 2006 aged 49.

Though each death is tragic in its own way, compared to events such as the Second World War it is amazing that from the time the Falkland Islands were invaded, throughout the war only three civilians died.

In 2022, as part of the Falkland Islands 40th Anniversary Place Names Project, Milly was honoured with 'Bonner Bay', a small sandy bay next to Beach Point on the Port Harriet coastline mainland East Falkland.

Her name lives on…

Mary Ann Goodwin 22 December 1900 ~ 13 June 1982 Age 81

Mary Ann Cartmell was born in the Falkland Islands on 22 December 1900; she married John Hewitt in 1919 and had two children. Mary became a widow when John passed away on 24 July 1923.

On 7 June 1926 Mary Married William ('Bill') Goodwin and later had two sons, William ('Nutt') and Laurence ('Laurie') and lived in the camp for some time.

Eventually Mary and Bill moved into Stanley where they successfully ran a dairy herd and supplied fresh milk to the residents. After Bill's death Mary and Laurie carried on with the dairy until age and ill health defeated them. This didn't deter Mary; she then took in lodgers and cooked hot lunches for many of the single men who came to the Falklands, including teachers and BAS personnel.

Mary died on 13 June 1982 as a result of injuries sustained during the bombing of Stanley in the final days of the war.

Mary was much loved by her family and still missed to this day.

The above information was kindly provided by Mary's granddaughter Jackie.

At 81 years of age Mary was unable to recover from her injuries. She was the only civilian who did not die instantly, a testament to her strength.

In 2022, as part of the Falkland Islands 40th Anniversary Place Names Project, Mary was honoured with 'Goodwin Islet', an islet north of Gull Island at the entrance to Walker Creek, East Falkland.

Her name lives on…

Susan Whitley 25 January 1950 ~ 12 June 1982 Age 32

Susan Giles was born on 25 January 1950 in Llandrindod Wells, Radnorshire, Mid-Wales.

Sue trained as a domestic science teacher at Gloucester College.

At some point Sue heard about the Falkland Islands and fell in love with what the islands had to offer. She applied for a teaching job in the Falklands, which she was eventually offered.

Sue left the United Kingdom on 29 August 1976 for a new life in the Falkland Islands. She met Steve Whitley, a veterinarian working locally, and they married in 1981. They had no children.

Sue was killed on 12 June 1982, the youngest of the three civilians to die when the British naval shell exploded over the house in which they were sheltering.

Sue was buried at Sea Lion Island, which is reflected in the place named after her forty years later. Later, the people of Llandrindod Wells organised the Susan Whitley Trust which was active from December 1983 until December 2019. The trust was aimed at advancing the education of children of school age resident in the Falkland Islands within the field of art, craft, domestic science or sport.

In 2022, as part of the Falkland Islands 40th Anniversary Place Names Project, Susan was honoured with 'Whitley Point', the western point of Sea Lion Island in the Sea Lion Islands Group.

Her name lives on…

AFTERWORD

To those of us who fought, loved, and lost men and women we cared about in 1982, the memories are forever etched into the caverns of our minds. The Falklands War was a traditional war fought in the old-fashioned way, at times with 'fixed bayonets'. We must make sure that future generations remember the sacrifice of those we lost and those who came home. They were all only a footstep or a bullet away from the same end.

This book has been a 'labour of love'; its inception, as with many things, seemed to be by accident. Once underway, however, the enormity of the commitment of seven years of research took its toll, as did the emotions which arose along the road with all its twists and turns. It was impossible for me to be detached as each story unfolded, wanting to do the best for each individual and those who knew them. Sometimes that was impossible. Tracing people forty years after an event, of course has its challenges.

As momentum gathered, synchronicity came into play by way of chance encounters and contact from different corners of the globe.

I was born in a War Memorial Hospital, perhaps an indication of things to come. Interests in the spiritual side of life were always in conflict with the soldier who swept me off my feet. As teenagers a veritable truce was drawn with regards to our differences of opinion over politics and religion. Perhaps one day humanity may follow suit.

In the words of the late philosopher George Santayana: 'Those who cannot remember the past are condemned to repeat it'.

INFOMATION SOURCES

www.gro.gov.uk (All)
www.cwgc.org (Various)
www.thegazette.co.uk (Various)
www.irishgenealogy.ie (Various)
www.scotlandspeople.gov.uk (Various)
www.veterans.mod.uk (All)
www.iwm.org.uk/memorials (Various)
www.newmp.org.uk North East War Memorials Project (Dent)
www.barnardcastleschool.org.uk (Dent)
www.spink.com (Various)
www.scotsguards.org (Various)
www.walesonline.co.uk (Various)
www.dailypost.co.uk (Various)
www.goadby-marwood-history.co.uk (Fitton)
www.ohclub.co.uk (Forge)
www.warmemorialsonline.org.uk (Various)
www.paradata.org.uk (Various)
www.bbc.com (Various)
www.hmsardent.org (Various)
www.en.wikipedia.org
www.dailymail.co.uk (Various)
www.uk.forceswarrecords.com (Various)
www.newmp.org.uk (Various)
www.sama82.org.uk (Various)
www.roll-of-honour.com (Various)
www.doyrms.com (Various)
www.royalnavy.mod.uk (Various)
www.dailyrecord.co.uk (Various)
www.flyingmarines.co.uk (Nunn)
www.boxingnewsonline.net (Vickers E)
www.welshguardscharity.co.uk (Various)
www.hmscoventry.co.uk (Various)
www.thenorthernecho.co.uk (White)
www.lancashiretelegraph.co.uk (Various)

INFOMATION SOURCES

www.victoriacross.org.uk (Sephton)
www.thefreelibrary.com (Dunphy)
www.sappers.co.uk (Gandhi)
www.historypoints.org (Various)
www.midweekherald.co.uk (Banfield)
www.belfasttelegraph.co.uk (Johnston)
www.scmp.com (Various)
www.thecourier.co.uk (Various)
www.hansard.parliament.co.uk (Various)

Anon. 2022. Commemorative Map for the 40th Anniversary of the Liberation of the Falkland Islands. Falkland Islands Government Design Office, Stanley, Falkland Islands.

With thanks and gratitude to all family, friends, comrades and the community who have contributed to the stories of the fallen.